Other Titles in This Series

(Continued in the back of this publication)

Proceedings of Symposia in APPLIED MATHEMATICS

Volume 50

Different Aspects of Coding Theory

American Mathematical Society
Short Course
January 2–3, 1995
San Francisco, California

Robert Calderbank
Editor

American Mathematical Society
Providence, Rhode Island

LECTURE NOTES PREPARED FOR THE
AMERICAN MATHEMATICAL SOCIETY SHORT COURSE
CODING THEORY

HELD IN SAN FRANCISCO, CALIFORNIA
JANUARY 2–3, 1995

The AMS Short Course Series is sponsored by the Society's Program
Committee on National Meetings. The Series is under the direction of the
Short Course Subcommittee of the Program Committee
for National Meetings.

1991 *Mathematics Subject Classification.* Primary 62K05, 68Q25, 68Q68, 93B15,
94A05;
Secondary 05B25, 51A35, 51A40, 58F03, 68P25, 68Q15, 94A14, 94A40, 94A60,
94B12, 94B27.

Library of Congress Cataloging-in-Publication Data
Different aspects of coding theory : American Mathematical Society short course, January 2–3,
1995, San Francisco, California / Robert Calderbank, editor.
   p.   cm. — (Proceedings of symposia in applied mathematics, ISSN 0160-7634; v. 50)
   Includes bibliographical references and index.
   ISBN 0-8218-0379-4
   1. Coding theory—Congresses.   I. Calderbank, Robert, 1954– .   II. Series.
QA268.D54 1995
003′.54—dc20
                                                                      95-35165
                                                                      CIP

Table of Contents

Table of Contents

Preface

The lectures at the Short Course in San Francisco and the different chapters of this book emphasize connections between coding theory and coding practice, and between coding theory and different parts of mathematics.

The principal purpose of coding theory is the reliable transmission or storage of data. The introductory chapter provides the basics of algebraic coding theory, and the design of codes for the Gaussian channel. It is intended to set the stage for the contributions that follow. The chapter by Marcus, Roth and Siegel focuses on magnetic recording, where binary data written on a disk is required to satisfy certain constraints. The encoding of random data as constrained sequences is accomplished by means of a finite state machine. Shannon, in 1948, introduced the notion of capacity; the maximum data rate supported by the universe of constrained sequences. However methods of encoding and decoding at or very close to this achievable rate were developed more recently through connections with symbolic dynamics. Here we also see connections with finite automata since the constrained sequences can be thought of as a language that is accepted by the encoder. In fact many basic concepts have grown up independently in coding theory, linear systems theory and automata theory. The multilingual dictionary compiled by Forney, Marcus, Sindhushayana and Trott connects these different worlds and how they have evolved in parallel. One of the objectives of the Short Course and this book was to promote more crosspollination between these different mathematical communities.

One of the most interesting connections between coding theory and other parts of mathematics is the use of algebraic geometry to construct efficient error-correcting codes. The contribution by Stichtenoth relates these geometric Goppa codes to the polynomial codes constructed by Reed and Solomon that are now found everywhere from computer hard disks to compact disk players. Reed-Solomon and algebraic geometry codes are particular examples of linear codes, but it is sometimes the case that nonlinear codes are more efficient. Examples include the Kerdock and Preparata codes which are closely related to quadratic forms. The chapter by Kantor connects these codes with orthogonal and symplectic geometry, and with extremal families of lines in Euclidean space.

A different geometric perspective is evident in the chapter by Hardin and Sloane. Here we are concerned with approximating the properties of a large universe (such as the surface of a sphere) with a small ensemble or design (such as a discrete subset of points). This connects with the construction of experimental designs in statistics, which are used to optimize industrial processes. However there are also fascinating connections with Waring's Problem in number theory.

The last chapter by Feigenbaum explores the use of codes in theoretical computer science. Here codes are used to improve algorithmic efficiency, in program testing and correction, and to obtain characterizations of complexity classes. It is an opportunity for coding theorists to see familiar constructs at work in a very different context.

I would like to use this opportunity to thank all the lecturers at the Short Course, and all the contributors to this volume. I hope that all readers, whether they be coding theory novices or experts in the field, will find something to interest them in the different chapters. I would also like to thank Wayne Drady for the time and energy he invested in making the Short Course run smoothly. Finally I would like to thank Susan Pope for creating a coherent whole out of the individual contributions.

A. R. Calderbank
AT&T Bell Laboratories
Murray Hill, NJ 07974
May 15, 1995

Proceedings of Symposia in Applied Mathematics
Volume **50**, 1995

Coding Theory as Discrete Applied Mathematics

A. R. Calderbank

ABSTRACT. This paper provides an introduction to algebraic coding theory
and to the design of codes for Gaussian channels. It covers basic definitions,
soft-decision decoding of block codes, code construction in the frequency domain, the theory of designs, finite dimensional lattices, trellis codes and the
duality between data transmission and source compression. These topics have
been selected to emphasize connections to different areas of mathematics, and
connections to real applications.

1. Introduction

Classical coding theory is concerned with the representation of information that
is to be transmitted over some noisy channel. There are only two resources available
to the code designer; memory and redundancy. This general framework includes
the algebraic theory of error-correcting codes, where codewords are strings of symbols taken from some finite field, and it includes data transmission over Gaussian
channels, where codewords are vectors in Euclidean space. Coding theory is an
important example of discrete applied mathematics. Compact disk players, hard
disk drives, and high speed modems are examples of consumer products that make
essential use of coding to improve reliability. Innovation in coding and signal processing can translate to a significant competitive advantage in the marketplace. For
example, every time a consumer buys a compact disk a contribution of several cents
is made to Philips and Sony. The revenue stream that results amounts to hundreds
of millions of dollars every year. The importance of these applications has served
to refocus the coding theory community on the complexity of coding techniques.
It is entirely appropriate that performance should be valued as a function of delay
and decoding complexity. The special features of telephone channels and recording
channels have also led to new connections between coding theory, dynamical systems, and linear systems theory. These are described in the contribution by Marcus
[**53**].

1991 *Mathematics Subject Classification.* Primary 94A05; Secondary 94A14, 94B05, 94B12,
62K05.

Parts of this paper are reprinted from the manuscript of *The Art of Signaling: Mathematical
Foundations of Bandwidth Efficient Communication* with permission of the author.

Shannon's information theory [61] characterizes a channel by a single parameter; the channel capacity. Shannon demonstrated that it is possible to send information at any rate below channel capacity with an arbitrarily low probability of error. The method of proof is random coding; the existence of a good code is shown by averaging over all possible codes. Details can be found in the text by Cover and Thomas [18], which is packed with insights about different aspects of information theory. Practical considerations make it important that we consider codes with some special structure that simplifies decoding. Algebraic coding theory emphasizes linear codes. Here codewords are vectors with entries in some finite field, and the code is closed under vector addition and multiplication by scalars in the finite field. The linear structure makes encoding very simple, and sometimes facilitates decoding. However this author believes that the main reason algebraic coding theory emphasizes linear codes is that they are easier to discover. Optimal codes need not have this special linear structure, and nonlinear codes such as the Kerdock and Preparata codes have fascinating mathematical properties. The contribution by Kantor connects these nonlinear codes with quadratic forms and finite geometry. Ever since Shannon's original paper, coding theorists have attempted to construct structured codes that achieve channel capacity, but this problem remains open. Perhaps it is more profitable to ask a slightly different question. We mention here recent work of Spielman [64] that fixes the complexity of decoding and seeks to maximize transmission rate. This perspective is shared by the algebraic geometry codes described in the contribution by Stichtenoth, that achieve the Gilbert-Varshamov lower bound on transmission rate, for reasonable decoding complexity.

The text by van Lint [49] requires some mathematical sophistication, but is a very lucid introduction to the subject of error-correcting codes. The most comprehensive reference is still the text by MacWilliams and Sloane [51]. For more information about connections with discrete mathematics and finite geometry we refer the reader to Cameron and van Lint [13] and to Assmus and Key [2]. Conway and Sloane [16] is a treasury of information about codes and lattices; our treatment of the binary Golay code is inspired by Chapter 11 of this book. Calderbank [7] is intended as a text on the mathematical foundations of bandwidth efficient communication. For more information about the applications to magnetic recording we refer the reader to the contributions by Marcus [53] and by Marcus, Roth and Siegel [54].

2. Algebraic Coding Theory

Let $\mathbb{F}_q$ denote the finite field with q elements, and let $\mathbb{F}_q^N$ denote the set of N-tuples $(a_1, \ldots, a_N)$, where $a_i \in \mathbb{F}_q$. The *Hamming weight* $wt(x)$ of a vector $x \in \mathbb{F}_q^N$ is the number of nonzero entries. The *Hamming distance* $D(x, y)$ between two vectors $x, y \in \mathbb{F}_q^N$ is the number of places where x and y differ. Thus $D(x, y) = wt(x + y)$.

DEFINITION 2.1. An (N, M, D) *code* C over the alphabet $\mathbb{F}_q$ is a collection of M vectors from $\mathbb{F}_q^N$ (called *codewords*) such that

$$D(x, y) \geq D \text{ for all } x, y \in C ,$$

and D is the largest number with this property. The parameter D is called the *minimum distance* of the code.

Vector addition turns the set $\mathbb{F}_q^N$ into an N-dimensional vector space. A *linear code* is just a subspace of $\mathbb{F}_q^N$. The notation $[N, k, D]$ indicates a linear code with block length N, dimension k, and minimum distance D. The next result is fundamental, but it follows directly from the above definitions.

THEOREM 2.2. *The minimum distance of a linear code is the minimum weight of a nonzero codeword.*

It is possible to describe any code by just listing the codewords, and if the code has no structure, then this may be the only way. What makes an $[N, k, D]$ linear code easier to discover is that it is completely determined by any choice of k linearly independent codewords.

DEFINITION 2.3. A *generator matrix* G for an $[N, k]$ linear code C is a $k \times N$ matrix with the property that every codeword of C is some linear combination of the rows of G.

EXAMPLE 2.4. If I_{N-1} denotes the identity matrix of size $N - 1$, then the $(N-1) \times N$ matrix

$$G = \left[\begin{array}{c|c} & -1 \\ I_{N-1} & \vdots \\ & -1 \end{array} \right]$$

generates the $[N, N-1, 2]$ zero-sum code Z_N, where

$$Z_N = \left\{ (x_1, \ldots, x_N) \in \mathbb{F}_q^N \ \Big| \ \sum_{i=1}^{N} x_i = 0 \right\}. \quad \square$$

DEFINITION 2.5. Given an $[N, k]$ linear code C, the *dual code* $C^\perp$ is the $[N, N-k]$ linear code given by

$$C^\perp = \{ x \in \mathbb{F}_q^N \mid (x, c) = 0 \text{ for all } c \in C \},$$

where

$$((x_1, \ldots, x_N), (y_1, \ldots, y_N)) = \sum_{i=1}^{N} x_i y_i$$

is the standard inner product.

An $[N, k]$ linear code C is also completely determined by any choice of $N - k$ linearly independent codewords from $C^\perp$. For example, if $\mathbf{1} = (1, \ldots, 1)$, then $Z_N^\perp = \langle \mathbf{1} \rangle$, and $Z_N = \{ x \in \mathbb{F}_q^N \mid (x, \mathbf{1}) = 0 \}$.

DEFINITION 2.6. A *parity check matrix* H for an $[N, k]$ linear code C is an $(N-k) \times N$ matrix with the property that a vector $x \in \mathbb{F}_q^N$ is a codeword in C if and only if $Hx^T = 0$.

Thus a generator matrix for C is a parity check matrix for $C^\perp$ and vice versa. A linear code C is said to be *self-orthogonal* if $(x, y) = 0$ for all $x, y \in C$. If C is self-orthogonal, then $C \subseteq C^\perp$ and we can construct a parity check matrix for C by adding rows to a generator matrix. If $C = C^\perp$, then C is said to be *self-dual*. In this case a single matrix serves as both a generator matrix and a parity check matrix.

Hamming distance is not changed by *monomial transformations* which consist of permutations of the coordinate positions followed by diagonal transformations $\text{diag}[\lambda_1, \ldots, \lambda_N]$ that multiply coordinate i by the scalar λ_i. Monomial transformations preserve the Hamming metric and we shall say that two codes C_1 and C_2 are *equivalent* if one is obtained from the other by applying a monomial transformation.

The contribution by Kantor discusses nonlinear binary codes, called Kerdock codes, that can be very simply constructed as binary images under a certain natural map, called the Gray map, of linear codes over $\mathbb{Z}_4$, the integers modulo 4. The new perspective illuminates isometries of first order Reed-Muller codes that are not described by monomial transformations.

Bounds on the Size of a Code. The sphere $S_e(a)$ of radius e centered at the vector $a \in \mathbb{F}_q^N$ is the set

$$S_e(a) = \{x \in \mathbb{F}_q^N | D(x, a) \le e\} .$$

Since there are $q - 1$ ways to change an individual entry we have

$$|S_e(a)| = \sum_{i=0}^{e} \binom{N}{i} (q-1)^i .$$

THEOREM 2.7 (The Sphere Packing Bound). *Let C be a code in $\mathbb{F}_q^N$ with minimum Hamming distance D. If $e = \lfloor (D-1)/2 \rfloor$, then*

$$|C| \left(\sum_{i=0}^{e} \binom{N}{i} (q-1)^i \right) \le q^N .$$

PROOF. The spheres of Hamming radius e centered at the codewords of C are disjoint, and the union of these spheres is a subset of $\mathbb{F}_q^N$. □

DEFINITION 2.8. An e-error correcting code C for which equality holds in the sphere packing bound is said to be *perfect*.

EXAMPLE 2.9. Here we find all perfect single error correcting linear codes C over $\mathbb{F}_q$. These are the Hamming codes.

The sphere packing bound gives

$$|C|(1 + (q-1)N) = q^N .$$

Since C is linear, there is a dual code $C^\perp$ satisfying $|C^\perp| = q^N/|C| = q^s$ for some s, and so $N = (q^s - 1)/(q-1)$. The columns h_i, $i = 1, 2, \ldots, N$ in a parity check matrix H for C are vectors in $\mathbb{F}_q^s$. If $\lambda h_i = h_j$ for some $\lambda \in \mathbb{F}_q$, then $(e_i - \lambda e_j)H^T = 0$. This means $e_i - \lambda e_j \in C$, which contradicts the fact that C is a code with minimum Hamming weight $D = 3$. Hence different columns of H must determine different 1-dim. subspaces of $\mathbb{F}_q^s$. Since there are exactly $N = (q^s - 1)/(q-1)$ distinct 1-dim. subspaces of $\mathbb{F}_q^s$, we must choose exactly one vector from each subspace. Note that given s, any two codes of length $(q^s - 1)/(q-1)$ obtained in this way are equivalent. □

It is natural to start the search for other perfect codes by looking for instances where $\sum_{i=0}^{e} \binom{N}{i} (q-1)^i$ is a power of q. For $e = 2$, $q = 3$, $N = 11$ we find

$$3^6 \left(1 + 11 \cdot 2 + \binom{11}{2} \cdot 4 \right) = 3^{11} ,$$

and for $e = 3$, $q = 2$, $N = 23$ we find

$$2^{12}\left(1 + 23 + \binom{23}{2} + \binom{23}{2}\right) = 2^{23} .$$

In each case there was a code waiting to be found; the $[11, 6, 5]$ ternary Golay code, and the $[23, 12, 7]$ binary Golay code.

The Golay codes [**32**] were discovered in 1949, but their rich algebraic structure was not revealed until much later. The $[24, 12, 8]$ binary Golay code is obtained from the perfect $[23, 12, 7]$ code by adding an overall parity check, and it is a most extraordinary code. The codewords of any given weight form beautiful geometric configurations that continue to fascinate combinatorial mathematicians. The symmetry group of this code plays a central role in finite group theory, for it is the Mathieu group M_{24}, which is perhaps the most important of the 26 sporadic simple groups. Conway and Sloane [**16**] is a treasury of information concerning the Golay codes and the Leech lattice. We shall use the $[24, 12, 8]$ Golay code to introduce the Nordstrom-Robinson code, which is a nonlinear $(16, 2^8, 6)$ code. This code is the first member of the classical family of Kerdock codes considered by Kantor.

DEFINITION 2.10. Let $A_q(N, D)$ be the maximum size of a code defined over the alphabet $\mathbb{F}_q$ with block length N and minimum distance D.

The binary alphabet is of primary importance in coding theory, and the numbers $A_2(N, D)$ are central to the theory of binary codes, and to extremal set theory (which is only natural since binary vectors of length N represent subsets of the set of N coordinate positions). However these numbers take no account of decoding complexity, and for fixed transmission rate R, a $(2N, 2^{2RN}, 2\delta N)$ code with minimal decoding complexity might well be preferred to an $(N, 2^{RN}, \delta N)$ code that was more difficult to decode. We should of course be careful to normalize decoding complexity per dimension.

We fix the transmission rate R, and we increase the block length N in order to drive the error probability to zero. If the symbol error probability is p, then the average number of errors in a received vector of length N is Np. The minimum distance D must grow at least as fast as $2Np$. This explains the importance of the quantity $\alpha(\delta)$ given by

$$\alpha(\delta) = \limsup_{N\to\infty} \frac{\log_q A_q(N, \delta N)}{N} ,$$

which measures achievable rate. To study $\alpha(\delta)$ we need to estimate the number of vectors $V_q(N, e)$ in a sphere of radius e in $\mathbb{F}_q^N$.

LEMMA 2.11. *If $0 \le \lambda \le (q-1)/q$, then*

$$\log_q \frac{V_q(N, \lfloor \lambda N \rfloor)}{N} = H_q(\lambda) ,$$

where $H_q(x)$ defined on $[0, (q-1)/q]$ is the appropriate generalization of the binary entropy function, and is given by

$$H_q(0) = 0 ,$$
$$H_q(x) = x\log_q(q-1) - x\log_q x - (1-x)\log_q(1-x), \text{ for } 0 < x \le \frac{q-1}{q} .$$

THEOREM 2.12 (The Gilbert-Varshamov Bound). *If $0 \leq \delta \leq (q-1)/q$, then*

$$\alpha(\delta) \geq 1 - H_q(\delta) \ .$$

PROOF. It is sufficient to prove

$$A_q(N, D) \geq q^N / V_q(N, D-1) \ .$$

Let C be an (N, M, D) code in $\mathbb{F}_q^N$, where $M = A_q(N, D)$. Then by definition, there is no vector in $\mathbb{F}_q^N$ with Hamming distance D or more to all codewords in C. This means that

$$\mathbb{F}_q^N = \bigcup_{c \in C} S_{D-1}(c)$$

which implies $|C| V_q(N, D-1) \geq q^N$. $\square$

The proof shows it is possible to construct a code with at least $q^N / V_q(N, D-1)$ codewords by adding vectors to a code with minimum distance D until no further vectors can be added. It is possible to show that certain restricted families of codes contain members which meet the Gilbert-Varshamov bound (see MacWilliams and Sloane [51], Chapter 17).

Of course perfect codes are best possible since equality holds in sphere-packing bound. However Tietäväinen [67] and van Lint [48] have shown that only perfect multiple error correcting codes are the binary and ternary Golay codes, and the binary repetition codes. These classification results use a theorem of Lloyd [50] which has been generalized by many authors (see Cvetković and van Lint [21]). Lloyd's theorem states that a certain polynomial associated with a group theoretic decomposition of the Hamming metric space must have integral zeros. Delsarte [22] used this group theoretic decomposition to create an entire structural framework for algebraic coding theory in his Ph.D. thesis. The mathematical structures he introduced are called association schemes, and they were used by McEliece et al. [55] to derive the strongest bounds on achievable rate $\alpha(\delta)$ that are presently known. This asymptotic upper bound is sometimes called the linear programming bound since this was the method of proof. The upper bound for binary codes is as follows:

THEOREM 2.13 (McEliece, Rodemich, Rumsey and Welch). *For $q = 2$, the achievable rate $\alpha(\delta)$ satisfies*

$$\alpha(\delta) \leq \min\{1 + g(u^2) - g(u^2 + 2\delta u + 2\delta) | 0 \leq u \leq 1 - 2\delta\} \ ,$$

where

$$g(x) = H_2\left(\frac{1 - \sqrt{1-x}}{2}\right) \ .$$

Figure 1 plots the lower and upper bounds on the achievable rate of binary codes that are given by the Gilbert-Varshamov bound and the McEliece-Rodemich-Rumsey-Welch bound.

The last decade has seen the construction of algebraic geometry codes that can be encoded and decoded in time polynomial in the block length N, and with performance that matches or exceeds the Gilbert-Varshamov bound (certainly this is true for $q > 49$, but this numerical restriction does not appear essential). All this began with a paper published by Tsfasman, Vladut and Zink [68] in 1982.

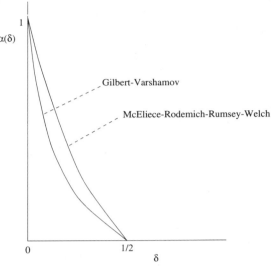

FIGURE 1. Asymptotic upper and lower bounds on achievable rate.

Soft-Decision Decoding of Block Codes. Here for simplicity we consider only binary codes. If C is a binary code, then we suppose that for transmission, 0 and 1 are mapped into 1 and -1 respectively. The entries of the received vector $(r_1, \ldots, r_N)$ are real numbers. Now

$$\|r - c\|^2 = \|r\|^2 - 2(r,c) + \|c\|^2 \ ,$$

and if c is a codeword, then $\|c\|^2$ is equal to the block length N. A maximum likelihood decoder for C finds a codeword $c \in C$ that maximizes the inner product (r,c). The *symbol metric* is $-r_j$ for 0 and r_j for 1, the smaller (more negative) metric being better. By contrast, *hard decision decoding* first quantizes each r_j to the nearest binary value (± 1) and then finds the closest codeword c' to this binary vector. Hard decision decoding is suboptimal, since c' may not be the closet codeword to r in the Euclidean metric. Maximum likelihood or soft-decision decoding of block codes is a subject of increasing importance, since electronic circuits can now perform the necessary arithmetic at the required speeds.

EXAMPLE 2.14. The first order Reed-Muller code $RM(1,m)$. The parity check matrix H_m for the binary Hamming code of length $2^m - 1$ is the $m \times (2^m - 1)$ matrix where the columns are the $2^m - 1$ different nonzero binary m-tuples. The extended Hamming code is obtained by adding an overall parity check to every Hamming codeword, and the matrix

$$W_m = \begin{bmatrix} 1 & \cdots & \cdots & \cdots & 1 \\ 0 & & & & \\ \vdots & & H_m & & \\ 0 & & & & \end{bmatrix}$$

is a parity check matrix for this code. The *first-order Reed-Muller code* $RM(1, m)$ is the dual of the extended Hamming code, and is generated by the matrix W_m. Codewords in $RM(1, m)$ correspond to polynomials in m binary variables $x_1, \ldots, x_m$ of degree at most 1; the entries of the codeword $(\epsilon, a_1, \ldots, a_m)W_m$ are the values taken by the polynomial $\epsilon + \sum_{i=1}^{m} a_i x_i$ at the different binary m-tuples. If $(a_1, \ldots, a_m) \neq (0, \ldots, 0)$ then the weight of this codeword will be 2^{m-1}, since exactly half of the entries will be equal to 1. Hence the weight distribution of $RM(1, m)$ is as follows:

Weight i	0	2^{m-1}	2^m
Number of Codewords	1	$2^{m+1} - 2$	1

We shall consider decoding algorithms that take advantage of the recursion

$$W_m = \begin{bmatrix} 1 \cdots 1 & 0 \cdots 0 \\ W_{m-1} & W_{m-1} \end{bmatrix}$$

satisfied by the generator matrix W_m.   □

We now describe efficient algorithms that successively determine the best estimate for partial codewords from a set of candidates that can easily be searched. These decoding algorithms will be represented by simple trellis diagrams with relatively few states. This is the approach taken by Forney [**27**] and we shall explain how it applies to the first order Reed-Muller code $RM(1, m)$.

The sequence of N coordinate positions is significant in trellis decoding of a binary $[N, k]$ code, because it determines the partial decoding decisions that can be made. For any position ℓ, we shall refer to the first ℓ coordinates as the *past*, and the remaining $N - \ell$ coordinates as the *future*. The decoder states are equivalence classes of past histories modulo future possibilities; the probability of a particular future given the entire past is the same as the probability of that future given the state. Our objective is to divide time into past and future so as to minimize the number of decoder states.

Let C be a binary $[N, k]$ code, and let ℓ be some coordinate position. We define C_ℓ^P to be the set of all codewords $c = (c_1, \ldots, c_N)$, where $c_{\ell+1} = \cdots = c_N = 0$. Then C_ℓ^P is a subspace of C and we let k_ℓ^P denote the dimension of this subspace. Sometimes it will be convenient to suppress the last $N - \ell$ coordinates, and to view C_ℓ^P as $[\ell, k_\ell^P]$ code. Similarly let $C_\ell^F = \{c = (c_1, \ldots, c_N) \in C | c_1 = \cdots = c_\ell = 0\}$ and let k_ℓ^F denote the dimension of C_ℓ^F. Again it will sometimes be convenient to view C_ℓ^F as an $[N - \ell, k_\ell^F]$ code. The states are the cosets of the subspace spanned by C_ℓ^P and C_ℓ^F. The vector space $\Sigma_\ell = [C : \langle C_\ell^P, C_\ell^F \rangle]$ of these cosets is called the *state space*. The dimension k_ℓ of the state space is given by

$$k_\ell = k - k_\ell^P - k_\ell^F \ ,$$

and there are 2^{k_ℓ} states. The decoding trellis is shown below

We associate possible decoder paths with cosets $[c]$ in Σ_ℓ, where $c = (a, z) \in C$, $a \in \mathbb{F}_2^\ell$ and $z \in \mathbb{F}_2^{N-\ell}$. Let $C[1, \ldots, \ell]$ denote the projection of C onto the first ℓ coordinates, and let $C[\ell + 1, \ldots, N]$ denote the projection of C onto the last $N - \ell$ coordinates. Then we may associate the first path segment with a coset of C_ℓ^P in $C[1, \ldots, \ell]$, and the second path segment with a coset of C_ℓ^F in $C[\ell + 1, \ldots, N]$. This division of time into past and future reduces the problem of decoding C to

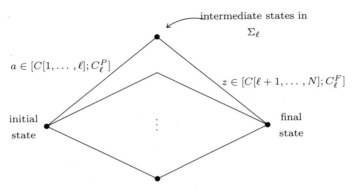

FIGURE 2. Divide and conquer decoding.

2^{k_ℓ} smaller problems, each of the form a decoding problem for (a coset of) C_ℓ^P, followed by a decoding problem for (a coset of) C_ℓ^F.

EXAMPLE 2.14 (continued). The Reed-Muller code $RM(1,3)$ is equal to the extended $[8,4,4]$ Hamming code. This code is generated by the matrix

$$W_3 = \begin{bmatrix} 0 & 0 & 0 & 0 & 1 & 1 & 1 & 1 \\ 1 & 1 & 1 & 1 & 1 & 1 & 1 & 1 \\ 1 & 0 & 1 & 0 & 1 & 0 & 1 & 0 \\ 1 & 0 & 0 & 1 & 1 & 0 & 0 & 1 \end{bmatrix}.$$

For $\ell = 2$, $C_2^P = \{0\}$, $C_2^F = \langle (111100), (001111) \rangle$, $k_2 = 4 - 0 - 2 = 2$, and the decoding trellis is shown below.

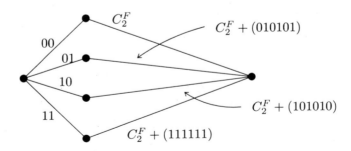

For $\ell = 4$, $C_4^P = C_4^F = \{(0000), (1111)\}$, $k_4 = 4 - 1 - 1 = 2$, and the decoding trellis is shown below.

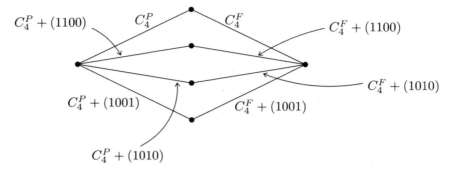

For $\ell = 6$, $C_6^P = \langle (111100), (110011) \rangle$, $C_6^F = \{0\}$, $k_6 = 4 - 2 - 0 = 2$, and the decoding trellis is shown below.

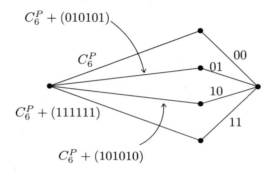

Let $a \in \Sigma_2$, $b \in \Sigma_4$ and $c \in \Sigma_6$, and join a to b to c if there is a single codeword in R_3 that passes through a, b and c. The decoding trellis that results is shown below in Figure 3.

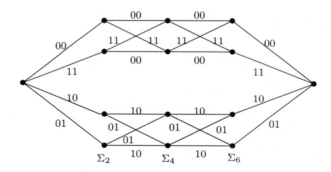

FIGURE 3. A decoding trellis for the $[8, 4, 4]$ Hamming code. □

The Viterbi Algorithm. The origin of the term *trellis code* is that the graph of state transitions looks like the structures used by gardeners to support climbing plants. Codewords are represented as paths through this trellis.

The decoder has a copy of the trellis. It processes the noisy samples and tries to find the path taken by the binary data. The decoding algorithm is dynamic programming. Every trellis stage, the decoder calculates and stores the most likely path terminating in a given state. The decoder also calculates the path metric, which measures distance from the partial received sequence to the partial codeword corresponding to the most likely path. At time $\ell = 4$ in Figure 3, the decoder only needs to update 2 path metrics and make 1 comparison to determine the most likely path terminating in a given state.

Viterbi [72] originally introduced this decoding method only as a proof technique, but it soon became apparent that it was really useful for decoding trellis codes of moderate complexity. The importance of this application is the reason the decoding method is called the Viterbi algorithm by communication theorists. Forney [26] recognized that the Viterbi algorithm is a recursive optimal solution to the problem of estimating the state sequence of a discrete time finite state Markov process observed in memoryless noise. Many problem in digital communication can be cast in this form.

EXAMPLE 2.14 (continued). Now we interpret the recursive definition of first order Reed-Muller codes in terms of decoding trellises. The code $RM(1,2)$ is the zero-sum code Z_4 and the decoding trellis for this code is shown below.

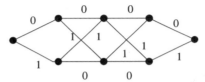

FIGURE 4. The decoding trellis for the zero-sum code Z_4.

The recursion for W_3 in terms of W_2 allows us to write $RM(1,3) = C_1 \cup C_2$, where

$$C_1 = \{(u,u)|u \in RM(1,2)\} \text{ and } C_2 = \{(u, u+1)|u \in RM(1,2)\} .$$

If we write coordinate positions in the order $4+1, 1, 4+2, 2, 4+3, 3, 4+4, 4$ then after replacing the edge label a in Figure 4 by aa, we obtain a decoding trellis for C_1. If we replace the edge label a by $\bar{a}a$, then we obtain a decoding trellis for C_2. After merging the initial and final states of these trellises, we obtain the decoding trellis for $RM(1,3)$ shown in Figure 3. Now we can use the recursion for W_m in terms of W_{m-1} once more, to produce the decoding trellis for $RM(1,4)$ shown below (for simplicity, most edge labels have been suppressed).

Decoding algorithms are assembled from basic binary operations such as real addition, real subtraction, comparing 2 real numbers, and taking an absolute value. For simplicity we might assign unit cost to each of these operations, and we might neglect the complexity of say multiplication by 2 (since this can be accomplished by merely shifting a binary expansion). It is then possible to compare different algorithms, and to show for example, that this iterative decoding procedure for Reed-Muller codes is less complex than the standard procedure using the fast Hadamard transform.

What is important in a code is the existence of a simple procedure for searching through the codewords. What makes trellis codes attractive is that they come with their own decoding algorithm. The trellis structure of Reed-Muller codes is revealed in Example 2.14, but surely this analysis extends to other families of block codes. The recursive definition of Reed-Muller codes leads to a simple decoding procedure,

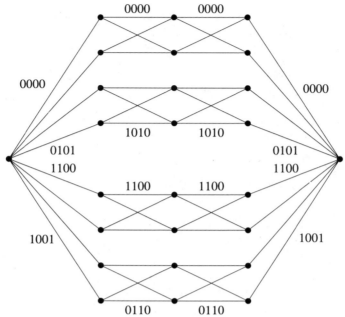

FIGURE 5. The decoding trellis for $RM(1,4)$.   □

and it is important to note that linearity of these codes is simply not relevant to decoding complexity.

It is also worthwhile to think more incisively about the tradeoff between decoding complexity and delay. Suppose that we are asked to choose between a $[2N, N, D]$ code C_1 and a $[4N, 2N, D]$ code C_2. Contemporary coding theory tends to emphasize C_1 and ignore C_2, placing the emphasis on minimizing block length, which is a measure of delay. But how important is it that information be decoded with a delay of 20 clock cycles rather than 40 clock cycles? Because there is "more room" in $2N$-dimensional space than in N-dimensional space, it may be possible to significantly reduce decoding complexity while still achieving minimum distance D. In these circumstances this author would advocate choosing code C_2 over code C_1.

The recursive definition of Reed-Muller codes is a particular case of the $|u|u+v|$ *construction*: let U be a binary linear code with block length N and minimum Hamming distance $d(U)$, and let V be a linear subcode with minimum distance $d(V)$. The $|u \mid u+v|$ construction combines U and V to give the code $|U \mid U+V|$, where

$$|U \mid U + V| = \{(u, u + v) \mid u \in U \text{ and } v \in V\} \ .$$

It is easy to see that $|U \mid U + V|$ is a linear code, that

$$\dim |U \mid U + V| = \dim(U) + \dim(V) \ ,$$

and that the minimum distance $D(|U|U + V|)$ is equal to $\min(2D(U), D(V))$. The first order Reed-Muller code $RM(1, m) = |RM(1, m - 1)|RM(1, m - 1) + \langle \mathbf{1} \rangle|$. Nonprimitive cyclic codes are also examples of the $|u|u + v|$ construction, and it would be interesting to compare them against primitive cyclic codes in terms of performance, decoding complexity and delay.

Spectral Constraints that Separate Codewords. We begin by considering integer valued sequences $e = (e_0, e_1, \ldots, e_{N-1})$ which we represent as polynomials $e(D) = \sum_{i=0}^{N-1} e_i D^i$. We shall say that the sequence $e(D)$ has a Kth order spectral null at $\theta = 2\pi\ell/M$, if $e(D)$ is divisible by $(e^{i\theta} - D)^K$. A collection of sequences with this property is called a *spectral null code*. To show that it is possible to separate vectors in Euclidean space by placing spectral constraints in the frequency domain, we consider the case $\theta = 0$. We say that the sequence $e(D)$ has *a sign change at position* u if $e_u \neq 0$, and $\text{sign}(e_u) = -\text{sign}(e_t)$, where $t = \max\{i < u | e_i \neq 0\}$.

THEOREM 2.15. (Descartes Rule of Signs). *Let $e(D)$ be a real polynomial with K positive real roots, not necessarily distinct. Then the number of sign changes in the sequence e of coefficients of $e(D)$ is at least K.*

For a proof we refer the reader to Householder [**37**]. Now consider a code with a Kth order spectral null at $\theta = 0$. It follows directly from Descartes Rule of Signs that the minimum squared distance between codewords is at least 8K. This simple observation is the starting point for the construction of many codes used in magnetic recording applications; more details can be found in Immink and Beenker [**38**], Karabed and Siegel [**40**], Eleftheriou and Cideciyan [**23**], and the contribution by Marcus, Roth and Siegel [**54**].

Now we consider frequency domain techniques involving finite fields (cf. Blahut [**5**]). First we observe that the binary $[2^m - 1, 2^m - m - 1, 3]$ Hamming code may be defined as the collection of binary vectors $(a_0, a_1, \ldots, a_{2^m-2})$ that satisfy

$$\sum_{i=0}^{2^m-2} a_i \alpha^i = 0 \, ,$$

where α is a primitive $(2^m - 1)$th root of unity in the extension field $\mathbb{F}_{2^m}$. (Recall that the Hamming code is the unique binary $[2^m - 1, 2^m - m - 1, 3]$ code, and the new definition certainly determines a code with these parameters.) We may think of the matrix

$$[1, \alpha, \alpha^2, \ldots, \alpha^{2^m-2}]$$

as a parity check matrix for this Hamming code. We may increase minimum distance by adding a second spectral constraint:

$$\begin{bmatrix} 1, & \alpha, & \alpha^2, & \ldots, & \alpha^{2^m-2} \\ 1, & \alpha^3, & \alpha^6, & \ldots, & \alpha^{3(2^m-2)} \end{bmatrix} .$$

This is the parity check matrix for the 2-error-correcting BCH code. More generally we may define a *BCH code with designed distance d* by means of the parity check matrix

$$H = \begin{bmatrix} 1 & \alpha & \alpha^2 & \cdots & \alpha^{2^m-2} \\ 1 & \alpha^2 & \alpha^4 & \cdots & \alpha^{2(2^m-2)} \\ 1 & \alpha^3 & \alpha^6 & \cdots & \alpha^{3(2^m-2)} \\ \vdots & \vdots & \vdots & & \vdots \\ 1 & \alpha^{d-2} & \alpha^{2(d-2)} & \cdots & \alpha^{(d-2)(2^m-2)} \end{bmatrix} .$$

Note that the rows of H are not linearly independent: some spectral constraints are inferred by others: for example $\sum_{i=0}^{2^m-2} a_i \alpha^i = 0$ implies $\sum_{i=0}^{2^m-2} a_i \alpha^{2i} = 0$. The assertion that the minimum distance is at least d amounts to proving that every set of $d-1$ columns is linearly independent. This is a Vandermonde argument.

The Hamming code and the BCH codes with designed distance d are examples of cyclic codes. These codes play an important role in coding practice, and are good in the sense that there are cyclic codes that meet the Gilbert-Varshamov bound. A linear code is *cyclic* if the set of codewords is fixed by a cyclic shift of the coordinates: if $(c_0, \ldots, c_{N-1})$ is a codeword, then so is $(c_{N-1}, c_0, \ldots, c_{N-2})$. To verify that the above codes are indeed cyclic, we apply the identity

$$\alpha^\ell \sum_{i=0}^{2^m-2} a_i \alpha^{\ell i} = \sum_{i=0}^{2^m-2} a_{i+1} \alpha^{\ell i} \,,$$

where subscripts are read modulo $2^m - 1$. The theory of cyclic codes identifies the sequence $(a_0, a_1, \ldots, a_{N-1})$ with the polynomial $a_0 + a_1 x + \cdots + a_{N-1} x^{N-1}$. Cyclic codes then correspond to ideals in the residue class ring $\mathbb{F}_2[x]/(x^N - 1)$, and the structure theory of principal ideal rings can be brought to bear.

We can also use the above parity check matrices to define codes over subfields of $\mathbb{F}_{2^m}$ other than the binary field $\mathbb{F}_2$. The codes defined over $\mathbb{F}_{2^m}$ itself are called *Reed-Solomon codes*. These codes were proposed by Reed and Solomon [59] and variants are now found everywhere from computer hard-disk drives to CD players. Note that Reed-Solomon codes did not go into use immediately, for at that time fast digital electronics did not exist. Reed-Solomon codes led to the development of geometric Goppa codes, and that is where the contribution by Stichtenoth begins. Note also that the Kerdock and Preparata codes discovered by Hammons et al. [34] are defined by transforms on Galois rings.

The Golay Code and the Nordstrom-Robinson Code. The most extraordinary binary code is the [24, 12] Golay code which we denote by $\mathcal{C}_{24}$. We shall introduce $\mathcal{C}_{24}$ using the Miracle Octad Generator (MOG), and the hexacode $\mathcal{C}_6$, which is a [6,3,4] code over the field with 4 elements. The MOG and the hexacode are computational tools developed by Curtis [19, 20] and Conway and Sloane [16] that make calculation within the Golay code very easy. The Leech lattice can be constructed using the Golay code $\mathcal{C}_{24}$, and the problems of designing maximum likelihood decoding algorithms for the code $\mathcal{C}_{24}$ and the lattice Λ_{24} are closely related. The importance of the Golay code and the Leech lattice has meant that these problems have been investigated extensively. We refer the reader to [1, 4, 15, 63, 66, 72] for more information.

The elements of the field $\mathbb{F}_4$ are named $0, 1, \omega$ and $\overline{\omega}$, where

$$1 + w = \overline{w}, 1 + \overline{w} = w, w + \overline{w} = 1, w^2 = \overline{w}, \overline{w}^2 = w, \text{ and } w^3 = 1 \,.$$

DEFINITION 2.16. The *hexacode* $\mathcal{C}_6$ is a 3-dimensional linear code over $\mathbb{F}_4$ consisting of all vectors $(ab\ cd\ ef)$ for which

$$a + b = c + d = e + f = s$$

and

$$a + c + e = ws \,.$$

We have separated the 6 entries into 3 *couples* to better display certain symmetries.

LEMMA 2.17. *The hexacode $\mathcal{C}_6$ has the following symmetries:*
(*i*) *scalar multiplication by any power of w,*
(*ii*) *interchanging the two entries in any two of the couples, and*
(*iii*) *any permutation of the 3 couples that preserves the ordering of the entries within each couple.*

The symmetries listed in Lemma 2.17 generate a group $\mathcal{G}$ of order 72.

LEMMA 2.18. *Every codeword in the hexacode $\mathcal{C}_6$ can be obtained from one of the 5 representatives listed below by applying some symmetry in $\mathcal{G}$.*

$$(01\ 01\ w\overline{w}) \quad (w\overline{w}\ w\overline{w}\ w\overline{w}) \quad (00\ 11\ 11) \quad (11\ ww\ \overline{w}\overline{w}) \quad (00\ 00\ 00)$$

36 *images*   12 *images*   9 *images*   6 *images*   1 *image*

PROOF. Simply check that each representative c is a hexacodeword, and calculate the size of the stabilizer within $\mathcal{G}$ of the hexacodeword c. $\qquad\square$

The Miracle Octad Generator or MOG. We shall arrange the entries of Golay codewords in a 4×6 array. This array is shown below, and is called the Miracle Octad Generator or MOG for short.

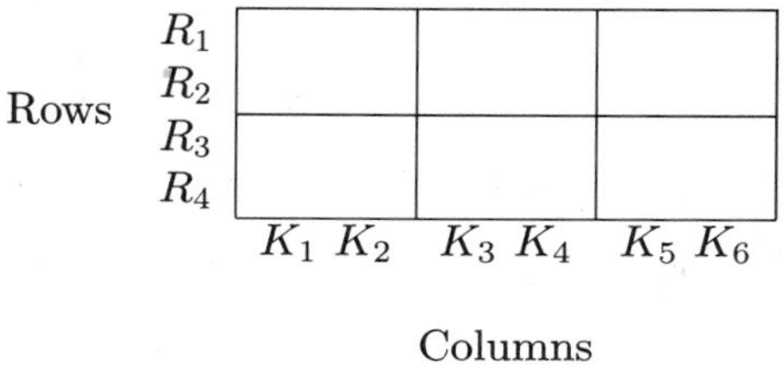

FIGURE 6. The 4×6 MOG array.

We specify vectors in $\mathbb{F}_2^{24}$ by starring the position of the nonzero entries as shown below

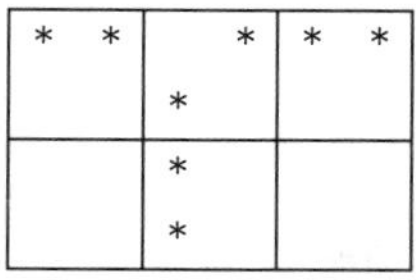

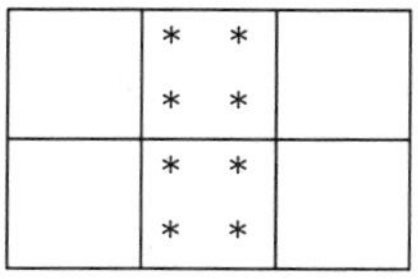

The binary world and the $\mathbb{F}_4$ world are connected by the *scoring* map φ from $\mathbb{F}_2^4$ to $\mathbb{F}_4$ given by

$$\varphi \begin{pmatrix} a \\ b \\ c \\ d \end{pmatrix} \longrightarrow a \cdot 0 + b \cdot 1 + c \cdot w + d \cdot \overline{w}\,.$$

By inverting the map φ, we obtain a $1 : 4$ map between field elements in $\mathbb{F}_4$ and binary 4 tuples. Figure 7 shows the 4 different ways to *interpret* a given field element as a binary 4-tuple. The *parity* of the interpretation is the parity of the weight of the corresponding 4-tuple.

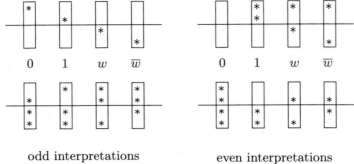

odd interpretations
of $0, 1, w$ and $\overline{w}$

even interpretations
of $0, 1, w$ and $\overline{w}$

FIGURE 7. Representing field elements by binary 4-tuples.

By scoring the columns of the MOG we obtain a map from $\mathbb{F}_2^{24}$ to $\mathbb{F}_4^6$, which we shall also denote by φ. Note that φ respects binary addition.

DEFINITION 2.19. We shall say that a vector v in $\mathbb{F}_2^{24}$ is *balanced* if

$$(v, R_1) = (v, K_1) = (v, K_2) = \cdots = (v, K_6) .$$

The set $\mathcal{B}$ of balanced vectors is a linear code, and in fact

$$\mathcal{B} = \langle K_1 + K_i, \ K_1 + R_1 \mid i = 2, 3, \ldots, 6 \rangle^\perp .$$

DEFINITION 2.20. The *Golay code* $\mathcal{C}_{24}$ is the set of all balanced vectors v in $\mathbb{F}_2^{24}$ such that $\varphi(v)$ is a hexacodeword.

The advantage of this definition is that given some familiarity with the hexacode $\mathcal{C}_6$, it is straightforward to check whether a binary vector is a Golay codeword. For example, the vectors

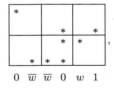

$$0 \ \ \overline{w} \ \ \overline{w} \ \ 0 \ \ w \ \ 1$$

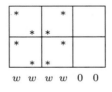

$$w \ \ w \ \ w \ \ w \ \ 0 \ \ 0$$

and

$$w \ \ \overline{w} \ \ w \ \ \overline{w} \ \ w \ \ \overline{w}$$

are all Golay codewords.

The set $\mathcal{B}$ of balanced codewords is a linear code, and since φ respects binary addition, the inverse image $\varphi^{-1}(\mathcal{C}_6)$ is also a linear code. Hence $\mathcal{C}_{24} = \mathcal{B} \cap \varphi^{-1}(\mathcal{C}_6)$ is linear. We shall say that codewords in $\mathcal{C}_{24}$ have odd parity or even parity according as the interpretation of each hexacodeword entry is odd or even. For example

$$K_1 + K_2 =$$

(even parity)

, and $K_1 + R_1 =$

(odd parity)

The Golay codewords with even parity form a subcode of index 2.

Figure 8 shows the codes that have been defined in this section. Edges indicate containment, and edge labels specify the index of the subcode. We see that $\dim \mathcal{C}_{24} = 12$.

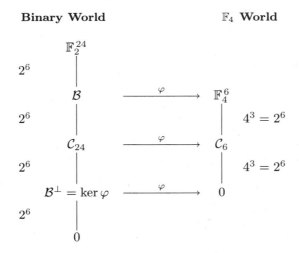

Binary World $\mathbb{F}_4$ **World**

FIGURE 8. Towers of linear codes.

THEOREM 2.21. *The Golay code $\mathcal{C}_{24}$ is a self-dual $[24, 12, 8]$ binary code. The Hamming weight of every codeword is divisible by 4.*

PROOF. We have shown that $\mathcal{C}_{24}$ is a 12-dim. linear code. Now let E denote the subcode of $\mathcal{C}_{24}$ consisting of all codewords with even parity. We begin by showing that all weights in E are divisible by 4.

If $e \in E$, then Lemma 2.18 implies that the hexacodeword $\varphi(e)$ has Hamming weight 0, 4 or 6. We see from Figure 7 that a nonzero entry in $\varphi(e)$ is represented by a binary 4 tuple with Hamming weight 2. We also see that a zero entry in $\varphi(e)$ is represented by a binary 4 tuple with Hamming weight 0 or 4. Hence

$$wt(e) \equiv 2wt(\varphi(e)) \equiv 0 \ (\text{mod} \ 4)$$

as required.

Next we prove that E is self-orthogonal. If $x, y \in E$ then $x + y \in E$, and the identity

$$wt(x + y) = wt(x) + wt(y) - 2wt(x \cap y)$$

implies $(x, y) \equiv wt(x \cap y) \equiv 0 \ (\text{mod} \ 2)$ as required.

The Golay code $\mathcal{C}_{24} = \langle E, K_1 + R_1 \rangle$. If $e \in E$, then balance requires $(e, K_1) = (e, R_1)$, so that $(e, K_1 + R_1) = 0$. Now $(K_1 + R_1, K_1 + R_1) = 0$, $(K_1 + R_1, E) = 0$, and $(E, E) = 0$, so that $\mathcal{C}_{24}$ is self-dual. The identity

$$wt(K_1 + R_1 + e) = wt(K_1 + R_1) + wt(e) - 2wt((K_1 + R_1) \cap e)$$

implies that all weights in $\mathcal{C}_{24}$ are divisible by 4.

It remains to prove that the minimum weight $D = 8$. Suppose for a contradiction that there is a codeword c in $\mathcal{C}_{24}$ with $wt(c) = 4$. Odd parity requires $wt(c) \geq 6$, so the codeword c has even parity, and hence $wt(\varphi(c)) \leq 2$. Since the hexacode has minimum weight 4, we must have $\varphi(c) = 0$. Now $c = K_i$ for some i and this violates the balance condition. $\qquad\square$

The Nordstrom-Robinson Code. This is a nonlinear $(16, 256, 6)$ code, which we denote by $\mathcal{N}_{16}$. We begin by defining a subset Ω of the $[24, 12]$ Golay code $\mathcal{C}_{24}$:

$$\Omega = \{c \in \mathcal{C}_{24} \mid \text{either } c|_{K_1+K_2} = 0 \text{ or } wt(c|_{K_1+K_2}) = 2$$
and the top left entry of c equals $1\}$.

The codewords in the Nordstrom-Robinson code $\mathcal{N}_{16}$ are obtained from the codewords in Ω by deleting the 8 coordinates in $K_1 + K_2$. It is easy to verify that codewords $c \in \mathcal{C}_{24}$ for which $c|_{K_1+K_2} = 0$ determine a copy of the Reed-Muller code $RM(1,4)$ in this way. Hence $\mathcal{N}_{16}$ is the union of 8 cosets of $RM(1,4)$. Soft decision decoding of $\mathcal{N}_{16}$ can then be reduced to solving 8 easy decoding problems for $RM(1,4)$.

We write $\mathcal{N}_{16} = \bigcup_{i=1}^{8} (RM(1,4) + y_i)$, where $y_1 = 0$. For $i \geq 2$, every weight in $RM(1,4) + y_i$ is congruent to 2 modulo 4, and lies in the interval $[\mathbf{6, 10}]$. It follows easily that the weight distribution of $\mathcal{N}_{16}$ is given by

weight i	0	6	8	10	16
Number of Codewords	1	112	30	112	1

The appearance of the Nordstrom-Robinson code $\mathcal{N}_{16}$ inside the Golay code $\mathcal{C}_{24}$ is a particular instance of the antipode construction of Conway and Sloane [**17**], which was inspired by examples found earlier by Vardy [**70**]. The idea here is to take a very good code or lattice (in this case $\mathcal{C}_{24}$), to take a subset of coordinates (in this case $K_1 + K_2$), and to take a collection of vectors defined on the distinguished subset that are pairwise close. Now consider the vectors in the original code or lattice that project onto the vectors z_i, and look at the projection C (in this case $\mathcal{N}_{16}$) on the complementary subset (in this case $K_3 + K_4 + K_5 + K_6$). Since we started with a very good code or lattice, and since the vectors z_i are pairwise close, the projection C is also a very good code or lattice.

We have seen that codewords in $RM(1,4)$ correspond to polynomials $\epsilon + s_1 x_1 + s_2 x_2 + s_3 x_3 + s_4 x_4$, where ϵ, s_1, s_2, s_3 and $s_4 = 0$ or 1. We label the 16 coordinate positions with the elements of a 4-dimensional vector space as shown below.

		0	e_3	e_4	$e_3 + e_4$
	e_1	$e_1 + e_3$	$e_1 + e_4$	$e_1 + e_3 + e_4$
	e_2	$e_2 + e_3$	$e_2 + e_4$	$e_2 + e_3 + e_4$
	$e_1 + e_2$	$e_1 + e_3 + e_3$	$e_1 + e_2 + e_4$	$e_1 + e_2 + e_3 + e_4$

Now we show that the coset representatives y_i correspond to quadratic functions of the binary variables x_1, x_2, x_3 and x_4. It is easy to verify that the codeword

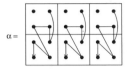

corresponds to the quadratic form $x_1 + x_2 + x_3 + x_4 + x_1 x_2 + x_3 x_4$. Coset representatives for the 7 nontrivial cosets of $RM(1,4)$ in $\mathcal{B}_{16}$ are obtained by applying powers of the automorphism α of $\mathcal{C}_{24}$ given by

$$\alpha =$$

Since α is described by the linear map

$$\begin{pmatrix} x_1 \\ x_2 \\ x_3 \\ x_4 \end{pmatrix} \longrightarrow \begin{pmatrix} 1 & 1 & 0 & 0 \\ 1 & 1 & 1 & 0 \\ 1 & 0 & 1 & 0 \\ 0 & 0 & 0 & 1 \end{pmatrix} \begin{pmatrix} x_1 \\ x_2 \\ x_3 \\ x_4 \end{pmatrix}$$

it follows that every codeword in $\mathcal{B}_{16}$ is described by a quadratic function of x_1, x_2, x_3 and x_4. The Nordstrom-Robinson code is the first member of the infinite family of Kerdock codes. We have now connected with the contribution by Kantor that describes Kerdock codes in terms of collections of quadratic forms.

3. The Theory of Designs

We begin in real Euclidean space with the game of soccer. The members of each team try to propel a round ball into the opposing team's goal using any part of the body except the hands or arms. In fact a soccer ball is a truncated icosahedron, and not a perfect sphere. This is a polytope with 60 vertices and two types of face; regular pentagons that are usually colored black, and regular hexagons that are usually colored white. The game of soccer evolved from medieval contests between villages involving an inflated animal bladder. It would be preverse to argue against the assertion that the truncated icosahedron is closer to a perfect sphere than an inflated bladder. However it is worthwhile to ask for a mathematical criterion that measures how well a sphere is approximated by a finite point set.

Recall that the kth moments of a vector (x, y, z) in $\mathbb{R}^3$ with respect to the origin are the monomials $x^a y^b z^c$ of total degree $k = a + b + c$ in x, y, z. There are $(k+1)(k+2)/2$ such moments. Our criterion for an approximation of strength t to the unit sphere Ω_d in $\mathbb{R}^d$ by a point set $\mathcal{P}$ is that the kth moments of $\mathcal{P}$ should equal the kth moments of Ω_d for $k \leq t$.

DEFINITION 3.1. Let $\mathcal{P} = \{P_1, \dots, P_N\}$ be a set of N points on the unit sphere $\Omega_d = \{x = (x_1, \dots, x_d) \in \mathbb{R}^d \mid x \cdot x = 1\}$. Then $\mathcal{P}$ is a *spherical t-design* if

the identity

$$\int_{\Omega_d} f(x)d\mu(x) = \frac{1}{N} \sum_{i=1}^{N} f(P_i)$$

(where μ is uniform measure on Ω_d normalized to have total measure 1) holds for all polynomials f of degree $\leq t$.

The 60 vertices of the soccer ball form a spherical 5-design. However in 1981, Goethals and Seidel [31] showed that a slight perturbation of these vertices changes them to a 9-design. More recently Hardin and Sloane [35] have found a spherical 9-design with only 48 points, and a 10-design with 60 points shown in Figure 9 (which is taken from [35]). The latter is the union of 5 snub tetrahedra with 174

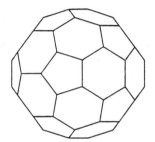 

FIGURE 9. The regular truncated icosahedron (or soccer ball) and the new 60 point spherical 10-design.

edges and 116 triangular faces. Hardin and Sloane do not expect it to immediately replace the standard soccer ball. More information about spherical designs and connections to number theory and the design of statistical experiments can be found in the contribution by Hardin and Sloane [36].

The purpose of a design is to capture with a small ensemble the regularity properties of a much larger universe. Note that this is also a feature of the small-bias probability spaces described in the contribution by Feigenbaum [25]. Designs are concerned with approximating a universe closely, whereas codes are concerned with separating an ensemble widely. Questions in coding theory are packing problems, whereas questions in design theory are covering problems. There is a duality between packing and covering that can be made mathematically precise (see for example Levenshtein [47]).

We now return to the discrete world where a $t - (v, k, \lambda)$ design is a collection $\mathcal{B}$ of subsets of a v-element set such that every member of $\mathcal{B}$ contains k points and every subset of t points is in λ blocks. Here we are looking at the universe of k-point subsets, and we are approximating the regularity properties of this universe with respect to t-subsets of coordinates. We now consider 2-designs in greater detail. If b denotes the number of blocks, and if r denotes the number of blocks containing a given point, then the identities

$$bk = vr \text{ and } r(k - 1) = (v - 1)\lambda$$

restrict the possible parameter sets. These identities are trivial in that they are obtained by elementary counting arguments. It is natural to impose the restriction

$k < v$, and in this case we have Fisher's inequality $b \geq v$. Designs with $b = v$ are called symmetric designs. In a symmetric design there is just one intersection number; two distinct blocks always intersect in λ points. Conversely it is easily shown that a 2-design with one intersection number is a symmetric design. The Bruck-Ryser-Chowla theorem provides a nontrivial restriction on the parameter sets of symmetric designs. Here "nontrivial" means an algebraic condition that is not a consequence of simple counting arguments. The Bruck-Ryser-Chowla theorem also provides a connection between the theory of designs and the algebraic theory of error-correcting codes. The symmetric design determines a self-dual code with respect to some nondegenerate scalar product. The restrictions provided by the theorem are necessary conditions for the existence of these self-dual codes. More information can be found in the monograph by Lander [42] and in Blokhuis and Calderbank [6].

The most important theorem relating codes and designs is the Assmus-Mattson theorem. The statement of this theorem given below differs from the statement given elsewhere (for example in Assmus and Mattson [3] or MacWilliams and Sloane [51]) where the conclusion applies only to codewords of sufficiently low weight. This restriction is to exclude designs with repeated blocks. Since we mean to allow t-designs with repeated blocks, we may drop the extra restriction.

THEOREM 3.2 (Assmus-Mattson). *Let C be a linear $[v, k, d]$ code over $\mathbb{F}_q$, where the weights of the nonzero codewords are $w_1 = d$, $w_2, \ldots, w_s$. Let $s'_1, w'_2, \ldots, w'_{s'}$ be the nonzero weights in $C^{\perp}$. Let t be the greatest integer in the range $0 < t < d$, such that there are at most $d-t$ weights w'_i with $0 < w'_i \leq v-t$. Then the codewords of any weight w_i in C form a t-design.*

For generalizations of this theorem we refer the reader to Calderbank, Delsarte and Sloane [8], and to Calderbank and Delsarte [9, 10].

The fundamental question in design theory is usually taken to be: Given v, k, λ does there exist a $t-(v, k, \lambda)$ design? This is certainly a natural question to ask from the perspective of extremal set theory, but it does not involve the idea of approximation in an essential way. Designs play an important role in applied mathematics and statistics. This author believes that questions involving fundamental limits on the quality of approximation are more fundamental to design theory.

4. The Band-Limited Gaussian Channel

The system model described here is taken from Forney and Eyuboglu [30]. A *Gaussian channel* combines a linear filter with additive Gaussian noise as shown in Figure 10. In the time domain the output $z(t)$ is given by

$$z(t) = x(t) * h(t) + n(t) ,$$

where $x(t)$ is the input waveform, $h(t)$ is the *channel impulse response*, $x(t) * h(t)$ is the convolution of $x(t)$ with $h(t)$, and $n(t)$ is zero-mean colored Gaussian noise.

The Fourier transform of $h(t)$ is the *frequency response $H(f)$* of the channel, and the *power spectrum $S_h(f)$* is given by $S_h(f) = |H(f)|^2$. In the frequency domain the signal $x(t)$ and the noise $n(t)$ are characterized by their Fourier transforms $X(f)$ and $N(f)$ respectively, and by their power spectra $S_x(f)$ and $S_n(f)$. An essential feature of the model is a power constraint

$$\int S_x(f) df \leq P$$

on the power spectrum $S_x(f)$ of the input waveform $x(t)$. The *channel signal to noise function* $SNR_h(f)$ is given by $SNR_h(f) = S_h(f)/S_n(f)$, and is measured in dB by taking $10\log_{10} SNR_h(f)$.

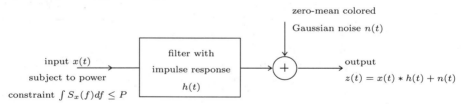

FIGURE 10. The Gaussian channel model.

The model is limited in that the output $z(t)$ is assumed to depend linearly on the input $x(t)$, and to be time-invariant. In magnetic recording applications, this linearity assumption becomes less valid once the recording density exceeds a certain threshold. In modem applications, the noise $n(t)$ starts to depend on the input $x(t)$ once the transmission rate exceeds threshold. However these caveats should not subtract from the importance of the basic model.

We think of the input $x(t)$ and the output $z(t)$ as random variables. The mutual information between $x(t)$ and $z(t)$ is the conditional entropy of $z(t)$ given $x(t)$. Channel capacity results from maximizing mutual information. Information theorists use what are called "waterfilling arguments" to show that there is a constant K and a frequency band $\mathcal{W} = \{f | K \geq 1/SNR_h(r)\}$, such that the capacity achieving input power spectrum $S_x^*(f)$ is given by

$$S_x^*(f) = \begin{cases} K - 1/SNR_h(f), & \text{if } f \in \mathcal{W}, \\ 0, & \text{if } f \notin \mathcal{W}. \end{cases}$$

This is shown in Figure 11, and for more details we refer the reader to Cover and Thomas [18]. The capacity achieving bandwidth is given by $W = \int_{\mathcal{W}} df$.

The sampling theorem of Nyquist and Shannon allows us to replace a continuous function limited to the frequency band $\mathcal{W}$ by a discrete sequence of W equally spaced samples, without loss of any information. This allows us to convert our continuous channel to a discrete time channel with signaling interval $T = 1/W$. The input $x(t)$ is generated as a filtered sequence $\sum x_k p(t - kT)$, where x_k is complex and the pulse p has power spectrum proportional to $S_x^*(f)$ on $\mathcal{W}$. The output $z(t)$ is sampled every T seconds and the decoder operates on these samples.

The capacity achieving bandwidth of an optical fiber is approximately 10^9 Hz, which is too large for sophisticated signal processing. By contrast the capacity achieving bandwidth of a telephone channel is approximately 3300 Hz. If a modem is to achieve data rates of 19.2 kb/s and above, then every time we signal, we must transmit multiple bits. Mathematics has a role to play here because now there is time for sophisticated signal processing.

An *ideal band-limited Gaussian channel* is characterized by a "brickwall" linear filter $H(f)$ that is equal to a constant over some frequency band of width W Hz and equal to zero elsewhere, and by white Gaussian noise with a constant power spectrum over the channel bandwidth. The equivalent discrete-time ideal channel represents the complex output sequence z_k as

$$z_k = x_k + n_k,$$

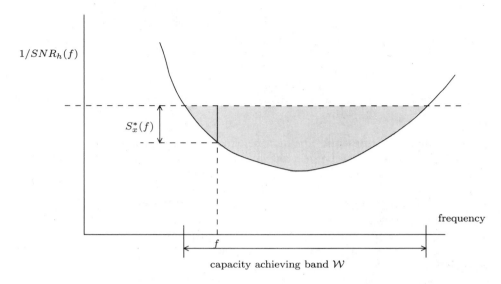

FIGURE 11. Representation of the input power spectrum that achieves capacity.

where (x_k) is the complex input sequence and (n_k) is a sequence of independent identically distributed complex zero-mean Gaussian random variables. We let S_x denote the average energy of the input samples (x_k), and we let S_n denote the average energy of the noise samples. Shannon proved that the channel capacity of this ideal channel is given by

$$C = \log_2(1 + S_x/S_n) \text{ bits/Hz },$$

or

$$\tilde{C} = CW = W \log_2(1 + S_x/S_n) \text{ bits/sec.}$$

We may transmit m bits/Hz by selecting x_k from a fixed constellation of 2^m points in the complex plane. This method of signaling is called 2^m-*Quadrature Amplitude Modulation* (2^m-QAM), and Figure 12 shows standard constellations for 16-QAM and 32-QAM. Note this is uncoded transmission since there is no redundancy.

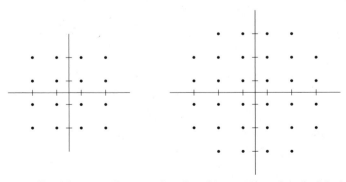

FIGURE 12. Signal constellations for Quadrature Amplitude Modulation.

There is a gap between capacity of this ideal channel and the rate that can be achieved by uncoded QAM transmission. The size of this gap varies with channel SNR and for sufficiently high SNR it is approximately 3 bits/Hz. This can also be expressed as an SNR group of approximately 9 dB since the extra rate changes S_x to $S_x/8$ and $10\log_{10} 8 \approx 9$ dB. The coding and shaping schemes described in this section are worth approximately 5 dB, and they make possible robust transmission at data rates up to 33.6 kb/s.

Constellation Design. Shannon recognized that signals input to a Gaussian channel should themselves be selected with a Gaussian distribution; the statistics of the signals should match that of the noise. We start by choosing a lattice Λ in real N-dimensional space $\mathbb{R}^N$. The signal constellation Ω consists of all lattice points within a region $\mathcal{R}$. The reason we consider signal constellations drawn from lattices is that signal points are distributed regularly throughout N-dimensional space. This means that the average signal power P of the constellation Ω is approximately the average power $P(\mathcal{R})$ of a probability distribution that is uniform within $\mathcal{R}$ and zero elsewhere. This approximation is called the *continuous approximation* and we shall use it extensively. If we fix the size of the signal constellation, then the average signal power depends on the choice of lattice and on the shape of the region that bounds the constellation. We obtain a Gaussian distribution by choosing the bounding region to be an N-dimensional sphere.

We shall also study implementation issues. At the encoder we consider the problem of addressing the signal constellation. At the decoder we consider the problem of finding the closest lattice point to a received vector in N-dimensional space.

Signal Power. Let Ω be an N-dimensional signal constellation and let $q(y)$ be the probability of transmitting the signal y. Let $\Omega_{i_1,\ldots,i_k}$ be the projection of Ω on coordinates $i_1,\ldots,i_k$, and let $q_{i_1,\ldots,i_k}(\ )$ be the induced probability distribution.

An N-dimensional signal is transmitted as N consecutive 1-dimensional signals or (in QAM transmission) as $N/2$ consecutive 2-dimensional signals modulating amplitude and phase of a carrier signal. This means that the projections Ω_i and $\Omega_{2i-1,2i}$ are particularly important.

DEFINITION 4.1. We shall usually consider signal constellations for which $q_i(\ )$ or $q_{2i-1,2i}(\ )$ are independent of i. In this case the projections Ω_i or $\Omega_{2i-1,2i}$ are identical. This common projection is called the *constituent 1- or 2-dimensional constellation* and is denoted by $\Omega_{[1]}$ or $\Omega_{[2]}$ respectively.

DEFINITION 4.2. Given an N-dimensional signal constellation Ω, the *average signal power P* (normalized per dimension) is given by

$$P = \frac{1}{N} \sum_{y \in \Omega} q(y)\|y\|^2 \,,$$

where $q(y)$ is the probability of transmitting the signal y. For QAM transmission we shall sometimes normalize power *per 2-dimensional symbol*. The *ratio of peak to average power* (PAR) measures the sensitivity of a signal constellation to nonlinearities and other signal dependent perturbations. Peak power is measured in the projection Ω_i, or in the projection $\Omega_{2i-1,2i}$, according as the basic signal is 1- or 2-dimensional.

EXAMPLE 4.3. Table 1 describes a 4-dimensional signal constellation with 512 lattice points that is bounded by a 4-dim. sphere. Signal points are drawn from the translate $\mathbb{Z}^4 + (1/2, 1/2, 1/2, 1/2)$ of the integer lattice $\mathbb{Z}^4$. These signal points are obtained from the representatives listed in Table 1 by applying all permutations of coordinates and all possible sign changes. We suppose that all these 4-dimensional signals are equiprobable.

TABLE 1. Representatives from a spherical 4-dimensional constellation with 512 signal points.

Representative y	$\|y\|^2$	$\frac{1}{16} \times$ Number
$(1111)/2$	1	1
$(3111)/2$	3	4
$(3311)/2$	5	6
$(5111)/2$	7	4
$(3331)/2$	7	4
$(5311)/2$	9	12
$(3333)/2$	9	1

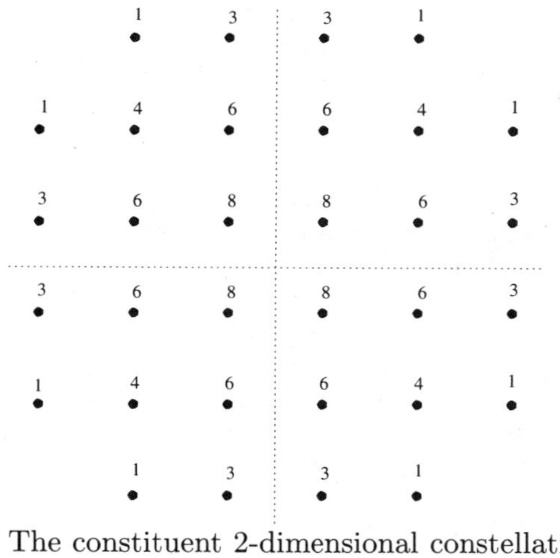

FIGURE 13. The constituent 2-dimensional constellation $\Omega_{[2]}$ and the induced probability distribution $q_{[2]}(\ )$ (in multiples of $1/128$).

The lattice $\mathbb{Z}^4 + (1/2, 1/2, 1/2, 1/2)$ and the spherical boundary are left invariant by all coordinate permutations. This means that the projections $\Omega_{2i-1,2i}$ are identical, and we may calculate average signal power using the constituent 2-dimensional constellation $\Omega_{[2]}$. Figure 10 shows $\Omega_{[2]}$ and the induced probability distribution $q_{[2]}(\ )$. It also makes the point that a spherical 4-dimensional constellation induces a non-uniform probability distribution on the constituent 2-dimensional constellation. It is easy to verify that

$$P = \frac{1}{2} \sum_{y \in \Omega_2} q_{[2]}(y) \|y\|^2 = \frac{27}{16} ,$$

$$PAR_1(\Omega) = \frac{25}{4} \times \frac{16}{27} = 3.7037\ldots ,$$

and

$$PAR_2(\Omega) = \frac{1}{2} \times \frac{(25+9)}{4} \times \frac{16}{27} = \frac{68}{27} = 2.5185\ldots ,$$

where the subscript indicates the projection where peak power is measured.

The Fundamental Volume of a Lattice.

DEFINITION 4.4. A *lattice* Λ in real N-dimensional space is a discrete additive subgroup of $\mathbb{R}^N$. A basis for the lattice Λ is a set of m vectors $v_1, \ldots, v_m$ such that

$$\Lambda = \left\{ \sum_{i=1}^{m} \lambda_i v_i \mid \lambda_i \in \mathbb{Z}, \ i = 1, \ldots, m \right\} .$$

The lattice Λ is said to be m-dimensional and usually we have $m = N$. If $w_1, \ldots, w_m$ is another choice of basis then there exists a unimodular integral matrix Q such that $w_i = Q v_i$ for all $i = 1, \ldots, m$.

DEFINITION 4.5. A *fundamental region* $\mathcal{R}$ for a lattice Λ is a region of $\mathbb{R}^N$ that contains one and only one point from each equivalence class modulo Λ. In other words $\mathcal{R}$ is a complete system of coset representatives for Λ in $\mathbb{R}^N$.

If $v_1, \ldots, v_m$ are a basis for a lattice Λ then the parallelotope consisting of the points

$$\mu_1 v_1 + \cdots + \mu_m v_m \ (0 \le \mu_i < 1)$$

is an example of a fundamental region of Λ. This region is called a *fundamental parallelotope*.

DEFINITION 4.6. If $\Lambda \subseteq \mathbb{R}^N$ is a lattice, and $y \in \Lambda$ is a lattice point, then the *Voronoi region* $\mathcal{R}(y)$ consists of those points in $\mathbb{R}^N$ that are at least as close to y as to any other $y' \in \Lambda$. Thus

$$\mathcal{R}(y) = \left\{ x \in \mathbb{R}^N \mid \|x - y\|^2 \le \|x - y'\|^2 \text{ for all } y' \in \Lambda \right\} .$$

The interiors of different Voronoi regions are disjoint though two neighboring Voronoi regions may share a face. These faces lie in the hyperplanes midway between two neighboring lattice points. Translation by $y \in \Lambda$ maps the Voronoi region $\mathcal{R}(w)$ to the Voronoi region $\mathcal{R}(w + y)$, so that all Voronoi regions are congruent.

A maximum likelihood decoding algorithm for the lattice Λ finds the Voronoi region $\mathcal{R}(y)$ that contains the received vector $v \in \mathbb{R}^N$. The Voronoi regions $\mathcal{R}(y)$ are the decision regions for this algorithm. We may create a fundamental region for the lattice Λ by deleting faces from a Voronoi region. Different ways of deleting faces correspond to different rules for resolving ties in a maximum likelihood decoding algorithm. Figure 14 shows a fundamental region for the integer lattice $\mathbb{Z}^2$ that is obtained by deleting faces from a Voronoi region. The corresponding rule for resolving ties in the first quadrant is that 1/2-integers are rounded down.

Given a lattice $\Lambda \subseteq \mathbb{R}^N$, there are many ways to choose a fundamental region. But the volume of the fundamental region is uniquely determined by the lattice Λ.

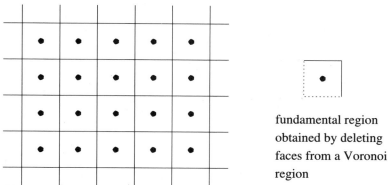

fundamental region
obtained by deleting
faces from a Voronoi
region

FIGURE 14. The plane tiled by Voronoi regions of the integer lattice $\mathbb{Z}^2$.

This volume is called the *fundamental volume* and we denote it by $V(\Lambda)$. There is a simple formula for the fundamental volume. Let $v_i = (v_{i1}, \ldots, v_{iN})$, $i = 1, \ldots, m$ be a basis for $V(\Lambda)$, and let

$$A = \begin{bmatrix} v_{11} & \cdots & v_{1N} \\ \vdots & & \vdots \\ v_{m1} & \cdots & v_{mN} \end{bmatrix}.$$

Then the fundamental volume $V(\Lambda)$ is given by

$$V(\Lambda)^2 = \det(AA^T),$$

and $V(\Lambda)^2$ is called the *determinant* or *discriminant* of the lattice. Note that the fundamental volume $V(\Lambda)$ is independent of the basis v_i, $i = 1, \ldots, m$, since any other basis w_i, $i = 1, \ldots, m$ is of the form $w_i = Qv_i$, where Q is a unimodular integral matrix. The matrix A is called *a generator matrix* for Λ since every lattice point is an integer linear combination of the rows of A.

EXAMPLE 4.7. The Gosset lattice E_8 was discovered in the last third of the nineteenth century by the Russian mathematicians A. N. Korkin and E. I. Zolotaroff, and by the English lawyer and amateur mathematician Thorold Gosset;

$$E_8 = \{(z_1, \ldots, z_8) | z_i \in \mathbb{Z}, \ i = 1, \ldots, 8 \text{ or } z_i \in \mathbb{Z} + 1/2, \ i = 1, \ldots, 8,$$

$$\text{and } z_1 + \cdots + z_8 \in 2\mathbb{Z}\}.$$

To see that the matrix A given by

$$A = \begin{bmatrix} 2 & 0 & 0 & 0 & 0 & 0 & 0 & 0 \\ -1 & 1 & 0 & 0 & 0 & 0 & 0 & 0 \\ 0 & -1 & 1 & 0 & 0 & 0 & 0 & 0 \\ 0 & 0 & -1 & 1 & 0 & 0 & 0 & 0 \\ 0 & 0 & 0 & -1 & 1 & 0 & 0 & 0 \\ 0 & 0 & 0 & 0 & -1 & 1 & 0 & 0 \\ 0 & 0 & 0 & 0 & 0 & -1 & 1 & 0 \\ 1/2 & 1/2 & 1/2 & 1/2 & 1/2 & 1/2 & 1/2 & 1/2 \end{bmatrix}$$

generates the lattice E_8, let $v_1, \ldots, v_8$ be the rows of A. We have to prove that any lattice point $z = (z_1, \ldots, z_8)$ in E_8 is an integral linear combination of these rows. If

$$w = z - 2z_8 v_8 = (w_1, w_2, \ldots, w_8)$$

then $w_8 = 0$, and

$$w = (w_7 + w_8)v_7 + (w_6 + w_7 + w_8)v_6 + \cdots + (w_2 + \cdots + w_8)v_2$$

$$+\frac{1}{2}(w_1 + \cdots + w_u)v_1 ,$$

as required. The fundamental volume $V(E_8)$ is given by

$$V(E_8)^2 = \det(AA^T) = (\det A)^2 = 1 ,$$

so that $V(E_8) = 1$.   □

DEFINITION 4.8. We shall say that a lattice $\Lambda \subseteq \mathbb{R}^N$ is *integral* if the inner product of any two lattice points is an integer. An integral lattice Λ with determinant $\det(\Lambda) = 1$ is called *unimodular*. If Λ is an integral lattice, and if the inner product $(x, x) \in 2\mathbb{Z}$ for all $x \in \Lambda$ then Λ is said to be *even*. It happens that E_8 is the unique 8-dimensional even unimodular lattice (see Conway and Sloane [16] for more details).

We let $d^2(\Lambda)$ denote the minimum squared Euclidean distance between two distinct points in the lattice Λ. Then $d^2(\Lambda)$ equals the minimum norm of a nonzero lattice point. For the lattice E_8 we have $d^2(E_8) = 2$. Every lattice point in E_8 has 240 nearest neighbors; the neighbors of the origin (the point 0^8) are the 112 points $(\pm 1)^2 0^6$, and the 128 points $(\pm 1/2)^8$ where the number of minus signs is even. This means that E_8 offers a way of arranging unit spheres in 8-dimensional space so that 240 spheres touch any given sphere. Levenshtein [46] and Odlyzko and Sloane [57] proved that it is impossible to exceed this. We can start to appreciate that the lattice E_8 is a fascinating mathematical object, and this large *kissing number* contributes to its allure.

But in communication systems, the large number of nearest neighbors is a serious liability. If the lattice E_8 had only a single nearest neighbor then a noise vector e with norm $\|e\|^2 \approx 1$ would only produce a decoding error if it pointed in the direction of the nearest neighbor. This is the reason the probability of decoder error increases with the number of nearest neighbors.

Codes and Lattices. Leech [44] showed how to use error-correcting codes to construct dense sphere packings in N-dimensional space. The idea is to specify a set of vectors with integer entries by constraining the binary expansion of those entries.

DEFINITION 4.9. The *coordinate array* of a vector $x = (x_1, \ldots, x_N)$ with integer coordinates is obtained by writing the binary expansion of the coordinates x_i in columns starting with the least significant digit. The first row of the coordinate array is the 2^0 row, the second row is the 2^1 row, the third row is the 2^2 row, and so on. To find the binary expansion (a_l) of a negative number $-a$, simply write

$$-a = \sum_{l \geq 0} a_l 2^l$$

and for $i = 1, 2, \ldots$ solve the equation $-a \equiv \sum_{l \geq 0} a_l 2^l \pmod{2^i}$. The coordinate array of the vector $(4, 2, -1, 1, 0, -2, 3, -3)$ is

$$
\begin{bmatrix}
0 & 0 & 1 & 1 & 0 & 0 & 1 & 1 \\
0 & 1 & 1 & 0 & 0 & 1 & 1 & 0 \\
1 & 0 & 1 & 0 & 0 & 1 & 0 & 1 \\
0 & 0 & 1 & 0 & 0 & 1 & 0 & 1 \\
& \cdots & & \cdots & & & \cdots &
\end{bmatrix}
\begin{array}{l}
2^0 \quad \text{row} \\
2^1 \quad \text{row} \\
2^2 \quad \text{row} \\
2^3 \quad \text{row}
\end{array} .
$$

In row 2^0, the entry 1 represents an odd integer, and the entry 0 represents an even integer. We define subsets of the integer lattice $\mathbb{Z}^N$ by constraining the first L rows of the coordinate array.

DEFINITION 4.10. Given L binary codes $C_1, \ldots, C_L$ with block length N, the sphere packing $\Lambda(C_1, \ldots, C_L)$ consists of all vectors $x \in \mathbb{Z}^N$ for which the ith row of the coordinate array of x is a codeword in C_i.

If $L = 1$, and if C_1 is a binary linear code, then

$$\Lambda(C_1) = \{ x \in \mathbb{Z}^N \mid x \equiv c \pmod{2}, \text{ for some } c \in C_1 \} .$$

Here $\Lambda(C_1)$ is a lattice, since it is closed under addition. This construction is described by Leech and Sloane [45], where it is called *Construction A*. Forney [28] uses the term mod 2 lattice to distinguish lattices constructed in this way. In general $\Lambda(C_1, \ldots, C_L)$ is not a lattice.

EXAMPLE 4.11. Here C is the extended $[8, 4, 4]$ Hamming code. The fundamental volume $V(\Lambda(C)) = 16$, and the minimum squared distance $d^2(\Lambda(C)) = 4$.

The code C contains the zero vector, 14 codewords of weight 4, and the all-one vector $\mathbf{1}$ of weight 8. There are 14×2^4 vectors in $\Lambda(C)$ of type $(\pm 1)^4 0^4$, and 16 vectors in $\Lambda(C)$ of type $(\pm 2) 0^7$. This gives 240 vectors in $\Lambda(C)$ with minimum norm 4, and it is easily seen that there are no others. This second appearance of the number 240 is not happenstance. The lattice $\Lambda(C)$ is a realization of the Gosset lattice E_8 on a different scale. There is a linear transformation $\Phi : \mathbb{R}^8 \to \mathbb{R}^8$ satisfying $\|\Phi(x)\|^2 = 2\|x\|^2$ that transforms the original realization of E_8 into $\Lambda(C)$. $\qquad\square$

The Continuous Approximation. The problem of designing an N-dimensional signal constellation Ω based on a lattice Λ is that of choosing the region $\mathcal{R}$ that bounds the signal constellation. The fact that a lattice has a fundamental volume $V(\Lambda)$ means that we can specify the size of the signal constellation by specifying the volume of the region $\mathcal{R}$. The volume $V(\mathcal{R})$ of the region $\mathcal{R}$ is given by

$$V(\mathcal{R}) = |\Omega| V(\Lambda) .$$

Points in a lattice Λ are distributed regularly throughout N-dimensional space. The average signal power P of the constellation Ω is approximately the average power $P(\mathcal{R})$ of a probability distribution that is uniform within $\mathcal{R}$ and zero elsewhere. We introduce this approximation principle with an example.

EXAMPLE 4.12. Let $\Lambda = \mathbb{Z}$. Then the fundamental volume $V(\Lambda) = 1$ and any interval $[y, y + 1)$ is a fundamental region. The signal constellation Ω consists of the $2L$ points $\pm(2i + 1)/2$, $i = 0, 1, \ldots, L - 1$ drawn from the translate $\mathbb{Z} + 1/2$ of the integer lattice. This translate is chosen to minimize average signal power. The region $\mathcal{R}$ is the interval $[-L, L]$. If we assume that signals are equiprobable, then the true average signal power P is given by

$$P = \frac{1}{4L} \sum_{i=0}^{L-1} (2i+1)^2 = \frac{4L^2 - 1}{12} .$$

The approximation $P([L, L])$ is given by

$$P([-L, L]) = \frac{1}{2L} \int_{-L}^{L} t^2 dt = L^2/3 ,$$

since the probability distribution takes the value $1/2L$ throughout $[-L, L]$ (the volume of the interval $[-L, L]$ equals $2L$). The agreement between the exact value and the approximation is quite good. $\square$

DEFINITION 4.13 (The Continuous Approximation). Let Ω be an N-dimensional signal constellation consisting of all points from a lattice Λ that lie within a region $\mathcal{R}$, with centroid the origin. If signals are equiprobable, then the average signal power P is approximately the average power $P(\mathcal{R})$ of a continuous distribution that is uniform within $\mathcal{R}$ and zero elsewhere. Thus

$$P \approx P(\mathcal{R}) = \frac{1}{NV(\mathcal{R})} \int_{\mathcal{R}} \|x\|^2 dv ,$$

where

$$V(\mathcal{R}) = \int_{\mathcal{R}} dv$$

is the volume of the region $\mathcal{R}$.

We rewrite this expression for average signal power P as

$$P \approx G(\mathcal{R})V(\mathcal{R})^{2/N} ,$$

where

$$G(\mathcal{R}) = \frac{\int_{\mathcal{R}} \|x\|^2 dv}{NV(\mathcal{R})^{1+2/N}}$$

is the normalized or dimensionless second moment. The second moment $G(\mathcal{R})$ results from taking the average squared distance from a point in $\mathcal{R}$ to the centroid, and normalizing to obtain a dimensionless quantity.

We see that the average signal power P depends on the choice of lattice, and on the shape of the region that bounds the signal constellation. The formula $P \approx G(\mathcal{R})V(\mathcal{R})^{2/N}$ separates these two contributions.

Equation (1) gives $V(\mathcal{R}) = |\Omega|V(\Lambda)$, so that the second factor is determined by the choice of lattice. Since different lattices require different volumes to enclose the same number of signal points, it is possible to save on signal power by choosing the lattice appropriately.

Since the second moment $G(\mathcal{R})$ is dimensionless, it is not changed by scaling the region $\mathcal{R}$. Therefore the first factor $G(\mathcal{R})$ measures the effect of the shape of the region $\mathcal{R}$ on average signal power.

Methods for Reducing Average Transmitted Signal Power. We consider signal constellations that consist of all lattice points that fall within some region $\mathcal{R}$. If the region $\mathcal{R}$ is an N-cube with faces parallel to the coordinate axes, then the induced probability distribution on an arbitrary M-dimensional projection is uniform. Changing the shape of the region $\mathcal{R}$ induces a nonuniform probability distribution on this M-dimensional projection (see Example 4.3). Thus gains derived from shaping an N-dimensional constellation can be achieved in M-dimensional space by nonequiprobable signaling.

Calderbank and Ozarow [11] introduced the method of shaping on rings, where the region $\mathcal{R}$ is partitioned into T subregions so as to obtain T equal subconstellations with increasing average power. A shaping code then specifies sequences of subregions, and it is designed so that subconstellations with lower average power are more frequent. The purpose of the shaping code is to create a good approximation to the desired Gaussian distribution. It is of great importance to minimize the complexity of the shaping code. For more information about the shell mapping algorithm used in the V.34 modem standard, we refer to Laroia, Farvardin and Tretter [43].

Trellis Codes. A *trellis code* is a sliding window method of encoding a binary data stream as a sequence of signals that are input to a noisy transmission channel. The sliding window encoder introduces memory and redundancy in order to gain immunity to noise. In Figure 14 the encoder slides a window of size $\nu + k$ over k parallel input bit streams. In each signaling interval, the content of the window determines the signal generated by the encoder. The v bits preceding the most recent block of k data bits determine one of 2^v states of the encoder. The shape of the window determines the possible transitions between states. Note that redundant transmission implies that the size of the signal constellation will be greater than 2^k.

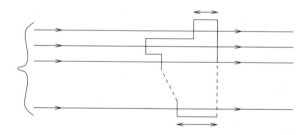

FIGURE 15. A sliding window encoder.

Let $v_i + 1$ denote the number of bits in the ith bit stream that appear in the sliding window. We say that v_i is the ith *constraint length*, and that $\nu = \sum_{i=1}^{k} \nu_i$ is the *overall constraint length*, or *total memory*.

We have defined trellis codes so that convolutional codes are included as a special case. For convolutional codes, the signal constellation is $\mathbb{F}_2^N$ for some $N > k$, and the encoder mapping $f : \mathbb{F}_2^{\nu+k} \to \mathbb{F}_2^N$ is linear.

We shall introduce convolutional codes by following an example in which $k = 1$, $\nu = 2$, and $N = 2$.

EXAMPLE 4.14. Here $k = 1$, $\nu = 2$, and $N = 2$. The encoder mapping $f :$ $\mathbb{F}_2^3 \to \mathbb{F}_2^2$ is given by $f(a, b, c) = (a + c, a + b + c)$. Figure 15 shows the encoder state diagram. The state of the encoder is the pair of prior input bits, and the window determines the possible transitions between states. If the triple abc appears in the window, then the present state is ab, and the next state will be bc. The corresponding encoder output $f(abc)$ labels the edge from ab to bc. The great

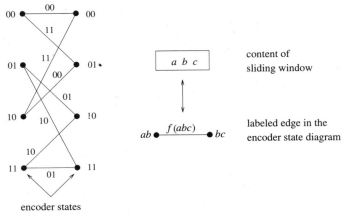

encoder states

FIGURE 16. An encoder state diagram.

advantage of convolutional codes is that they come with a decoding algorithm — the Viterbi algorithm outlined in Section 2. In fact the key property of a trellis code is that it is an ensemble of codewords that can be searched efficiently.

Set Partitioning. In 1976 Ungerboeck [69] constructed simple trellis codes for the Gaussian channel that provided coding gains of between 3 and 6 dB. His original paper has transformed the subject of coding for the Gaussian channel. We shall describe his method, which is to specify an underlying convolutional code, and a rule (mapping by set partitioning) that maps the output of this code onto a fixed signal constellation.

DEFINITION 4.15. An *L-level partition* is a sequence of partitions $\Gamma_0, \Gamma_1, \ldots, \Gamma_L$ where the partition Γ_i is a refinement of the partition Γ_{i-1}. This structure determines a rooted tree with $L + 1$ levels. The root of this tree is the entire signal constellation Γ_0, and in general, the vertices of the tree at level i are the subsets that constitute the partition Γ_i. A vertex y at level i is joined to the unique vertex at level $i - 1$ containing y, and to every vertex z at level $i + 1$ that is contained in y. The leaves of this tree are the subsets that form the partition Γ_L.

For simplicity we insist on a little more regularity. Every subset at level i will be joined to p_{i+1} subsets at level $i + 1$, and the numbers $0, 1, \ldots, p_{i+1} - 1$ will be used to label the edges to these subsets. Subsets in the partition Γ_i can then be labelled by paths $(a_1, a_2, \ldots, a_i)$, $0 \leq a_j \leq p_j - 1$ from the root to the corresponding vertex.

DEFINITION 4.16. The *intra subset squared distance* δ_i^2 is the minimum squared distance between different signals that are in the same subset at level i. It is given by

$$\delta_i^2 = \min_{\substack{S \in \Gamma_i \\ a,b \in S \\ a \neq b}} \{\|a - b\|^2\} .$$

EXAMPLE 4.17. Figure 16 shows a 2-level partition of the 1/2-integers in the interval $[-2, 2]$. The intra subset squared distances are $\delta_0^2 = 1$, $\delta_1^2 = 4$, and $\delta_2^2 = \infty$.

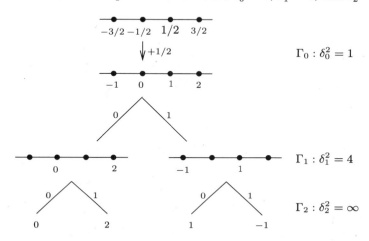

FIGURE 17. A 2-level partition.

Observe that two signals x and y are in the same subset at level i if and only if $x \equiv y \pmod{2^i}$. A signal x that falls in the subset labelled (a_1, a_2) at level 2 satisfies the congruences

$$x + 1/2 \equiv a_1 \pmod{2} \text{ and } x + 1/2 \equiv a_1 + 2a_2 \pmod{4} .$$

The components of the label (a_1, a_2) are the first two entries in the binary expansion of $x + 1/2$. The partitions Γ_0, Γ_1 and Γ_2 are determined by the Leech coordinate array introduced in Chapter 2.   □

Given any L-level partition, there is a lower bound on squared Euclidean distance between signals that depends only on the binary sum of the signal labels. This property is of fundamental importance in set partitioning. Let $x = (x_1, \ldots, x_L)$ and $y = (y_1, \ldots, y_L)$ label the signals $\alpha(x)$ and $\alpha(y)$. If i is the first index for which $x_i \neq y_i$ then

$$\|\alpha(x) - \alpha(y)\|^2 \geq \delta_{i-1}^2,$$

since the signals $\alpha(x)$ and $\alpha(y)$ belong to the same subset at level i in the partition tree. Table 2 gives squared Euclidean distance between signals $\alpha(x)$ and $\alpha(y)$ in Figure 17 as a function of the sum $x \oplus y$.

We shall use binary linear codes to select an ensemble of signal sequences. Let

$$C = \{x | x = (x_k), x_k \in \mathbb{F}_2^L\}$$

be a binary linear code, and let

$$\alpha(C) = \{\alpha(x) = (\alpha(x_k)) | x = (x_k) \in C\}$$

TABLE 2. Relating Euclidean distance between signals to Hamming distance between labels.

Label Sum $x \oplus y$	Lower Bound on $\|\alpha(x) - \alpha(y)\|^2$
00	0
01	4
11	1
10	1

be the corresponding ensemble of signal sequences. The Euclidean distance between signal sequences $\alpha(x)$ and $\alpha(y)$ is bounded below by a function of $x \oplus y$. If

$$\Delta(x_k) = \begin{cases} 0, & \text{if } x_k = 0, \\ \delta_{i-1}^2 & \text{if the first nonzero entry of } x_k \text{ is in position } i, \end{cases}$$

then the minimum squared distance $d^2(C)$ satisfies

$$d^2(C) = \inf_{\substack{x, y \in C \\ x \neq y}} \left\{ \|\alpha(x) - \alpha(y)\|^2 \right\} \geq \inf_{\substack{x \in C \\ x \neq 0}} \left\{ \sum_k \Delta(x_k) \right\}.$$

We can bound the Euclidean distance between sequences $\alpha(x)$ and $\alpha(y)$ by assuming that x is the zero sequence. This means that minimum Euclidean distance can be determined in much the same way as minimum Hamming distance for binary linear codes.

Figure 18 shows Ungerboeck's vision of trellis coded modulation. The linear code C is a rate $(L-1)/L$ convolutional code, and finding the best code requires an exhaustive search. This optimal code will depend on the intra subset distances δ_i and is unlikely to be a code that is optimal with respect to Hamming distance.

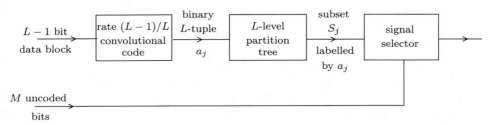

FIGURE 18. Encoder structure for trellis coded modulation.

Trellis Codes Based on Lattices and Cosets. Calderbank and Sloane [12] abstracted the idea of redundant signaling based on lattices and cosets. The signal points are taken from an N-dimensional lattice Λ, and the signal constellation contains an equal number of points from each coset of a sublattice Λ'. One part of the binary data stream selects cosets of Λ' in Λ, and the other part selects points from these cosets. All the redundancy is in the coset selection procedure, and the bits that select the signal point once the coset has been chosen are referred to as *uncoded bits*. Forney [**28**] coined the name *coset code* to describe redundant signaling based on lattices and cosets, and it is a good name because it captures the essential property of these signaling schemes. Coset coding provides a level of abstraction that makes it possible for a code designer to handle complicated codes and large signal constellations.

EXAMPLE 4.18. In this example the lattice Λ is the integer lattice $\mathbb{Z}$, and the sublattice Λ' is $4\mathbb{Z}$. Figure 19 shows the encoder trellis where the edges have been relabelled by the four residue classes modulo 4. All the redundancy is in the coset (residue class modulo Λ') selection procedure; one bit chooses from 4 cosets. In Figure 19 the symbol $[i]$ represents the coset $\{z | z \equiv i (\mathrm{mod}\ 4)\}$. For transmission all cosets are translated by $-1/2$. All the redundancy is in the coset selection

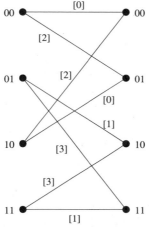

FIGURE 19. Labelling edges by cosets in $[\mathbb{Z} : 4\mathbb{Z}]$.

procedure, and we can achieve any transmission rate by just increasing the number of uncoded bits.

Coding Gain. Switching from uncoded transmission using Λ to coded transmission using a coset code C based on the lattice partition Λ/Λ' requires that the N-dim. signal constellation be expanded by a factor $2^{N\rho(C)}$, where $\rho(C)$ is the redundancy of the coset code C. Note that all redundancy is in the method of selecting cosets, so this quantity is easy to calculate. We assume that the constellation is expanded by scaling a bounding region, so that the power penalty incurred by expansion is $4^{\rho(C)}$. The coding gain $\gamma(C)$ of the coset code C is then given by

$$\gamma(C) = d^2(C)4^{-\rho(C)} .$$

This is the gain over uncoded transmission using the N-dim. lattice Λ. We shall refer to $\gamma(C)$ as the *nominal coding gain*, since this quantity does not take into account the path multiplicity of a coset code C. The coding gain is expressed in dB by taking $10\log_{10}\gamma(C)$.

EXAMPLE 4.14 ((continued)). Here $\Lambda = \mathbb{Z}$, $\Lambda' = 4\mathbb{Z}$ and we calculate the nominal coding gain of the coset code over uncoded QAM transmission. It is not hard to prove that the minimum squared distance $d^2(C) = 9$. To calculate the redundancy $\rho(C)$, we observe that every 1-dim. signalling interval, one input bit selects one of 4 cosets in $[\mathbb{Z} : 4\mathbb{Z}]$. The redundancy $\rho(C) = \log_2 4 - 1 = 1$, and the nominal coding gain $\gamma(C)$ is given by

$$\gamma(C) = 10 \log_{10} \frac{9}{4^1} = 3.3 \text{ dB} . \quad \square$$

The power and simplicity of the lattice/coset viewpoint comes from viewing the signal constellation as a finite subset of an infinite lattice. By focusing on the infinite lattice, we eliminate the influence of constellation boundary effects on code structure and code performance.

For channels with high SNR the performance of a trellis code C is determined by the minimum squared distance $d^2(C)$ between output sequences corresponding to distinct input sequences. For coset codes this minimum squared distance is determined by the minimum nonzero norm in the sublattice Λ' and by the method of selecting cosets.

For channels with moderate SNR (symbol error probability $\sim 10^{-6}$) performance is determined by the minimum squared distance $d^2(C)$, and by the path multiplicity $Mult(C)$. A telephone channel is an example of a channel with moderate SNR. Here Motorola Information Systems has proposed a rule of thumb that reducing the path multiplicity by a factor of two produces a coding gain of 0.2 dB. When discounting the coding gain of a coset code we compare against the path multiplicity of uncoded transmission using the same lattice. The result of discounting nominal coding gain by path multiplicity in this way is called *effective coding gain*, and is denoted $\gamma_{eff}(C)$.

One reason that trellis coded modulation has had an enormous impact on communications practice is that digital electronics are now sufficiently advanced to implement codes of the type proposed by Ungerboeck. A second reason, also very important, is that consumers were waiting for new products, like high speed modems, that this invention made possible. With all the benefits of hindsight we may look back and find the principles of set partitioning in earlier mathematical work by Leech [44], at a time when digital electronics were not ready for this innovation. However Leech's work lacked any connection with communications practice, and Ungerboeck made the link explicit between his mathematical theory of set partitioning and real applications.

It is instructive to look back at the work of Slepian [62] who constructed codes for the Gaussian channel by taking a finite group of $N \times N$ matrices, and applying each matrix to a fixed vector in $\mathbb{R}^N$. It is remarkable that Ungerboeck codes are examples of Slepian signal sets. One minor difference is that the group of isometries has become infinite. A more important difference is our emphasis on the complexity of the group. This was not an issue that concerned Slepian, but it is of paramount importance today, because it determines decoding complexity.

The contributions by Marcus [53] and by Marcus, Roth and Siegel [54] are concerned with properties of sequence based methods of data transmission. Both authors consider codes that are generated by finite state machines, and are interested in encoders with minimal complexity. Another interesting issue is whether it is possible to effectively distinguish between different codewords. A third issue is whether it is possible to decode by passing a sliding window over the codewords, and what features of the window are required.

On Duality Between Transmission and Quantization. The lattice decoding algorithms described in previous sections can be used to represent a source sequence x as the sum of a lattice point v, and an error sequence $e = (e_i)$. In quantization the objective is the lattice point v, and the expected value $E(e_i^2)$ is the *mean squared error* (m.s.e.) normalized per dimension. The error sequence e is distributed over the Voronoi region $\mathcal{R}$ of the lattice, and if this distribution is uniform, then the mean squared error $E(e_i^2)$ is equal to the second moment $G(\mathcal{R})$. In quantization, the quantity $\gamma(\mathcal{R}) = 1/12G(\mathcal{R})$ is called the cell shape gain, and it measures the reduction in mean squared error that comes from choosing the shape of the quantization cell. The baseline for comparison is uniform scalar quantization (using the integer lattice) where the quantization cell is the N-cube C_N with second moment $G(C_N) = 1/12$.

By contrast, the objective in transmission is not the lattice point v, but the error sequence e. The idea is to choose a suitable discrete set of source sequences x, so that the entries of the error sequence e have a Gaussian distribution.

This duality between transmission and quantization is central to Conway and Sloane [14, 16]. See also [24], [43], and [52].

References

[1] O. Amrani, Y. Be'ery, A. Vardy, F.-W. Sun, and H. C. A. van Tilborg, *The Leech Lattice and the Golay Code: Bounded-distance decoding and multilevel constructions*, IEEE Trans. Inform. Theory 40, 1994, pp. 1030–1043.

[2] E. F. Assmus, Jr. and J. D. Key, *Designs and their Codes*, Cambridge University Press, 1992.

[3] E. F. Assmus, Jr. and H. F. Mattson, Jr., *New 5-designs*, J. Combinatorial Theory 6, 1969, pp. 122–151.

[4] Y. Be'ery and J. Snyders, *Optimal soft decision block decoders based on the fast Hadamard transform*, IEEE Trans. Inform. Theory 32, 1986, pp. 355–364.

[5] R. E. Blahut, *Algebraic Methods for Signal Processing and Communications Coding*, Springer-Verlag, 1991.

[6] A. Blokhuis and A. R. Calderbank, *Quasi-symmetric designs and the Smith Normal Form*, Designs, Codes and Cryptography 2, 1992, pp. 189–206.

[7] A. R. Calderbank, *The Art of Signaling: Mathematical Foundations of Bandwidth Efficient Communication*, in preparation.

[8] A. R. Calderbank, P. Delsarte and N. J. A. Sloane, *A strengthening of the Assmus-Mattson Theorem*, IEEE Trans. Inform. Theory 37, 1991, pp. 1261–1268.

[9] A. R. Calderbank and P. Delsarte, *On error-correcting codes and invariant linear forms*, SIAM J. Discrete Math. 6, 1993, pp. 1–23.

[10] A. R. Calderbank and P. Delsarte, *Extending the t-design concept*, Trans. A.M.S. 338, 1993, pp. 941–962.

[11] A. R. Calderbank and L. H. Ozarow, *Nonequiprobable signaling on the Gaussian Channel*, IEEE Trans. Inform. Theory 36, 1990, pp. 726–740.

[12] A. R. Calderbank and N. J. A. Sloane, *New trellis codes based on lattices and cosets*, IEEE Trans. Inform. Theory 33, 1987, pp. 177–195.

[13] P. J. Cameron and J. H. van Lint, *Designs, Graphs, Codes and their Links*, Cambridge University Press, 1991.

[14] J. H. Conway and N. J. A. Sloane, *A fast encoding method for lattice codes and quantizers*, IEEE Trans. Inform. Theory 29, 1983, pp. 820–824.

[15] J. H. Conway and N. J. A. Sloane, *Soft decoding technique for codes and lattices including the Golay Code and the Leech Lattice*, IEEE Trans. Inform. Theory 32, 1986, pp. 41–50.

[16] J. H. Conway and N. J. A. Sloane, *Sphere Packings Lattices and Groups*, Springer-Verlag, 1988.

[17] J. H. Conway and N. J. A. Sloane, *The antipode construction for sphere packings*, 1994, preprint.

[18] T. M. Cover and J. A. Thomas, *Elements of Information Theory*, Wiley, 1991.

[19] R. T. Curtis, *On subgroups of O,I: lattice stabilizers*, J. Algebra 27, 1973, pp. 549–573.

[20] R. T. Curtis, *A new combinatorial approach to M_{24}*, Mathematical Proc. of the Cambridge Philosophical Soc. 79, 1976, pp. 25–42.

[21] D. M. Cvetković and J. H. van Lint, *An elementary proof of Lloyd's theorem*, Proc. Kon. Ned. Akad. v. Wet. 80, 1977, pp. 6–10.

[22] P. Delsarte, *An algebraic approach to the association schemes of coding theory*, Philips Research Reports Supplements, No. 10, 1973.

[23] E. Eleftheriou and R. Cideciyan, *On codes satisfying Mth order running digital sum constraints*, IEEE Trans. Inform. Theory 37, 1991, pp. 1294–1313.

[24] M. V. Dyuboglu and G. D. Forney, Jr., *Lattice and trellis quantization with lattice- and trellis-bounded codebooks. High-rate theory for memoryless sources*, IEEE Trans. Inform. Theory 39, 1993, pp. 46–59.

[25] J. Feigenbaum, *The use of coding theory in computational complexity*, 1994, preprint.

[26] G. D. Forney, Jr., *The Viterbi Algorithm*, Proc. of the IEEE 61, 1973, pp. 268–278.

[27] G. D. Forney, Jr., *Coset codes — Part I: Introduction and geometrical classification*, IEEE Trans. Inform. Theory 34, 1988, pp. 1123–1151.

[28] G. D. Forney, Jr., *Coset codes — Part II: Binary lattices and related codes*, IEEE Trans. Inform. Theory 34, 1988, pp. 1152–1187.

[29] , G. D. Forney, Jr., *Geometrically uniform codes*, IEEE Trans. Inform. Theory 37, 1991, pp. 1241–1260.

[30] G. D. Forney, Jr. and M. V. Eyuboglu, *Combined equalization and coding using precoding*, IEEE Comm. Mag. 30, 1991, pp. 25–35.

[31] J.-M. Goethals and J. J. Seidel, *The football*, Nieuw. Arch. Wiskunde 29, pp. 50–58.

[32] M. J. E. Golay, *Notes on digital coding*, Proc. IEEE 37, 1949, pp. 657.

[33] R. W. Hamming, *Error detecting and error correcting codes*, Bell System Tech. J. 29, 1950, pp. 147–160.

[34] A. R. Hammons, P. V. Kumar, A. R. Calderbank, N. J. A. Sloane and P. Solé, *The $\mathbb{Z}_4$ linearity of Kerdock, Preparata, Goethals and related codes*, IEEE Trans. Inform. Theory 40, 1994, pp. 301–319.

[35] R. H. Hardin and N. J. A. Sloane, *An improved snub cube and other new spherical designs in three dimensions*, 1994, preprint.

[36] R. H. Hardin and N. J. A. Sloane, *Codes (spherical) and designs (experimental)*, 1994, preprint.

[37] A. S. Householder, *Principles of Numerical Analysis*, McGraw-Hill, 1953.

[38] K. A. S. Immink and G. Beenker, *Binary transmission codes with higher order spectral nulls at zero frequency*, IEEE Trans. Inform. Theory 33, 1987, pp. 452–454.

[39] W. M. Kantor, *Codes, quadratic forms and finite geometries*, 1994, preprint.

[40] R. Karabed and P. H. Siegel, *Matched spectral null codes for partial response channels*, IEEE Trans. Inform. Theory 37, 1991, pp. 818–855.

[41] A. M. Kerdock, *A class of low-rate nonlinear binary codes*, Information and Control 20, 1972, pp. 182–187.

[42] E. S. Lander, *Symmetric Designs: An Algebraic Approach*, London Math. Soc. Lecture Notes 74, Cambridge Univ. Press, 1983.

[43] R. Laroia, N. Farvardin, and S. Tretter, *On optimal shaping of multidimensional constellations*, IEEE Trans. Inform. Theory 40, 1994, pp. 1044–1056.

[44] J. Leech, *Notes on sphere packings*, Canadian J. Math. 19, 1967, pp. 251–267.

[45] J. Leech and N. J. A. Sloane, *Sphere packings and error-correcting-codes*, Canadian J. Math. 23, 1971, pp. 718–745.

[46] V. I. Levenshtein, *On bounds for packing spheres in n-dimensional Euclidean space*, Doklady Akademii Nauk 245, pp. 1299–1303.

[47] V. I. Levenshtein, *On relationships between the minimal code distance and the maximal design strength*, to appear in Proc. Conf. on Algebraic Combinatorics, Fukuoka, Japan, 1993.

[48] J. H. van Lint, *Nonexistence theorems for perfect error-correcting-codes*. In: Computers in Algebraic and Number Theory, vol. IV, SIAM-AMS Proceedings, 1971.

[49] J. H. van Lint, *Introduction to Coding Theory*, Graduate Texts in Math. 86, Springer, 1982.

[50] S. P. Lloyd, *Binary block coding*, Bell System Tech. J. 36, 1957, pp. 517–535.

[51] F. J. MacWilliams and N. J. A. Sloane, *The Theory of Error-Correcting-Codes*, North-Holland, 1977.

[52] M. W. Marcellin and T. R. Fischer, *Trellis coded quantization of memoryless and Gauss-Markov sources*, IEEE Trans. Commun. 38, 1990, pp. 82–93.

[53] B. H. Marcus, *Symbolic dynamics and connections to coding theory, automata theory and system theory*, 1994, preprint.

[54] B. H. Marcus, R. M. Roth and P. H. Siegel, *Modulation codes for digital data storage*, 1994, preprint.

[55] R. J. McEliece, E. R. Rodemich, H. C. Rumsey, Jr., and L. R. Welch, *New upper bounds on the rate of a code via the Delsarte-MacWilliams inequalities*, IEEE Trans. Inform. Theory 23, 1977, pp. 157–166.

[56] A. W. Nordstrom and J. P. Robinson, *An optimum nonlinear code*, Information and Control 11, 1967, pp. 613–616.

[57] A. M. Odlyzko and N. J. A. Sloane, *New bounds on the number of unit spheres that can touch a unit sphere in n-dimensions*, J. Combinatorial Theory (A) 26, 1979, pp. 210–214.

[58] F. P. Preparata, *A class of optimum nonlinear double-error correcting codes*, Information and Control 13, 1968, pp. 378–400.

[59] I. S. Reed and G. Solomon, *Polynomial codes over certain finite fields*, SIAM Journal 8, 1960, pp. 300–304.

[60] J. J. Seidel, *Discrete noneuclidean geometry*, Handbook of Incidence Geometry, ed. F. Buekenhout, North-Holland, to appear.

[61] C. E. Shannon, *A mathematical theory of communication*, Bell System Tech. J. 27, 1948, pp. 379–423 and 623–656.

[62] D. Slepian, *Group codes for the Gaussian channel*, Bell System Tech. J. 47, 1968, pp. 575–602.

[63] J. Snyders and Y. Be'ery, *Maximum likelihood soft decoding of binary block codes and decoders for the Golay codes*, IEEE Trans. Inform. Theory 35, 1989, pp. 963–975.

[64] D. A. Spielman, *Linear-time encodable and decodable error-correcting codes*, Proc. 27th ACM Symposium on the Theory of Computing, 1995.

[65] H. Stichtenoth, *Algebraic geometric codes*, 1994, preprint.

[66] F.-W. Sun, H. C. A. van Tilborg and A. Vardy, *The Leech Lattice, the octacode and decoding algorithms*, 1994, preprint.

[67] A. Tietäväinen, *On the nonexistence of perfect codes over finite fields*, SIAM J. Applied Math. 24, 1973, pp. 88–96.

[68] M. A. Tsfasman, S. G. Vladut and T. Zink, *On Goppa codes which are better than the Gilbert-Varshamov bound*, Math. Nachr. 109, 1982, pp. 21–28.

[69] G. Ungerboeck, *Channel coding with multilevel/phase signals*, IEEE Trans. Inform. Theory 28, 1982, pp. 55–67.

[70] A. Vardy, *A new sphere packing in 20 dimensions*, 1994, preprint.

[71] A. Vardy and Y. Be'ery, *More efficient soft-decision decoding of the Golay codes*, IEEE Trans. Inform. Theory 37, 1991, pp. 667–672.

[72] A. J. Viterbi, *Error bounds for convolutional codes and an asymptotically optimum decoding algorithm*, IEEE Trans. Inform. Theory 13, 1967, pp. 260–269.

MATHEMATICAL SCIENCES RESEARCH CENTER, AT&T BELL LABORATORIES, MURRAY HILL, NEW JERSEY 07974-0636

E-mail address: rc@research.att.com

Proceedings of Symposia in Applied Mathematics
Volume **50**, 1995

Modulation Codes for Digital Data Storage

Brian Marcus, Ron M. Roth, and Paul H. Siegel

ABSTRACT. These lecture notes address aspects of the theory and design of
constrained codes that find applications in digital data storage devices. The
notes provide background for the material presented in a lecture in the short
course on "Coding Theory" held in conjunction with the AMS meeting in
San Francisco, California, January 1995. The notes are largely extracted from
references [**MSW92**] and [**MRS95**]

1. Constrained codes and recording channels

1.1. Introduction. During the past decade, digital data storage devices have
become ubiquitous. They are found not only in computer centers at business locations, but in desk-top workstations in office, portable personal computers, and many
home entertainment applications, such as multimedia computers and high-fidelity
music systems. The variety of such devices is impressive, including conventional
diskette and hard disk drives; optical read-only drives such as audio compact disc
(CD) and mini-disc systems, CD-ROM drives, and erasable magneto-optic drives;
as well as conventional magnetic tape drives, digital audio tape (DAT) systems,
and digital compact cassette (DCC) audio tape systems.

If one were to examine the manner in which information is stored in any of
these systems, one would find that the information is represented by sequences of
binary symbols with particular restrictions, or constraints, imposed. For example,
the maximum length of runs of identical symbols may be limited, or the imbalance
over time between the number of occurrences of each of the binary symbols may be
bounded.

To understand the motivation for representing the stored information in such a
form, one must step back and view the entire data recording and retrieval process,
as illustrated in the diagram of Figure 1.

As can be seen in the schematic, the digital recording system uses, in addition
to the perhaps more familiar data compression and error correction coding, this
additional kind of constrained coding – sometimes called modulation coding – that
governs the general features of the binary patterns reflected on the storage medium.
In the most general terms, the purpose of a constrained code is to help maximize the
storage density while ensuring reliable data recovery by matching the characteristics
of the recorded signals to the physical properties of the medium and transducers,

---

1991 *Mathematics Subject Classification.* Primary 94A05; Secondary 58F03, 68Q68, 94A14,
94A40, 94B12.

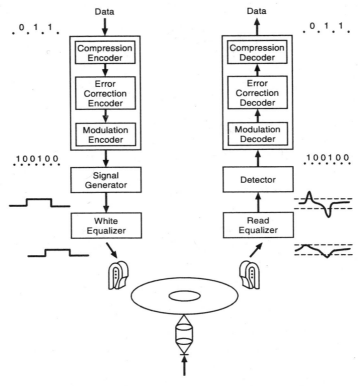

FIGURE 1. Data recording schematic. Reprinted with permission from the IEEE Transactions on Information Theory; Introduction to the Special Issue on Coding for Storage Devices, May 1991. © 1991 IEEE, Piscataway, New Jersey.

as well as to the signal processing and detection methods used to write and read back the binary symbol sequences.

In this lecture, we will describe some of the mathematics underlying the characterization and analysis of such constrained systems of sequences, as well as key mathematical results that pertain to the construction of mapping algorithms, or "codes", between the constrained sequences and the information sequences they represent.

1.2. Outline of the lecture. In the remainder of Section 1, we motivate the problem of modulation coding with examples of constrained systems of sequences that arise in the context of digital data recording. We also present a historical and technical overview of results pertaining to the constrained coding problem. Section 2 contains the basic mathematical concepts regarding constrained sets of sequences that are required to rigorously formulate the coding problem and its solutions. Section 3 addresses finite-state encoders and various types of decoders, and states the corresponding fundamental theorems on code existence. In Section 4, we give an overview of the state-splitting algorithm, which gives a systematic procedure for designing finite-state encoders for constrained systems. We briefly discuss issues pertaining to the construction of encoders with decoders of the various types. We also mention techniques that may be used to simplify the implementation of the encoders and decoders. In Section 5, we introduce some advanced topics that offer problems for research in the area of constrained coding. We summarize the lecture in Section 6, and conclude the notes with an extensive list of references.

1.3. Constraints for recording. In this section, we describe several classes of constraints that have arisen in digital recording applications.

1.3.1. *Runlength constraints.* In digital magnetic and optical recording systems, a widely used family of constraints are the (d, k)-runlength-limited (RLL) constraints, where the run of 0's between consecutive 1's in a binary sequence must have length at least d and no more than k. For example, many commercial systems today use a code with the constraint $(d, k) = (1, 7)$. An example of a sequence satisfying this constraint is

$$\cdots 00100001010000000100 \cdots .$$

Other existing recording standards include the $(1, 3)$-RLL constraint (which can be found in flexible and Winchester-type magnetic disk drives) and the $(2, 10)$-RLL constraint (which appears in the compact disk). The parameter k is imposed to guarantee sufficient sign-changes in the recorded waveform which are required for clock synchronization during readback to prevent clock drifting. The parameter d is required to prevent inter-symbol interference.

The set of all sequences satisfying a (d, k)-RLL constraint is conveniently described by reading the labels off of paths in the labeled directed graph in Figure 2. We will have much more to say about such graphs in Section 2.

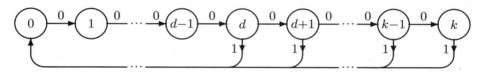

FIGURE 2. (d, k)-RLL constraint.

A related family of constraints that arise in practice is the class of multiple-spaced RLL codes. These codes are characterized by parameters (d, k, s), where d and k again define the minimum and maximum allowable runlengths of 0's, and s indicates that the runlengths of 0's must be of the form $d + is$, with i a nonnegative integer.

These constraints were originally investigated by Funk [**Funk82**]. In the context of magnetic recording, he showed that multiple-spaced RLL codes with $s = 2$ might have some practical value. More recently, and independently, $(d, k, 2)$ constraints were shown to play a natural role in magneto-optic recording systems using a resonant-bias coil direct-overwrite technique [**RuS89**]. A graph presentation for the $(d, k, s) = (2, 18, 2)$ constraint is shown in Figure 3.

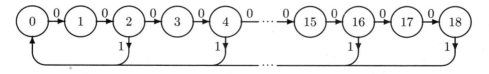

FIGURE 3. $(d, k, s) = (2, 18, 2)$.

1.3.2. *Spectral-null constraints.* Another commonly encountered constraint requires that the recording input waveforms have no spectral content at a particular frequency f. The code is said to have a spectral null at f in the code power-density spectrum. Let T denote the time duration of one bit and let S be a set of sequences generated by a finite labeled directed graph with edge labels over the bipolar alphabet $\{+1, -1\}$. A necessary and sufficient condition for S to have a spectral null at frequency $f = (m/n)(1/T)$ is that there exist a constant B such that for all sequences $\mathbf{w} = w_0 w_1 \ldots w_{\ell-1}$ in S and $0 \le i \le i' < \ell$ we have

$$(1) \qquad \left| \sum_{h=i}^{i'} w_h e^{-j2\pi hm/n} \right| \le B ,$$

where $j = \sqrt{-1}$ [**Pie84**], [**MS87**], [**YY76**].

For example, sequences with a spectral null at $f = 0$, often called *dc-free* or *charge-constrained* sequences, have been used in many magnetic tape recording systems employing rotary-type recording heads, such as the R-DAT digital audio tape systems. This constraint is also imposed in optical recording to reduce interaction between the recorded data and the servo system, and also to allow filtering of noise resulting from finger-prints [**Imm91**, Ch. 2]. In this case, the parameter B in (1) is called the *digital sum variation (DSV)* of the set of dc-free sequences. The larger the value of B, the less reduction there will be in the spectral content at frequencies approaching the spectral null frequency $f = 0$. The set of all sequences with DSV B is generated by the labeled directed graph of Figure 4.

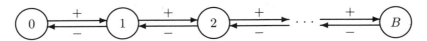

FIGURE 4. $DSV = B$ charge constraint.

Graphs generating sequences with spectral nulls at rational submultiples of the symbol frequency are described in [**MS87**]. Higher-order spectral-null constraints, which further restrict the spectral content in the vicinity of spectral-null frequencies, are discussed in [**ImmB87**], [**KS91a**], [**EC91**], [**RSV94**].

1.3.3. *Charge and runlength constraints.* Runlength and spectral-null constraints may be combined. One example is the class of charge–RLL constraints — sometimes denoted $(d, k; c)$ constraints — and defined as follows. In recording systems using peak detection (see Section 1.5.1) a (d, k)-constrained binary sequence $\mathbf{z} = z_0 z_1 z_2 \cdots$ is typically transformed into a sequence $\mathbf{w} = w_0 w_1 w_2 \cdots$ over the bipolar alphabet $\{+1, -1\}$ through an intermediate binary sequence $\mathbf{x} = x_0 x_1 x_2 \cdots$ according to the rules:

$$x_i = x_{i-1} \oplus z_i \quad \text{and} \quad w_i = (-1)^{x_i} ,$$

where $\oplus$ denotes addition modulo 2 and $x_{-1} = 0$.

The set of binary $(d, k; c)$ sequences $\mathbf{z}$ satisfy (d, k)-RLL constraints, with the additional restriction that the corresponding bipolar sequences $\mathbf{w}$ will be dc-free with DSV no larger than $B = 2c$. As an example, $(1, 3; 3)$ and $(1, 5; 3)$ constraints have found application in commercial tape recording systems [**Patel75**], [**MM77**], [**Mill77**]. A graph presentation for the $(1, 3; 3)$ constraint is shown in Figure 5.

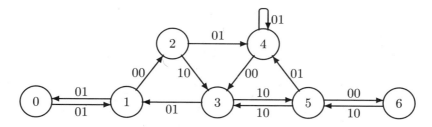

FIGURE 5. $(d, k; c) = (1, 3; 3)$.

1.3.4. *Constraints for PRML.* Recently, magnetic recording systems using digital signal processing methods have appeared on the scene. These systems typically employ a scheme, denoted PRML, based on partial-response (PR) signaling, with maximum-likelihood (ML) sequence detection. See [**Cid92**], [**Dol89**], [**DMU79**], [**KobT70**], [**WoodP86**]. As discussed in more detail below, it proves to be desirable in PRML systems to use binary sequences which satisfy not only a "global" k constraint, denoted **G**, but also a separate "interleaved" k constraint on the even index and odd index subsequences, denoted **I**. To help distinguish the PRML (**G**, **I**) constraints from the (d, k)-RLL constraints, we will use the notation $(0, \mathbf{G}/\mathbf{I})$. An example of a sequence satisfying the $(0, 4/4)$ constraint is

$$\cdots 001000010010001001100 \cdots .$$

We can represent $(0, \mathbf{G}/\mathbf{I})$ constraints by labeled directed graphs based on states (vertices) which reflect the three relevant quantities, the number g of 0's since the last occurrence of 1 in the sequence and the numbers a and b which denote the number of 0's since the last 1 in the two interleaved subsequences. Note that g is a function of a and b, denoted $g(a, b)$:

$$g(a, b) = \begin{cases} 2a + 1 & \text{if } a < b \\ 2b & \text{if } a \geq b \end{cases} .$$

We name the states by pairs (a, b), where a is the number of 0's in the interleaved subsequence containing the next to last bit, and b is the number in the subsequence containing the last bit. In the (a, b) notation, the set of states V for a $(0, \mathbf{G}/\mathbf{I})$ constraint is given by

$$V = \{(a, b) : 0 \leq a, b \leq \mathbf{I} \text{ and } g(a, b) \leq \mathbf{G}\}$$

and the edges between states are given by

$$(a, b) \xrightarrow{0} (b, a + 1) , \quad \text{provided } (b, a + 1) \in V$$
$$(a, b) \xrightarrow{1} (b, 0) .$$

A graph presentation for the $(0, \mathbf{G}/\mathbf{I}) = (0, 4/4)$ constraint is shown in Figure 6, where state labels (omitted) agree with integer grid coordinates, starting with $(0, 0)$ at the lower left. For the sake of clarity, only the 0-labeled edges are shown in the figure.

1.4. Constrained coding: overview and history. Once the set of constrained sequences is specified, one needs an encoder that translates incoming information into the sequences that obey the constraint. The encoder typically takes the form of a finite-state machine, shown schematically in Figure 7.

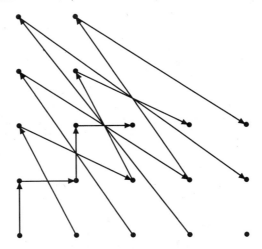

FIGURE 6. PRML $(0, \mathbf{G}/\mathbf{I}) = (0, 4/4)$ constraint: 0-labeled edges in graph presentation.

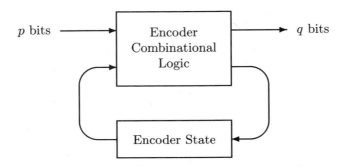

FIGURE 7. Finite-state encoder schematic.

A rate $p : q$ finite-state encoder accepts an input block of p user bits and generates a length-q codeword depending on the input block and the current internal state of the encoder. The sequences obtained by concatenating the length-q codewords generated by the encoder satisfy the constraint. There are of course only finitely many states. (This structure is ideally suited to digital logic implementation using combinatorial logic or look-up tables.)

As is customary in the literature, we sometimes use the term *rate* to mean the ratio p/q, instead of the pair of block sizes $p : q$. It will be clear from the context which version of the term rate we mean.

The encoders that we construct will automatically be decodable. The weakest type of decoder that we consider is a *state-dependent decoder* which accepts, as input, codewords of length q and generates a block of p user bits depending on the internal state, the input codeword, as well as finitely many upcoming codewords. Such a decoder will invert the encoder when applied to valid code sequences, effectively retracing the state sequence followed by the encoder in generating the code sequence. However, when the code is used in the context of a noisy channel, the state-dependent decoder may run into a serious problem. The noise causes errors in the detection of the code sequences, and the decoder must cope with erroneously detected sequences, including sequences that are not even valid code strings. It is generally very important that the decoder confine the propagation of errors at the decoder output resulting from such an error at the decoder input. Unfortunately, an error at the input to a state-dependent decoder can cause the decoder to lose track of the encoder state sequence, with no guarantee of recovery and with the possibility of unbounded error propagation.

The decoder therefore needs to have additional properties. Specifically, any input symbol error should give rise to a bounded number of output (decoded) bit errors. We call an encoder, for which there is such a decoder, *noncatastrophic*. This is a standard concept in the theory of convolutional codes. In that setting, this definition constrains the time span in which the bounded number of errors must occur. However, in general it does not. Since, in practice, it is preferable to have these output errors occur within a bounded time interval, we often seek a decoder that is defined by a *sliding-block* mapping. Such a decoder (called a *sliding-block decoder*) makes a decision on a given received length-q codeword on the basis of the local context of that codeword in the received sequence: the codeword itself, as well as a fixed number m of preceding codewords and a fixed number a of later codewords. The preceding symbols constitute what is called the *memory* (m) of the decoder, and the following symbols are called the *anticipation* (a). Figure 8 shows a schematic diagram of a sliding-block decoder.

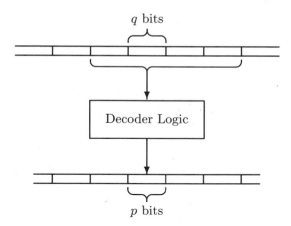

FIGURE 8. Sliding-block decoder schematic.

(This function can be realized as a shift register with combinatorial logic attached.) It is easy to see that a single error at the input to a sliding-block decoder can only affect the decoding of codewords that fall in a "window" of length at most m+a+1 codewords.

The problem for the code designer is to construct a code with these encoder/decoder attributes. In addition, it is desirable that the code be *efficient*, where efficiency has a very precise meaning, established by Shannon in his classic paper [**Sha48**]. Shannon proved that the rate $R = p/q$ of a constrained code cannot exceed a quantity, now referred to as the Shannon capacity C, that depends only upon the constraint. He also gave a nonconstructive proof of the existence of codes at rates less than, but arbitrarily close to, the capacity. The measure of efficiency of a code is the ratio R/C.

Progress was made in the 50's, 60's and 70's in finding techniques for generating practical, efficient modulation codes. In his pioneering work, Franaszek [**Fra67**], [**Fra69**], [**Fra70**], [**Fra72**], [**Fra79**], [**Fra80a**], [**Fra80b**], [**Fra82**] (see also Béal [**Béal90a**]) developed construction methods that advanced the theory of code design and invented specific codes that played important roles in the digital data recording industry. In addition, Tang and Bahl [**TB70**], Jacoby [**JAC77**], [**JK**], [**CJB**], Lempel and Cohn [**LemCo82**], Patel [**Patel75**], and others made many important contributions. Nevertheless, there remained certain fundamental questions: For a given rate R, what are the block sizes p, q such that $R = p/q$ can be realized? When and how can encoders with sliding-block decoders be found? If the Shannon capacity is a rational number $C = p/q$, can a 100% efficient sliding-block code be designed?

In the 80's, many of these basic questions were answered. The major breakthrough occurred with the introduction by Adler, Coppersmith, and Hassner [**ACH83**] of techniques that originated from a mathematical discipline called symbolic dynamics. This approach has brought to recording code design a new level of mathematical rigor and generality. In [**ACH83**], as well as subsequent papers by Marcus [**Mar85**], and Karabed-Marcus [**KarM88**], practical properties of encoder and decoder mappings were translated into mathematical terms, families of sequences that play a distinguished role in coding were precisely characterized, and definitive theorems about the existence of code mappings were formulated and proved. Moreover, the proofs of the theorems provided a set of code construction techniques that have proven to be of practical value to code designers. Reference [**ACH83**] provides an algorithm – the state-splitting algorithm – for constructing efficient encoders with sliding-block decoders for the family of *finite type* constraints that includes, for example, all RLL (d, k) constraints and PRML $(0, \mathbf{G/I})$ constraints. References [**Mar85**] and [**KarM88**] develop additional techniques, and they extend the sliding-block code existence results to the larger family of *almost-finite type* systems, such as the spectral-null constraints. They also show the existence of *noncatastrophic* codes (which, we recall, are slightly weaker than sliding-block codes in terms of error propagation) for systems not included in the previous families.

1.5. Background on magnetic recording. This section is not essential to the remainder of these lecture notes. It is intended for those readers who might be interested in understanding in more detail the signal processing methods used in digital magnetic recording and the motivation for introducing the constraints described in Section 1.3. For a description of the respective background on optical recording, the reader is referred to [**Bouw85**], [**Heem82**], [**Imm91**, Ch. 2], [**Pohl92**].

1.5.1. *Peak detection.* Digital data storage systems using magnetic disks and tapes typically use a recording technique called "saturation" recording. In this approach, the magnetic material at a given position along a track can be magnetized in one of two possible, opposing directions. The normalized input signal applied to the recording transducer (head) in this process can be thought of as a two-level waveform which assumes the values $+1$ and -1 over consecutive time intervals of duration T. In the waveform, the transitions from one level to another, which effectively carry the digital information, are therefore constrained to occur at integer multiples of the time period T, and we can describe the waveform digitally as a sequence $\mathbf{w} = w_0 w_1 w_2 \cdots$ over the bipolar alphabet $\{+1, -1\}$, where w_i is the signal amplitude in the time interval $(iT, (i+1)T]$.

For most practical purposes, the input-output relationship of the digital magnetic recording channel can be viewed as linear. Denote by $2h(t)$ the output signal (readback voltage), in the absence of noise, corresponding to a single transition from, say, -1 to $+1$ at time $t = 0$. Then, the output signal $y(t) = y_{\mathbf{w}}(t)$ generated by the waveform represented by the sequence $\mathbf{w}$ is given by:

$$y(t) = \sum_{i=0}^{\infty} (w_i - w_{i-1}) \, h(t - iT) \,,$$

with $w_{-1} = 1$. Note that the "derivative" sequence $\mathbf{w}'$ of coefficients $w_i' = w_i - w_{i-1}$ consists of elements taken from the ternary alphabet $\{0, \pm 2\}$, and the nonzero values, corresponding to the transitions in the input signal, alternate in sign.

A frequently used model for the transition response $h(t)$ is the function

$$h(t) = \frac{1}{1 + (2t/\tau)^2} \,,$$

often referred to as the Lorentzian isolated-step response. The output signal $y(t)$ is therefore the linear superposition of time-shifted Lorentzian pulses with coefficients of magnitude 2 and alternating polarity. Provided that the density of transitions — reflected in the so-called density ratio τ/T — is small enough, the locations of peaks in the output signal will closely correspond to the locations of the transitions in the recorded input signal. With a synchronous clock of period T, one could then, in principle, reconstruct the ternary sequence $\mathbf{w}'$ and the recorded bipolar sequence $\mathbf{w}$.

The detection method used to implement this process in the potentially noisy digital recording device is known as *peak detection* and it operates roughly as follows. The peak detector determines the location of peaks in the (possibly noisy) output signal whose amplitude exceeds a prespecified level. This ensures that low-amplitude, spurious peaks due to noise will be excluded from consideration. A timing recovery circuit — known as a phase-lock loop (PLL) — generates a synchronous clock whose frequency and phase are adaptively adjusted to ensure that the peak locations occur, on average, at time positions that are integral multiples of T.

At moderate densities, peak detection errors may occur as a result of the combined effects of noise, shifting of peak locations due to interference between nearby pulses, and drifting of clock phase due to an inadequate number of detected peak locations. The latter two problems are pattern dependent, and the class of RLL constraints are intended to address them both. Specifically, in order to reduce the effects of pulse interference, one can demand that the sequence $\mathbf{w}'$ contain at least d symbols of value zero between consecutive nonzero values. Similarly, to prevent loss of clock synchronization, one can require that there be no more than k symbols of value zero between consecutive nonzero values in $\mathbf{w}'$.

The constraint on $\mathbf{w}'$ can be translated directly into a constraint on binary information sequences $\mathbf{z} = z_0 z_1 z_2 \cdots$ by means of a simple operation known as Non-Return-to-Zero Inverse (NRZI) precoding. This operation transforms a sequence $\mathbf{z}$ over $\{0, 1\}$ into a sequence $\mathbf{w} = w_0 w_1 w_2 \cdots$ over the bipolar alphabet $\{+1, -1\}$, where $\mathbf{w}$ is given in terms of an intermediate binary sequence $\mathbf{x} = x_0 x_1 x_2 \cdots$ by

$$x_i = x_{i-1} \oplus z_i \quad \text{and} \quad w_i = (-1)^{x_i} ,$$

with $x_{-1} = 0$. It thus follows that

$$w_i' = w_i - w_{i-1} = (-1)^{x_{i-1}}((-1)^{z_i} - 1) = -(-1)^{x_{i-1}} \cdot 2 z_i .$$

So,

$$|w_i'| = 2 z_i$$

and the constraints on the runlengths of consecutive zero symbols in $\mathbf{w}'$ are reflected in corresponding (d, k)-RLL constraints on the binary sequences $\mathbf{z}$. (We remark that this precoding convention also permits use of a peak detector that can ignore the polarity of.peaks because the symbols 1 and 0 in $\mathbf{z}$ indicate simply the presence or absence of transitions in the input signal, respectively.)

1.5.2. *PRML detection.* The PRML approach to be discussed here has been shown to provide increased reliability at high recording densities relative to peak detection. The motivation for using $(0, \mathbf{G}/\mathbf{I})$ constraints can be found in the operation of the PRML system, which we now describe in simplified terms. As in the case of peak detection, the saturation recording approach is used with PRML. The key difference between PRML and peak detection systems is that PRML reconstructs the recorded information from the sequence of *sample values* of the output signal at times $t = 0, T, 2T, 3T, \ldots$, rather than from peak locations. Denote by $\mathrm{sinc}(x)$ the real function $(\sin(\pi x))/(\pi x)$. The PRML system uses an electronic filter to transform the output pulse $2h(t)$ resulting from an isolated transition at time $t = 0$ into a modified pulse $2f(t)$ where

$$(2) \qquad\qquad f(t) = \mathrm{sinc}\left(\frac{t}{T}\right) + \mathrm{sinc}\left(\frac{t - T}{T}\right) .$$

Note that at the consecutive sample times $t = 0$ and $t = T$, the function $f(t)$ has the value 1, while at all other times which are multiples of T, the value is 0. This particular partial-response filtering is referred to as "Class-4" [**Kretz67**]. Through linear superposition, the output signal $y(t) = y_{\mathbf{w}}(t)$ generated by the waveform represented by the bipolar sequence $\mathbf{w}$ is given by:

$$y(t) = \sum_{i=-1}^{\infty} (w_i - w_{i-1}) f(t - iT) ,$$

where we set $w_{-2} = w_{-1} = w_0$. Therefore, *at sample times*, the Class-4 transition response results in *controlled interference*, leading to output signal samples $y_i = y(iT)$ that, in the absence of noise, assume values in $\{0, \pm 2\}$. Hence, in the noiseless case, the recorded bipolar sequence $\mathbf{w}$ can be recovered from the output sample values $y_i = y(iT)$, because the interference between adjacent transitions is prescribed. Therefore, unlike the peak detection system, PRML does not require the separation of transitions.

The $(0, \mathbf{G}/\mathbf{I})$ constraints arise from the following considerations. The first parameter, 0, may be thought of as a $d = 0$ constraint, emphasizing that interference between adjacent transition responses is acceptable. The parameter $\mathbf{G}$ is comparable to the k constraint in peak detection constraints, ensuring effective operation of the PRML timing recovery and gain control circuits, which typically rely upon frequent occurrence of nonzero output samples. Specifically, the **G** constraint represents the maximum number of consecutive zero samples allowed in the sample sequence $y_0 y_1 y_2 \cdots$.

The parameter **I** is intimately related to the maximum-likelihood detection method used in PRML. Before discussing the ML detection algorithm, it is useful to rewrite the output signal as

$$y(t) = \sum_{i=0}^{\infty} (w_i - w_{i-2}) \operatorname{sinc}\left(\frac{t - iT}{T}\right),$$

where, we recall, $w_{-2} = w_{-1} = w_0$. This form can be obtained by simple arithmetic from the original expression for the Class-4 transition response (2). This implies the following relation between the noiseless output samples $y_0 y_1 y_2 \cdots$ and the input bipolar sequence $\mathbf{w}$:

$$y_i = w_i - w_{i-2}, \quad i \geq 0.$$

A trellis diagram presenting the possible output sample sequences is shown in Figure 9. Each state is denoted by a pair of symbols that can be interpreted as the last pair of inputs, $w_{i-2} w_{i-1}$. There is an edge connecting each pair of states $w_{i-2} w_{i-1}$ and $w_{i-1} w_i$, and the label of this edge is $y_i = w_i - w_{i-2}$.

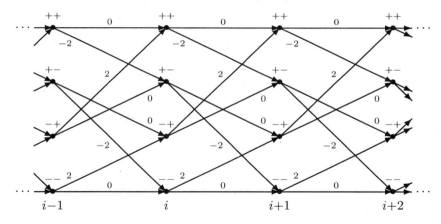

FIGURE 9. Trellis diagram for Class-4 output sequences.

The iterative ML detection algorithm is based upon the technique of dynamic programming in an embodiment of the *Viterbi algorithm*, familiar from decoding of convolutional codes. As shown by Forney [**For72**] and Kobayashi [**Koba71a**], the Viterbi algorithm is an optimal detector for partial-response (in particular, Class-4) output-signal sample sequences, in the presence of additive white Gaussian noise.

The behavior of the ML detector can be described in terms of the trellis diagram in Figure 9. Denote by $r_0 r_1 r_2 \cdots$ the sequence of (possibly noisy) received samples. Assume an initial state $u = w_{-2} w_{-1}$ is specified. For each state $v = w_{\ell-2} w_{\ell-1}$ in the diagram that can be reached from u by a path of length ℓ, the ML detector determines the allowable noiseless output sample word $\hat{y}_0 \hat{y}_1 \ldots \hat{y}_{\ell-1}$, generated by a path of length ℓ from u to v, that minimizes the Euclidean distance

$$\sum_{i=0}^{\ell} (r_i - \hat{y}_i)^2.$$

The words so determined are referred to as *survivor words*.

The representation of the output samples as $y_i = w_i - w_{i-2}$ permits the detector to operate independently on the output subsequences at even and odd time indices. Note that, within each interleave, the nonzero sample values y_i must alternate in sign. Figure 10 shows a trellis diagram presenting the possible sequences in each of the interleaves.

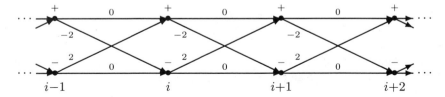

FIGURE 10. Trellis diagram for interleaved sequences.

There are several formulations of the Viterbi algorithm applied to this system. See [**FC89**], [**Koba71b**], [**SW91**], [**WoodP86**], [**Ze87**]. The motivation for the **I** constraint is clear from the following description of the ML detection algorithm, essentially due to Ferguson [**Ferg72**]. It can be interpreted in terms of a "dynamic threshold detection scheme," as described by Wood [**Wood90**]. We will outline the detector operation on the subsequence of received samples at even time indices. The procedure for the odd time indices is entirely analogous.

The detector may operate in one of two modes, denoted by the variable m which takes values in $\{+1, -1\}$, according to whether the detector expects the next non-zero sample value to be positive or negative. In mode $m = +1$ (resp. $m = -1$), the detector uses a variable R to store the *value* of the largest (resp. smallest) sample since the last change of the mode variable m. It also maintains a variable J to store the *time index* i of the largest (resp. smallest) sample value since the last change of the mode m.

The detector mode and variables are initialized by setting $m \leftarrow +1$, $R \leftarrow -\infty$, and $J \leftarrow -1$.

At each successive time instant $i = 2j$, $j \geq 0$, the detector takes one of three possible actions, as determined by m, R, J, and the new noisy sample r_{2j}:

1. If $m \cdot r_{2j} \geq m \cdot R$, then do $\hat{y}_J \leftarrow 0$, $R \leftarrow r_{2j}$, and $J \leftarrow 2j$;
2. else if $m \cdot R - 2 < m \cdot r_{2j} < m \cdot R$, then do $\hat{y}_{2j} \leftarrow 0$;
3. else if $m \cdot r_{2j} \leq m \cdot R - 2$, then do $\hat{y}_J \leftarrow 2m$, $R \leftarrow r_{2j}$, $J \leftarrow 2j$, and $m \leftarrow -m$.

Case 1 corresponds to the situation in which the survivor words at time $2j$ for both states in Figure 10 are obtained by extending the survivor word at time $2(j-1)$ for state $u = m$. Case 2 corresponds to the situation in which the survivor word at time $2j$ for each state u is the extension of the survivor word at time $2(j-1)$ for state u. Finally, case 3 corresponds to the situation in which the survivor words at time $2j$ for both states are obtained by extending the survivor word at time $2(j-1)$ for state $u = -m$.

Cases 1 and 3 correspond to "merging" of survivor paths, thereby determining the estimated value $\hat{y}_J$ for the channel output at the index of the previous merge. In the noiseless case, the merges occur when the output sample value is either $+2$ or -2. Case 2, on the other hand, defers the decision about this estimated value. In the noiseless case, this arises when the output sample value is 0. Since the latter case could arise for an arbitrary number of successive time indices, one could encounter a potentially unbounded time span between time J and the generation of the estimated channel output $\hat{y}_J$ — even in the noiseless case. The **I** constraint on the maximum runlength of consecutive zero samples in each interleave of the output sequence is introduced to reduce the probability of such a long delay (or eliminate the possibility in the noiseless case).

In analogy to the RLL constraints, the **G** and **I** constraints on the output sample sequences $y_0 y_1 y_2 \cdots$ can be translated directly into a constraint on recorded binary sequences **z** by applying NRZI precoding to each of the interleaves. This interleaved NRZI (INRZI) precoding transforms **z** into a bipolar sequence **w** through an intermediate binary sequence **x** according to the rules:

$$x_i = x_{i-2} \oplus z_i \quad \text{and} \quad w_i = (-1)^{x_i} \, ,$$

where $x_{-2} = x_{-1} = 0$ and, as before, $\oplus$ denotes addition modulo 2. The constraint on the runlengths of consecutive 0's in the output sample sequence and in the even/odd subsequences are then reflected in corresponding $(0, \mathbf{G}/\mathbf{I})$ constraints in the binary sequences **z**.

2. Constrained systems

2.1. Labeled graphs and constraints. First, we introduce a convenient diagrammatic method used to present the set of constrained words allowed in a given channel. An encoder for the channel, in turn, may generate words only from this set.

A *labeled graph* (or a *finite labeled directed graph*) $G = (V, E, L)$ consists of —

- a finite set of states $V = V_G$;
- a set of edges $E = E_G$ where each edge e has an *initial state* $\sigma_G(e)$ and a *terminal state* $\tau_G(e)$, both in V;
- edge labels $L = L_G : E \to \Sigma$ drawn from a finite alphabet Σ.

We will also use the notation $u \xrightarrow{a} v$ to denote an edge labeled a from state u to state v in G.

Figure 11 shows a "typical" labeled graph.

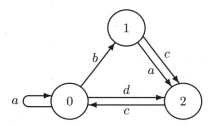

FIGURE 11. Typical labeled graph.

While some of the properties of interest to us do not depend on the labeling L, most do. We will omit the labeling qualifier from the term 'graph' in those cases where the labeling is immaterial.

There are a few features worth highlighting. Since the graph is directed, each edge can be traversed in only one direction, as indicated by the arrow. *Self-loops*, meaning edges that start and terminate at the same state, are allowed. Also, there

can be more than one edge connecting a given state to another state; these are
called *parallel edges*. However, we assume that distinct edges that share the same
initial and terminal states have distinct labels. A graph is called *essential* if every
state has at least one outgoing edge and at least one incoming edge. The *out-
degree* of a state in a graph is the number of edges outgoing from that state. The
minimum out-degree of a graph is the smallest among all out-degrees of the states
in that graph.

A path γ in a graph G is a finite sequence of edges $e_1 e_2 \ldots e_\ell$ such that
$\sigma_G(e_{i+1}) = \tau_G(e_i)$ for $i = 1, 2, \ldots, \ell-1$. The length of a path γ is the number
of edges along the path and is denoted by $\ell(\gamma)$. The *state sequence* of a path
$e_1 e_2 \ldots e_\ell$ is the sequence of states $\sigma_G(e_1)\sigma_G(e_2) \ldots \sigma_G(e_\ell)$. A *cycle* in a graph is
a path $e_1 e_2 \ldots e_\ell$ where $\tau_G(e_\ell) = \sigma_G(e_1)$. We will also use the term right-infinite
path for an infinite sequence of edges $e_1 e_2 \cdots$ in G such that $\sigma_G(e_{i+1}) = \tau_G(e_i)$ for
$i \geq 1$. Similarly, a bi-infinite path is a bi-infinite sequence of edges $\cdots e_{-1} e_0 e_1 e_2 \cdots$
with $\sigma_G(e_{i+1}) = \tau_G(e_i)$ for all i.

A labeled graph can be used to generate finite symbol sequences, by reading
off the labels along paths in the graph, thereby producing a *word* or a *string* or a
block. For example, in Figure 11, the word $a\ b\ c\ c\ d$ can be generated by following
a path along edges with state sequence 0 0 1 2 0. The length of a word $\mathbf{w}$ will be
denoted by $\ell(\mathbf{w})$. A word of length ℓ generated by G will be called an ℓ-*block*.

We regard two labeled graphs as the same if there is a *labeled graph isomorphism*
from one to the other — i.e., maps from states to states and edges to edges which
preserve initial states, terminal states, and labels.

The underlying finite directed graph of a labeled graph is conveniently described
by a matrix as follows. Let G be a graph. The *adjacency matrix* $A = A_G =
[(A_G)_{u,v}]_{u,v \in V_G}$ is the $|V_G| \times |V_G|$ matrix where the entry $(A_G)_{u,v}$ is the number of
edges from state u to state v in G. For instance, the adjacency matrix of the graph
in Figure 11 is

$$A_G = \begin{bmatrix} 1 & 1 & 1 \\ 0 & 0 & 2 \\ 1 & 0 & 0 \end{bmatrix}.$$

The adjacency matrix of course has nonnegative, integer entries. It is a useful
artifice; for example, the number of paths of length ℓ from state u to state v is
simply $(A_G^\ell)_{u,v}$, and the number of cycles of length ℓ is simply the trace of A_G^ℓ.

The fundamental object considered in the theory of constrained coding is the
set of words generated by a labeled graph. A *constrained system* (or *constraint*),
denoted S, is the set of all words (i.e., finite sequences) obtained from reading the
labels of paths in a labeled graph G. We say that G *presents* S or is a *presentation*
of S, and we write $S = S(G)$. If a path γ is labeled by a word $\mathbf{w}$, we say that γ
generates $\mathbf{w}$ and denote $L_G(\gamma) = \mathbf{w}$. The *alphabet* of S is the set of symbols that
actually occur in words of S and is denoted $\Sigma = \Sigma(S)$.

As central examples of constrained systems, we have the RLL and charge-
constrained systems presented by the labeled graphs in Figures 2 and 4.

A constrained system is equivalent in automata theory to a regular language
which is recognized by an automaton, the states of which are all accepting [**Hopc79**].
A constrained system is called a *sofic system* (or *sofic shift*) in symbolic dynamics [**KarM88**] — except that a sofic system usually refers to the bi-infinite symbol
sequences generated by a labeled graph.

A constrained system should not be confused with any particular labeled graph, because a given constrained system can be presented by many different labeled graphs. For example, the $(0,1)$-RLL constrained system is presented by all labeled graphs in Figures 12 through 15, which are very different from one another. This is good: one presentation may be preferable because it has a smaller number of states, while another presentation might be preferable because it could be used as an encoder.

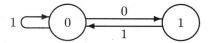

FIGURE 12. Labeled graph for $(0,1)$-RLL constrained system.

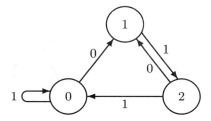

FIGURE 13. Another labeled graph for $(0,1)$-RLL constrained system.

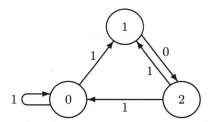

FIGURE 14. Yet another labeled graph for $(0,1)$-RLL constrained system.

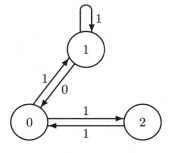

FIGURE 15. One more labeled graph for $(0,1)$-RLL constrained system.

2.2. Properties of labelings.

2.2.1. *Deterministic presentation.* For purposes of encoder construction, it will be important to consider labelings with special properties. The most fundamental special property is as follows.

A labeled graph is *deterministic* if at each state the outgoing edges are labeled distinctly. In other words, at each state, any label generated from that state uniquely determines an outgoing edge from that state. The labeled graphs in Figures 2, 4, 12, and 13 are deterministic while the labeled graphs in Figures 14 and 15 are not. Constrained systems in the engineering literature are usually presented by deterministic graphs. In fact, any constrained system can be presented in this way, as stated in the next proposition.

PROPOSITION 2.1. *Any constrained system can be presented by some deterministic labeled graph.*

We also have the notion of *co-deterministic*, obtained by replacing "outgoing" with "incoming" in the definition.

'Deterministic' is called *right resolving* in symbolic dynamics.

A *Shannon cover* of a constrained system is a deterministic presentation with a smallest number of states. Such a distinguished representation is often useful in analyzing properties of constrained systems and, moreover, arises naturally in describing RLL and spectral-null constraints.

2.2.2. *Finite anticipation.* Encoder synthesis algorithms usually begin with a deterministic presentation and transform it into a presentation which satisfies the following weaker version of the deterministic property.

A labeled graph G has *finite local anticipation* (or, in short, *finite anticipation*), if there is an integer N such that any two paths of length $N+1$ with the same initial state and labeling must have the same initial edge. The *(local) anticipation* $\mathcal{A}(G)$ of G is the smallest N for which this holds. Hence, knowledge of the initial state of a path and the first $\mathcal{A}(G)+1$ symbols that it generates is sufficient information to determine the initial edge of the path. In case G does not have finite anticipation, we define $\mathcal{A}(G) = \infty$.

We also define the *(local) co-anticipation* of a labeled graph G as the anticipation of the labeled graph obtained by reversing the directions of the edges in G.

Note that to say that a labeled graph is deterministic is to say that it has zero anticipation. The labeled graph in Figure 14 is a presentation of the $(0,1)$-RLL constrained system with anticipation 1 but not 0. Figure 15 depicts a presentation which does not have finite anticipation.

'Finite anticipation' is also called *right closing* (in symbolic dynamics [**BMT87**]) or *lossless of finite order* [**Huff59**], [**Even65**].

Similarly, a labeled graph G is said to have *finite memory* if there is an integer N such that the paths in G of length N that generate the same word, all terminate at the same state. The smallest N for which this holds is called the *memory* of G and denoted $\mathcal{M}(G)$.

2.2.3. *Definite graphs.* A labeled graph is (m,a)-*definite* if, given any word $\mathbf{w} = w_{-\mathsf{m}}w_{-\mathsf{m}+1}\ldots w_0 \ldots w_{\mathsf{a}}$, the set of paths $e_{-\mathsf{m}}e_{-\mathsf{m}+1}\ldots e_0 \ldots e_{\mathsf{a}}$ that generate $\mathbf{w}$ all agree in the edge e_0. We say that a labeled graph is definite if it is (m,a)-definite for some finite nonnegative m and a. Definite graphs are referred to in the literature also as graphs with *finite memory-and-anticipation*.

Note the difference between this concept and the concept of finite anticipation: we have replaced knowledge of an initial state with knowledge of a finite amount of memory. Actually, definiteness is a stronger condition.

Figure 13 shows a labeled graph that is $(2,0)$-definite, while Figure 16 shows a labeled graph that has finite anticipation (in fact is deterministic and co-deterministic) but is not definite.

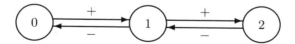

FIGURE 16. Labeled graph for some charge constraint.

Note that, in contrast to the anticipation and the memory, we did not require a and m to be minimal in any sense while talking about (m, a)-definiteness. It would be natural to require that m+a be minimal, but even that does not specify m and a uniquely; for instance, the labeled graph in Figure 17 is $(1,0)$-definite and also $(0, 1)$-definite.

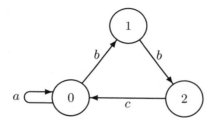

FIGURE 17. Labeled graph which is both $(1,0)$-definite and $(0, 1)$-definite.

2.2.4. *Lossless graphs.* A labeled graph is *lossless* if any two distinct paths with the same initial state and terminal state have different labelings. All of the pictures of labeled graphs that we have presented so far are lossless. Figure 18 shows a presentation of the $(0, 1)$-RLL constrained system that is not lossless.

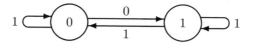

FIGURE 18. Graph which is not lossless.

2.3. Power of a graph. As mentioned in Section 1.4, a rate $p : q$ finite-state encoder will generate a word, composed of length-q codewords (q-blocks) hooked together, that belongs to the desired constrained system S. For a constrained system S presented by a labeled graph G, it will be very useful to have an explicit description of the words in S, grouped into such non-overlapping "chunks" of length q.

Let G be a labeled graph. The *qth power of G*, denoted G^q, is the labeled graph with the same set of states as G, but one edge for each path of length q in G, labeled by the q-block generated by that path. For a constrained system S

presented by a labeled graph G, the qth *power of S*, denoted S^q, is the constrained system presented by G^q. So, S^q is the constrained system obtained from S by grouping the symbols in each word into non-overlapping "chunks" of length q (in particular, the definition of S^q does not depend on which presentation G of S is used).

For example, Figure 19 shows the third power G^3 of the labeled graph G in Figure 12 that presents the $(0, 1)$-RLL constrained system (multiple labeling on an edge indicates parallel edges).

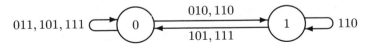

FIGURE 19. Third power of labeled graph in Figure 12.

Finally, we state a result which asserts that the power operation introduced in this section preserves the properties of labelings introduced in Section 2.2. We leave the proof to the reader.

PROPOSITION 2.2. *The power of a graph preserves the deterministic, finite anticipation (co-anticipation), and definiteness properties.*

2.4. Finite-type and almost-finite-type constraints. In this section, we consider some special classes of constraints that play a distinguished role in the statement of the coding theorems and the encoder construction algorithms.

A constrained system S is *finite-type* (in symbolic dynamics, *shift of finite type*) if it can be presented by a definite graph. As an example, the (d, k)-RLL constraint is finite-type: the labeled graph in Figure 2 is $(k, 0)$-definite — i.e., for any given word $\mathbf{w}$ of length at least $k+1$, all paths that generate $\mathbf{w}$ end with the same edge.

It is important to recognize that there are "bad" presentations of finite-type constrained systems, meaning labeled graphs that are not definite. For example, the labeled graph in Figure 15 represents the $(0, 1)$-RLL constrained system, but it is not definite, as can be seen by considering the paths that generate words consisting of all 1's.

Given the existence of bad labeled graphs, one might begin to worry about potential problems in determining whether or not a constrained system is finite-type. However, there is an intrinsic characterization of finite-type constrained systems that resolves this difficulty.

A constrained system S is said to have *finite memory* if there is an integer N such that, for any symbol $b \in \Sigma(S)$ and any word $\mathbf{w} \in S$ of length at least N, we have $\mathbf{w}b \in S$ if and only if $\mathbf{w}'b \in S$ where $\mathbf{w}'$ is the suffix of $\mathbf{w}$ of length N. The smallest such integer N, if any, is called the *memory* of S and is denoted by $\mathcal{M}(S)$.

It is can be readily verified that the (d, k)-RLL constrained system has memory k.

LEMMA 2.3. *A constrained system S has finite memory if and only if there is a presentation G of S with finite memory. Furthermore, the memory of S is the smallest memory of any presentation of S with finite memory.*

PROPOSITION 2.4. *A constrained system is finite-type if and only if it has finite memory.*

Not every constrained system of practical interest is finite-type. For example, the charge constraint described by Figure 16 is not. This can be seen easily by considering the condition above: the symbol '+' can be appended to the word

$$- + - + - + \cdots - +$$

but not to the word

$$+ + - + - + - + \cdots - + \, .$$

However, this constrained system falls into a natural broader class of constrained systems, called almost-finite-type systems; these systems should be thought of as "locally finite-type" (perhaps that would have been a better name). A constrained system is *almost-finite-type* if it can be presented by a labeled graph that has both finite anticipation and finite co-anticipation.

Since definiteness implies finite anticipation and finite co-anticipation, every constrained system which is finite-type is also almost-finite-type, and so the almost-finite-type systems do indeed include the finite-type systems. From Figure 16, we see that the charge-constrained systems are presented by labeled graphs with zero anticipation (i.e., deterministic) and zero co-anticipation (i.e., co-deterministic); thus, these systems are almost-finite-type, but not finite-type. Most every constrained system that has been used in practical applications is in fact almost-finite-type.

Recall that every constrained system has a deterministic presentation (and hence finite anticipation); likewise, every constrained system has a co-deterministic presentation (and hence finite co-anticipation). So, the essential feature of the almost-finite-type definition is that there is a presentation that simultaneously has finite anticipation and finite co-anticipation.

As with finite-type systems, we have the problem that a given constrained system may have some presentation that satisfies the finite anticipation and co-anticipation conditions and another presentation that does not. There is an intrinsic condition that defines almost-finite-type, but it is a bit harder to state [**Will88**]. An example of a constrained system which is not almost-finite-type is given in [**KarM88**].

2.5. Irreducibility.

2.5.1. *Irreducible graphs.* A graph G is *irreducible* (or *strongly connected*), if for any ordered pair of states u, v, there is a path from u to v in G. A graph is *reducible* if it is not irreducible. Note our use of the term 'ordered': for a given pair of states u, v, we must be able to travel from u to v and from v to u.

All of the graphs in Figures 12 through 15 are irreducible, while Figure 20 shows a reducible graph which presents the system of unconstrained binary words.

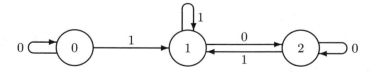

FIGURE 20. Reducible labeled graph for unconstrained binary words.

Observe that the property of being irreducible does not depend on the labeling and can be described in terms of the adjacency matrix: namely, for every (ordered) pair of states u, v, there exists some ℓ such that $(A_G^\ell)_{u,v} > 0$.

It will be useful later to know that any reducible graph can, in some sense, be broken down into "maximal" irreducible pieces. To make this more precise we introduce the concept of an irreducible component. An *irreducible component* of a graph G is a maximal (with respect to inclusion) irreducible subgraph of G. The irreducible components of a graph are simply the subgraphs consisting of all edges whose initial and terminal states both belong to an equivalence class of the following relation: $u \sim v$ if there is a path from u to v and a path from v to u (we allow paths to be empty so that $u \sim u$).

An *irreducible sink* is an irreducible component H such that any edge which originates in H must also terminate in H. An *irreducible source* is an irreducible component H such that any edge which terminates in H must also originate in H.

Any graph can be broken down into irreducible components with 'transient' connections between the components. The irreducible sinks can have transient connections entering but not exiting. Every graph has at least one irreducible sink (and, similarly, at least one irreducible source). To see this, we argue as follows. Pick an irreducible component and check if it is an irreducible sink. If so, stop. If not, there must be a path leading to another irreducible component. Repeat the procedure on the latter component. The process must eventually terminate at an irreducible sink H; otherwise, the original decomposition into irreducible components would be contradicted. The picture of the irreducible components and their connections is perhaps best illustrated via the adjacency matrix: by reordering the states, $A = A_G$ can be written in block upper triangular form with the adjacency matrices of the irreducible components as block diagonals, as shown in Figure 21.

$$
A = \begin{bmatrix}
A_1 & B_{1,2} & B_{1,3} & \cdots & & B_{1,k} \\
 & A_2 & B_{2,3} & \cdots & & B_{2,k} \\
 & & A_3 & \ddots & & \vdots \\
 & & & \ddots & & B_{k-1,k} \\
 & & & & & A_k
\end{bmatrix}.
$$

FIGURE 21. Writing matrix in upper triangular form.

Figure 22 shows the irreducible components of the graph in Figure 20; one is an irreducible sink and the other is an irreducible source.

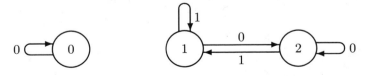

FIGURE 22. Irreducible components of labeled graph in Figure 20.

From the point-of-view of finite-state encoder construction, it turns out that, by passing to irreducible components, we can concern ourselves primarily with irreducible labeled graphs; we explain why in Section 3.1.

There are times when the qth power of a graph G will not be irreducible, even when G is. For example, Figure 16 shows a labeled graph describing a charge-constrained system. Its second power G^2, shown in Figure 23, has two irreducible components. This example illustrates the general situation: it can be shown that, if G is an irreducible graph, then any power G^q is either irreducible or decomposes into isolated, irreducible components (see also Figures 12 and 19).

FIGURE 23. Second power of labeled graph in Figure 16.

2.5.2. *Irreducible constrained systems.* A constrained system S is *irreducible*, if for every pair of words $\mathbf{w}, \mathbf{w}'$ in S, there is a word $\mathbf{z}$ such that $\mathbf{wzw}'$ is in S. A constrained system that is not irreducible is called *reducible*.

The following shows that irreducibility of a constrained system can be reformulated in terms of irreducible labeled graphs.

LEMMA 2.5. *Let S be a constrained system. The following are equivalent:*
(*a*) *S is irreducible;*
(*b*) *S is presented by some irreducible (in fact, deterministic) labeled graph.*

We will also make use of the following result.

LEMMA 2.6. *Let S be an irreducible constrained system and let G be a labeled graph such that $S \subseteq S(G)$. Then for some irreducible component G' of G, $S \subseteq S(G')$.*

All of the constrained systems that we have considered so far are irreducible, while Figure 24 presents a reducible constrained system.

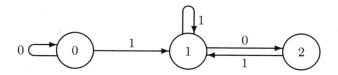

FIGURE 24. Reducible constrained system.

In general, the Shannon cover is not unique. However, it can be shown that, for an irreducible system, the Shannon cover is indeed unique up to labeled graph isomorphism.

2.6. Capacity. We need to discuss one more concept, namely the *Shannon capacity* or simply *capacity* of the constrained system S, before we can state the fundamental coding theorems.

2.6.1. *Combinatorial characterization of capacity.* Let S be a constrained system. The Shannon capacity $\mathsf{cap}(S)$ of S measures the growth rate of the number $N(\ell; S)$ of words of length ℓ in S, in the sense that the $N(\ell; S)$ is well-approximated by $2^{\ell \, \mathsf{cap}(S)}$ for large enough ℓ. More precisely, the *base-α Shannon capacity*, or simply *base-α capacity* of S, is defined by

$$\mathsf{cap}_\alpha(S) \;=\; \lim_{\ell \to \infty} \frac{1}{\ell} \log_\alpha N(\ell; S) \,.$$

We omit the base notation unless we want to emphasize the specific base used.

That the limit actually exists can be shown in two ways. The most direct method is as follows: first, one shows that $\log N(\ell; S)$ is a *subadditive function* — i.e., for all ℓ and m, $(\log N(\ell+m; S)) \leq (\log N(\ell; S)) + (\log N(m; S))$; then one shows that for any subadditive function $f(\ell)$, the limit $\lim_{\ell \to \infty} (\log f(\ell))/\ell$ exists (see [**Walt82**]). An alternative method is provided by Theorem 2.12 below.

The analysis of constrained systems – in particular, the computation of capacity – as well as the encoder construction algorithms, both make heavy use of Perron-Frobenius theory. Therefore, we make a short break in our treatment of constrained systems and summarize here the basic results of this theory, tailored to our needs.

2.6.2. *Perron-Frobenius Theorem.* A nonnegative real square matrix A is called *irreducible* if for every row index u and column index v there exists a nonnegative integer ℓ such that $A_{u,v}^\ell > 0$. A nonnegative real square matrix which is not irreducible is called *reducible*.

For a square real matrix A, we denote by $\lambda(A)$ the spectral radius of A — i.e., the largest of the absolute values of the eigenvalues of A.

THEOREM 2.7. (*Perron-Frobenius Theorem for irreducible matrices* [**Gant60**, Ch. XIII], [**Minc88**, Ch. 1], [**Sen80**, Ch. 1], [**Var62**, Ch. 2]) *Let $A = [(A)_{u,v}]_{u,v}$ be an irreducible matrix.*

(a) $\lambda(A)$ *is an eigenvalue of A and A has positive (i.e., all components are positive) right and left eigenvectors associated with the eigenvalue $\lambda(A)$;*

(b) $\lambda(A)$ *is a simple eigenvalue of A; i.e., $\lambda(A)$ appears as a root of the characteristic polynomial of A with multiplicity 1. In particular, all right (respectively left) eigenvectors associated with the eigenvalue $\lambda(A)$ are scalar multiples of one another.*

(c) $\min_u \sum_v (A)_{u,v} \leq \lambda(A) \leq \max_u \sum_v (A)_{u,v}$.

Irreducibility of a nonnegative square matrix A depends on the locations (row and column indices) of the nonzero entries in A, and not on their specific values. For example, irreducibility will be preserved if we changed each nonzero entry in A to 1. Therefore, the following definition is useful.

Let $A = [(A)_{u,v}]$ be a nonnegative real square matrix. The *support graph* of A is a graph G with a state for each row in A and an edge $u \to v$ if and only if $(A)_{u,v} > 0$. Note that A is irreducible if and only if its support graph G is irreducible, and G is irreducible if and only if its adjacency matrix A_G is irreducible.

In analogy with graphs, we can now define an *irreducible component* of a nonnegative real square matrix A as an irreducible submatrix of A whose support graph is an irreducible component of the support graph of A. The term *irreducible sink* extends to matrices in a straightforward manner. By applying the same permutation on both the rows and columns of A, we can obtain a matrix in block upper triangular form with the irreducible components as the block diagonals, as in Figure 21. This implies the following.

THEOREM 2.8. (*Perron-Frobenius Theorem for nonnegative matrices*) *Let A be a nonnegative square matrix. Then,* (*a*) *the set of eigenvalues of A is the union (with multiplicity) of the sets of eigenvalues of the irreducible components of A;*

(*b*) *hence, $\lambda(A)$ is an eigenvalue of A and there are nonnegative right and left eigenvectors associated with $\lambda(A)$.*

Since $\lambda(A)$ is actually an eigenvalue of A, we will refer to $\lambda(A)$ as the *largest eigenvalue of A*.

2.6.3. *Approximate eigenvectors.* Given a nonnegative integer square matrix A and an integer n, an (A, n)-*approximate eigenvector* is a nonnegative integer vector $\mathbf{x} \neq \mathbf{0}$ such that

$$A\mathbf{x} \geq n\mathbf{x},$$

where the (weak) inequality holds componentwise. We refer to this inequality as the *approximate eigenvector inequality*. The set of all (A, n)-approximate eigenvectors is denoted $\mathcal{X}(A, n)$.

Approximate eigenvectors play an essential role in the construction and the analysis of finite-state encoders.

For a vector $\mathbf{x} = [x_u]_u$, we will use the notations $\|\mathbf{x}\|_1$ and $\|\mathbf{x}\|_\infty$ for $\sum_u |x_u|$ and $\max_u |x_u|$, respectively. The transpose of $\mathbf{x}$ will be denoted $\mathbf{x}^\top$.

We state the following important theorem without proof.

THEOREM 2.9. *Let A be a nonnegative integer square matrix and let n be a positive integer. Then,*

$$\mathcal{X}(A, n) \neq \emptyset \quad \text{if and only if} \quad \lambda(A) \geq n.$$

Furthermore, if A is irreducible and $\lambda(A) = n$, then every (A, n)-approximate eigenvector is a right eigenvector associated with the eigenvalue n.

When A is the adjacency matrix of a graph G, the approximate eigenvector inequality has a very simple meaning in terms of G. Think of the vector $\mathbf{x} = [x_u]_{u \in V_G}$ as assigning *state weights*: the weight of state u is x_u. Now assign *edge weights* to the edges of the graph according to their terminal states: the weight of an edge e is given by $x_{\tau_G(e)}$. Let E_u denote the set of outgoing edges from state u in G. Then the approximate eigenvector inequality can be written as the set of simultaneous scalar inequalities, one for each state u,

$$\sum_{e \in E_u} x_{\tau_G(e)} \geq n x_u \quad \text{for every } u \in V_G.$$

That is, the sum of the weights of the outgoing edges from a given state u is at least n times the weight of the state u itself.

EXAMPLE 2.10. Let G be the presentation of the $(0, 1)$-RLL constrained system shown in Figure 12. The third power of G is shown in Figure 19, and the adjacency matrix of G^3 is given by

$$A_G^3 \begin{bmatrix} 2 \\ 1 \end{bmatrix} = \begin{bmatrix} 3 & 2 \\ 2 & 1 \end{bmatrix} \begin{bmatrix} 2 \\ 1 \end{bmatrix} = \begin{bmatrix} 8 \\ 5 \end{bmatrix} \geq 4 \begin{bmatrix} 2 \\ 1 \end{bmatrix}.$$

Therefore, the vector $\mathbf{x} = [\,2\ 1\,]^\top$ is an $(A_G^3, 4)$-approximate eigenvector.

For a graph G, the all-1's vector $\mathbf{1}$ is an (A_G, n)-approximate eigenvector if and only if G has minimum out-degree at least n. Also, a 0–1 vector is an (A_G, n)-approximate eigenvector if and only if G has a subgraph with minimum out-degree at least n.

2.6.4. *Computing approximate eigenvectors.* In this section, we describe an algorithm for computing (A, n)-approximate eigenvectors. The algorithm is due to Franaszek [**Fra82**, Appendix] (see also [**ACH83**, Appendix]), and its running time is proportional to the *values* (rather than the size of the bit representations) of the computed approximate eigenvector [**MR91**].

The input to the following algorithm (Franaszek algorithm) is a nonnegative integer square matrix A, a positive integer n, and a nonnegative integer vector $\boldsymbol{\xi}$. The output is a nonnegative integer vector $\mathbf{x}$, the properties of which are summarized in Proposition 2.11 (part (b)) below.

> $\mathbf{y} \leftarrow \boldsymbol{\xi}$;
> $\mathbf{x} \leftarrow \mathbf{0}$;
> **while** $\mathbf{x} \neq \mathbf{y}$ **do**
> **begin**
> > $\mathbf{x} \leftarrow \mathbf{y}$;
> > $\mathbf{y} \leftarrow \min \left\{ \left\lfloor \frac{1}{n} A\mathbf{x} \right\rfloor, \mathbf{x} \right\}$
> > /* both $\lfloor \cdot \rfloor$ and $\min\{\cdot, \cdot\}$ are applied componentwise.   */
> **end** ;
> **output: x** .

For a nonnegative integer square matrix A, a positive integer n, and a nonnegative integer vector $\boldsymbol{\xi} = [\xi_u]_u$, let $\mathcal{X}(A, n; \boldsymbol{\xi})$ denote the set of all elements $\mathbf{x} = [x_u]_u$ of $\mathcal{X}(A, n)$ that are dominated by $\boldsymbol{\xi}$ (i.e., $x_u \leq \xi_u$ for all u, or, in short, $\mathbf{x} \leq \boldsymbol{\xi}$).

PROPOSITION 2.11. *Let A be a nonnegative integer square matrix and let n be a positive integer.*

(a) *If $\mathbf{x}, \mathbf{x}' \in \mathcal{X}(A, n)$, then the vector defined by $[\max(x_u, x'_u)]_u$ belongs to $\mathcal{X}(A, n)$. Thus, for any nonnegative integer vector $\boldsymbol{\xi}$ there is a largest (componentwise) element of $\mathcal{X}(A, n; \boldsymbol{\xi})$.*

(b) *Franaszek algorithm eventually halts for any input vector $\boldsymbol{\xi}$; and the output is either the zero vector (if $\mathcal{X}(A, n; \boldsymbol{\xi}) = \emptyset$) or the largest (componentwise) element of $\mathcal{X}(A, n; \boldsymbol{\xi})$.*

2.6.5. *Algebraic characterization of capacity.* We now return to the calculation of capacity. The following theorem expresses the capacity of an irreducible constrained system S in terms of the adjacency matrix of a lossless presentation of S.

THEOREM 2.12. *Let S be an irreducible constrained system and let G be an irreducible lossless (in particular, deterministic) presentation of S. Then,*

$$\mathsf{cap}(S) = \log \lambda(A_G) .$$

We break the proof of Theorem 2.12 into two lemmas.

LEMMA 2.13. *Let A be an irreducible matrix. Then, for every row index u,*

$$\lim_{\ell \to \infty} \frac{1}{\ell} \log \left(\sum_v (A^\ell)_{u,v} \right) = \log \lambda(A) .$$

Furthermore,

$$\lim_{\ell \to \infty} \frac{1}{\ell} \log \left(\sum_{u,v} (A^\ell)_{u,v} \right) = \log \lambda(A) .$$

LEMMA 2.14. *Let S be an irreducible constrained system and let G be an irreducible lossless presentation of S. Then*

$$\mathsf{cap}(S) \;=\; \lim_{\ell \to \infty} \frac{1}{\ell} \log \Big(\sum_{u,v} (A_G^\ell)_{u,v} \Big).$$

For the $(0,1)$-RLL constrained system presented by the deterministic labeled graph in Figure 12, the adjacency matrix is

$$A \;=\; \left[\begin{array}{cc} 1 & 1 \\ 1 & 0 \end{array} \right]$$

with largest eigenvalue

$$\lambda = \frac{1+\sqrt{5}}{2}\,,$$

and capacity

$$\mathsf{cap}_2(S) \;=\; \log_2 \lambda \;=\; .6942\ldots$$

Actually, Theorem 2.12 holds for any constrained system, irreducible or reducible.

We conclude the discussion of capacity by stating the following useful and easily verified fact.

PROPOSITION 2.15. *For any constrained system S,*

$$\mathsf{cap}(S^q) \;=\; q\,\mathsf{cap}(S)\,.$$

3. Coding theorems

3.1. Finite-state encoders. As was described in Section 1, an encoder takes the form of a synchronous finite-state-machine (see Figure 7). We make the definition of encoder precise as follows.

Let S be a constrained system and n be a positive integer. An *(S,n)-encoder* is a labeled graph $\mathcal{E}$ such that —

- each state of $\mathcal{E}$ has out-degree n;
- $S(\mathcal{E}) \subseteq S$;
- $\mathcal{E}$ is lossless.

A *tagged (S,n)-encoder* is an (S,n)-encoder $\mathcal{E}$ where the outgoing edges from each state in $\mathcal{E}$ are assigned distinct *input tags* from an alphabet of size n. The notation $u \xrightarrow{s/a} v$ stands for an edge in $\mathcal{E}$ from state u to state v which is labeled a and tagged by s. We will sometimes use the same symbol $\mathcal{E}$ to denote both a tagged (S,n)-encoder and the underlying (S,n)-encoder.

A *rate $p:q$ finite-state (S,α)-encoder* is a tagged (S^q, α^p)-encoder, where we assume that the input tags are the α-ary p-blocks. For the typical case $\alpha = 2$, we will abbreviate and call such an encoder a *rate $p:q$ finite-state encoder for S*.

A tagged (S,n)-encoder (or a rate $p:q$ finite-state (S,α)-encoder) is deterministic or has finite anticipation or is definite according to whether the (S,n)-encoder (or (S^q,α^p)-encoder) has these properties. In particular, only the (output) labels (and not the input tags) play a role in these properties.

EXAMPLE 3.1. Figure 25 depicts a rate $1:2$ two-state encoder for the $(1,3)$-RLL constrained system. The input tag assigned to each edge is written before the slash, followed by the label of the edge. The encoder in the figure is known as the

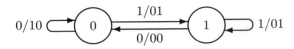

FIGURE 25. Rate $1 : 2$ two-state encoder for $(1,3)$-RLL constrained system.

Modified Frequency Modulation (MFM) code and is due to Miller [**Mill63**]. This encoder is deterministic and $(1,0)$-definite.

Given a rate $p : q$ finite-state (S, α)-encoder $\mathcal{E}$, encoding is accomplished as follows.

1. Select an arbitrary initial state u_0 in $\mathcal{E}$.
2. If the current state is u and the input data is the p-block $\mathbf{s}$, find the outgoing edge e from state u in $\mathcal{E}$ with input tag $\mathbf{s}$. The *codeword* generated is the q-block that labels the edge e. The next encoder state is $\tau_{\mathcal{E}}(e)$.
3. Repeat Step 2 as long as input is provided.

With only the losslessness assumption, decoding can be implemented, but it is terribly impractical because one cannot decode any symbols at all until an entire codeword sequence is received; also, one can decode only those codewords (i.e., q-blocks) that are labels of paths that start at u_0 and terminate at a particular state. However, if an encoder $\mathcal{E}$ has finite anticipation $\mathcal{A} = \mathcal{A}(\mathcal{E})$, then we can decode in a state-dependent manner as follows.

1. Use the initial state u_0 of $\mathcal{E}$ as the initial state of the decoder.
2. If the current state is u, then the current codeword to be decoded, together with the $\mathcal{A}$ upcoming codewords, constitute a word of length $\mathcal{A}+1$ (measured in q-blocks) that is generated by a path that starts at u; by definition of anticipation, the initial edge e of such a path is uniquely determined; the reconstructed (decoded) data is the input tag of e; the next decoder state is $\tau_{\mathcal{E}}(e)$.
3. Repeat Step 2 as long as codewords are provided.

Such a decoder will invert the encoder when applied to valid codeword sequences, effectively retracing the state sequence followed by the encoder in generating the codeword sequence. The output of the decoder will be identical to the input to the encoder — up to a shift of $\mathcal{A}$ input p-blocks; that is, the output of the decoder at time $i \geq \mathcal{A}$ is the p-block $\mathbf{s}_{i-\mathcal{A}}$ that was input to the encoder at time $i - \mathcal{A}$. Hence, the anticipation of an encoder $\mathcal{E}$ measures the *decoding delay* of the state-dependent decoder we have just outlined.

A rate $p : q$ finite-state (S, α)-encoder is called a *rate $p : q$ <u>block</u> (S, α)-encoder* if it contains only one state. Shannon [**Sha48**] showed that whenever there is a rate $kp : kq$ block encoder, for some k, we must have $p/q \leq \mathsf{cap}_\alpha(S)$. Conversely, he proved (nonconstructively) that whenever $p/q < \mathsf{cap}_\alpha(S)$, there is an integer k and a rate $kp : kq$ block encoder. The following result improves this.

THEOREM 3.2. (Finite-state coding theorem) *Let S be a constrained system. If $p/q \leq \mathsf{cap}_\alpha(S)$, then there exists a rate $p : q$ finite-state (S, α)-encoder <u>with finite anticipation</u>.*

Theorem 3.2 is proven in Section 4. It can be derived as a weaker version of the main theorem of [**ACH83**]. It improves upon the earlier coding results, in particular Shannon's result mentioned above, in three important ways:

- It is fairly constructive: it effectively provides encoders with number of states which is close to the smallest possible.
- It proves the existence of finite-state (S, α)-encoders that achieve rate equal to the capacity $\mathsf{cap}_\alpha(S)$, when $\mathsf{cap}_\alpha(S)$ is rational.
- For any positive integers p and q satisfying the inequality $p/q \leq \mathsf{cap}_\alpha(S)$, there is a rate $p : q$ finite-state (S, α)-encoder that operates at rate $p : q$. In particular, choosing p and q relatively prime, one can design an encoder/decoder using the smallest possible codeword length (namely, q) compatible with the chosen rate p/q.

We remarked earlier (Section 2.5.1) that, for the purposes of constructing (S, n)-encoders, we could restrict our attention to irreducible components of a labeled graph presenting S. We do not pay any price in terms of achievable rate in doing so, because we can always choose an irreducible component with a maximum largest eigenvalue.

Moreover, when G is irreducible, but G^q decomposes into irreducible components, then the components are isolated and all have the same largest eigenvalue. So, for encoding purposes, we are free to use any such component, although some components may result in simpler encoders than others. See [**How89**], [**WW91**].

The following is the converse of Theorem 3.2.

THEOREM 3.3. (Finite-state inverse-to-coding theorem) *Let S be a constrained system. Then, there exists a rate $p : q$ finite-state (S, α)-encoder only if $p/q \leq \mathsf{cap}_\alpha(S)$.*

Proof. Let $\mathcal{E}$ be an (S^q, α^p)-encoder. The number of paths of length ℓ in $\mathcal{E}$ equals $|V_\mathcal{E}|(\alpha^p)^\ell$. Since $\mathcal{E}$ is lossless, it follows that the number of words of length ℓ in $S(\mathcal{E})$ is bounded from above by $|V_\mathcal{E}|(\alpha^p)^\ell$ and from below by $(1/|V_\mathcal{E}|)(\alpha^p)^\ell$. So, $\mathsf{cap}_\alpha(S(\mathcal{E})) = p$. On the other hand, since $S(\mathcal{E}) \subseteq S^q$ we have, by Proposition 2.15,

$$p = \mathsf{cap}_\alpha(S(\mathcal{E})) \leq \mathsf{cap}_\alpha(S^q) = q\,\mathsf{cap}_\alpha(S)\,,$$

as claimed. $\square$

In Example 3.1, we showed a rate $1 : 2$ finite-state encoder for the $(1, 3)$-RLL constrained system. So, the base-2 capacity of this system must be at least $1/2$. Indeed, using Theorem 2.12, we can find that the base-2 capacity is $\approx .5515$.

3.2. Block encoders. Before getting to the general framework of encoder construction (which will be discussed in detail in Section 4), we present two basic types of encoders, namely, block encoders and deterministic encoders. These encoders are *not* suitable in many cases, since, in order to obtain a rate $p : q$ finite-state (S, α)-encoder with rate close to capacity, we may need to take extremely large values of q. Also, these encoding methods might not achieve the capacity even when it is rational. Yet, the cases where these methods fail illuminate the motivation to the general method which will be presented in Section 4.

Perhaps the most basic type of encoders is that of block encoders, namely, finite-state encoders with one state. A block (S^q, α^p)-encoder $\mathcal{E}$ can be represented as a *dictionary* $\mathcal{L}$, consisting of α^p codewords that label the edges of the encoder, where each such label is a word of length q in S. Denote by $\mathcal{L}^*$ the set of words that are obtained by concatenation of words in $\mathcal{L}$. Clearly, $\mathcal{L}^* = S(\mathcal{E}) \subseteq S^q$, which means that the codewords of the dictionary $\mathcal{L}$ are *free-concatenatable*: every concatenation of the codewords in $\mathcal{L}$ produces a word in S.

Let S be an irreducible constrained system presented by a deterministic graph G and let α and q be positive integers. We can obtain a block (S^q, α^p)-encoder as follows. (Recall that, to this end, there is no loss of generality in assuming that S is irreducible.) We pick an arbitrary state u in G and find the largest integer p such that $(A_G^q)_{u,u} \geq \alpha^p$. Then, we construct the encoder dictionary by taking α^p words of length q that are generated by cycles in G that start and terminate at u. In fact, if we choose these words in consecutive lexicographic order, then a codeword can be reconstructed efficiently from its index in the dictionary. This technique is known as *enumerative coding* (see [**Imm91**, p. 117], [**TB70**]). The question is whether the attainable rate p/q can be made large enough so that we can approach capacity. The answer turns out to be positive, as summarized in the following theorem.

THEOREM 3.4. (Block coding theorem [**Sha48**]) *Let S be an irreducible constrained system and let α be a positive integer. There exists a sequence of rate $p_m : q_m$ block (S, α)-encoders such that $\lim_{m \to \infty} p_m/q_m = \mathsf{cap}_\alpha(S)$.*

Yet, we might need to take values of q which are extremely large to get rates p/q which are close enough to capacity.

The following result provides a characterization of all block encoders for a given constrained system.

PROPOSITION 3.5. *Let S be a constrained system with a deterministic presentation G and let n be a positive integer. Then there exists a block (S, n)-encoder if and only if there exists a subgraph H of G and a dictionary $\mathcal{L}$ with n symbols of $\Sigma(S)$, such that $\mathcal{L}$ is the set of labels of the outgoing edges from each state in H.*

Based on Proposition 3.5, Freiman and Wyner describe in [**FW64**] a procedure for finding whether there exists a block (S^q, α^p)-encoder for a given constrained system S with finite memory $\leq q$. See also [**MSW92**, Section V and Appendix B]. This procedure is not efficient in general. However, given α and q, for certain constrained systems S, such as the (d, k)-RLL constrained systems, it does allow to effectively compute the largest p for which there exists a block (S^q, α^p)-encoder.

3.3. Deterministic encoders. As pointed out earlier, block encoders, although conceptually simple, may not be suitable in many cases, since they might require a prohibitively large value of q in order to achieve the desired rate. An extreme case is shown in the following simple example.

EXAMPLE 3.6. Consider the constrained system S over the alphabet $\{a, b, c, d\}$ which is presented by the labeled graph G of Figure 26. The adjacency matrix of

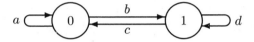

FIGURE 26. Graph presentation for Example 3.6.

G is the all-1's 2×2 matrix and $\lambda(A_G) = 2$. In fact, G is a rate $1 : 1$ two-state encoder for S.

Now, suppose we would like to construct a rate $p : q$ block encoder for S. Since the follower sets of the two states in G are disjoint, then, by Proposition 3.5, the codewords of the dictionary must all be generated by cycles that start and terminate at the very same state of G. However, for each of the two states u in G, there are $(A_G^q)_{u,u} = 2^{q-1}$ cycles of length q that start and terminate at u. Hence, the best we could end up with is a rate $(q-1) : q$ block encoder for S, which, apparently, does not achieve the capacity $\mathsf{cap}_2(S) = 1$.

In Example 3.6, the deterministic presentation G of the constrained system is also a deterministic encoder. In general, if each state in G^q has out-degree at least α^p, then we can delete excess edges and obtain a deterministic (S^q, α^p)-encoder. In fact, it would suffice for G^q to have a subgraph where each state has out-degree at least α^p. It turns out that this condition is also necessary. The following result is stated by Franaszek in [**Fra67**].

PROPOSITION 3.7. *Let S be a constrained system with a deterministic presentation G and let n be a positive integer. Then there exists a deterministic (S, n)-encoder if and only if there exists such an encoder which is a subgraph of G.*

However, not always can we find a deterministic encoder with the desired rate. We illustrate this in the next example.

EXAMPLE 3.8. Let S be the $(0, 1)$-RLL constrained system which is presented by Figure 12. The capacity of S is given by

$$\mathsf{cap}_2(S) \;=\; \log_2\left(\frac{1+\sqrt{5}}{2}\right) \;\approx\; .6942 \;>\; \frac{2}{3}\,.$$

A rate $2 : 3$ two-state encoder for S is shown in Figure 27. However, the encoder

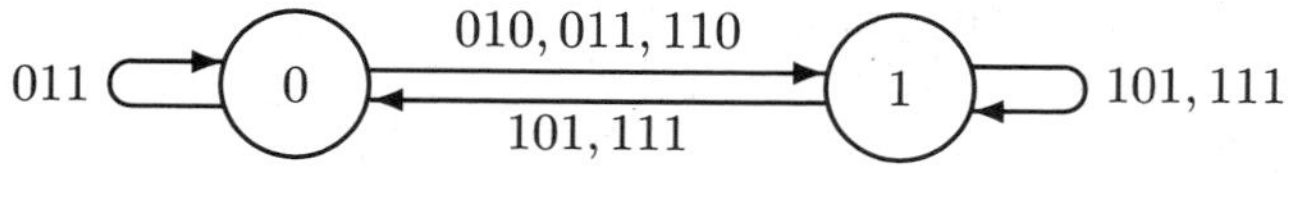

FIGURE 27. Rate 2 : 3 two-state encoder for $(0,1)$-RLL constrained system.

in the figure is not deterministic. We now claim that there is no deterministic rate $2 : 3$ finite-state encoder for S. If there were one, then, by Proposition 3.7, there would be an $(A_G^3, 4)$-approximate eigenvector whose entries are either zero or one. However, it is easy to verify that neither of the vectors $[0\ 1]^\top$, $[1\ 0]^\top$, or $[1\ 1]^\top$, is an $(A_G^3, 4)$-approximate eigenvector. (Applying Franaszek algorithm of Section 2.6.4 to $A = A_G^3$, $n = 4$, and $\boldsymbol{\xi} = [1\ 1]^\top$, yields the all-zero output vector.) Note, on the other hand, that the set $\mathcal{X}(A_G^3, 4)$ is nonempty; in fact, we have shown in Example 2.10 that $[2\ 1]^\top$ is an $(A_G^3, 4)$-approximate eigenvector.

3.4. Stronger forms of decodability. As mentioned in Section 1, when a finite-state encoder is used in the context of a noisy channel, the state-dependent decoder may run into a serious problem. The noise causes errors in the received sequence of symbols, and the decoder must cope with erroneous sequences, including sequences that could not be generated by the encoder in the first place. Consider the simple (and, admittedly, artificial) example given in Figure 28. If we set the initial state to be state 0 and encode the word $0000000\cdots$, we obtain the constrained word

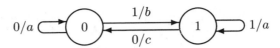

FIGURE 28. Encoder susceptible to catastrophic decoder failure.

$aaaaaaa \cdots$. If the first symbol a is corrupted into the symbol b, then the received word will be $baaaaaa \cdots$, which is decoded to the word $1111111 \cdots$. Thus, one channel error caused the decoder to make an unbounded number of errors because the decoder lost track of the correct state.

Thus, it is desirable that the encoder be decodable in a somewhat state-independent manner. Block encoders are simple examples of encoders that can be decoded this way, but they are certainly not the only ones.

3.4.1. *Sliding-block decodable encoders.* A tagged (S, n)-encoder is (m, a)-*sliding block decodable*, if the following holds: for any two paths $e_{-\mathsf{m}}e_{-\mathsf{m}+1} \cdots e_0 \cdots e_{\mathsf{a}}$ and $e'_{-\mathsf{m}}e'_{-\mathsf{m}+1} \cdots e'_0 \cdots e'_{\mathsf{a}}$ that generate the same word, the edges e_0 and e'_0 have the same (input) tag. We will use the shorter term sliding-block decodable encoder to call a tagged encoder which is (m, a)-*sliding block decodable* for some m and a.

A *sliding-block decoder* for a tagged (S, n)-encoder is a mapping $\mathcal{D}$ from the set $(\Sigma(S))^{\mathsf{m}+\mathsf{a}+1}$ to the set of input tags, such that, if $\mathbf{w} = w_1 w_2 \cdots$ is any symbol sequence generated by the encoder from the input tag sequence $\mathbf{s} = s_1 s_2 \cdots$, then, for $i > \mathsf{m}$,

$$s_i = \mathcal{D}(w_{i-\mathsf{m}}, \ldots, w_i, \ldots, w_{i+\mathsf{a}}) \, .$$

We call a the *look-ahead* of $\mathcal{D}$ and m the *look-behind* of $\mathcal{D}$. The sum $\mathsf{m}+\mathsf{a}+1$ is called the *decoding window length* of $\mathcal{D}$.

It is easy to verify that a tagged (S, n)-encoder has a sliding-block decoder if and only if it is sliding-block decodable.

A $(0, 0)$-sliding-block decodable encoder is called *block decodable*.

The following proposition is straightforward.

PROPOSITION 3.9. *If a tagged (S, n)-encoder is (m, a)-definite, then it is (m, a)-sliding-block decodable for any tagging of the edges.*

The encoder of Example 3.1 is $(1, 0)$-definite. Hence, it is $(1, 0)$-sliding-block decodable for any tagging of the edges. Moreover, for the specific tagging shown in Figure 25, the encoder is block decodable: the second bit in each label equals the input tag.

PROPOSITION 3.10. *If an essential tagged (S, n)-encoder is (m, a)-sliding-block decodable, then it has anticipation at most a.*

Notions of sliding-block decodability naturally extend to rate $p : q$ finite-state (S, α)-encoders: A *sliding-block decoder* for a rate $p : q$ finite-state (S, α)-encoder is a mapping

$$\mathcal{D} : \Sigma(S^q)^{\mathsf{m}+\mathsf{a}+1} \to \{0, 1, \ldots, \alpha-1\}^p$$

such that, if $\mathbf{w} = w_1 w_2 \cdots$ is any sequence of q-blocks generated by the encoder from the input tag sequence of p-blocks $\mathbf{s} = s_1 s_2 \cdots$, then, for $i > \mathsf{m}$,

$$s_i = \mathcal{D}(w_{i-\mathsf{m}}, \ldots, w_i, \ldots, w_{i+\mathsf{a}}) \, .$$

Figure 8 shows a schematic diagram of a sliding-block decoder.

Recall that a single error at the input to a sliding-block decoder can only affect the decoding of q-blocks that fall in a "window" of length at most m+a+1, measured in q-blocks. Thus, error propagation is controlled by sliding-block decoders.

Now, we improve Theorem 3.2 for finite-type constrained systems.

THEOREM 3.11. (Adler, Coppersmith, and Hassner [**ACH83**]) *Let S be a finite-type constrained system. If $p/q \leq \mathsf{cap}_\alpha(S)$, then there exists a rate $p : q$ finite-state (S, α)-encoder with a sliding-block decoder.*

This result is proven in Section 4.4.

We point out that there is an algorithm for testing whether a given tagged (S, n)-encoder is (m, a)-sliding-block decodable In contrast, however, we have the following.

THEOREM 3.12. (Siegel [**Sie85b**]) *Given an untagged (S, n)-encoder $\mathcal{E}$, the problem of deciding whether there is a tag assignment to the edges of $\mathcal{E}$ such that $\mathcal{E}$ is block decodable (namely, $(0, 0)$-sliding-block decodable) is NP-complete.*

We point out that Theorem 3.12 is NP-complete even when n is a fixed integer greater than 2. On the other hand, the problem becomes polynomial if we fix the size of the alphabet of S.

So far, we have assumed in the definition of (m, a)-sliding-block decodability that $\mathsf{m} \geq 0$. For any qualitative discussion, this may suffice. However, in order to reduce the error propagation, we do like to have the window length m+a+1 as small as possible. In order to achieve this, we may in practice let m be also negative (but still having $\mathsf{m}+\mathsf{a} \geq 0$). A value $\mathsf{m} < 0$ corresponds to the case where the sliding-block decoder reconstructs a tag which was input way back in the past — i.e., m time slots *earlier* than the 'oldest' symbol in the examined window. See [**Imm92**] and [**Holl93b**]. When we would like to emphasize that m can be negative, we will say that the encoder is (m, a)-sliding-block decodable *in the wide sense*.

3.4.2. *Block decodable encoders.* Block decodable encoders are a special case of (m, a)-sliding-block decodable encoders where both m and a are zero. The easily-verified relationship between block encoders, deterministic encoders, and block decodable encoders, is summarized in the following proposition.

PROPOSITION 3.13. *Let $\mathcal{E}$ be an encoder. Then,*

$\mathcal{E}$ *is a block encoder* $\Rightarrow \mathcal{E}$ *is block decodable* $\Rightarrow \mathcal{E}$ *is deterministic .*

In Example 3.8, we presented a rate $2 : 3$ two-state encoder for the $(0, 1)$-RLL constrained system, and that encoder was $(0, 1)$-sliding-block decodable. On the other hand, we proved that there is no rate $2 : 3$ deterministic encoder for this system. Hence, there is no block decodable encoder for the $(0, 1)$-RLL constrained system at that rate.

The next proposition is the analog of Proposition 3.7 for block decodable encoders and is proven is a similar way.

PROPOSITION 3.14. *Let S be a constrained system with a deterministic presentation G and let n be a positive integer. Then there exists a block decodable (S, n)-encoder if and only if there exists such an encoder which is a subgraph of G.*

By Theorem 3.12, there is most probably no efficient algorithm for deciding whether a particular subgraph of G can be tagged so as to obtain a block decodable encoder. This does not apply, however, for specific encoders for specific constrained systems. Luckily, the important class of (d,k)-RLL constrained systems falls into the latter category. In [**Fra67**] and [**Fra70**], Franaszek shows that, for certain irreducible constrained systems, including powers of (d,k)-RLL constrained systems, every deterministic encoder which is a subgraph of the Shannon cover can be tagged so that it is block decodable. As pointed out in Section 3.3, the set of states of a deterministic encoder (a set of principal states), if any, can be found efficiently using Franaszek algorithm of Section 2.6.4. Furthermore, by properly choosing the labels of the outgoing edges from each state in the encoder, we can use enumerative coding [**Imm91**, p. 117][**TB70**], so that the tagging of the edges can be efficiently computed.

Explicit description of such labeling, for (d,k)-RLL constrained systems, is given by Gu and Fuja in [**GuF94**], and also by Tjalkens in [**Tja94**]. They show that their labeling yields the largest rate attainable by any block decodable encoder for any given (d,k)-RLL constrained system. The Gu–Fuja construction is a generalization of a coding scheme due to Beenker and Immink [**BI83**].

We now describe the Beenker–Immink construction (see also [**Imm91**, pp. 116–117]). Let $\mathcal{L}(q; d, k; r)$ denote the set of all q-blocks in the (d,k)-RLL constrained system, with at least d leading zeroes and at most r trailing zeroes. We assume that $q > k \geq 2d$ and that $d \geq 1$, and set $r = k-d$. Encoding is carried out by a one-to-one mapping of the $p = \lfloor \log_2 |\mathcal{L}(q; d, k; k-d)| \rfloor$ input bits (tags) into q-blocks, or codewords, in $\mathcal{L}(q; d, k; k-d)$. Such a mapping can be implemented either by a look-up table (of size 2^p) or by enumerative coding. However, since the codewords in $\mathcal{L}(q; d, k; k-d)$ are not free-concatenatable, the encoded codeword needs to be adjusted: When the hooking-together of the previous codeword with the current codeword causes a violation of the (d,k)-RLL constraint, we invert one of the first d zeroes in the latter codeword. The condition $q > k \geq 2d$ guarantees that such inversion can always resolve the constraint violation. The first d bits in each codeword (which are initially zero) are referred to as *merging bits*. Since encoding of a current codeword depends on the previous codeword, the Beenker–Immink encoder is not a block encoder; however, it is block decodable.

We can use Example 3.1 to illustrate how this scheme works (even though the condition $q > k$ is not met). In the example, the set $\mathcal{L}(2; 1, 3; 2)$ consists of the two codewords 00 and 01. When the codeword 00 is to be followed by another 00, we resolve the constraint violation by changing the latter codeword into 10.

A well-known application of the Beenker–Immink method is that of the Eight-to-Fourteen Modulation (EFM) code, which is implemented in the compact disc (see [**Bouw85**, Ch. 7][**Heem82**][**Imm91**, Ch. 2][**IO85**]). The codewords of the EFM code are taken from the set $\mathcal{L}(16; 2, 10; 8)$, which is of size 257, thus yielding a rate $8:16$ block decodable encoder for the $(2,10)$-RLL constrained system. (The number 'fourteen' in the code name is the number of 'net' bits in each codeword — with the two merging bits excluded. In fact, the actual implementation in the compact disk uses three merging bits rather than two, resulting in a rate $8:17$ block decodable encoder with preferable spectral properties.)

In their paper [**GuF94**], Gu and Fuja show that, for any (d,k)-RLL constrained system S with $k > d \geq 1$, and for any $q \geq d$, a block decodable (S^q, n)-encoder exists if and only if $n \leq |\mathcal{L}(q; d, k; k-1)|$ (Tjalkens presents a similar result in [**Tja94**] for the range $q \geq k \geq 2d > 1$). Hence, the Beenker–Immink construction is optimal for $d = 1$ and sub-optimal for $d > 1$. The construction presented in [**GuF94**] that attains the equality $n = |\mathcal{L}(q; d, k; k-1)|$, requires more than just inverting a merging bit; still, as shown in [**GuF94**], it can be efficiently implemented. See also [**Tja94**].

3.4.3. *Non-catastrophic encoders.* A tagged (S, n)-encoder is a *non-catastrophic encoder* if it has finite anticipation and whenever the sequences of output labels of two right-infinite paths differ in only finitely many places, then the sequences of input tags also differ in only finitely many places. A rate $p : q$ finite-state tagged (S, α)-encoder is non-catastrophic if the corresponding tagged (S^q, α^p)-encoder is non-catastrophic.

Observe that non-catastrophic encoders restrict error propagation in the sense that they limit the <u>number</u> of decoded data errors spawned by an isolated channel error. In general, however, such encoders do not necessarily limit the *time span* in which these errors occur. On the other hand, tagged encoders which are sliding-block decodable do limit the time span as well and therefore are preferable.

The following result shows that, with the standard capacity assumption, we can always find non-catastrophic encoders and that whenever there is excess in capacity or whenever the constraint is almost-finite-type (such as the charge-constrained systems), the decoder can be made sliding-block, ensuring that decoder error propagation is limited in both number and time span.

THEOREM 3.15. *Let S be a constrained system. If $p/q \leq \mathsf{cap}_\alpha(S)$, then there exists a non-catastrophic rate $p : q$ finite-state (S, α)-encoder. Moreover, if, in addition, either $p/q < \mathsf{cap}_\alpha(S)$ or S is almost-finite-type, then the encoder can be chosen to be sliding-block decodable.*

So, for general constrained systems, the error propagation is guaranteed to be limited only in number. Indeed, in [**KarM88**] an example is given of a constrained system with rational capacity, for which there is <u>no</u> sliding-block decodable encoder with rate equaling capacity (of course, by Theorem 3.15, such a constrained system cannot be almost-finite-type). In the non-catastrophic encoders constructed in Theorem 3.15, the decoding errors generated by an isolated channel error are confined to two bounded bursts, although these bursts may appear arbitrarily far apart.

The notion of non-catastrophic is a standard concept in the theory of convolutional codes. In that setting, it coincides with sliding-block decodability [**LinCo83**, Ch. 10].

The proof of Theorem 3.15 is fairly complicated. Although it does not exactly provide a practical encoder synthesis algorithm, the proof makes use of some very powerful techniques that can be brought to bear in particular applications. Several of the ideas in the generalization to almost-finite-type systems have also played a role in the design of coded-modulation schemes based upon spectral-null constraints. See, for example, [**KS91a**].

The quest for a sliding-block decodable encoder with rate equaling capacity for a particular example provided the original motivation for Theorem 3.15. The example is as follows.

Let S be the $(1, 3; 3)$ combined charge-constrained run-length-limited system (see Section 1.3.3). The Shannon cover G of S has period 2, and an irreducible component G_0 of G^2 is shown in Figure 5. It can be readily checked that $\lambda(A_{G_0}) = 2$, with a respective positive eigenvector $\mathbf{x} = \begin{bmatrix} 1 & 2 & 3 & 3 & 3 & 4 & 2 \end{bmatrix}^\top$. Hence, we have $\mathsf{cap}(S) = 1/2$. For this constraint, Patel [**Patel75**] constructed a particular rate $1 : 2$ finite-state $(S, 2)$-encoder. So, the rate of this encoder is as high as possible.

Unfortunately, this encoder does not have finite anticipation. However, Patel was able to modify the encoder to have finite anticipation and even a sliding-block decoder with very small decoding window length, at the cost of only a small sacrifice in rate (although there is an additional cost in complexity). This modified encoder was used in an IBM tape drive [**Patel75**].

Recall that charge-constrained systems are almost-finite-type and that run-length-limited systems are finite-type and therefore almost-finite-type. It can be shown that the intersection of two almost-finite-type constrained systems is again almost-finite-type, and so the $(1, 3; 3)$-constrained system S is almost-finite-type. It then follows from Theorem 3.15 that there actually is a rate $1 : 2$ tagged finite-state $(S, 2)$-encoder which is sliding-block decodable. However, the encoding/decoding complexity of such a code appears to be enormous. On the other hand, there is a rate $4 : 8$ tagged finite-state $(S, 2)$-encoder which is sliding-block decodable, with only moderate encoding/decoding complexity (see [**KS91b**]).

Finally, we remark that Ashley [**Ash93**] has proven a far-reaching generalization of Theorem 3.15.

4. Code construction via state-splitting

In this section, we provide an introduction to the state-splitting algorithm, which implements the proof of Theorem 3.2, for constructing finite-state encoders. The steps in the algorithm are summarized in Section 4.4.

The approach we will follow uses graph construction techniques, based on state splitting and approximate eigenvectors, which have their roots in symbolic dynamics, where they were introduced by R.F. Williams [**Will73**] and Adler, Goodwyn, and Weiss [**AGW77**]. The first application of state-splitting ideas in constrained coding was Patel's construction of the Zero-Modulation (ZM) code [**Patel75**]. The state-splitting algorithm is also related to earlier ideas of Franaszek [**Fra82**], [**Fra89**].

For a given deterministic presentation G of a constrained system S and an achievable rate $p/q \leq \mathsf{cap}_\alpha(S)$, we will apply a state-splitting transformation iteratively beginning with the qth power graph G^q; the procedure culminates in a new presentation of S^q with minimum out-degree at least α^p; then, after deleting edges, we get an (S^q, α^p)-encoder, which, when tagged, gives our desired rate $p : q$ finite-state (S, α)-encoder.

Although the design procedure can be made completely systematic — in the sense of having the computer automatically generate an encoder and decoder for any valid code rate — the application of the method to just about any nontrivial code design problem will benefit from the interactive involvement of the code designers. There are some practical tools that can help the designer make "good" choices during the construction process. We will discuss some of these tools in Section 4.5.

It should be stressed that the general problem of designing codes that achieve, for example, the minimum number of encoder states, minimum sliding-block decoding window, or the less precise feature of minimum hardware complexity, is not solved. This remains an active research topic, as exemplified by recent papers where lower bounds on the number of encoder states [**MR91**] and the minimum sliding-block decoder window are studied [**Ash88**], [**Kam89**], [**Imm92**], [**Holl93b**]. See Sections 5.1 and 5.2 for more on this.

4.1. State splitting. In this section, we define state splitting of a labeled graph H and later apply it to $H = G^q$. We begin with a simplified special case.

Let $H = (V, E, L)$ be a labeled graph and denote by E_u the set of outgoing edges from state u in H. A *basic out-splitting* at state u is determined by a partition

$$E_u = E_u^{(1)} \cup E_u^{(2)}$$

of E_u into two disjoint sets. This partition is used to define a new labeled graph $H' = (V', E', L')$ that changes the local picture at state u. The set of states V' consists of all states $v \neq u$ in H, as well as two new states denoted $u^{(1)}$ and $u^{(2)}$:

$$V' = (V - \{u\}) \cup \{u^{(1)}, u^{(2)}\} \,.$$

The states $u^{(1)}$ and $u^{(2)}$ are called *descendant states* of state u, and state u is called the *parent state* of $u^{(1)}$ and $u^{(2)}$.

The edges in H' that do not involve states $u^{(1)}$ and $u^{(2)}$ are inherited from H. That is, if there is an edge e from state v to state v' in H, (with $v, v' \neq u$) there is a corresponding edge in H'. For edges involving state u, we consider three cases:

Case 1: Let edge e in H start at a state $v \neq u$ and terminate at state u. This edge is replicated in H' to produce two edges: an edge $e^{(1)}$ from v to $u^{(1)}$ and an edge $e^{(2)}$ from v to $u^{(2)}$.

Case 2: Let edge e in H start at state u and terminate at a state $v \neq u$, and suppose e belongs to the set $E_u^{(i)}$ in the partition of E_u. We draw in H' a corresponding edge from state $u^{(i)}$ to state v.

Case 3: Let edge e be a self-loop at state u in H, and suppose that e belongs to $E_u^{(i)}$. In H' there will be two edges from state $u^{(i)}$ corresponding to e: one edge to state $u^{(1)}$, the other to state $u^{(2)}$.

As with states, we refer to *descendant edges* in H' and *parent edges* in H. In all cases, the edge label of an edge in H' is the edge label of its parent edge in H.

In specifying the partitions in particular examples, we will refer to the edges by their edge labels in cases where this causes no ambiguity.

The change in the local picture at state u is shown in Figures 29 and 30. In the figures, we have partitioned the set of edges E_u into subsets, $E_u^{(1)} = \{a, b\}$ and $E_u^{(2)} = \{c\}$. The state u splits into two states, $u^{(1)}$ and $u^{(2)}$, according to the partition. It is evident that the anticipation at states v_1 and v_2 may increase by one symbol. So, H' need not be deterministic even if H is.

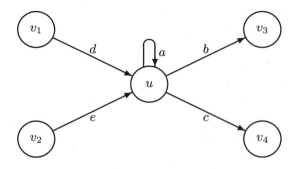

FIGURE 29. Local picture at state u before splitting.

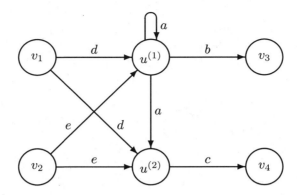

FIGURE 30. Basic out-splitting at state u for Figure 29.

In general, a state splitting may involve partitions into any number of subsets, and several states may be split simultaneously; so, we have the following more general notion of state splitting.

An *out-splitting* of a labeled graph H begins with a partition of the set, E_u, of outgoing edges for each state u in H into $N(u)$ disjoint subsets

$$E_u = E_u^{(1)} \cup E_u^{(2)} \cup \cdots \cup E_u^{(N(u))} .$$

From the partition, we derive a new labeled graph H'. The set of states $V_{H'}$ consists of the descendant states $u^{(1)}, u^{(2)}, \ldots, u^{(N(u))}$ for every $u \in V_H$. Outgoing edges from state u in H are partitioned among its descendant states and replicated in H' to each of the descendant terminal states as follows: for each edge e from u to v in H, determine the partition element $E_u^{(i)}$ to which e belongs, and endow H' with edges $e^{(r)}$ from $u^{(i)}$ to $v^{(r)}$ for $r = 1, 2, \ldots, N(v)$; the label of $e^{(r)}$ in H' is the same as the label of e in H.

Sometimes an out-splitting is called a *round* of out-splitting to indicate that several states may have been split simultaneously.

The labeled graph H' obtained from H by out-splitting is sometimes called an out-splitting of H. It has several important characteristics, relative to H, enumerated in the following proposition.

PROPOSITION 4.1. *Let H be a labeled graph and let H' be obtained from H by out-splitting. Then*

1. $S(H') = S(H)$.
2. *If H has anticipation $\mathcal{A}$, then H' has anticipation at most $\mathcal{A}+1$.*
3. *If H is (m, a)-definite, then H' is $(\mathsf{m}, \mathsf{a}+1)$-definite.*
4. *If H is irreducible, so is H'.*

The *complete out-splitting* of a labeled graph H is the out-splitting obtained from the partition in which each set in the partition consists of a single, distinct edge. The resulting graph is called the *edge graph of H*, since it contains one state for each edge in H. It is also referred to as the *higher 2-block graph of H*. Fig. 14 shows the edge graph for the RLL $(0,1)$ graph in Fig. 12.

We also have the notion of *in-splitting* obtained by reversing the roles of outgoing and incoming edges in the definition of out-splitting.

It is clear that, through state splitting, we can change the local picture, in particular the outdegree, of states in a labeled graph $H = G^q$ representing the constraint S^q. The remarkable fact is that, when $\mathsf{cap}(S) \geq p/q$, there is a sequence of state splittings that will generate a new labeled graph with outdegree at least 2^p. The tool that we will use to guide the evolution of this sequence of transformations is an approximate eigenvector inequality , as we now discuss.

4.2. x-consistent splitting. Let G be a labeled graph and let $\mathbf{x} = [x_v]_{v \in V_G}$ be an (A_G, n)-approximate eigenvector. A *basic* $\mathbf{x}$*-consistent partition* at state u is a partition of E_u into

$$E_u = E_u^{(1)} \cup E_u^{(2)} \, ,$$

with the property that

$$\sum_{e \in E_u^{(1)}} x_{\tau(e)} \geq n \, y^{(1)} \qquad \text{and} \qquad \sum_{e \in E_u^{(2)}} x_{\tau(e)} \geq n \, y^{(2)} \, ,$$

where $y^{(1)}$ and $y^{(2)}$ are positive integers and

$$y^{(1)} + y^{(2)} = x_u \, .$$

The out-splitting determined by this partition is called a *basic* $\mathbf{x}$*-consistent splitting* at state u, and we denote the resulting labeled graph by H'. It is straightforward to check that the induced vector $\mathbf{x}' = [x_v']_v$, indexed by the states of H', defined by

$$x_v' = \begin{cases} x_v & \text{if} \quad v \neq u \\ y^{(1)} & \text{if} \quad v = u^{(1)} \\ y^{(2)} & \text{if} \quad v = u^{(2)} \end{cases} \, ,$$

is an $(A_{H'}, n)$-approximate eigenvector.

The cube of the $(0, 1)$-RLL graph presentation is shown in Figure 31 (which is identical to Figure 19). Figure 32 shows the result of a basic $\mathbf{x}$-consistent splitting for Figure 31, with respect to the $(A_G^3, 2^2)$-approximate eigenvector $\mathbf{x} = [2 \ 1]^\mathsf{T}$. State 0 is split into two descendant states, $0^{(1)}$ and $0^{(2)}$, according to the partition $E_0^{(1)} = \{011, 110, 010\}$ and $E_0^{(2)} = \{101, 111\}$. The induced vector is $\mathbf{x}' = [1 \ 1 \ 1]^\mathsf{T}$, and the resulting labeled graph therefore has minimum out-degree at least $2^2 = 4$.

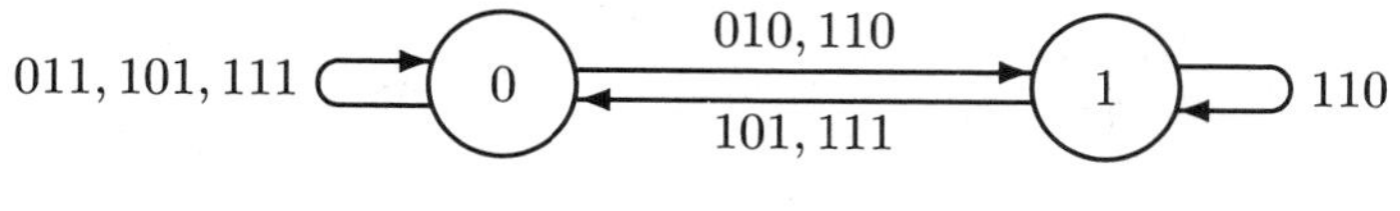

FIGURE 31. Cube of $(0, 1)$-RLL graph presentation.

The notion of $\mathbf{x}$-consistency can be extended to out-splittings in general as follows.

Given a labeled graph H, a positive integer n, and an (A_H, n)-approximate eigenvector $\mathbf{x} = [x_v]_{v \in V_H}$, an $\mathbf{x}$*-consistent partition* of H is defined by partitioning the set, E_u, of outgoing edges for each state u in H into $N(u)$ disjoint subsets

$$E_u = E_u^{(1)} \cup E_u^{(2)} \cup \cdots \cup E_u^{(N(u))} \, ,$$

such that

(3) $$\sum_{e \in E_u^{(r)}} x_{\tau(e)} \geq n x_u^{(r)} \qquad \text{for} \qquad r = 1, 2, \ldots, N(u) \, ,$$

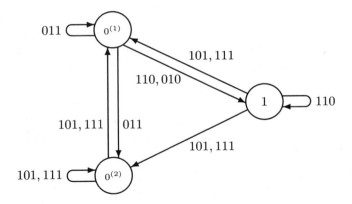

FIGURE 32. Basic **x**-consistent splitting for Figure 31.

where $x_u^{(r)}$ are nonnegative integers and

$$(4) \qquad \sum_{r=1}^{N(u)} x_u^{(r)} = x_u \quad \text{for every } u \in V_H.$$

The out-splitting based upon such a partition is called an **x**-*consistent splitting*. The vector **x**$'$ indexed by the states $u^{(r)}$ of the split graph H' and defined by $x'_{u^{(r)}} = x_u^{(r)}$ is called the *induced vector*.

An **x**-consistent partition or splitting is called *non-trivial* if $N(u) \geq 2$ for at least one state u. Observe that any basic **x**-consistent splitting is a non-trivial **x**-consistent splitting and that any non-trivial **x**-consistent splitting can be broken down into a sequence of basic **x**-consistent splittings.

Figures 33 and 34 give an example of an **x**-consistent splitting in which two states, 0 and 1, are split simultaneously. An $(A_G, 2)$-approximate eigenvector is $\mathbf{x} = [2\ 2\ 1]^\top$. An **x**-consistent splitting for states 0 and 1 can be carried out as follows. State 0 splits according to the partition $E_0^{(1)} = \{a\}$ and $E_0^{(2)} = \{b, c\}$. State 1 splits, simultaneously, according to the partition $E_1^{(1)} = \{d\}$ and $E_1^{(2)} = \{e, f\}$. Note that the subset $E_1^{(2)}$ has "excess weight." This yields a new labeled graph H' with induced vector $\mathbf{x}' = [1\ 1\ 1\ 1\ 1]^\top$, and the resulting labeled graph therefore has minimum out-degree at least 2.

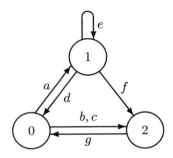

FIGURE 33. Labeled graph to be split.

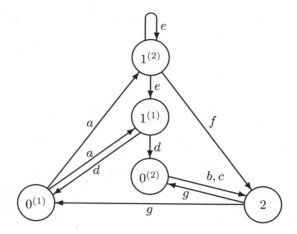

FIGURE 34. **x**-consistent splitting for Figure 33.

We summarize in Proposition 4.2 the important features of **x**-consistent out-splittings.

PROPOSITION 4.2. *Let H be a labeled graph and let* **x** *be an (A_H, n)-approximate eigenvector. Suppose that H' is obtained from H by an* **x**-*consistent splitting and* **x**$'$ *is the induced vector. Then*

1. **x**$'$ *is an $(A_{H'}, n)$-approximate eigenvector.*
2. $\sum_{u \in V_H} x_u = \sum_{v \in V_{H'}} x'_v$.

Proof. 1. The inequality (3) says precisely that $(A_{H'}\mathbf{x}')_{u^{(r)}} \geq n\, x'_{u^{(r)}}$ for each state $u^{(r)}$ of H'. So, **x**$'$ is an $(A_{H'}, n)$-approximate eigenvector.

2. This follows immediately from (4). □

4.3. Constructing the encoder. The key result needed for the construction of our encoders is as follows.

PROPOSITION 4.3. *Let H be an irreducible labeled graph and assume that the all-1's vector* **1** *is* <u>not</u> *an (A_H, n)-approximate eigenvector. Let* **x** *be a positive (A_H, n)-approximate eigenvector. Then, there is a basic* **x**-*consistent splitting of H.*

For the proof of this important result, we refer the reader to [**MSW92**]. We will now describe how we will make use of it in an iterative fashion to construct finite-state encoders with finite anticipation.

Let G be a deterministic labeled graph presenting S and let p and q be integers such that $p/q \leq \mathsf{cap}_\alpha(S)$. So, G^q is a deterministic labeled graph presenting S^q. Let **x** $= [x_v]_{v \in V_G}$ be an (A_G^q, α^p)-approximate eigenvector. If **x** is a 0–1 vector, then some subgraph of G^q has minimum out-degree at least α^p, and we are done. So, we may assume that there is no 0–1 (A_G^q, α^p)-approximate eigenvector. Let G' be the labeled subgraph of G^q induced by the states of G that correspond to the nonzero entries of **x**. The vector **x**$'$ obtained by restricting **x** to the states in G' is a positive $(A_{G'}, \alpha^p)$-approximate eigenvector.

If G' is irreducible, then we will be in a position to apply Proposition 4.3 for $H = G'$ and $n = \alpha^p$. Otherwise, we can restrict to a sink G_0 of G'; recall that a sink is an irreducible component all of whose outgoing edges terminate in the component, and recall that every graph has a sink. Since G_0 is an irreducible component of G', and, by assumption, there is no 0–1 (A_G^q, α^p)-approximate eigenvector, it follows that $\mathbf{1}$ is not an (A_{G_0}, α^p)-approximate eigenvector. Moreover, since G_0 is a sink, it follows that the restriction, $\mathbf{x}_0$, of $\mathbf{x}'$ to G_0 is a positive (A_{G_0}, α^p)-approximate eigenvector. Proposition 4.3 can now be applied to carry out a basic $\mathbf{x}_0$-consistent splitting of G_0, producing an irreducible labeled graph G_1.

By Proposition 4.2, an $\mathbf{x}_0$-consistent splitting decomposes entries of $\mathbf{x}_0$ into strictly smaller positive integers. So, iteration of this state-splitting procedure will produce a sequence of labeled graphs $G_1, G_2, \ldots, G_t$, where the graph G_t has an adjacency matrix A_{G_t} with an all-1's (A_{G_t}, n)-approximate eigenvector. Therefore, as described in Section 2.6.3, the graph G_t has minimum out-degree at least $n = \alpha^p$. Since, by Proposition 4.1, out-splitting preserves finite anticipation, the graph G_t has finite anticipation. Deleting excess edges, we pass to a subgraph of G'_t which is an (S^q, α^p)-encoder. Now, tag this encoder with input labels, and we have our rate $p:q$ finite-state (S, α)-encoder with finite anticipation.

Having now completely described the construction of the encoder, we have completed the proof of Theorem 3.2 modulo the proof of Proposition 4.3.

Note that the number of iterations required to arrive at the encoder graph is no more than $\sum_{v \in V_G}(x_v - 1)$, since a state v with entry x_v will be split into at most x_v descendant states throughout the whole iteration process. So, by Proposition 4.1, the anticipation of G_t is at most $\sum_{v \in V_G}(x_v - 1)$. For the same reason, the number of states in the encoder graph is at most $\sum_{v \in V_G} x_v$.

If we delete an edge $1 \xrightarrow{101} 0^{(1)}$ and assign input tags to the labeled graph in Figure 32, we obtain the rate 2:3 finite-state $(0,1)$-RLL encoder shown in Figure 35. We indicate, for this example, how the encoding and decoding is implemented.

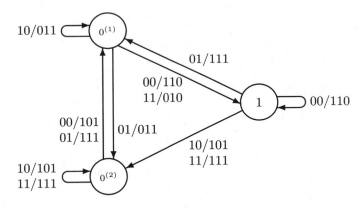

FIGURE 35. Tagged $(0,1)$-RLL encoder.

If we initialize to state $0^{(1)}$, the data string 10 00 10 11 encodes to the $(0,1)$-RLL string

$$011 \ 110 \ 101 \ 111 \ .$$

We decode the $(0,1)$-RLL code string just generated. Starting at state $0^{(1)}$, the edge determined by the codeword 011, with upcoming codeword 110, is the self-loop $0^{(1)} \xrightarrow{10/011} 0^{(1)}$, so the decoder will generate the input tag 10. Proceeding, the codeword 110, with upcoming word 101, determines the edge $0^{(1)} \xrightarrow{00/110} 1$. The reader can decode the next codeword 101 in a similar matter, and that is as far as we can go without knowing more upcoming codewords.

As we will see later on, the encoder of Figure 35 is not the smallest rate $2 : 3$ finite-state $(0, 1)$-RLL encoder in terms of number of states.

4.4. State-splitting algorithm. We summarize the steps in the encoder construction procedure.

1. Select a labeled graph G and integers p and q as follows:
   (a) Find a deterministic labeled graph G (or more generally a labeled graph with finite anticipation) which presents the given constrained system S (most constrained systems have a natural deterministic representation that is used to describe them in the first place).
   (b) Find the adjacency matrix A_G of G.
   (c) Compute the capacity $\mathsf{cap}_\alpha(S) = \log_\alpha \lambda(A_G)$.
   (d) Select a desired code rate $p : q$ satisfying

$$\mathsf{cap}_\alpha(S) \geq \frac{p}{q}$$

   (one usually wants to keep p and q relatively small for complexity reasons).
2. Construct G^q.
3. Using the algorithm of Section 2.6.4, find an (A_G^q, α^p)-approximate eigenvector $\mathbf{x}$.
4. Eliminate all states u with $x_u = 0$ from G^q, and restrict to an irreducible sink H of the resulting graph. Restrict $\mathbf{x}$ to be indexed by the states of H.
5. Iterate steps 5a–5c below until the labeled graph H has minimum out-degree at least α^p:
   (a) Find a non-trivial $\mathbf{x}$-consistent partition of the edges in H (the proof of Proposition 4.3, not included in these notes, shows how to find such a partition in at least one state).
   (b) Find the $\mathbf{x}$-consistent splitting corresponding to this partition, creating a labeled graph H' and an approximate eigenvector $\mathbf{x}'$.
   (c) Let $H \leftarrow H'$ and $\mathbf{x} \leftarrow \mathbf{x}'$.
6. At each state of H, delete all but α^p outgoing edges and tag the remaining edges with α-ary p-blocks, one for each outgoing edge. This gives a rate $p : q$ finite-state (S, α)-encoder.

We conclude this section by proving Theorem 3.11, thereby showing how to achieve sliding-block decodability for finite-type constraints.

The proof is obtained by applying the state-splitting algorithm to any presentation of S with finite memory. Recall from Propositions 2.2 and 4.1 that higher powers and out-splitting preserve definiteness (although the anticipation may increase under out-splitting). Thus, the (S^q, α^p)-encoder constructed in Section 4.3 is (m, a)-definite for some m and a and so is sliding-block decodable. This completes the proof of Theorem 3.11.

Note that we can decode a q-block $\mathbf{w}$ as follows: observe the m previous q-blocks and the a upcoming q-blocks to determine the unique edge that produced $\mathbf{w}$; then read off the input tag on this edge. This defines an (m, a)-sliding-block decoder.

As an example, by examining Figure 35, one can see that the $(0, 1)$-RLL encoder has a sliding-block decoder with window length 2, as shown in Figure 36. (For example, according to the table in Figure 36, the codeword 010 decodes to 11; the codeword 011 decodes to 01 if it is followed by 101 or 111, and it decodes to 10 if it is followed by 010, 011 or 110.)

Current Codeword	Next Codeword	Decoded Data
010	—	11
011	{101, 111}	01
011	{010, 011, 110}	10
101	{101, 111}	10
101	{010, 011, 110}	00
110	—	00
111	{101, 111}	11
111	{010, 011, 110}	01

FIGURE 36. Sliding-block decoding table for encoder in Figure 35.

4.5. Simplifications.

4.5.1. *State merging.* In practice, it is desirable to design fixed-rate encoders with a small number of states. For a given labeled graph $G = (V, E, L)$, with an (A_G, n)-approximate eigenvector $\mathbf{x} = [x_v]_{v \in V}$, we have shown that the state-splitting algorithm can produce an encoder $\mathcal{E}$ with $|V_\mathcal{E}|$ states where

$$|V_\mathcal{E}| \leq \sum_{v \in V} x_v .$$

This gives an upper bound on the number of states in the smallest (S, n)-encoder. Often, however, one can reduce this number substantially by means of state merging.

One situation where we can merge states in a labeled graph H is the following. Let u and u' be two states in H and suppose that there is a 1–1 correspondence $e_i \mapsto e_i'$ between the sets of outgoing edges $E_u = \{e_1, e_2, \ldots, e_t\}$ and $E_{u'} = \{e_1', e_2', \ldots, e_t'\}$ such that for $i = 1, 2, \ldots, t$ we have $\tau(e_i) = \tau(e_i')$ and $L(e_i) = L(e_i')$. Then, we can eliminate one of the states, say u', and all of its outgoing edges, and redirect into u all incoming edges to u'. Clearly, the new labeled graph presents the same constraint, but with one fewer state. Note that this procedure is precisely the inverse of an in-splitting.

As an example, we again consider the $(0, 1)$-RLL constrained system S. If we delete the self loop $1 \xrightarrow{110} 1$ from Figure 32, we can see that states $0^{(2)}$ and 1 can be merged, according to the merging criterion just discussed. The resulting two-state labeled graph is the one shown in Figure 37 (which is the same encoder shown in Figure 27). Tagging the latter, we obtain a tagged $(S^3, 2^2)$-encoder as shown in Figure 38 [**Sie85a**]. The respective decoding table is shown in Figure 39. Note that the encoder of Figure 38 has less states than the encoder previously shown in Figure 35. Although there is not yet a definitive solution to the problem of minimizing the number of encoder states, there are techniques and heuristics that have proven to be very effective in the construction of encoders.

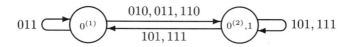

FIGURE 37. Deleting edges and merging states in Figure 32.

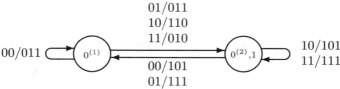

FIGURE 38. Rate 2 : 3 tagged two-state encoder for $(0,1)$-RLL constrained system.

Current Codeword	Next Codeword	Decoded Data
010	—	11
011	{101, 111}	01
011	{010, 011, 110}	00
101	{101, 111}	10
101	{010, 011, 110}	00
110	—	10
111	{101, 111}	11
111	{010, 011, 110}	01

FIGURE 39. Sliding-block decoder for encoder in Figure 38.

For further discussion of techniques for encoder simplification, the reader is referred to [**MSW92**] and [**MRS95**].

4.5.2. *Sliding-block decoder window.* When a finite-state encoder with sliding block decoder is used in conjunction with a noisy channel, the extent of error propagation is controlled by the size of the decoder window. How large is this window? Well, suppose that we start the state-splitting algorithm with some labeled graph G presenting a constrained system of finite-type and G^q has finite memory $\mathcal{M} = \mathcal{M}(G^q)$ (measured in q-blocks). If t is the number of (rounds of) out-splittings used to construct the encoder, then the encoder graph $\mathcal{E}$ is $(\mathcal{M}, t)$-definite (measured in q-blocks). It follows that we can design a sliding-block decoder with decoding window length W satisfying the bound

$$\mathsf{W} \leq \mathcal{M} + t + 1$$

(again, measured in q-blocks). Recall from Section 4.3 that an upper bound on the number of (rounds of) out-splittings required is

$$t \leq \sum_{v \in V_G} (x_v - 1),$$

so,

(5) $$\mathsf{W} \leq \mathcal{M} + \sum_{v \in V_G} (x_v - 1) + 1.$$

The guarantee of a sliding-block decoder when S is finite-type and the explicit bound on the decoder window length represent key strengths of the state-splitting algorithm. In practice, however, the upper bound (5) on the window length often is larger — sometimes much larger — than the shortest possible.

For the $(0, 1)$-RLL encoder in Figure 35, where (referring to Figure 31) $\mathcal{M} = 1$, $x_0 = 2$, and $x_2 = 1$, this expression gives an upper bound of 3 (codewords) on the window length. However, we saw, in Table 36, a decoder with window length of $W = 2$. For a rate $2 : 3$ $(1, 7)$-RLL encoder discussed in [**MSW92**], the labeled graph G^3 has memory $\mathcal{M} = 3$, and the approximate eigenvector is

$$\mathbf{x} = [2\,3\,3\,3\,2\,2\,2\,1]^\top .$$

The number of rounds of splitting turns out to be only 2, implying

$$W \leq \mathcal{M} + 3 = 6 ,$$

far less than the upper bound (5) gives. In fact, a window length of $W = 3$ was actually achieved [**AHM82**], [**WW91**]. For the rate $8 : 9$ PRML $(0, 3/3)$ encoder discussed in [**MSW92**], the bound (5) was 11, but a window length of $W = 2$ was achieved [**MSW92**].

These reduced window lengths were achieved by trying several possibilities for the choices of presentation, approximate eigenvector, out-splittings, elimination of excess edges and input tagging assignment (see, for instance [**MSW92**], [**WW91**]). In [**KarM88**] and [**AM93**], in-splitting was another tool used in reducing the window length — although for those codes, the ordinary state-splitting algorithm applied to a 'very large' approximate eigenvector will yield codes with the same sliding-block decoding window. Recently, Hollmann [**Holl93b**] has found an approach that combines aspects of the state-splitting algorithm with other approaches and has been demonstrated to be of use in further reducing the window length.

5. Advanced Topics and Research Areas

In this section, we offer some pointers for the interested reader toward several active areas of research pertaining to constrained coding and its applications.

5.1. General code construction methods. In Section 4, we focused on the state-splitting algorithm which gives a rigorous proof of the general existence theorems (Theorems 3.2 and 3.11) for constrained code constructions. The algorithm has other virtues: it is fairly easy to use, it has yielded many codes of practical interest, and, as shown in [**AM93**], it is in a certain sense a universal method of constructing every sliding-block decoder. (In this context, we take the state-splitting algorithm to mean a selection of deterministic presentation G of a constrained system S, an (A_G, n)-approximate eigenvector $\mathbf{x}$, a sequence of $\mathbf{x}$-consistent out-splittings, followed by deletion of excess edges, and finally an input tagging assignment, resulting in a tagged (S, n)-encoder.) However, as pointed out in Section 4.5, there are lots of choices in the algorithm: the presentation, the approximate eigenvector, the sequence of out-splittings, the deletion of excess edges, and the input-tagging assignment. It is not known how to make these choices to yield optimal encoders/decoders.

There have been many other important and interesting approaches to constrained code construction — far too many to mention here. We instead refer the reader to [**MRS95**] for a review, without proof, of some alternative methods for constructing constrained codes.

5.2. Complexity of encoders. There are various criteria, some already mentioned, that are used to measure the performance and complexity of encoders and their respective decoders. One very active area of research is the search for bounds on these parameters. A thorough discussion of this topic is beyond the scope of this lecture. Instead, we will simply list several of the key complexity criteria that are of mathematical and practical interest, and refer the reader to [**MRS95**] for an up-to-date survey of results and remaining problems in this area.

We list here the predominant factors that are usually taken into account while designing rate $p : q$ finite-state (S, α)-encoders.

The values of p and q: Typically, the rate p/q is chosen to be as close to $\mathsf{cap}_\alpha(S)$ as possible, subject to having p and q small enough: The reason for the latter requirement is minimizing the number of outgoing edges, α^p, from each state in the encoder and keeping to a minimum the number of input–output connections of the encoder.

Number of states in an encoder: In both hardware and software implementation of encoders $\mathcal{E}$, we will need $\lceil \log_2 |V_{\mathcal{E}}| \rceil$ bits in order to represent the current state of $\mathcal{E}$. This motivates an encoder design with a relatively small number of states [**Koh78**, Ch. 9].

Gate complexity: In addition to representing the state of a finite-state encoder, we need, in hardware implementation, to realize the next-state function and the output function as a gate circuit. Hardware complexity is usually measured in terms of the number of required gates (e.g., NAND gates), and this number also includes the implementation of the memory bit cells that represent the encoder state (each memory bit cell can be realized by a fixed number of gates).

The number of states in hardware implementation becomes more significant in applications where we run several encoders *in parallel* with a common circuit for the next-state and output functions, but with duplicated hardware for representing the state of each encoder.

Time and space complexity of a RAM program: When the finite-state encoder is to be implemented as a computer program on a random-access machine (RAM) [**AHU74**, Ch. 1], the complexity is usually measured by the space requirements and the running time of the program.

Encoder anticipation: One way to implement a decoder for an encoder $\mathcal{E}$ with finite anticipation $\mathcal{A}(\mathcal{E})$ is by accumulating the past $\mathcal{A}(\mathcal{E})$ symbols (in $\Sigma(S^q)$) that were generated by $\mathcal{E}$; these symbols, with the current symbol, allow the decoder to simulate the state transitions of $\mathcal{E}$ and, hence, to reconstruct the sequence of input tags (see Section 3.1). The size of the required buffer thus depends on $\mathcal{A}(\mathcal{E})$.

Window length of sliding-block decodable encoders: A typical decoder of an (m, a)-sliding-block decodable encoder consists of a buffer that accumulates the past m+a symbols (in $(\Sigma(S^q))$ that were generated by the encoder. A decoding function $\mathcal{D} : (\Sigma(S^q))^{(m+a+1)} \rightarrow \{0, 1, \ldots, \alpha^p - 1\}$ is then applied to the current symbol and to the contents of the buffer to reconstruct an input tag in $\{0, 1, \dots, \alpha-1\}^p$ (see Section 3.4.1). From a complexity point-of-view, the window length, m+a+1, determines the size of the required buffer.

5.3. Combined Error-Correction and Modulation Coding. The preceding sections of these notes have addressed the properties of constrained systems and the construction of codes into these constraints. In practice, these constrained codes, as applied in (binary) data recording systems, may be viewed as part of the modulation/demodulation process of input/output signals of the system. Most systems require the use of some form of error-correction coding in addition to any modulation coding of the input signal or symbol sequence. It is natural to investigate the interplay between these two forms of coding and the possibilities for efficiently combining their functions into a single coding operation, in analogy to the coded-modulation techniques now in wide use in data transmission. In this section we will simply discuss the predominant error mechanisms in recording systems and mention the associated metrics imposed upon constrained systems in connection with these.

Magnetic recording systems using peak detection, as described in Section 1.5.1, are subject to three predominant types of errors at the peak detector output. The most frequently observed error is referred to as a *bitshift error*, where a pair of recorded symbols 01 is detected as 10 (a *left bitshift*), or the pair 10 is detected as 01 (a *right bitshift*). Another commonly occurring error type is called a *drop-out error* or, sometimes, a *missing-bit error*, where a recorded symbol 1 is detected as a 0. Less frequently, a *drop-in error* or *extra-bit error* results in the detection of a recorded 0 as a 1. It is convenient to refer to the drop-in and drop-out errors as *substitution errors*.

Hamming-metric constrained codes are most pertinent in recording channels that behave like a binary symmetric channel, in which drop-in and drop-out errors occur with equal probability. However, there are alternative models of interest that suggest the use of codes designed with other criteria in mind beyond optimization of minimum Hamming distance. Among these models, the two that have received the most attention are: the asymmetric channel — where only drop-in errors or drop-out errors, but not both, are encountered; and, the bitshift channel — where a symbol 1 is allowed to shift position by up to a prespecified number of positions.

Another error type is a *synchronization error*, resulting in an insertion or deletion of a symbol 0 in the detected symbol sequence. In practical digital recording systems on disks and tape, this type of error can have catastrophic consequences with regard to recovery of information that follows the synchronization loss. As a result, recording devices use synchronization and clock generation techniques in conjunction with code constraints, such as the k constraint in RLL codes for peak detection and the **G** constraint in PRML $(0, \mathbf{G}/\mathbf{I})$ codes, to effectively preclude such errors. Nevertheless, RLL-constrained synchronization-error-correcting codes have some intrinsic coding-theoretic interest, and have received considerable attention. Codes capable of correcting more than one insertion and deletion error may also be used to protect against bitshift errors, which result from the insertion and deletion of 0's on either side of a 1. The Edit distance, or Levenshtein metric, and the Lee metric arise naturally in the context of synchronization errors.

In recording systems using partial-response with some form of sequence detection, exemplified by the PRML system described in Section 1.5.2, the maximum-likelihood detector tends to generate burst-errors whose specific characteristics can be determined from the error-events associated with the underlying trellis structure. Several authors have proposed trellis-coded modulation approaches for PRML that yield codes which combine $(0, \mathbf{G}/\mathbf{I})$ constraints with enhanced minimum Euclidean distance.

Upper and lower bounds on the size of codes which satisfy runlength or spectral-null constraints have been investigated by several researchers. There have also been numerous methods proposed for constructing such codes for possible application in storage systems.

A partial survey of results on the theory and construction of combined modulation and error-correction codes may be found in [**MRS95**].

6. Summary

The problem of constrained coding has its roots in the seminal 1948 paper of Claude Shannon from which information and coding theory originated. Its relevance to data transmission and storage has been a driving force behind major advances in the mathematical theory of constrained systems and the development of practical code construction methods. There has evolved a synergistic interplay between the research on constrained coding and such mathematical disciplines as symbolic dynamics, automata theory, algebra, and systems theory.

These notes provide an introduction to the theory and practice of constrained codes and their particular application to modulation coding for digital data storage.

References

[AW91]   K.A.S. ABDEL-GHAFFER, J.H. WEBER, *Bounds and constructions for run-length limited error-control block codes*, IEEE Trans. Inform. Theory, 37 (1991), 789–800.

[Ad87]   R.L. ADLER, *The torus and the disk*, IBM J. Res. Develop., 31 (1987), 224–234.

[ACH83] R.L. ADLER, D. COPPERSMITH, M. HASSNER, *Algorithms for sliding block codes — an application of symbolic dynamics to information theory*, IEEE Trans. Inform. Theory, 29 (1983), 5–22.

[AFKM86] R.L. ADLER, J. FRIEDMAN, B. KITCHENS, B.H. MARCUS, *State splitting for variable-length graphs*, IEEE Trans. Inform. Theory, 32 (1986), 108–113.

[AGW77] R.L. ADLER, L.W. GOODWYN, B. WEISS, *Equivalence of topological Markov shifts*, Israel J. Math., 27 (1977), 49–63.

[AHM82] R.L. ADLER, M. HASSNER, J. MOUSSOURIS, *Method and apparatus for generating a noiseless sliding block code for a $(1, 7)$ channel with rate 2/3*, U.S. Patent 4,413,251 (1982).

[AHU74] A.V. AHO, J.E. HOPCROFT, J.D. ULLMAN, *The Design and Analysis of Computer Algorithms*, Addison-Wesley, Reading, Massachusetts, 1974.

[Ash87a] J.J. ASHLEY, *On the Perron-Frobenius eigenvector for non-negative integral matrices whose largest eigenvalue is integral*, Linear Algebra Appl., 94 (1987), 103–108.

[Ash87b] J.J. ASHLEY, *Performance Bounds in Constrained Sequence Coding*, Ph.D. Thesis, University of California, Santa Cruz, 1987.

[Ash88] J.J. ASHLEY, *A linear bound for sliding block decoder window size*, IEEE Trans. Inform. Theory, 34 (1988), 389–399.

[Ash92] J.J. ASHLEY, *LR conjugacies of shifts of finite type are uniquely so*, Contemp. Math., 135 (1992), 57–84.

[Ash93] J.J. ASHLEY, *An extension theorem for closing maps of shifts of finite type*, Trans. AMS, 336 (1993), 389–420.

[AB94]   J.J. ASHLEY, M.-P. BÉAL, *A note on the method of poles for code construction*, IEEE Trans. Inform. Theory, 40 (1994), 512–517.

[AM93]   J.J. ASHLEY, B.H. MARCUS, *Canonical encoders for sliding block decoders, SIAM J. Discr. Math.* (1995), to appear.

[AMR93a]   J.J. ASHLEY, B.H. MARCUS, R.M. ROTH, *Construction of encoders with small decoding look-ahead for input-constrained channels, IEEE Trans. Inform. Theory,* 41 (1995), 55–76.

[AMR93b]   J.J. ASHLEY, B.H. MARCUS, R.M. ROTH, *On the decoding delay of encoders for input-constrained channels,* in preparation.

[BL91]   A.M. BARG, S.N. LITSYN, *DC-constrained codes from Hadamard matrices, IEEE Trans. Inform. Theory,* 37 (1991), 801–807.

[Béal90a]   M.-P. BÉAL, *The method of poles: a coding method for constrained channels, IEEE Trans. Inform. Theory,* IT-36 (1990), 763–772.

[Béal90b]   M.-P. BÉAL, *La méthode des pôles dans le cas des systèmes sofiques,* preprint, LITP Report, 29 (1990).

[Béal93a]   M.-P. BÉAL, *Codage Symbolique,* Masson, Paris, 1993.

[Béal93b]   M.-P. BÉAL, *A new optimization condition in the method of poles for code construction,* preprint, 1993.

[BI83]   G.F.M. BEENKER, K.A.S. IMMINK, *A generalized method for encoding and decoding run-length-limited binary sequences, IEEE Trans. Inform. Theory,* 29 (1983), 751–754.

[Be84]   E.R. BERLEKAMP, *Algebraic Coding Theory,* Revised Edition, Aegean Park Press, Laguna Hills, California, 1984.

[Blah90]   R.E. BLAHUT, *Digital Transmission of Information,* Addison-Wesley, Reading, Massachusetts, 1990.

[Blaum91]   M. BLAUM, *Combining ECC with modulation: performance comparisons, IEEE Trans. Inform. Theory,* 37 (1991), 945–949.

[BLBT93]   M. BLAUM, S. LITSYN, V. BUSKENS, H.C.A. VAN TILBORG, *Error-correcting codes with bounded running digital sum, IEEE Trans. Inform. Theory,* 39 (1993), 216–227.

[BvT89]   M. BLAUM, H.C.A. VAN TILBORG, *On error-correcting balanced codes, IEEE Trans. Inform. Theory,* 35 (1989), 1091–1093.

[Bours94]   P.A.H. BOURS, *Codes for correcting insertion and deletion errors,* Ph.D. dissertation, Dept. of Mathematics and Computing Science, Eindhoven University of Technology, Eindhoven, The Netherlands, June 1994.

[Bouw85]   G. BOUWHUIS, J. BRAAT, A. HUIJSER, J. PASMAN, G. VAN ROSMALEN, K.A.S. IMMINK, *Principles of Optical Disc Systems,* Adam Hilger, Bristol and Boston, 1985.

[BKM85]   M. BOYLE, B. KITCHENS, B.H. MARCUS, *A note on minimal covers for sofic systems, Proc. AMS,* 95 (1985), 403–411.

[BMT87]   M. BOYLE, B.H. MARCUS, P. TROW, *Resolving maps and the dimension group for shifts of finite type, Memoirs AMS,* 377 (1987).

[CHL86]   A.R. CALDERBANK, C. HEEGARD, T.-A. LEE, *Binary convolutional codes with application to magnetic recording, IEEE Trans. Inform. Theory,* 32 (1986), 797–815.

[CHT89]   A.R. CALDERBANK, M.A. HERRO, V. TELANG, *A multilevel approach to the design of dc-free codes, IEEE Trans. Inform. Theory,* 35 (1989), 579–583.

[CW71]   J.C.-Y. CHIANG, J.K. WOLF, *On channels and codes for the Lee metric, Inform. Control,* 19 (1971), 159–173.

[C70]   T.M. CHIEN, *Upper bound on the efficiency of DC-constrained codes, Bell Syst. Tech. J.,* (1970), 2267–2287.

[Cid92]   R. CIDECIYAN, F. DOLIVO, R. HERMANN, W. HIRT, W. SCHOTT, *A PRML system for digital magnetic recording, IEEE J. Sel. Areas Commun.,* 10 (1992), 38–56.

[CL91]   G.D. COHEN, S.N. LITSYN, *DC-constrained error-correcting codes with small running digital sum, IEEE Trans. Inform. Theory,* 37 (1991), 801–807.

[Dol89]   F. DOLIVO, *Signal processing for high density digital magnetic recoding,* in *Proc. COMPEURO'89,* Hamburg, Germany, 1989.

[DMU79]   F. DOLIVO, D. MAIWALD, G. UNGERBOECK, *Partial-response class-IV signaling with Viterbi decoding versus conventional modified frequency modulation in magnetic recording,* IBM Res. Zurich Lab., IBM Res. Rep. RZ 973–33865 (1979).

[EH78]   J. EGGENBERGER, P. HODGES, *Sequential encoding and decoding of variable length, fixed rate data codes,* U.S. Patent 4,115,768 (1978).

[EC91]   E. ELEFTHERIOU, R. CIDECIYAN, *On codes satisfying Mth order running digital sum constraints, IEEE Trans. Inform. Theory,* 37 (1991), 1294–1313.

[Even65] S. EVEN, *On information lossless automata of finite order, IEEE Trans. Elect. Comput.,* 14 (1965), 561–569.

[Even79] S. EVEN, *Graph Algorithms,* Computer Science Press, Potomac, Maryland, 1979.

[Ferg72] M.J. FERGUSON, *Optimal reception for binary partial response channels, Bell Sys. Tech. J.,* 51 (1972), 493–505.

[Fe84]   H.C. FERREIRA, *Lower bounds on the minimum-Hamming distance achievable with runlength constrained or DC-free block codes and the synthesis of a $(16,8)$ $d_{min} = 4$ DC-free block code, IEEE Trans. Magn.,* 20 (1984), 881–883.

[FL91]   H.C. FERREIRA, S. LIN, *Error and erasure control (d,k) block codes, IEEE Trans. Inform. Theory,* 37 (1991), 1399–1408.

[Fi75a]   R. FISCHER, *Sofic systems and graphs, Monats. fur Math.* 80 (1975), 179–186.

[Fi75b]   R. FISCHER, *Graphs and symbolic dynamics, Colloq. Math. Soc. János Bólyai, Topics in Information Theory,* 16 (1975), 229–243

[For72]   G.D. FORNEY, JR., *Maximum likelihood sequence detection in the presence of intersymbol interference, IEEE Trans. Inform. Theory,* 18 (1972), 363–378.

[FC89]   G.D. FORNEY, JR., A.R. CALDERBANK, *Coset codes for partial response channels; or, cosets codes with spectral nulls, IEEE Trans. Inform. Theory,* 35 (1989), 925–943.

[Fra67]   P.A. FRANASZEK, *Sequence-state coding for digital transmission, Bell Sys. Tech. J.,* 47 (1967), 143–155.

[Fra69]   P.A. FRANASZEK, *On synchronous variable length coding for discrete noiseless channels, Inform. Control,* 15 (1969), 155–164.

[Fra70]   P.A. FRANASZEK, *Sequence-state methods for run-length-limited coding, IBM J. Res. Develop.,* 14 (1970), 376–383.

[Fra72]   P.A. FRANASZEK, *Run-length-limited variable length coding with error propagation limitation,* U.S. Patent 3,689,899 (1972).

[Fra79]   P.A. FRANASZEK, *On future-dependent block coding for input-restricted channels, IBM J. Res. Develop.,* 23 (1979), 75–81.

[Fra80a] P.A. FRANASZEK, *Synchronous bounded delay coding for input restricted channels, IBM J. Res. Develop.,* 24 (1980), 43–48.

[Fra80b] P.A. FRANASZEK, *A general method for channel coding, IBM J. Res. Develop.,* 24 (1980), 638–641.

[Fra82]   P.A. FRANASZEK, *Construction of bounded delay codes for discrete noiseless channels, IBM J. Res. Develop.,* 26 (1982), 506–514.

[Fra89]   P.A. FRANASZEK, *Coding for constrained channels: a comparison of two approaches, IBM J. Res. Develop.,* 33 (1989), 602–607.

[FT93]   P.A. FRANASZEK, J.A. THOMAS, *On the optimization of constrained channel codes,* preprint, 1993.

[Fred89] L.J. FREDRICKSON, J.K. WOLF, *Error-detecting multiple block (d,k) codes, IEEE Trans. Magn.,* 25 (1989), 4096–4098.

[Fred94] L.J. FREDRICKSON, R. KARABED, P. SIEGEL, H. THAPAR, AND R. WOOD, *Improved trellis coding for partial-response channels, Proc. IEEE Magn. Rec. Conf.,* San Diego, California (1994), *IEEE Trans. Magn.,* 31 (1995), 1141–1148.

[FW64]   C. FREIMAN, A. WYNER, *Optimum block codes for noiseless input restricted channels, Inform. Control,* 7 (1964), 398–415.

[Fri84]   J. FRIEDMAN, *A note on state splitting, Proc. AMS,* 92 (1984), 206–208.

[Funk82] P. FUNK, *Run-length-limited codes with multiple spacing, IEEE Trans. Magn.,* 18 (1982), 772–775.

[Gall68] R.G. GALLAGER, *Information Theory and Reliable Communication,* John Wiley, New York, 1968.

[Gant60] F.R. GANTMACHER, *Matrix Theory, Volume II,* Chelsea Publishing Company, New York, 1960.

[GoW68]   S.W. GOLOMB, L.R. WELCH, *Algebraic coding and the Lee metric,* in: *Error Correcting Codes* (H.B. Mann, Editor), John Wiley, 1968, pp. 175–194.

[GoW70]   S.W. GOLOMB, L.R. WELCH, *Perfect codes in the Lee metric and the packing of polyominoes, SIAM J. Appl. Math.,* 18 (1970), 302–317.

[GuF93]   J. Gu, T. Fuja, *A generalized Gilbert-Varshamov bound derived via analysis of a code-search algorithm*, IEEE Trans. Inform. Theory, 39 (1993), 1089–1093.

[GuF94]   J. Gu, T. Fuja, *A new approach to constructing optimal block codes for runlength-limited channels*, IEEE Trans. Inform. Theory, 40 (1994), 774–785.

[Heeg91] C.D. Heegard, B.H. Marcus, P.H. Siegel, *Variable-length state splitting with applications to average runlength-constrained (ARC) codes*, IEEE Trans. Inform. Theory, 37 (1991), 759–777.

[Heem82] J.P.J. Heemskerk, K.A.S. Immink, *Compact disc: system aspects and modulation*, Philips Techn. Review, 40 (1982), 157–164.

[Hild91] H.M. Hilden, D.G. Howe, E.J. Weldon, Jr., *Shift error correcting modulation codes*, IEEE Trans. Magn., 27 (1991), 4600–4605.

[Hole91] K.J. Hole, *Punctured convolutional codes for the $1 - D$ partial-response channel*, IEEE Trans. Inform. Theory, 37 (1991), 808–817.

[Hole94] K.J. Hole, O. Ytrehus, *Improved coding techniques for partial-response channels*, IEEE Trans. Inform. Theory, 40 (1994), 482–493.

[Holl93a] H.D.L. Hollmann, *A block-decodable $(d,k) = (1,8)$ runlength-limited rate 8/12 code*, IEEE Trans. Inform. Theory, 40 (1994), 1292–1296.

[Holl93b] H.D.L. Hollmann, *On the construction of bounded-delay encodable codes for constrained systems*, IEEE Trans. Inform. Theory, to appear.

[Hopc79] J.E. Hopcroft, J.D. Ullman, *Introduction to Automata Theory, Languages, and Computation*, Addison-Wesley, Reading, Massachusetts, 1979.

[How84]   T.D. Howell, *Analysis of correctable errors in the IBM 3380 disk file*, IBM J. Res. Develop., 28 (1984), 206–211.

[How89]   T.D. Howell, *Statistical properties of selected recording codes*, IBM J. Res. Develop., 32 (1989), 60–73.

[Huff54] D.A. Huffman, *The synthesis of sequential switching circuits*, J. Franklin Inst., 257 (1954), 161–190 and 275–303.

[Huff59] D.A. Huffman, *Canonical forms for information lossless finite-state machine*, IRE Trans. Circuit Theory, 6, (1959, Special Supplement), 41–59.

[IKN80]   I. Iizuka, M. Kasahara, and T. Namekawa, *Block codes capable of correcting both additive and timing errors*, IEEE Trans. Inform. Theory, 26 (1980), 393–400.

[Imm90]   K.A.S. Immink, *Runlength-limited sequences*, Proc. IEEE, 78 (1990), 1745–1759.

[Imm91]   K.A.S. Immink, *Coding Techniques for Digital Recorders*, Prentice Hall, New York, 1991.

[Imm92]   K.A.S. Immink, *Block-decodable runlength-limited codes via look-ahead technique*, Philips J. Res., 46 (1992), 293–310.

[Imm93]   K.A.S. Immink, *Constructions of almost block decodable runlength-limited codes*, IEEE Trans. Inform. Theory, 41 (1995), 284–287.

[ImmB87] K.A.S. Immink, G.F.M. Beenker, *Binary transmission codes with higher order spectral zeros at zero frequency*, IEEE Trans. Inform. Theory, 33 (1987), 452–454.

[IO85]   K.A.S. Immink, H. Ogawa, *Method for encoding binary data*, U.S. Patent 4,501,000 (1985).

[JAC77]   G. Jacoby, *A new look-ahead code for increased data density*, IEEE Trans. Magn., 13 (1977), pp. 1202–4.

[JK]   G. Jacoby and R. Kost, *Binary two-thirds rate code with full work look-ahead*, IEEE Trans. Magn., 20 (1984), pp. 709–714.

[CJB]   M. Cohn, G. Jacoby and A. Bates III, *Data encoding method and system employing two-thirds code rate with full word look-ahead*, U.S. Patent 4,337,458 (1982).

[Jus82]   J. Justesen, *Information rates and power spectra of digital codes*, IEEE Trans. Inform. Theory, 28 (1982), 457–472.

[JusH84] J. Justesen, T. Høholdt, *Maxentropic Markov chains*, IEEE Trans. Inform. Theory, 30 (1984), 665–667.

[Kam89]   H. Kamabe, *Minimum scope for sliding block decoder mappings*, IEEE Trans. Inform. Theory, 35 (1989), 1335–1340.

[Kam94]   H. Kamabe, *Irreducible components of canonical diagrams for spectral nulls*, IEEE Trans. Inform. Theory, 40 (1994), 1375–1391.

[KarM88] R. Karabed, B.H. Marcus, *Sliding-block coding for input-restricted channels*, IEEE Trans. Inform. Theory, 34 (1988), 2–26.

[KS91a]   R. KARABED, P.H. SIEGEL, *Matched spectral null codes for partial response channels*, *IEEE Trans. Inform. Theory*, 37 (1991), 818–855.

[KS91b]   R. KARABED, P.H. SIEGEL, *A 100% efficient sliding-block code for the charge-constrained, runlength-limited channel with parameters $(d, k; c) = (1, 3; 3)$*, *Proc. 1991 IEEE Int'l Symp. Inform. Theory*, Budapest, Hungary (1991), p. 229.

[Khay89]   Z.-A. KHAYRALLAH, *Finite-State Codes and Input-Constrained Channels*, Ph.D. Thesis, University of Michigan, 1989.

[Khay90]   Z.-A. KHAYRALLAH, D. NEUHOFF, *Subshift models and finite-state codes for input-constrained noiseless channels: a tutorial*, preprint, 1990.

[Kit81]   B. KITCHENS, *Continuity Properties of Factor Maps in Ergodic Theory*, Ph.D. Thesis, University of North Carolina, Chapel Hill, 1981.

[Koba71a]   H. KOBAYASHI, *Application of probabilistic decoding to digital magnetic recording systems*, *IBM J. Res. Develop.*, 15 (1971), 64-74.

[Koba71b]   H. KOBAYASHI, *Correlative level coding and maximum-likelihood decoding*, *IEEE Trans. Inform. Theory*, 18 (1972), 363–378.

[KobT70]   H. KOBAYASHI, D.T. TANG, *Application of partial-response channel coding to magnetic recording systems*, *IBM J. Res. Develop.*, 14 (1970), 368–374.

[Koh78]   Z. KOHAVI, *Switching and Finite Automata Theory*, Second Edition, Tata McGraw-Hill, New Delhi, 1978.

[KolK90]   V.D. KOLESNIK, V.YU. KRACHKOVSKY, *Bounds on rates for limited bitshift-correcting codes*, in *Proc. Int'l Workshop Algebraic Combin. Coding Theory*, Leningrad, USSR, (1990), 100–104.

[KolK91]   V.D. KOLESNIK, V.YU. KRACHKOVSKY, *Generating functions and lower bounds on rates for limited error-correcting codes*, *IEEE Trans. Inform. Theory*, 37 (1991), 778–788.

[Kretz67]   E.R. KRETZMER, *Generalization of a technique for binary data transmission*, *IEEE Trans. Commun. Technol.*, 14 (1967), 67.

[Krusk83]   J.B. KRUSKAL, *An overview of sequence comparison: Time warps, string edits, and macromolecules*, *SIAM Review*, 25 (1983), 201–237.

[KuV93a]   A.V. KUZNETSOV AND A.J. HAN VINCK, *A coding scheme for single peak-shift correction in (d, k)-constrained channels*, *IEEE Trans. Inform. Theory*, 39 (1993), 1444-1450.

[KuV93b]   A.V. KUZNETSOV AND A.J. HAN VINCK, *The application of q-ary codes for the correction of single peak-shifts, deletions and insertions of zeros*, *Proc. 1993 IEEE Int'l Symp. Inform. Theory*, San Antonio, Texas, Jan. 1993, 128.

[LW87]   P. LEE, J.K. WOLF, *Combined error-correction/modulation codes*, *IEEE Trans. Magn.*, 23 (1987), 3681–3683.

[LW89]   P. LEE, J.K. WOLF, *A general error-correcting code construction for run-length limited binary channels*, *IEEE Trans. Inform. Theory*, 35 (1989), 1330–1335.

[LemCo82]   A. LEMPEL, M. COHN, *Look-ahead coding for input-restricted channels*, *IEEE Trans. Inform. Theory*, 28 (1982), 933–937.

[Lev65]   V.I. LEVENSHTEIN, *Binary codes capable of correcting deletions, insertions, and reversals*, (Russian), *Doklady Akademii Nauk SSSR*, 163 (1965), 845–848. (English), *Soviet Physics Doklady*, 10 (1966), 707–710.

[Lev67]   V.I. LEVENSHTEIN, *Asymptotically optimum binary code with correction for losses of one or two adjacent bits*, *Problems of Cybernetics*, 19 (1967), 298–304.

[Lev71]   V.I. LEVENSHTEIN, *One method of constructing quasilinear codes providing synchronizatin in the presence of errors*, (Russian), *Problemy Peredachi Informatsii*, 7 (1971), 30–40. (English), *Problems of Information Transmission*, 7 (1971), 215–222.

[Lev91]   V.I. LEVENSHTEIN, *On perfect codes in deletion and insertion metric*, (Russian), *Discretnaya. Mathematika*, 3 (1991), 3–20. (English), *Discrete Mathematics and Applications*, 2 (1992), 241–258.

[LV93]   V.I. LEVENSHTEIN AND A.J. HAN VINCK, *Perfect (d, k)-codes capable of correcting single peak-shifts*, *IEEE Trans. Inform. Theory*, 39 (1993), 656–662.

[LinCo83]   S. LIN, D.J. COSTELLO, JR., *Error Control Coding, Fundamentals and Applications*, Prentice-Hall, Englewood Cliffs, New Jersey, 1983.

[LM94]   D. LIND, B.H. MARCUS, *An Introduction to Symbolic Dynamics and Coding,* Cambridge University Press, 1995.

[MM77]   J.C. MALLINSON, J.W. MILLER, *Optimal codes for digital magnetic recording, Radio and Elec. Eng.,* 47 (1977), 172–176.

[Mar85]   B.H. MARCUS, *Sofic systems and encoding data, IEEE Trans. Inform. Theory,* 31 (1985), 366–377.

[MR91]   B.H. MARCUS, R.M. ROTH, *Bounds on the number of states in encoders graphs for input-constrained channels, IEEE Trans. Inform. Theory,* IT-37 (1991), 742–758.

[MR92]   B.H. MARCUS, R.M. ROTH, *Improved Gilbert-Varshamov bound for constrained systems, IEEE Trans. Inform. Theory,* 38 (1992), 1213–1221.

[MRS95]   B.H. MARCUS, R.M. ROTH, P.H. SIEGEL, *Constrained Systems and Coding for Recording Channels, Handbook of Coding Theory,* Elsevier, Amsterdam, 1995, to appear.

[MS87]   B.H. MARCUS, P.H. SIEGEL, *On codes with spectral nulls at rational submultiples of the symbol frequency, IEEE Trans. Inform. Theory,* 33 (1987), 557–568.

[MS88]   B. MARCUS, P.H. SIEGEL, *Constrained codes for partial response channels, Proc. Beijing Int'l Workshop on Information Theory* (1988), DI-1.1–1.4.

[MSW92]   B.H. MARCUS, P.H. SIEGEL, J.K. WOLF, *Finite-state modulation codes for data storage, IEEE J. Sel. Areas Commun.,* 10 (1992), 5–37.

[Mill63]   A. MILLER, *Transmission system,* U.S. Patent 3,108,261 (1963).

[Mill77]   J.W. MILLER, U.S. Patent 4,027,335 (1977).

[Minc88]   H. MINC, *Nonnegative Matrices,* Wiley, New York, 1988.

[MPi89]   C.M. MONTI, G.L. PIEROBON, *Codes with a multiple spectral null at zero frequency, IEEE Trans. Inform. Theory,* 35 (1989), 463–472.

[Moore56] E.F. MOORE, *Gedanken-experiments on sequential machines, Automata Studies,* Princeton University Press, Princeton, New Jersey, 1956, 129–153.

[NB81]   K. NORRIS, D.S. BLOOMBERG, *Channel capacity of charge-constrained run-length limited systems, IEEE Trans. Magn.,* 17 (1981), 3452–3455.

[Or93]   A. ORLITSKY, *Interactive communication of balanced distributions and of correlated files, SIAM J. Discr. Math.,* 6 (1993), 548–564.

[PK92]   A. PATAPOUTIAN, P. V. KUMAR, *The (d, k) subcode of a linear block code, IEEE Trans. Inform. Theory,* 38 (1992), 1375–1382.

[Patel75] A.M. PATEL, *Zero-modulation encoding in magnetic recording, IBM J. Res. Develop.,* 19 (1975), 366–378.

[PRS63]   M. PERLES, M.O. RABIN, E. SHAMIR, *The theory of definite automata, IEEE. Trans. Electron. Computers,* 12 (1963), 233–243.

[Pie84]   G.L. PIEROBON, *Codes for zero spectral density at zero frequency, IEEE Trans. Inform. Theory,* 30 (1984), 435–439.

[Pohl92]   K.C. POHLMANN, *The Compact Disc Handbook,* Second Edition, A–R Editions, Madison, Wisconsin, 1992.

[Rae94]   J.W. RAE, G.S. CHRISTIANSEN, R. KARABED, P.H. SIEGEL, H.K. THAPAR, AND S.-M. SHIH, *Design and performance of a VLSI 120 Mb/s trellis-coded partial response channel, Proc. IEEE Magn. Rec. Conf.,* San Diego, California (1994), *IEEE Trans. Magn.,* 31 (1995), 1208–1214.

[RS92]   R.M. ROTH, P.H. SIEGEL, *A family of BCH codes for the Lee metric, Proc. Thirtieth Annual Allerton Conf. on Communication, Control, and Computing,* Urbana-Champaign, Illinois, September 1992, 1–10.

[RS94]   R.M. ROTH, P.H. SIEGEL, *Lee-metric BCH codes and their application to constrained and partial-response channels, IEEE Trans. Inform. Theory,* 40 (1994), 1083–1096.

[RSV94]   R.M. ROTH, P.H. SIEGEL, A. VARDY, *High-order spectral-null codes: constructions and bounds, IEEE Trans. Inform. Theory,* 40 (1994), 1828–1840.

[Roth93]   R.M. ROTH, *Spectral-null codes and null spaces of Hadamard submatrices, Proc. First French–Israeli Workshop on Algebraic Coding,* Paris (July 1993), G. Cohen, S. Litsyn, A. Lobstein, G. Zémor (Eds.), Springer (LNCS 781, 1994), 141–153.

[RuS89]   D. RUGAR, P.H. SIEGEL, *Recording results and coding considerations for the Resonant bias coil overwrite technique, Optical Data Storage Topical Meeting,* G. R. Knight, C.N. Kurtz, Eds., *Proc. SPIE,* 1078 (1989), 265–270.

[Sa93a]   Y. SAITOH, *Theory and design of error-control codes for byte-organized/ input-restricted storage devices where unidirectional/peak-shift errors are predominant,* Ph.D. dissertation, Division of Electrical and Computer Engineering, Yokohama National University, Yokohama, Japan, February 1993.

[Sa93b]   Y. SAITOH, T. OHNO, H. IMAI, *Construction techniques for error-control runlength-limited block codes, IEICE Trans. Fundamentals,* E76-A (1993), 453–458.

[Sen80]   E. SENETA, *Non-negative Matrices and Markov Chains,* Second Edition, Springer, New York, 1980.

[SZ91]   S. SHAMAI, E. ZEHAVI, *Bounds on the capacity of the bit-shift magnetic recording channel, IEEE Trans. Inform. Theory,* 37 (1991), 863–871.

[Sha48]   C.E. SHANNON, *The mathematical theory of communication, Bell Sys. Tech. J.,* 27 (1948), 379–423.

[ST93]   D.B. SHMOYS, É. TARDOS, *Computational complexity,* in *The Handbook of Combinatorics,* L. Lovász, R.L. Graham, M. Grötschel (Editors), North Holland, Amsterdam, to appear.

[Shung91] C. SHUNG, P. SIEGEL, H. THAPAR, R. KARABED, *A 30 MHz trellis codec chip for partial-response channels, IEEE J. Solid-State Circ.,* 26 (1991), 1981–1987. San Francisco, February 1991, pp. 132–133.

[Sie85a]   P.H. SIEGEL, *Recording codes for digital magnetic storage, IEEE Trans. Magn.,* 21 (1985), 1344–1349.

[Sie85b]   P.H. SIEGEL, *On the complexity of limiting error propagation in sliding block codes, Proc. 2nd IBM Symp. on Coding and Error Control,* San Jose, California, January 1985.

[SW91]   P.H. SIEGEL, J.K. WOLF, *Modulation and coding for information storage, IEEE Commun. Magazine,* 29 (1991), 68–86.

[TK76]   E. TANAKA AND T. KASAI, *Synchronization and substitution error-correcting codes for the Levenshtein metric, IEEE Trans. Inform. Theory,* 22 (1976), 156–162.

[TB70]   D.T. TANG, L.R. BAHL, *Block codes for a class of constrained noiseless channels, Inform. Control,* 17 (1970), 436–461.

[Ten76]   G.M. TENENGOLTS, *Class of codes correcting bit loss and errors in the preceding bit,* (Russian), *Avtomatika i Telemekhanika,* 37 (1976), 174–179. (English), *Automation and Remote Control,* 37 (1966), 797–802.

[Ten84]   G.M. TENENGOLTS, *Nonbinary codes, correcting single deletion or insertion, IEEE Trans. Inform. Theory,* 30 (1984), 766–769.

[Tja94]   T.J. TJALKENS, *On the principal state method for runlength limited sequences, IEEE Trans. Inform. Theory,* 40 (1994), 934–941.

[Thap92]   H.K. THAPAR, J. RAE, C.B. SHUNG, R. KARABED, P.H. SIEGEL, *On the performance of a rate 8/10 matched spectral null code for class-4 partial response, IEEE Trans. Magn.,* 28 (1992), 2884–2889.

[Thap93]   H. THAPAR, C. SHUNG, J. RAE, R. KARABED, P.H. SIEGEL, *Real-time recording results for a trellis-coded partial response (TCPR) system, IEEE Trans. Magn.,* 29 (1993), 4009–4011.

[U66]   J.D. ULLMAN, *Near-optimal, single-synchronization-error-correcting code, IEEE Trans. Inform. Theory,* 12 (1966), 418–424.

[U67]   J.D. ULLMAN, *On the capabilities of codes to correct synchronization errors, IEEE Trans. Inform. Theory,* 13 (1967), 95–105.

[Var62]   R.S. VARGA, *Matrix Iterative Analysis,* Prentice-Hall, Englewood Cliffs, New Jersey, 1962.

[WN94]   H. WALDMAN, E. NISENBAUM, *Upper bounds and Hamming spheres under the dc-constraint,* submitted to *IEEE Trans. Inform. Theory,* 1994.

[Walt82]   P. WALTERS, *An Introduction to Ergodic Theory,* Graduate Texts in Mathematics 79, Springer, New York, 1982.

[WW91]   A.D. WEATHERS, J.K. WOLF, *A new 2/3 sliding block code for the (1,7) runlength constraint with the minimal number of encoder states, IEEE Trans. Inform. Theory,* 37 (1991), 908–913.

[Will73]   R.F. WILLIAMS, *Classification of subshifts of finite type, Annals Math.,* 98 (1973), 120–153; errata: *Annals Math.,* 99 (1974), 380–381.

[Will88]   S. WILLIAMS, *Covers of non-almost-finite-type systems*, *Proc. AMS,* 104 (1988), 245–252.

[WY93]   K. WINICK, S.-H. YANG, *Bounds on the size of error correcting runlength-limited codes*, preprint, 1993.

[WU86]   J.K. WOLF, G. UNGERBOECK, *Trellis coding for partial-response channels*, *IEEE Trans. Commun.,* 34 (1986), 765–773.

[Wood90]   R. WOOD, *Denser magnetic memory*, *IEEE Spectrum,* 27, No. 5 (May 1990), 32–39.

[WoodP86]   R. WOOD, D. PETERSON, *Viterbi detection of class IV partial response on a magnetic recoding channel*, *IEEE Trans. Commun.,* 34 (1986), 454–461.

[YY76]   S. YOSHIDA, S. YAJIMA, *On the relation between an encoding automaton and the power spectrum of its output sequence*, *Trans. IECE Japan,* 59 (1976), 1–7.

[Yt91a]   Ø. YTREHUS, *Upper bounds on error-correcting runlength-limited block codes*, *IEEE Trans. Inform. Theory,* 37 (1991), 941–945.

[Yt91b]   Ø. YTREHUS, *Runlength-limited codes for mixed-error channels*, *IEEE Trans. Inform. Theory,* 37 (1991), 1577–1585.

[Ze87]   E. ZEHAVI, *Coding for Magnetic Recording*, Ph.D. Thesis, University of California, San Diego, 1987.

[ZW88]   E. ZEHAVI, J.K. WOLF, *On runlength codes*, *IEEE Trans. Inform. Theory,* 34 (1988), 45–54.

IBM K53-802, 650 HARRY ROAD, SAN JOSE, CA 95120
E-mail address: marcus@almaden.ibm.com

COMPUTER SCIENCE DEPARTMENT, TECHNION — ISRAEL INSTITUTE OF TECHNOLOGY, HAIFA 32000, ISRAEL
E-mail address: ronny@csa.cs.Technion.AC.IL

IBM RESEARCH DIVISION, ALMADEN RESEARCH CENTER, 650 HARRY ROAD, SAN JOSE, CA 95120
E-mail address: siegelph@almaden.ibm.com

Proceedings of Symposia in Applied Mathematics
Volume **50**, 1995

Symbolic Dynamics and Connections to Coding Theory, Automata Theory and System Theory

Brian Marcus

1. Introduction

In this article, we give an introduction to symbolic dynamics and then discuss some common themes in coding theory, automata theory and system theory. Although these subjects have grown up somewhat independently, there is a strong connection among them. In particular, they all study systems, representations of systems, and transformations from one system to another. For additional reading on the connections among these subjects, we refer the reader to the Mutilingual Dictionary, hereafter referred to as the *Dictionary*, which appears in this volume. For ease of reading, most of the terms that we use are defined within this article.

For further background on symbolic dynamics than is contained in this article, we refer the reader to [**7**], [**10**], and the textbook [**30**].

2. Classical dynamical systems and the origins of symbolic dynamics

A *classical (discrete-time) dynamical system* or simply *classical system* is a pair (X, f) where X is a set and $f : X \to X$ is a map. The idea is that $x \in X$ describes the system at time $t = 0$ seconds, $f(x)$ describes it at time $t = 1$ seconds, $f^2(x) = f(f(x))$ at $t = 2$ seconds, and so on. We assume that f is *invertible*, and so $f^{-n}(x)$ describes the system at time $t = -n$. Of central interest is the study of the *orbit*, $\{\ldots, f^{-2}(x), f^{-1}(x), x, f(x), f^2(x), \ldots\}$, of an individual point x and how the orbits vary with x.

The definition of dynamical system that we have given here differs from the definition given in the Dictionary (I-1); we will discuss that definition in Section 8.

Given a classical system (X, f) and a partition (usually finite) P of X, we get a new system by 'coding' points in X relative to P as follows. Let $\Sigma = \Sigma(X, f)$ be the set of all bi-infinite sequences, $\ldots p_{-1} p_0 p_1 \ldots$, over the alphabet P, for which there is an $x \in X$ such that $f^i(x) \in p_i$ (of course, Σ depends on the partition P as well). Let $\sigma : \Sigma \to \Sigma$ denote the left shift map: $\sigma(\ldots p_{-1} p_0 p_1 \ldots) = \ldots q_{-1} q_0 q_1 \ldots$ where $q_i = p_{i+1}$. The action of f on points in X is represented by the action of σ on sequences in Σ. In this way, we represent the orbits of a classical system by

1991 *Mathematics Subject Classification*. Primary 58F03; Secondary 68Q68, 93B15, 94A40, 94B12.

sequences of symbols. For this reason, we call (Σ, σ) a *symbolic dynamical system.* Strictly speaking, the symbolic dynamical system that is considered in symbolic dynamics is a "closure" $(\overline{\Sigma}, \sigma)$ rather than (Σ, σ) itself (see the definition of shift space in Section 3.1).

What is the advantage of replacing an ordinary classical dynamical system with a symbolic dynamical system? The idea is that problems of isomorphism between two classical systems (X, f) and (Y, g) are then translated into coding problems between the corresponding symbolic dynamical systems $(\Sigma(X, f), \sigma)$ and $(\Sigma(Y, g), \sigma)$. In this way, the tools of discrete mathematics can be brought to bear on the problems of isomorphism.

In general, (Σ, σ) is only an approximation of (X, f). But for certain classical systems and certain carefully chosen partitions, (Σ, σ) contains "most" of the "essential" information about (X, f). This works very well for some interesting systems [4], [14]. Originally, the symbolic dynamics approach was developed in order to approximate certain continuous-time, rather than discrete-time, systems such as geodesic flows on surfaces of negative curvature [1], [36].

3. Symbolic dynamical systems

3.1. Shift spaces and sliding block codes.

The *full shift,* $W^{\mathcal{Z}}$, over a finite alphabet W is the set of all bi-infinite sequences over W. The finite sequences over W are called *blocks.* An *n-block* is a block of length n. For $x \in W^{\mathcal{Z}}$, we write $x = \ldots x_{-2} x_{-1} x_0 x_1 x_2 \ldots$, and for $\mathcal{J} \subseteq \mathcal{Z}$, define $x|_{\mathcal{J}}$ to be the restriction of x to its coordinates in $\mathcal{J}$.

The fundamental object in symbolic dynamics is a *shift space,* which is a shift-invariant subset X of a full shift defined by forbidding the appearance of blocks from a given list $\mathcal{U}$ (finite or infinite):

$$X = \{x \in W^{\mathcal{Z}} : x|_{\mathcal{J}} \notin \mathcal{U} \text{ for all finite intervals } \mathcal{J}\}.$$

The blocks of a shift space X are the sequences $x|_{\mathcal{J}}$, where x varies over X and $\mathcal{J}$ varies over all finite intervals.

Usually attention is focused on *irreducible* shift spaces, i.e. shift spaces X such that whenever u, v are blocks of X, there is a block w such that uwv is also a block of X. In many cases of interest, the study of general shift spaces can be reduced to the study of irreducible shift spaces.

The term "symbolic dynamical system" is often used as a synonym for a dynamical system (X, σ) where X is a shift space, although there is considerable interest in analogues of shift spaces where the sequences are indexed by $\mathcal{Z}^+$, $\mathcal{R}$ or $\mathcal{Z}^n$, rather than $\mathcal{Z}$ and/or where the alphabet is allowed to be infinite. We will focus only on a very special, concrete class of shift spaces and coding issues for these spaces. This neglects other very important aspects of symbolic dynamics.

In symbolic dynamics, we transform one shift space, X, to another, Y, via a *sliding block code,* i.e., a map $\phi : X \rightarrow Y$ which can be expressed as follows: there are integers m, a (*memory, anticipation*) and a map Φ from $(m + a + 1)$-blocks of X to 1-blocks of Y such that $\phi(x)_i = \Phi(x|_{[i-m, i+a]})$. We write $\phi = \Phi_\infty$.

A *conjugacy* is an invertible sliding block code, and two shift spaces are *conjugate* if there is a conjugacy from one to the other. In symbolic dynamics, two shift spaces are often regarded as being the "same" if they are conjugate. Since conjugacy is a rather robust concept, this perspective may appear strange to a coding theorist, automata theorist or system theorist.

Shift spaces and sliding block codes can be defined in topological terms as follows. A *cylinder set* is the set of all points $x \in W^{\mathbb{Z}}$ such that $x|_{\mathcal{J}} = w$ for some block w and some finite interval of coordinates $\mathcal{J}$. Endow the full shift with a topology by declaring the open sets to be unions of cylinder sets. Then the shift spaces are precisely the closed shift-invariant subset of the full shift. And the sliding block codes are precisely the continuous, shift-commuting maps. For the most part, we will not need this topological perspective.

3.2. Sofic shifts. A *sofic shift* is the set of bi-infinite sequences obtained by reading the labels of a labeled finite directed graph (G, L) (here, a *finite directed graph* or simply *graph* G is a finite set of states and edges, with each edge having an initial state and a terminal state; a *labeled finite directed graph* or simply *labeled graph* (G, L) is a finite directed graph, together with a map L from the edges of G to an alphabet). The sofic shift is said to be *presented* by the labeled graph, and the labeled graph is called a *presentation* of the sofic shift. The sofic shifts, presented by the labeled graphs in Figure 1 (resp., Figure 2) are the set of all binary sequences such that 1's are isolated (resp., such that 0's occur in even runs). Note that the full shift is a sofic shift, presented by a labeled graph with only one state.

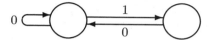

FIGURE 1. A sofic shift

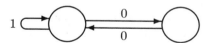

FIGURE 2. Another sofic shift

If a graph G is *irreducible* (i.e., there is a path from any state to any other state), then the sofic shift presented by any labeling of G is irreducible. Conversely, it can be shown that any irreducible sofic shift can be presented by a labeling of an irreducible graph.

An *edge shift* is a sofic shift defined by a presentation in which the edges are labeled distinctly. In this case, the underlying graph G itself completely defines the sofic shift, and so it makes sense to denote an edge shift by X_G. As an example of an edge shift X_G see Figure 3.

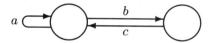

FIGURE 3. An edge shift

Note that any presentation (G, L) of a sofic shift X defines a sliding block code $\phi = L_{\infty}$, with zero memory and zero anticipation, from the edge shift X_G to X.

Given graphs G', G, a *graph homomorphism* $\Phi : G' \to G$ is a mapping from edges of G' to edges of G which respects initial, terminal states (and so induces an associated state mapping). A *graph isomorphism* is a graph homomorphism Φ in which both Φ and its associated state mapping are bijective. Any graph homomorphism Φ induces a sliding block code $\Phi_\infty : X_{G'} \to X_G$, and if Φ is a graph isomorphism, then Φ_∞ is a conjugacy. But these conjugacies are very special since they and their inverses have zero memory and zero anticipation.

A *shift of finite type* is a shift-invariant subset of the full shift defined by forbidding a <u>finite</u> list of blocks. It is not hard to show that every edge shift is a shift of finite type and that every shift of finite type is a sofic shift. The shift spaces that arise as symbolic models for classical dynamical systems tend to be shifts of finite type.

It is possible to "recode" any shift of finite type as an edge shift, in the sense that any shift of finite type is conjugate to an edge shift; as a result, in the literature, the distinction between edge shifts and shifts of finite type has often been blurred.

4. Minimal presentations of sofic shifts

In this section, we consider minimal presentations of sofic shifts. The simplest notion of minimality would be in terms of number of states, and so a unique minimal presentation of a sofic shift X would be a unique (up to relabeling) presentation of X with smallest number of states. Typically, there is no unique minimal presentation in this sense. However, within the following class of presentations, there is always a unique minimal one.

A presentation of a sofic shift is *right resolving* if at each state, all outgoing edges are labeled distinctly. Borrowing an idea (the "subset construction" [22]) from automata theory, one can show that every sofic shift has a right resolving presentation. The presentations in Figures 1, 2 and 3 are right resolving. Right resolving presentations are nice because, up to a choice of initial state, there is a one-to-one correspondence between right-infinite paths and right-infinite label sequences. Replacing the term "outgoing" by the term "incoming," we obtain the notion of *left resolving* presentation.

THEOREM 4.1 (Fischer [15], [16]). *Every irreducible sofic shift has a unique minimal (in terms of number of states) right resolving presentation, (G_X^+, L_X^+).*

(G_X^+, L_X^+) is often called the *(right) Fischer cover*. Likewise, there is a unique minimal left resolving presentation (G_X^-, L_X^-). We remark that N. Jonoska showed that Theorem 4.1 is false for (reducible) sofic shifts in general [23],[30].

There is an intrinsic description of (G_X^+, L_X^+). For a shift space X and $x \in X$, the *future* of $x|_{(-\infty,0)}$ is defined as follows:

$$F(x|_{(-\infty,0)}) = \{y|_{[0,\infty)} : x|_{(-\infty,0)}y|_{[0,\infty)} \in X\}.$$

It turns out that a shift space is sofic if and only if it has finitely many futures. Now, from the futures of a sofic shift X, we can directly construct a presentation of X: namely, the states are the futures of X and there is an edge from $F(x|_{(-\infty,0)})$ to $F(y|_{(-\infty,0)})$, labeled a, whenever $y|_{(-\infty,0)} = x|_{(-\infty,0)}a$. This labeled graph is called the *future cover* or *(right) Krieger cover* of X. It turns out that (G_X^+, L_X^+) is the subgraph of the future cover obtained by restricting to certain "synchronizing" states. See [24].

There is another notion of minimality which is perhaps more meaningful than minimality of the number of states. Roughly speaking, a unique minimal presentation (G, L) of X is one such that every presentation of X "collapses" onto (G, L).

To be more precise, we endow the set of presentations of a sofic shift X with the following ordering: $(G, L) \leq (G', L')$ if there is a label-preserving graph homomorphism Φ from (G', L') to (G, L) such that Φ_∞ is onto (this is what we mean by saying that (G', L') "collapses" onto (G, L)). This becomes a partial ordering once we identify presentations which are equivalent via label-preserving graph isomorphism. For a class $\mathcal{C}$ of presentations of a sofic shift, we say that a presentation is $\mathcal{C}$-minimal if it is a minimal element with respect to the ordering restricted to $\mathcal{C}$. Note that if a sofic shift has a unique $\mathcal{C}$-minimal presentation, then it is the unique smallest (in terms of number of states) presentation within the class $\mathcal{C}$. The classes of interest to us are

1. $\mathcal{A}$, the class of *all presentations*
2. $\mathcal{I}$, the class of *irreducible presentations* (i.e., presentations where the underlying graph is irreducible)
3. $\mathcal{R}$, the class of *irreducible, right resolving presentations*.

Of course, $\mathcal{I}$-minimality and $\mathcal{R}$-minimality can apply only to irreducible sofic shifts. The presentation (G_X^+, L_X^+) above turns out to be the unique $\mathcal{R}$-minimal presentation of an irreducible sofic shift X [15], [16]. The following result characterizes the irreducible sofic shifts for which there is a unique $\mathcal{I}$-minimal presentation.

THEOREM 4.2 (Jonoska, Marcus [24]). *For an irreducible sofic shift X, the following are equivalent.*

1. *X has a unique $\mathcal{I}$-minimal presentation*
2. *$(G_X^+, L_X^+) = (G_X^-, L_X^-)$ (up to a label-preserving graph isomorphism)*
3. *(G_X^+, L_X^+) is left resolving (as well as right resolving).*

We refer the reader to [24] for the characterization of sofic shifts with unique $\mathcal{A}$-minimal presentation; that result is essentially a result in system theory (see Theorem 8.1). Theorem 4.2 above was motivated by Theorem 8.1 as well as a result which involves a more robust notion of minimality that is more natural for symbolic dynamics; this is expressed in Theorem 4.3 below, which requires the following definitions. Let X be a sofic shift. For presentations (G, L) and (G', L') of X, we say that (G', L') *factors through* (G, L) if there is an onto sliding block code $\phi : X_{G'} \to X_G$ such that $L'_\infty = L_\infty \circ \phi$. Since the map ϕ is allowed to have memory or anticipation, this condition is much weaker than $(G, L) \leq (G', L')$. We say that a presentation is *right closing* if it is "right resolving with delay," more precisely, if for some N, any two paths of length N with the same initial state and the same label must have the same initial edge. Clearly, right closing is a weakening of right resolving. Replacing the term "initial" with "terminal" in the definition, we obtain the notion of *left closing*. For presentations (G, L) and (G', L') of X, we say that (G', L') and (G, L) are **-equivalent* if there is a conjugacy $\phi : X_{G'} \to X_G$ such that $L'_\infty = L_\infty \circ \phi$.

THEOREM 4.3 (Boyle, Kitchens, Marcus [9]). *For an irreducible sofic shift X, the following are equivalent.*

1. *X has an irreducible presentation (G, L) such that every irreducible presentation (G', L') of X factors through (G, L)*
2. *(G_X^+, L_X^+) is *-equivalent to (G_X^-, L_X^-)*
3. *(G_X^+, L_X^+) is left closing (as well as right resolving).*

5. Coding from one sofic shift to another

One of the major problems of symbolic dynamics is to classify shift spaces up to conjugacy. The property of being a sofic shift or of being a shift of finite type is a conjugacy invariant; that is, if a shift space X is conjugate to a sofic shift (resp., of finite type), then X itself is sofic (resp., of finite type). Here, we focus mostly on the special class of edge shifts, where many of the difficulties already arise. We use the notation $X \cong Y$ to denote conjugacy.

Now, there are some simple invariants (i.e., necessary conditions) of conjugacy between shift spaces: (1) they must have the same number of periodic sequences of all periods; (2) they must have the same entropy (the *entropy* of a shift space is $\lim_{n \to \infty} \frac{\log(N_n(X))}{n}$ where $N_n(X)$ is the number of n-blocks that occur in X); (3) if one shift is irreducible, then so is the other. For edge shifts, these conditions can be described concretely using the *adjacency matrix* $A(G)$, i.e., the matrix indexed by the states of G and defined by $A(G)_{IJ} = $ the number of edges from I to J; for instance, the entropy of an edge shift X_G is the *log* of the largest eigenvalue of $A(G)$. If G and H are both irreducible and $A(G)$ and $A(H)$ have the same set of non-zero eigenvalues (with multiplicity), then it turns out that all three of the necessary conditions for conjugacy of X_G and X_H mentioned above are satisfied [**30**]. However, these conditions are not sufficient. This is a consequence of how conjugacies between edge shifts can be generated by the following basic operations.

An *out-splitting* of a graph G is a graph H obtained by splitting (partitioning) the outgoing edges and replicating the incoming edges at each state. Likewise, we have *in-splittings* by reversing the roles of 'outgoing' and 'incoming.' Also, we have the inverse operations of *out-amalgamation* and *in-amalgamation*. It is not hard to show that if H is obtained from G via any one of these operations, then $X_G \cong X_H$. The following result shows that all conjugacies are generated by combining these operations:

THEOREM 5.1 (Williams [**48**]). *Let G and H be irreducible graphs. Then $X_G \cong X_H$ iff H can be obtained from G by a sequence of splittings and amalgamations (out and in).*

In a sense, this solves the conjugacy problem for edge shifts; moreover, there is a way to generalize this result to sofic shifts [**37**]. However, since there may be no way of telling how many splittings/amalgamations are needed to reach H from G, Theorem 5.1 does not appear to give a finite algorithm (efficient or not) for deciding conjugacy between edge shifts. Indeed, no such algorithm is known, and in this sense the conjugacy problem for edge shifts is not solved.

Nevertheless, Theorem 5.1 can be used to give a very strong necessary condition for conjugacy and to give examples of irreducible graphs G, H such that $A(G)$ and $A(H)$ have the same eigenvalues (including multiplicity), but $X_G \not\cong X_H$; see [**48**] and [**30**].

While conjugacy is perhaps the most natural coding notion in symbolic dynamics, there are other meaningful notions: for instance, sofic shifts X and Y are *finitely equivalent* if there is an edge shift X_G and finite-to-one, onto sliding block codes $X_G \to X$, $X_G \to Y$. If the sliding block codes can also be made "one-to-one almost everywhere", then we say that X and Y are *almost topologically conjugate*. Classification up to these notions has met with greater success than the conjugacy problem in the sense that there is a simple algorithm based on relatively simple invariants to decide, for a given pair of sofic shifts X, Y, whether such a coding is possible. For example,

THEOREM 5.2 (Parry[**38**]). *Two irreducible sofic shifts X and Y are finitely equivalent if and only if they have the same entropy.*

The almost topological conjugacy problem was solved by Adler and Marcus [**3**]. For expositions of work on these and other coding problems, we refer the reader to [**7**], [**30**]; the original solutions to these problems are contained in [**5**], [**8**], [**10**], [**27**], [**28**], [**37**], [**45**], among many others.

6. Symbolic dynamics and coding theory

6.1. Algebraic coding. In symbolic dynamics, the term "code" means some kind of mapping such as "sliding block code." In contrast, coding theory usually uses the term "code" to mean a set (elements of which are called "codewords") of sequences with "good" error-correcting properties, used to transmit information over noisy channels.

Coding theory focuses on the construction of good codes. Nevertheless, once one constructs a code, one must find a method to encode arbitrary messages to codewords and to decode codewords back to arbitrary messages. In coding theory, the domain of an encoder is usually a full shift (which represents arbitrary messages).

The two major classes of codes considered in coding theory are *block codes*, in which the codewords are finite sequences all of the same length, and *convolutional codes*, in which the codewords are infinite (or bi-infinite) sequences. Here, we focus on convolutional codes.

Usually, convolutional codes are defined in a concrete manner, via generator matrices [**29**]. We define convolutional codes, in terms of symbolic dynamics, as follows. Let F be a finite field. Then the full F^k-shift, $(F^k)^{\mathbb{Z}}$, may be regarded as a vector space over F. A *rate $k : n$ convolutional encoder* is a linear sliding block code from the full F^k-shift into the full F^n-shift. A *convolutional code* is the image of a convolutional encoder. Since images of linear spaces by linear maps are linear, a convolutional code is a linear subspace of $(F^n)^{\mathbb{Z}}$.

Sliding block codes preserve the properties of being a shift space and irreducibility, and so every convolutional code is an irreducible linear shift space; in fact, the converse is true as well: the convolutional codes are precisely the irreducible linear shift spaces.

The convolutional encoder clearly plays the role of a transformation from one system to another: it maps a full shift onto a convolutional code. But it can also be used to represent the convolutional code as a sofic shift: the images of certain basis vectors in the full F^k-shift can be used to construct a labeled graph which presents the convolutional code as a sofic shift.

For every convolutional code X, there is a unique $\mathcal{A}$-minimal convolutional encoder [**17**]; the sense of minimality described in [**17**] is stated differently, but the minimal encoder constructed there is $\mathcal{A}$-minimal as a presentation. Moreover, this minimal encoder is a conjugacy, and so it can be used to encode data into the convolutional code in an invertible way. In summary, we have:

THEOREM 6.1 (Forney [17]).   1. *Every convolutional code X has a unique $\mathcal{A}$-minimal presentation.*

2. *Every convolutional code is conjugate to a full shift, via a linear conjugacy.*

Recently, it has become evident that some very powerful codes, which "look algebraic," do indeed have algebraic structure, in spite of the fact that they are not convolutional codes [12], [20]. This motivates the study of the following more general class of shift spaces.

Let C be a finite group. A *group shift* over C is a shift space which is a subgroup of $C^{\mathcal{Z}}$ (with the coordinatewise group operation). Convolutional codes are examples of group shifts where the group $C = F^n$.

In analogy with Theorem 6.1, one might expect that for every irreducible group shift X, there is finite group D and a homomorphic (i.e., addition-preserving) conjugacy form $D^{\mathcal{Z}}$ onto X. This turns out to be false [26], [32]. Moreover, unlike convolutional codes, group shifts can fail to be irreducible. Nevertheless, the following version of Theorem 6.1 holds for group shifts.

THEOREM 6.2.   1. *Every group shift has a unique $\mathcal{A}$-minimal presentation*

2. *Every irreducible group shift is conjugate to a full shift*

Various versions of this result can be found in Forney and Trott [20], Kitchens [26], Loeliger and Mittelholzer [32], and Miles and Thomas [35].

There is a further natural generalization that goes beyond group shifts. Let C be a finite group, and let S be a finite set. A *group action* of C on S is a homomorphism from C into the permutation group of S. Given a group action of C on S, any group shift X over C acts on $S^{\mathcal{Z}}$ (coordinatewise). A *homogeneous shift* is a shift space $Y \subseteq S^{\mathcal{Z}}$ such that the action of X preserves Y and X acts transitively on Y. We then say that X *presents* Y as a homogeneous shift.

A homogeneous shift need not be a group shift, but it does inherit a good deal of algebraic structure from the acting group. *Geometrically uniform codes* [19], which are of interest in problems of transmission over channels with white Gaussian noise, are central examples of homogeneous shifts in which the acting group C is a finite group of Euclidean isometries and S is a finite set of points in Euclidean space.

It turns out that homogeneous shifts do not always have unique minimal presentations (either $\mathcal{A}$-minimal or $\mathcal{I}$-minimal) [42], [46]. Nevertheless, up to conjugacy, their structure is as simple as group shifts and convolutional codes. In particular:

THEOREM 6.3 (Sindhushayana [42]). *Every irreducible homogeneous shift is conjugate to a full shift.*

Now, let's specialize to the case where the group shift $X = X_G$ and the homogeneous shift $Y = X_H$ are irreducible edge shifts. It follows from Theorems 5.1, 6.2 (part 2) and 6.3 that both G and H can be obtained from a 1-state graph via a sequence of splittings/amalgamations (out and in). Theorem 6.4 below refines this in a way that sheds some light on the structure of the graphs G and H.

We use the notation (G, H) to denote the group shift X_G, the homogeneous shift X_H, and the action of X_G on X_H (which is really generated by an action of the edge set $\mathcal{E}_G$ of G on the edge set $\mathcal{E}_H$ of H).

We say that (G', H') is an *action-preserving out-splitting* of (G, H) if G' (resp., H') is an out-splitting of G (resp., H) and the action of $\mathcal{E}_{G'}$ on $\mathcal{E}_{H'}$ is consistent with the action of $\mathcal{E}_G$ on $\mathcal{E}_H$ via the out-splittings.

A graph G' formed from a graph G by replacing each edge of G by a constant number of parallel edges is called a *parallel-edgification* of G. We say that (G', H') is an *action-preserving parallel-edgification* of (G, H) if G' (resp., H') is a parallel-edgification of G (resp. H) and the action of $\mathcal{E}_{G'}$ on $\mathcal{E}_{H'}$ is consistent with the action of $\mathcal{E}_G$ on $\mathcal{E}_H$ via the parallel-edgifications.

THEOREM 6.4 (Marcus, Sindhushayana). *Let G and H be irreducible graphs such that X_G is a group shift which presents a homogeneous shift X_H. Then (G, H) is obtained from the trivial action of the 1-state, 1-edge graph on itself via a sequence of action-preserving out-splittings and action-preserving parallel-edgifications.*

Recently, Sindhushayana [**43**] has used a version of this result to give a procedure to decide if a given sofic shift X is literally (not merely up to conjugacy) a homogeneous shift, and how to find the complete set of symmetries of X. See Sindhushayana, Marcus and Trott [**44**] for more on this subject.

6.2. Constrained coding. In certain communication channels, it turns out that some sequences are more likely to be corrupted by noise than other sequences. Thus, it is desirable to design encoders which encode arbitrary messages into constrained messages that are well-adapted to the channel. This is the subject of *constrained coding*.

A specific application where constrained coding is used is that of data storage: data is recorded on a storage medium, to be retrieved by a user at some later time. This can be regarded as a noisy communication channel, where recording is viewed as "sending" and retrieval is viewed as "receiving."

For instance, in magnetic recording, a '1' is recorded (i.e., "sent") as a change in magnetic polarity, and a '0' is recorded (i.e., "sent") as absence of change in magnetic polarity. For retrieval of the information, 1's are detected by magnetic flux, but 0's are detected indirectly: the number of 0's in between two 1's is inferred by information provided by a clock. To prevent loss of clock synchronization, it is desirable that strings of consecutive 0's not be too long. To prevent intersymbol interference (i.e., interference between two consecutive 1's), it is also desirable that strings of consecutive 0's not be too short. Thus, one records only those messages that satisfy a (d, k) *run-length-limited (RLL)* constraint, i.e., the set of all binary sequences such that the number of consecutive zeros between two ones is at least d and at most k. This constraint can be formulated as a sofic shift (see Figure 4).

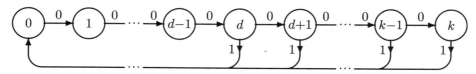

FIGURE 4. (d, k)-RLL constraint.

Since a storage device should be able to store any message, it is necessary to encode arbitrary binary sequences into sequences that obey a specific RLL constraint. It is important that the encoder encode data at a high rate, that the decoder not propagate channel errors, and that the complexity of encoding and decoding be low.

There are several methods that can be used for construction of such encoders. One such method is called the *state-splitting algorithm* [**2**] (see [**30**] and [**34**] for expository treatments). This algorithm begins with a presentation of a sofic shift and iteratively performs a sequence of out-splittings to arrive at a new presentation which can be used as an encoder. The algorithm evolved from work on the coding problems discussed in Section 5.

The state-splitting algorithm has several desirable features: it can produce codes for any desired constraint whatsoever; the encoders encode data at as high a rate as is theoretically possible; the decoders have limited error propagation; and the encoders and decoders tend to have low complexity.

For further information on constrained coding, see Paul Siegel's article in this volume and the forthcoming book chapter [**33**].

7. Symbolic dynamics and automata theory

Automata theory is primarily concerned with languages: a *language* is simply a set of finite sequences (of arbitrary lengths) over a finite alphabet A. Of particular interest are regular languages; this is the set of languages obtained from finite languages by certain basic operations (union, concatenation, star) [**22**]. Just as for sofic shifts, there is a more concrete way to define regular languages in terms of labeled graphs as follows. A *finite automaton* is a labeled graph with two distinguished subsets of states: a set of initial states and a set of terminal states; a *regular language* is the set of all finite sequences obtained from a finite automaton as labels of paths which begin at an initial state and end at a terminal state. A finite automaton can be viewed as a "presentation" of a regular language.

Using all states as both initial states and terminal states, we see that the language of a sofic shift (i.e., the set of finite sequences that appear in elements of a sofic shift) is a regular language. Moreover, there is a simple way to convert any regular language into the language of a sofic shift.

A *deterministic finite automaton* (abbr., *DFA*) is a finite automaton such that at each state all of the outgoing edges are labeled distinctly and there is a unique initial state. Clearly, the concept of determinism in automata theory is the (much older) analogue of right resolving in symbolic dynamics.

The following is a classical result of automata theory:

THEOREM 7.1 ([**22**]). *Every regular language has a unique minimal (in terms of number of states) DFA.*

The unique minimal right resolving presentation (G_X^+, L_X^+) of an irreducible sofic shift, described in Section 4, is the analogue of the unique minimal DFA. The construction of (G_X^+, L_X^+) was based, to some extent, on ideas used in constructing the minimal DFA. But Theorem 4.1 is a more difficult result since presentations of sofic shifts do not have a uniquely specified initial state.

A finite automaton is called *nonambiguous* if no two distinct paths share the same initial state, label and terminal state [**7**]. Note that every DFA is nonambiguous, but typically nonambiguity is much weaker than determinism. Symbolic dynamics (Theorem 7.2 below) gives a different perspective on what it means for a presentation to be nonambiguous. To understand this, we first extend the definition of nonambiguity to labeled graphs by allowing all states to be both initial states and terminal states. Then right resolving presentations of sofic shifts are nonambiguous.

THEOREM 7.2. *If* (G, L) *is irreducible, then* $\phi = L_\infty$ *is finite-to-one if and only if* (G, L) *is nonambiguous.*

This result is implicit in [13], [21] (see [7] and [30] for expositions).

Now, recall that sofic shifts X and Y are called finitely equivalent if there is an edge shift X_G and finite-to-one, onto sliding block codes $X_G \to X$ and $X_G \to Y$. Recall also that two irreducible sofic shifts X and Y are finitely equivalent if and only if they have the same entropy (Theorem 5.2). From Theorem 7.2, it follows that any finite equivalence between sofic shifts can be replaced by another one of the following form, familiar in automata theory: there is a graph G with two labelings L_X and L_Y such that (G, L_X) presents X, (G, L_Y) presents Y, and both labeled graphs are nonambiguous (such a structure is called a *transducer*; transducers are the objects in automata theory which transform one language to another). In this way, a finite equivalence may be viewed as an "input-state-output" system (i.e., X_G represents the state sequences, X represents the input sequences and Y represents the output sequences). The proof of Theorem 5.2 actually shows that whenever there is a finite equivalence between irreducible sofic shifts it can be taken to be a transducer where one of the labelings is right resolving (deterministic) and the other is left resolving ("co-deterministic") [38].

The book [7] treats some aspects of the interaction between symbolic dynamics and automata theory in detail. See also [6], [30], [40], [41].

8. Symbolic dynamics and system theory

Traditionally, system theory has been concerned with input/output systems and notions of control. Such a system is usually specified as a difference equation or differential equation with input, state and output variables. Major issues have centered around *controllability* (for any given pair of states, there is a finite sequence of inputs that drive the system from one state to the other) and *observability* (the state of the system can be deduced by observing a finite sequence of outputs) [11], [25].

More recently, Willems [47] has developed a theory of systems in which the emphasis is on the evolutionary behavior of the combined system of variables. He defines a *dynamical system* or simply *system* as a triple $(T, W, \mathcal{B})$ where T is a time axis, W is an alphabet, and the behavior $\mathcal{B} \subseteq W^T$ is a set of sequences with index set T and alphabet W (this is Definition I-1 in the Dictionary). For instance, when $T = \mathcal{Z}^+$, the behavior $\mathcal{B}$ is a set of right-infinite sequences, and when $T = \mathcal{Z}$, the behavior $\mathcal{B}$ is a set of bi-infinite sequences.

In system theory, usually $T = \mathcal{Z}$ (discrete-time), or $T = \mathcal{R}$ (continuous-time), while W and $\mathcal{B}$ are arbitrary. In linear system theory, W is usually a finite dimensional vector space and $\mathcal{B}$ is a subspace of W^T.

Hereafter, we assume $T = \mathcal{Z}$ and that all systems are *time-invariant*, i.e., the shift map preserves the behavior $\mathcal{B}$.

Symbolic dynamics fits into this perspective: namely, a shift space is a time-invariant system in Willems' sense where $T = \mathcal{Z}$, W is finite, and $\mathcal{B}$ is closed. Observe how the symbolic dynamics approach, described in Section 2, transforms an invertible dynamical system (X, f), in the classical sense, to a dynamical system in Willems' sense: given a partition P of X, set the time axis to be $T = \mathcal{Z}$, the alphabet to be $W = P$ and the behavior $\mathcal{B}$ to be the set of sequences Σ, obtained by coding points of X relative to P.

In Willems' theory, a *state realization* or simply *realization* $(\mathcal{Z}, W, X, \mathcal{B}_s)$ is a system $(\mathcal{Z}, W \times X, \mathcal{B}_s)$ such that whenever $(w, x), (w', x') \in \mathcal{B}_s$ and $x_0 = x'_0$, then $(w, x)|_{(-\infty,0)}(w, x)|_{[0,\infty)} \in \mathcal{B}_s$. The *external behavior* of a state realization is the system $(\mathcal{Z}, W, \mathcal{B})$ where $\mathcal{B} = \{w : (w, x) \in \mathcal{B}_s \text{ for some } x\}$. The state realization may be regarded as a presentation of its external behavior, with the elements of X as states. A state realization of a system is closely related to a presentation of a sofic shift; in fact, any labeled graph may be regarded as a state realization.

A realization of an external behavior is *minimal* if (roughly speaking) no other realization of the same external behavior can be obtained by "merging" states [47]. Willems characterized the time-invariant systems with unique minimal realization, using the notion of futures $F(x|_{(-\infty,0)})$ that we described in Section 4. We state this in Theorem 8.1 below. The *past induced canonical realization* of a time-invariant system $(\mathcal{Z}, W, \mathcal{B})$ is the state realization $\Sigma_p = (\mathcal{Z}, W, X, \mathcal{B}_p)$ where

$$\mathcal{B}_p = \{(w, x) \in W^{\mathcal{Z}} \times X^{\mathcal{Z}} : x_i = F(w|_{(-\infty,i]})\}.$$

Likewise there is the notion of *future induced canonical realization*.

THEOREM 8.1 (Willems [47], and references therein). *A time-invariant system has a unique minimal realization if and only if its future induced and past induced canonical realizations are equivalent in the sense that there is a bijection from states of one realization to states of the other that transforms one realization to the other. The unique minimal realization is the past induced canonical realization.*

Note how similar this result is to the characterization of irreducible sofic shifts with unique $\mathcal{I}$-minimal presentation (Theorem 4.2 $(1 \Leftrightarrow 2)$).

The Dictionary gives many concepts in system theory which are closely related to concepts in symbolic dynamics. For instance, an *input-state-output system* is defined to be a state realization $(\mathcal{Z}, U \times Y, X, \mathcal{B})$ subject to certain natural restrictions (see Definition VI-1 in the Dictionary). Here, U, Y, and X play the role of input, output and state. Such systems are closely related to finite equivalences in symbolic dynamics and transducers in automata theory (as discussed in Section 7). Also, the notions of observability (Definitions II-3 and II-4) are very similar to the idea of shift of finite type, and the notions of controllability (Definitions II-7 and II-8) are very similar to the idea of irreducibility for sofic shifts; see the remarks in the Dictionary.

9. Conclusion

We have given an introduction to symbolic dynamics and brought out common themes and interconnections with coding theory, automata theory and system theory. We have seen the notion of minimal representation of systems in symbolic dynamics (Theorems 4.1, 4.2 and 4.3), coding theory (Theorems 6.1 (part 1), 6.2 (part 1)) automata theory (Theorem 7.1) and system theory (Theorem 8.1). And we have seen how the notion of transformation of systems is viewed in symbolic dynamics (sliding block code, finite equivalence), coding theory (encoder), automata theory (transducer) and in system theory (input-state-output system).

References

[1] R.L. Adler, Geodesic flows, interval maps and symbolic dynamics, published in Ergodic theory, symbolic dynamics and hyperbolic spaces, Oxford U. Press, 1991, 93-124.

[2] R.L. Adler, D. Coppersmith and M. Hassner, Algorithms for sliding block codes — an application of symbolic dynamics to information theory, IEEE Trans. Inform. Theory, 29 (1983), 5–22

[3] R. Adler and B. Marcus, Topological entropy and equivalence of dynamical systems, Memoirs AMS, 219 (1979)

[4] R. Adler and B. Weiss, Similarity of automorphisms of the torus, Memoirs AMS, 98 (1970).

[5] J. J. Ashley, Resolving factor maps for shifts of finite type with equal entropy, Ergodic Theory and Dynamical Systems, 11 (1991), 219–240.

[6] J. Ashley, B. Marcus, D. Perrin, S. Tuncel, Surjective extensions of sliding-block codes, SIAM J. Discrete Math. 6 (1993) 582-611.

[7] M.-P. Béal, Codage Symbolique, Masson, Paris, 1993.

[8] M. Boyle, Lower entropy factors of sofic systems, Ergodic Theory and Dynamical Systems, 4 (1984), 541–557.

[9] M. Boyle, B. Kitchens and B. H. Marcus, A note on minimal covers for sofic systems, Proceedings AMS, 95 (1985), 403–411.

[10] M. Boyle, B. Marcus and P. Trow, Resolving maps and the dimension group for shifts of finite type, Memoirs AMS, 377 (1987).

[11] R. Brockett, Finite dimensional linear systems, Wiley, 1970.

[12] A.R. Calderbank, A. R. Hammons, P. V. Kumar, N. J. Sloane, P. Sole, A linear construction of certain Kerdok and Preparata codes, Bulletin AMS, 29 (1993), 218-222.

[13] E. Coven and M. Paul, Finite procedures for Sofic systems, Monats. Math., 83 (1977), 265–278.

[14] R. Devaney, An Introduction to Chaotic Dynamical Systems, Addison-Wesley, 1987.

[15] R. Fischer, Graphs and symbolic dynamics Colloq. Math. Soc. János Bólyai, Topics in Information Theory 16 (1975) 229–243

[16] R. Fischer, Sofic systems and graphs, Monats. fur Math., 80 (1975), 179–186.

[17] G. D. Forney, Jr., Convolutional Codes I: Algebraic structure, IEEE Transactions on Information Theory. 16 (1970) 720–738.

[18] G. D. Forney, Jr., Algebraic structure of convolutional codes, and algebraic system theory, published in Mathematical System Theory, A. C. Antoulas, ed., Spring-Verlag, (1991), 527–558.

[19] G. D. Forney, Jr., Geometrically uniform codes, IEEE Transactions on Information Theory, IT-37, 1991, 1241-1260.

[20] G. D. Forney, Jr. and M. D. Trott, "The dynamics of linear codes over groups: state spaces, trellis diagrams and canonical encoders," IEEE Transactions on Information Theory, 39 (1993), 1491–1513.

[21] G. A. Hedlund, Endomorphisms and automorphisms of the shift dynamical system, Math Systems Theory, 3 (1969), 320–375.

[22] J. E. Hopcroft and J. D. Ullman, Introduction to Automata Theory, Languages, and Computation, Addison-Wesley, Reading, Massachusetts, 1979.

[23] N. Jonoska, Sofic shifts with synchronizing presentations, Theoretical Computer Science, to appear.

[24] N. Jonoska and B. Marcus, Minimal presentations of sofic shifts, IEEE-Information Theory, IT-40, 1994, 1818–1827.

[25] T. Kailath, Linear Systems, Prentice-Hall, 1980.

[26] B. Kitchens, Expansive dynamics on zero-dimensional groups, Ergodic Theory and Dynamical Systems, 7 (1987), 249–261.

[27] B. Kitchens, B. Marcus and P. Trow, Eventual factor maps and compositions of closing maps, Ergodic Theory and Dynamical Systems, 11 (1991), 85–113.

[28] W. Krieger, On the subsystems of topological Markov chains, Ergodic Theory and Dynamical Systems, 2 (1982), 195–202.

[29] S. Lin and D. Costello, Error Control Coding: Fundamentals and Applications, Prentice-Hall, 1983.

[30] D. Lind and B. Marcus, An Introduction to symbolic dynamics and coding, Cambridge University Press, 1995.

[31] H.-A. Loeliger, G. D. Forney, Jr., T. Mittelholzer, and M. D. Trott, "Minimality and observability of group systems," Journal of Linear Algebra and its Applications, 205–206 (1994), 937–963.

108   BRIAN MARCUS

[32] H. A. Loeliger and T. Mittelholzer, Convolutional codes over groups, preprint, 1992.
[33] B. H. Marcus, R.M. Roth, and P. H. Siegel, "Constrained systems and coding for recording channels," to appear as book chapter in Handbook for Coding Theory, ed. R. Brualdi, C. Huffman, and V. Pless, Elsevier Press.
[34] B. H. Marcus, P. H. Siegel and J. K. Wolf, "Finite-state modulation codes for data storage," IEEE Journal on Selected Areas in Communications, 10 (1992), 5–37.
[35] G. Miles and R. K. Thomas, The breakdown of automorphisms of compact topological groups, Studies in Probability and Ergodic Theory, Advances in Mathematics Supplementary Studies, Academic Press, New York-London 2 (1978), 207–218.
[36] M. Morse and G. A. Hedlund, Symbolic Dynamics, American Journal of Math, 60 (1938), 815–866.
[37] M. Nasu, Topological conjugacy for sofic systems, Ergodic Theory and Dynamical Systems, 6 (1986), 265–280.
[38] W. Parry, A finitary classification of topological Markov chains and sofic systems, Bull. Lond. Math. Soc., 9 (1977), 86–92.
[39] W. Parry and R. F. Williams, Block coding and a zeta function for Markov chains, Proc. Lon. Math. Soc., 35 (1977), 483–495.
[40] D. Perrin and M-P Schutzenberger, Synchronizing prefix codes and automata and the road coloring problem, published in Symbolic Dynamics and its Applications, Contemporary Mathematics, ed. P. Walters, 135 (1992), 295–318.
[41] D. Perrin, Arbes et series rationnelles, C.R. Acad. Sci. Paris 309, Serie 1 (1989), 713–716.
[42] E. Rossin, N. T. Sindhushayana, and C. Heegard, "Trellis group codes for the Gaussian channel, to appear, IEEE-Information Theory.
[43] N. T. Sindhushayana, Symbolic dynamic techniques for trellis group codes, PhD Thesis, Cornell University, 1994.
[44] N. T. Sindhushayana, B. Marcus and M. Trott, "Homogeneous shifts," preprint, 1995.
[45] P. Trow and S. Williams, Core dimension group constraints for factors of sofic shifts, Ergodic Theory and Dynamical Systems, 13 (1993), 213–224
[46] M. D. Trott, The Algebraic Structure of Trellis Codes, Ph.D. thesis, Stanford University, 1992.
[47] J. C. Willems, Models for Dynamics, Dynamics Reported, 2 (1989), 171–269.
[48] R. F. Williams, Classification of subshifts of finite type, Annals of Math. 98 (1973), 120-153; Errata, Annals of Math. 99 (1974), 380-381.

IBM K53-802, 650 HARRY ROAD, SAN JOSE, CA 95120
E-mail address: marcus@almaden.ibm.com

Proceedings of Symposia in Applied Mathematics
Volume **50**, 1995

Multilingual Dictionary: System Theory, Coding Theory, Symbolic Dynamics, and Automata Theory

Dave Forney, Brian Marcus, N.T. Sindhushayana, and Mitchell Trott

Introduction

System theory, coding theory, symbolic dynamics and automata theory are subjects which have a lot in common, but have developed somewhat independently. So, it is not surprising that very similar concepts with very different terminology have arisen in these subjects. This dictionary is an attempt to bring together the various terms for these concepts.

We have divided the material into several sections. Within each section, the items are displayed in an $n \times 4$ table; each row represents a concept, and the columns represent the four subjects of this dictionary. Following the table, you will find, for each concept, a definition together with (sometimes) a brief discussion. The definition is usually given in terms of system theory, but occasionally in the more natural mother tongue. As with natural languages, often something is lost in the translation; in the discussion, we try to explain how the terms for each concept differ (if they do) as well as to indicate some relations among the different concepts. Most of the terms in this dictionary are fairly well established, but some were made up to meet the needs of the dictionary.

There is an *Index of Terms*, in alphabetical order, at the end of the Dictionary.

For the purposes of this dictionary, system theory is interpreted to mean the behavioral theory of systems. Coding theory is taken to mean coding theory and information theory. And within symbolic dynamics, we have included terminology from the field of constrained coding (which has adopted some terms from the theory of state machines popular in the '50's and '60's).

While we have not made any specific references in this paper, we drew heavily from the papers listed in the bibliography of the article by B. Marcus in this volume.

We are happy to thank Natasha Jonoska, Andi Loeliger, Jan Willems and Susan Williams for their helpful comments on the Dictionary. We thank Yvonne Marcus for help with the index, useful remarks and various wisecracks.

An earlier version of this dictionary was presented at the IEEE-IT Workshop on Coding, System Theory and Symbolic Dynamics, held in Mansfield, MA., October

1991 *Mathematics Subject Classification.* Primary 58F03, 68Q68, 93B15.

18-20, 1993. We thank the National Science Foundation and National Security Agency for their support of that workshop.

Before we begin, we would like to present one instance where the same term has been used for different concepts in two of the subjects:

code (kōd) *n.* 1. [Coding Th.] A set of sequences. 2. [Symbolic Dyn.] A rule for mapping one set of sequences to another set of sequences.

Actually, the usage in symbolic dynamics corresponds to an old usage in coding theory; "Morse code" refers not just to a set of signal sequences, but also a rule for mapping text into signal sequences. In modern coding theory, a mapping rule is called an "encoder."

TABLE OF CONTENTS

KEY:

ST = System theory (behavioral)

CT = Coding theory

SD = Symbolic dynamics (including constrained coding)

AT = Automata theory

I. Basic concepts of system

Sect.	System Theory	Coding Theory	Symbolic Dynamics	Automata Theory
I-1	Dynamical system	Code	—	Language
I-2	Complete	—	Closed (compact)	—
I-3	Completion	—	Closure	—
I-4	Time-invariant	Time-invariant	Shift-invariant	—
I-5	Trim	—	—	—
I-6	Finite alphabet, discrete time, complete, time-invariant system	—	Shift space (subshift)	—

I-1.
ST. Dynamical system (system)
CT. Code
SD. —-
AT. Language

DEFINITION. A *dynamical system* (or *system*) is a triple $(T, W, \mathcal{B})$ where T is a *time axis*, W is a *signal alphabet* (or simply *alphabet*), and the *behavior* $\mathcal{B} \subseteq W^T$ is a set of sequences with index set T and alphabet W.

For instance, when $T = \mathcal{Z}$, the set of integers, the behavior $\mathcal{B}$ is a set of bi-infinite sequences.

In system theory, usually $T = \mathcal{Z}$ (discrete time), or $T = \mathcal{R}$, the set of real numbers (continuous time), while W and $\mathcal{B}$ are arbitrary. In linear system theory, W is usually a finite dimensional real vector space and $\mathcal{B}$ is a subspace of W^T.

In coding theory, usually $T = \mathcal{Z}$ (corresponding to convolutional codes, defined in VII-1) or T is a finite subinterval of $\mathcal{Z}$ (corresponding to block codes). A *code* is a set of sequences defined on one of these time axes T. Usually, W is finite, or at least discrete, and has some algebraic structure such as vector space, module or group structure. Then $\mathcal{B}$ is usually an algebraic sub-object (subspace, submodule, subgroup) of W^T.

In symbolic dynamics, usually $T = \mathcal{Z}$ and W is finite. The behavior $\mathcal{B}$ must satisfy some additional conditions (see I-6 below). But there has been significant work done for time axes $T = \mathcal{Z}^+, \mathcal{R}, \mathcal{Z}^n$ and for infinite alphabets as well.

In automata theory, $T = \mathcal{Z}$, W is finite, and the behavior is defined by a *language* $\mathcal{L}$, which is a set of finite sequences (of arbitrary lengths) over a finite alphabet A; more precisely, given a language $\mathcal{L}$, introduce a symbol e, not in A, and define $\mathcal{B}$ to be the set of all bi-infinite sequences over $W = A \cup \{e\}$ of the form

$$\ldots eeeweee \ldots, \ w \in \mathcal{L},$$

where the 'time 0' coordinate can appear anywhere. In automata theory, the focus is on the language $\mathcal{L}$, not the behavior $\mathcal{B}$. There has also been significant work done in automata theory on infinite sequences.

Useful Notation: For a subset $J \subseteq T$ and $x \in W^T$, $x|_J$ denotes the sequence x restricted to the indices in J. In particular, when $T = \mathcal{Z}$ and $i \leq j$, $x|_{[i,j]}$, called a *block* or *word*, denotes the restriction of the sequence x to the indices $k : i \leq k \leq j$. For $J \subseteq T$, we have the *projection*

$$\mathcal{B}|_J = \{x|_J : x \in \mathcal{B}\}.$$

Whenever the alphabet W of a system $(T, W, \mathcal{B})$ is decomposed as a direct product $W = W_1 \times W_2$, we denote

$$P_{W_1}\mathcal{B} = \{w_1 : (w_1, w_2) \in \mathcal{B} \text{ for some } w_2\}.$$

and similarly for $P_{W_2}\mathcal{B}$.

I-2.
ST. Complete
CT. —
SD. Closed or Compact
AT. —

DEFINITION. A system is *complete* if

$$x \in \mathcal{B} \text{ iff for all finite } J \subset T, \ x|_J \in \mathcal{B}|_J.$$

Suppose that $T = \mathcal{Z}$, W is finite and we endow W^T with any metric d such that $d(x, y)$ is 'small' iff for 'large' n, $x|_{[-n,n]} = y|_{[-n,n]}$; for instance, let ρ be any metric on W, and define

$$d(x, y) = \sum_{k=-\infty}^{\infty} \frac{\rho(x_k, y_k)}{2^{|k|}}.$$

Then complete = closed = compact (as subsets of the metric space W^T).

I-3.
ST. Completion
CT. —
SD. Closure
AT. —

DEFINITION. The *completion* $(T, W, \bar{\mathcal{B}})$ of a system $(T, W, \mathcal{B})$ is the smallest complete system that contains the system.

Equivalently, $(T, W, \bar{\mathcal{B}})$ is the set of all $x \in W^T$ such that for all finite $J \subset T$ $x|_J \in \mathcal{B}|_J$.

I-4.
ST. Time-invariant
CT. Time-invariant
SD. Shift-invariant
AT. —

DEFINITION. Suppose that T has some notion of addition (e.g., $T = \mathcal{Z}, \mathcal{Z}^+, \mathcal{R}, \mathcal{Z}^n, \mathcal{R}^n$). Define the shift map $\sigma_i : W^T \to W^T$ by $(\sigma_i(x))_k = x_{i+k}$, $k, i \in T$. A system is *time-invariant* if $\forall i \ \sigma_i(\mathcal{B}) = \mathcal{B}$.

Some prefer inclusion rather than equality in the definition of time-invariance.

Observe that for a time-invariant system, $\forall k \in T$, $J \subset T$, we have $\mathcal{B}|_{k+J} = \mathcal{B}|_J$. Note that when $T = \mathcal{Z}$ a system is time-invariant iff $\sigma_1(\mathcal{B}) = \mathcal{B}$.

In coding theory, the delay operator $D = \sigma^{-1}$. In symbolic dynamics, σ_1 is denoted simply σ.

I-5.
ST. Trim
CT. —
SD. —
AT. —

DEFINITION. A system $(T, W, \mathcal{B})$ is *trim* if each element of W appears in some element of $\mathcal{B}$.

I-6.
ST. Finite-alphabet, complete, time-invariant system, with $T = \mathcal{Z}$
CT. —
SD. Shift space
AT. —

DEFINITION. A *shift space* is a finite-alphabet, complete, time-invariant system with $T = \mathcal{Z}$.

Note on classical dynamical systems: The notion of dynamical system that we have given here differs from the classical notion. A classical (discrete-time) dynamical system is a pair (X, f) where X is a set and $f : X \to X$ is an invertible mapping; usually, X has some structure and f respects that structure. Given a partition P of X, we get a time-invariant system in the sense of this dictionary by setting $T = \mathcal{Z}$, $W = P$ and $\mathcal{B}_P$ to be the subset of $P^{\mathcal{Z}}$ which describes the orbits of f – i.e., $\mathcal{B}_P$ is the set of all sequences $\dots p_{-1} p_0 p_1 \dots$ for which there is an $x \in X$ such that $f^i(x) \in p_i$. Symbolic dynamics models classical systems (X, f) using finite partitions P, by replacing (X, f) with a shift space $\mathcal{B}$ that is roughly (but not exactly) the completion of $\mathcal{B}_P$. Noninvertible f are also considered (giving rise to systems with $T = \mathcal{Z}^+$).

For ease of exposition, we hereafter make the following

STANDING ASSUMPTIONS:

1. Discrete time ($T = \mathcal{Z}$)

2. Time-Invariance

3. Trim

This leaves out some very important cases: continuous-time systems in system theory, block codes in coding theory, and multidimensional systems. However, many of the concepts in the dictionary can be extended to these settings.

II. Concepts of memory

Sect.	System Theory	Coding Theory	Symbolic Dynamics	Automata Theory
II-1	L-complete system	—	L-step Shift of Finite Type (L-step SFT)	—
II-2	Strongly complete system	—	Shift of Finite Type (SFT)	—
II-3	L-observable system	—	—	—
II-4	Strongly observable system	—	—	—
II-5	Memoryless system	—	—	—
II-6	Free system	Sequence space	Fullshift	—
II-7	Controllable system	—	Irreducible (Topologically transitive) shift space	—
II-8	Strongly controllable system	Finite-constraint length code	Mixing shift space	—

II-1.
ST. L-complete system
CT. —
SD. L-step Shift of Finite Type (abbr., L-step SFT)
AT. —

DEFINITION. A system is *L-complete* if

$$x \in \mathcal{B} \text{ iff } \forall i \in T \ x|_{[i,i+L]} \in \mathcal{B}|_{[0,L]}.$$

In other words, if a sequence looks like an element of $\mathcal{B}$ through all windows of length $L+1$, then it is in fact in $\mathcal{B}$.

The term 'L-step SFT' usually assumes finite alphabet.

FACT. L-complete $\Rightarrow$ complete.

Note that completeness is invariant under reordering of the time axis; L-completeness is not.

II-2.
ST. Strongly complete
CT. —
SD. Shift of finite type (abbr., SFT) or Finite memory system
AT. —

DEFINITION. A system is *strongly complete* if it is L-complete for some L.

The term 'SFT' usually assumes finite alphabet. The term 'finite memory system' is used in constrained coding.

II-3.
ST. L-observable system
CT. —-
SD. —-
AT. —-

DEFINITION. A system is *L-observable* if whenever

$$x, y \in \mathcal{B} \text{ and } x|_{[0,L)} = y|_{[0,L)}$$

then

$$x|_{(-\infty,0)} y|_{[0,\infty)} \in \mathcal{B}.$$

FACT. L-observable + complete = L-complete.
An L-observable system is sometimes called L-finite memory.

II-4.
ST. Strongly observable system
CT. —-
SD. —-
AT. —-

DEFINITION. A system is *strongly observable* if it is L-observable for some L. The least such L is called the *observability index* or *observer memory* of the system.

FACT. Strongly observable + complete = Strongly complete. So, a shift of finite type is the same as a strongly observable shift space.

II-5.
ST. Memoryless system
CT. —-
SD. —-
AT. —-

DEFINITION. A system is *memoryless* if it is 0-observable.

II-6.
ST. Free system
CT. Sequence space
SD. Full shift
AT. —-

DEFINITION. A system is *free* if it is 0-complete.

The term 'Full shift' usually assumes finite alphabet.

FACT. Free = Memoryless + Complete

FACT. A free system is the Cartesian product W^T.

EXAMPLE 1. Let W be a group with identity element e. Let $W_f^{\mathcal{Z}}$ be the system which consists of all sequences $x \in W^{\mathcal{Z}}$ such that $x_n = e$ for all sufficiently large $|n|$ (the subscript 'f' stands for 'finite' indicating that $W_f^{\mathcal{Z}}$ really represents the set of all finite sequences over the alphabet W). Observe that W_f^T is memoryless, but unless W is the trivial group it is not complete and therefore not free.

II-7.
ST. Controllable system
CT. —-
SD. Irreducible shift space or Topologically transitive shift space
AT. —-

DEFINITION. A system is *controllable* if $\forall x, y \in \mathcal{B}$, $\exists M \in \mathcal{Z}^+, z \in \mathcal{B}$ such that $z|_{(-\infty,0]} = x|_{(-\infty,0]}$ and $z|_{[M,\infty)} = y|_{[0,\infty)}$.[1]

In symbolic dynamics, a shift space X is *irreducible* if whenever u, v are blocks that appear in elements of X, then there is a block w such that uwv appears in some element of X. This agrees with controllability for the special (but distinguished) class of sofic shifts defined in III-6 below.

II-8.
ST. Strongly controllable system
CT. Finite-constraint length code
SD. Mixing shift space
AT. —-

DEFINITION. A system is *strongly controllable* if $\exists M \in \mathcal{Z}^+$ satisfying: $\forall x, y \in \mathcal{B}$, $\exists z \in \mathcal{B}$ such that $z|_{(-\infty,0]} = x|_{(-\infty,0]}$ and $z|_{[M,\infty)} = y|_{[0,\infty)}$. The least such M is called the *controllability index* or *controller memory*.

FACT. 0-controllable = 0-observable = memoryless
The term 'mixing' assumes shift space and agrees with strong controllability for sofic shifts, defined in III-6 below.

---

[1]This definition does not appear to generalize in a straightforward way to the time-varying case.

III. Concepts of State Representation

Sect.	System Theory	Coding Theory	Symbolic Dynamics	Automata Theory
III-1	State space system	Realization	—	—
III-2	External behavior	Code generated by a realization	—	—
III-3	State behavior	State code generated by a realization	—	—
III-4	Evolution law	Trellis section	Labeled graph (Finite state transition diagram)	automaton
III-5	State space system of an evolution law	Trellis	—	—
III-6	External behavior of an evolution law	Code generated by a trellis	Sofic shift (sofic system) (constrained system)	Regular language
III-7	—	—	Graph shift (Edge sequence shift)	—
III-8	Finite state, complete, state behavior	—	Topological Markov shift (State sequence shift)	—

III-1.
ST. State space system
CT. Realization
SD. —-
AT. —-

DEFINITION. A *state space system* $(T, W, X, \mathcal{B}_s)$ is a system $(T, W \times X, \mathcal{B}_s)$ that satisfies the *Axiom of State* – i.e., whenever

$$(w, x), (w', x') \in \mathcal{B}_s \text{ and } x_0 = x'_0,$$

then

$$(w, x)|_{(-\infty, 0)} (w', x')|_{[0, \infty)} \in \mathcal{B}_s.$$

III-2.
ST. External behavior
CT. Code generated by a realization
SD. —-
AT. —-

DEFINITION. The *external behavior* of a state space system $(T, W, X, \mathcal{B}_s)$ is the system $(T, W, P_W \mathcal{B}_s)$.

III-3.
ST. State behavior
CT. State code generated by a realization
SD. —
AT. —

DEFINITION. The *state behavior* of a state space system $(T, W, X, \mathcal{B}_s)$ is the system $(T, X, P_X \mathcal{B}_s)$.

III-4.
ST. Evolution law
CT. Trellis section
SD. Labeled graph or Finite-state transition diagram (FSTD)
AT. Finite automaton

DEFINITION. An *evolution law* is a quadruple (T, W, X, ∂) where T is a time axis, W is an alphabet, X is a set called the *state space*, and $\partial \subseteq X \times W \times X$, called the *next state relation*.

In linear system theory, the alphabet, state space and next state relation are usually finite-dimensional vector spaces. In coding theory, symbolic dynamics and automata theory, they are usually finite sets.

A *trellis section* is essentially the same as an evolution law, but the emphasis is on finite state spaces. The states are sometimes called nodes. Elements of the next state relation are sometimes called branches.

A *labeled graph* is a finite-alphabet, finite-state evolution law (although, strictly speaking, a labeled graph may have multiple copies of the same (x, w, x')). In symbolic dynamics, a labeled graph is usually defined as a pair $(G, \mathcal{L})$. Here, G is a *graph* ('finite directed graph' in graph theory) and $\mathcal{L}$ is a *labeling*; that is, $G = (\mathcal{V}, \mathcal{E}, s, t)$ consists of a finite set $\mathcal{V}$ of vertices (states), a finite set $\mathcal{E}$ of edges, initial state, terminal state functions $s, t : \mathcal{E} \to \mathcal{V}$, and $\mathcal{L}$ is a function on $\mathcal{E}$; the next state relation is then $\{(s(e), \mathcal{L}(e), t(e)) : e \in \mathcal{E}\}$. One usually makes the harmless assumption that each state has at least one outgoing edge and one incoming edge (roughly corresponding to the 'trim' concept). A *path* or *edge sequence* in a graph is a sequence (finite, bi-infinite, or semi-infinite) of edges e_i such that $t(e_i) = s(e_{i+1})$. A *state sequence* is the sequence of states of a path.

Finite-state transition diagram (FSTD) is the term used in constrained coding.

A *finite automaton* is a labeled graph, usually endowed with a specific subset of states called the *initial states* and a specific subset of states called the *terminal states*. However, the properties in section IV of finite automata are properties of the underlying labeled graph and do not involve the specific initial state and terminal states.

III-5.
ST. State space system of an evolution law
CT. Trellis or Trellis diagram
SD. —
AT. —

DEFINITION. The *state space system* $(T, W, X, \mathcal{B}_s)$ *of an evolution law* (T, W, X, ∂) is defined by

$$\mathcal{B}_s = \{(w, x) \in W^T \times X^T : (x_k, w_k, x_{k+1}) \in \partial \text{ for each } k \in T\}.$$

The term *trellis* usually assumes finite-state.

III-6.
ST. External behavior of an evolution law
CT. Code generated by a trellis
SD. Sofic shift or sofic system or constrained system
AT. Regular language

DEFINITION. The *external behavior of an evolution law* is the external behavior of the state space system of the evolution law.

A *sofic shift* is the external behavior of a finite-alphabet, finite-state evolution law – equivalently, the set of label sequences of bi-infinite paths in a labeled graph. A sofic shift is automatically a shift space. 'Sofic' is a Hebrew word meaning finite. The terms 'sofic shift,' 'sofic system,' and 'constrained system' (a term from constrained coding) are synonyms except that 'constrained system' is often taken to mean the set of label sequences of <u>finite</u> paths in a labeled graph.

A *regular language* is the language consisting of all label sequences of finite paths in a finite automaton that begin with an initial state of the automaton and end with a terminal state of the automaton.

The set of finite sequences that occur in a sofic shift is a special kind of regular language: it is closed under subwords and prolongable in the sense that for every word w that occurs there are symbols a and b such that awb also occurs.

FACT. The state space system of an evolution law is complete (and conversely).

FACT. The external behavior of an evolution law need not be complete, but the external behavior of a finite-state evolution law is always complete (see also VII-3 and VII-8).

III-7.
ST. —
CT. —
SD. Graph shift or Edge sequence shift
AT. —

(Recall the notions of graph and labeled graph from III-4).

DEFINITION. A *graph shift* is the set of all bi-infinite paths of a graph – in other words, a sofic shift presented by a labeled graph in which all the edges are labeled distinctly.

III-8.
ST. Finite-state, complete state behavior
CT. —
SD. Topological Markov shift or State sequence shift
AT. —

DEFINITION. A *topological Markov shift* is the set of all bi-infinite <u>state</u> sequences of a graph – equivalently, a finite-state complete state behavior.

FACT. Every graph shift is a topological Markov shift, every topological Markov shift is an SFT, every SFT is a sofic shift, and every sofic shift is a shift space; these inclusions are all proper.

IV. Properties of state representation (state realization)

Sect.	System Theory	Coding Theory	Symbolic Dynamics	Automata Theory
IV-1	Point controllable state behavior	—	Irreducible graph	—
IV-2	Strongly point controllable state behavior	—	Primitive graph	—
IV-3	Deterministic evolution law	Instantaneously invertible trellis	Right resolving labeled graph	Deterministic finite automaton
IV-4	—	Trellis that is invertible with delay	Right closing (Lossless of finite order) labeled graph	—
IV-5	—	—	Lossless labeled graph	Non-ambiguous finite automaton
IV-6	Externally induced (observable) state space system	Invertible realization	Conjugacy-inducing labeled graph	Local finite automaton
IV-7	Past-induced state space system	—	Right resolving, conjugacy inducing labeled graph	Local DFA
(cont'd)	(cont'd)	(cont'd)	(cont'd)	(cont'd)
IV-8	Past-induced canonical realization	—	Right Krieger cover (Future cover) (Shannon cover)	Minimal DFA
IV-9	—	—	Right Fischer cover	
IV-10	—	Tom cover	—	—

IV-1.
ST. Point controllable state behavior
CT. —

SD. Irreducible graph
AT. —-

DEFINITION. A state behavior $(T, X, \mathcal{B}_x)$ is *point controllable* if for each $u, u' \in X$, there is an $x \in \mathcal{B}_x$ and $M \geq 0$ such that $x_0 = u$ and $x_M = u'$.

A graph G is *irreducible* if, for each pair of states I, I' in G, there is a path in G from I to I'.

FACT. A topological Markov shift, viewed as a state behavior, is point controllable iff its underlying graph is irreducible.

IV-2.
ST. Strongly point controllable state behavior
CT. —-
SD. Primitive graph
AT. —-

DEFINITION. A state behavior $(T, X, \mathcal{B}_x)$ is *strongly point controllable* if $\exists M$ such that $\forall u, u' \in X$, there is an $x \in \mathcal{B}_x$ such that $x_0 = u$ and $x_M = u'$.

A graph G is *primitive* if there is a positive integer M such that for each pair of states I, I', there is a path in G from I to I' of length M.

A topological Markov shift, viewed as a state behavior, is strongly point controllable iff its underlying graph is primitive.

In symbolic dynamics, primitive graphs are sometimes called *aperiodic* since a graph is primitive iff it is irreducible and the gcd of its cycle lengths is 1.

FACT. A sofic shift is irreducible (resp., mixing) iff it can be presented by an irreducible (resp., primitive) graph.

IV-3.
ST. Deterministic evolution law
CT. Instantaneously invertible trellis
SD. Right resolving labeled graph
AT. Deterministic finite automaton (DFA)

DEFINITION. An evolution law is *deterministic* if the initial state and label determine the terminal state – in other words, whenever $(x, w, x'), (x, w, x'') \in \partial$, then $x' = x''$.

The term 'unifilar' is used for a similar way of presenting functions of Markov chains (in source coding theory).

A *deterministic finite automaton* is a finite automaton with a single initial state and whose labeling is deterministic i.e., at each state, distinct outgoing edges have distinct labels.

IV-4.
ST. —-
CT. Trellis that is invertible with delay
SD. LFO labeled graph or Right closing labeled graph
AT. —-

DEFINITION. A labeled graph is *lossless of finite order* (LFO) if $\exists D$ (the 'delay') such that whenever two paths of length $D + 1$ present the same sequence and have the same initial state, then they have the same initial edge.

Equivalently, an LFO labeled graph is a finite-alphabet finite-state evolution law such that $\exists D$ satisfying: whenever

$$(x_0, w_0, x_1)(x_1, w_1, x_2), \ldots, (x_{D-1}, w_{D-1}, x_D) \in \partial,$$

$$(x_0', w_0, x_1'), (x_1', w_1, x_2'), \ldots, (x_{D-1}', w_{D-1}, x_D') \in \partial,$$

and

$$x_0 = x_0',$$

then

$$x_1 = x_1'.$$

This is a notion of 'determinism with delay.' 'LFO' is a term adopted by constrained coding, while 'right closing' is the term usually used in symbolic dynamics (see also V-7).

IV-5.
ST. —
CT. —
SD. Lossless labeled graph or Labeled graph with no diamonds
AT. Non-ambiguous finite automaton

DEFINITION. A labeled graph is *lossless* if whenever two paths present the same label sequence and have the same initial and terminal states, then the paths coincide.

Equivalently, a lossless labeled graph is a finite-alphabet finite-state evolution law such that whenever

$$(x_0, w_0, x_1), (x_1, w_1, x_2), \ldots, (x_{n-1}, w_{n-1}, x_n) \in \partial,$$

$$(x_0', w_0, x_1'), (x_1', w_1, x_2'), \ldots, (x_{n-1}', w_{n-1}, x_n') \in \partial$$

and

$$x_0 = x_0', x_n = x_n',$$

then

$$x_i = x_i'$$

for $i = 0, \ldots, n$.

In a labeled graph, a *diamond* is a pair of paths with the same initial state, terminal state and label sequence – hence, a lossless labeled graph is the same as a labeled graph with no diamonds. The term 'lossless' has been adopted by constrained coding, while the phrase 'no diamonds' is usually used in symbolic dynamics.

FACT. If a labeled graph is lossless, then each bi-infinite sequence is the label sequence of only finitely many bi-infinite paths. The converse is true provided that the underlying graph is irreducible.

FACT. Deterministic $\Rightarrow$ Lossless of Finite Order $\Rightarrow$ Lossless

IV-6.
ST. Externally Induced state space system or Observable state space system
CT. Invertible realization
SD. Conjugacy-inducing labeled graph
AT. Local finite automaton

DEFINITION. A state space system $(T, W, X, \mathcal{B}_s)$ is *externally induced* if the external behavior determines the state sequence – in other words, whenever $(w, x), (w, x') \in \mathcal{B}_s$, then $x_0 = x_0'$ (equivalently, $x = x'$ because of time invariance).

See V-9 for more on the term 'conjugacy.'

FACT. When the state space system is induced by a finite-state evolution law, (as in much of coding theory, symbolic dynamics and automata theory), 'externally induced' is equivalent to the condition that for some n, knowledge of $w|_{[-n,n]}$ is sufficient to determine the state x_0 at time 0.

FACT. A shift space is an SFT iff it can be presented by a conjugacy-inducing labeled graph.

IV-7.
ST. Past-Induced state space system
CT. —-
SD. Right resolving conjugacy-inducing labeled graph
AT. Local DFA

DEFINITION. A state space system $(T, W, X, \mathcal{B}_s)$ is *past-induced* if whenever $(w, x), (w', x') \in \mathcal{B}_s$ and $w|_{(-\infty,0]} = w'|_{(-\infty,0]}$, then $x_0 = x_0'$.

Similarly, there is the notion of Future-induced state system $\approx$ Left resolving conjugacy-inducing labeled graph $\approx$ Co-deterministic local automaton

IV-8.
ST. Past-Induced canonical realization
CT. —-
SD. Right Krieger cover or Future cover or Shannon cover
AT. Minimal DFA

DEFINITION. For a system $(T, W, \mathcal{B})$ and $w \in \mathcal{B}$, the *follower set* of w is defined

$$\mathcal{F}(w) = \mathcal{F}(w|_{(-\infty,0]}) = \{u \in \mathcal{B}|_{(0,\infty)} : w|_{(-\infty,0]}u|_{(0,\infty)} \in \mathcal{B}\}$$

Say that $w, w' \in \mathcal{B}$ are *past equivalent* if $\mathcal{F}(w) = \mathcal{F}(w')$. Let X denote the set of equivalence classes $[w]$ of this equivalence relation. The *Past-Induced Canonical Realization* of $(T, W, \mathcal{B})$ is the state space system $\Sigma_s^{\approx} = (T, W, X, \mathcal{B}_s)$ where

$$\mathcal{B}_s = \{(w, x) \in W^T \times X^T : x_i = [\sigma_i(w)]\}.$$

In symbolic dynamics, for a sofic shift, the completion of the past-induced canonical realization is called the *Right Krieger cover* (sometimes, called the *future cover*). The *Shannon cover* is the same as the Right Krieger cover except that it is usually defined by follower sets of blocks rather than follower sets of left semi-infinite sequences.

The *minimal DFA* of a regular language $\mathcal{L}$ is the smallest (in terms of number of states) deterministic finite automaton that presents $\mathcal{L}$.

FACT. The minimal DFA of a regular language is unique. When the regular language comes from a sofic shift, the right Krieger cover coincides with a particular subgraph of the minimal DFA.

FACT. When $(T, W, \mathcal{B})$ is an SFT, then $\Sigma_{\tilde{s}}^{\simeq}$ is automatically complete and is therefore the Right Krieger cover.

Similarly, there is the notion of Future-Induced Canonical Realization $\approx$ Left Krieger Cover.

IV-9.
ST. —
CT. —
SD. Right Fischer cover
AT. —

DEFINITION. For an irreducible sofic shift S, the *right Fischer cover* is the minimal (in terms of number of states) right resolving labeled graph which presents S.

FACT. The right Fischer cover is unique, and it is a particular subgraph of the right Krieger cover.

The uniqueness of the right Fischer cover is closely related to the uniqueness of the minimal DFA. But neither result implies the other.

IV-10.
ST. —
CT. Tom cover
SD. —
AT. —

DEFINITION. An information theorist at Stanford.

V. Concepts of input/output

Sect.	System Theory	Coding Theory	Symbolic Dynamics	Automata Theory
V-1	Input/Output system	—	—	—
V-2	I/O system with output observable from input .	—	—	—
V-3	Non-anticipating I/O system	Encoder	—	—
V-4	—	Feedbackfree encoder	Sliding block code (Continuous, shift-commuting map)	—
V-5	—	Causal encoder	—	—
V-6	—	—	Right resolving sliding block code	—
V-7	—	—	Right closing sliding block code	—
	(cont'd)	(cont'd)	(cont'd)	(cont'd)
V-8	—	—	Finite-to-one sliding block code	—
V-9	—,	—	(Topological) Conjugacy	—

V-1.
ST. Input/output system
CT. —
SD. —
AT. —

DEFINITION. An *input/output system* $(T, U, Y, \mathcal{B})$ is a system $(T, U \times Y, \mathcal{B})$, with corresponding *input system* $(T, U, P_U \mathcal{B})$ and corresponding *output system* $(T, Y, P_Y \mathcal{B})$ satisfying the following:

1. The input system is memoryless
and

2. The input sequence and the past of the output sequence determine the future of the output sequence; more precisely, whenever $(u, y), (u, y') \in \mathcal{B}$ and $y|_{(-\infty, 0]} = y'|_{(-\infty, 0]}$, then $y = y'$.

V-2.
ST. Input/output system with output observable from input
CT. —
SD. —
AT. —

DEFINITION. An input/output system $(T, U, Y, \mathcal{B})$ has *output observable from input* if for each $u \in P_U \mathcal{B}$, there is a unique y such that $(u, y) \in \mathcal{B}$.

V-3.
ST. Non-anticipating input/output system
CT. Encoder
SD. —
AT. —

DEFINITION. A *non-anticipating input/output system* is an input/output system $(T, U, Y, \mathcal{B})$ such that whenever $(u, y) \in \mathcal{B}$, $u' \in P_U \mathcal{B}$, and $u'|_{(-\infty, 0]} = u|_{(-\infty, 0]}$, there is a (unique) y' such that $(u', y') \in \mathcal{B}$ and $y'|_{(-\infty, 0]} = y|_{(-\infty, 0]}$.

V-4.
ST. —
CT. Feedbackfree encoder
SD. Sliding block code or Continuous, shift-commuting map
AT. —

DEFINITION. Let X and Y be shift spaces (recall that a shift space is a finite-alphabet complete time-invariant system). A *sliding block code* $\phi : X \to Y$ is a map which can be expressed as follows: there are integers m, a (*memory, anticipation*) and a map Φ from $(m + a + 1)$-blocks of X to 1-blocks of Y such that $\phi(x)_i = \Phi(x|_{[i-m, i+a]})$. We write $\phi = \Phi_\infty$.

In coding theory, the term 'feedbackfree encoder' is used instead of the term 'sliding block code.'

FACT. A map from one shift space to another is a sliding block code iff it is continuous and commutes with the shift map σ.

Note that for a labeled graph $(G, \mathcal{L})$, the map $\mathcal{L}_\infty$ from bi-infinite paths in G to bi-infinite label sequences is a sliding block code with $m = a = 0$.

V-5.
ST. —
CT. Causal encoder
SD. —
AT. —

DEFINITION. A feedbackfree encoder is *causal* if the anticipation $a = 0$.

Of course, any feedbackfree encoder can be shifted so that it becomes causal. But usually feedbackfree encoders are assumed to be causal anyway.

V-6.
ST. —
CT. —
SD. Right resolving sliding block code
AT. —

DEFINITION. A sliding block code $\phi : X \to Y$ is *right resolving* if $m = a = 0$ and $\Phi(x_0 x_1) = \Phi(x_0 x_1')$ implies $x_1 = x_1'$.

V-7.
ST. —
CT. —
SD. Right closing sliding block code
AT. —

DEFINITION. A sliding block code $\phi : X \to Y$ is *right closing* if whenever $x, x' \in X$, $x|_{(-\infty,0]} = x'|_{(-\infty,0]}$, and $\phi(x) = \phi(x')$, then $x = x'$.

V-8.
ST. —
CT. —
SD. Finite-to-one sliding block code
AT. —

DEFINITION. A sliding block code is *finite-to-one* if each point in the image has only finitely many preimages.

The terms right resolving, right closing, and finite-to-one for sliding block codes correspond to the terms right resolving, right closing, and lossless for irreducible labeled graphs (i.e., a labeled graph $(G, \mathcal{L})$ is right resolving (resp., right closing, lossless) iff the sliding block code $\mathcal{L}_\infty$ is right resolving (resp., right closing, finite-to-one).

FACT. For a sliding block code, $\phi : X \to Y$, the behavior $\{(x, \phi(x)) : x \in X\}$ defines an input/output system with output observable from input iff
(1) The domain of ϕ is a full shift
and
(2) ϕ is right closing.

V-9.
ST. —
CT. —
SD. Conjugacy or Topological conjugacy
AT. —

DEFINITION. A *conjugacy* is a sliding block code which is 1-1 and onto.

FACT. Up to conjugacy, the concepts Shift of finite type, Graph shift, and Topological Markov shift all coincide.
We also have the related notions:

DEFINITION. A *factor map* or *factoring* is a sliding block code which is onto.

DEFINITION. An *imbedding* is a sliding block code which is 1-1.

FACT. A sliding block code is an imbedding iff $\exists n$ such that $\phi(x)|_{[-n,n]} = \phi(x')|_{[-n,n]} \Rightarrow x_0 = x_0'$.

Note on minimal realizations: A realization of a system $(T, W, \mathcal{B})$ is a state space system $(T, W, X, \mathcal{B}_s)$ whose external behavior is $\mathcal{B}$. A realization $(T, W, X, \mathcal{B}_s)$ of $\mathcal{B}$ is *minimal* if no other realization of $\mathcal{B}$ can be obtained by 'collapsing' $\mathcal{B}_s$ (via merging states in a way that can be made precise). Now, it is a fact that a system has a unique minimal realization iff its past-induced and future-induced canonical realizations coincide.

There is the following analogous result in symbolic dynamics. For an irreducible sofic shift Y, an irreducible SFT presentation is an SFT X and a factor map $\phi : X \rightarrow Y$. An irreducible SFT presentation of Y is minimal if no other irreducible SFT presentation of Y can be obtained by 'collapsing' ϕ (via sliding block codes in a way that can be made precise). It is a fact that an irreducible sofic shift has a unique minimal irreducible SFT presentation iff its Right and Left Fischer covers coincide. Such a sofic shift is called 'almost of finite type.'

VI. Concepts of input/output machine

Sect.	System Theory	Coding Theory	Symbolic Dynamics	Automata Theory
VI-1	Input/State/ Output system	State space encoder	—	—
VI-2	I/S/O evolution law	Encoder trellis section	Finite-state code (encoder)	Transducer
VI-3	—	Encoder with finite-memory decoder	Sliding block decodable finite-state code	—
VI-4	—	Noncatastrophic encoder	Noncatastrophic finite-state code	—

VI-1.
ST. Input/State/Output system (abbr., I/S/O system)
CT. State space encoder
SD. —
AT. —

DEFINITION. An *Input/State/Output System* is a state space system $(T, U \times Y, X, \mathcal{B})$ (with corresponding *input system* $(T, U, P_U \mathcal{B})$ and corresponding *output system* $(T, Y, P_Y \mathcal{B})$) such that

(1) the input system is memoryless
and

(2) the current state, together with the future of the input sequence, determine the future state sequence and future output sequence; more precisely, whenever $a \in P_X \mathcal{B}|_0$ and $b|_{[0,\infty)} \in P_U \mathcal{B}|_{[0,\infty)}$, there is a unique $(u, y, x)|_{[0,\infty)} \in \mathcal{B}|_{[0,\infty)}$ such that $x_0 = a$ and $u|_{[0,\infty)} = b|_{[0,\infty)}$.

This is equivalent to the condition that both systems $(T, U, Y \times X, \mathcal{B})$ and $(T, U, X, P_{U \times X} \mathcal{B})$ are nonanticipating input/output systems.

VI-2.
ST. Input/State/Output (I/S/O) evolution law
CT. Encoder trellis section
SD. Finite-state code or Finite-state encoder
AT. Transducer

DEFINITION. An *Input/State/Output Evolution Law* is an evolution law $(T, U \times Y, X, \partial)$ for which there are functions $f : X \times U \to X$ (the 'next state function') and $g : X \times U \to Y$ (the 'output function') such that $(x, (u, y), x') \in \partial$ iff

$$(1) \qquad x' = f(x, u)$$

and

$$(2) \qquad y = g(x, u)$$

The corresponding *input evolution law* to an I/S/O evolution law is (T, U, X, ∂_U) with next state relation $(x, u, x') \in \partial_U$ iff $\exists y$ such that $(x, (u, y), x') \in \partial$. The corresponding *output evolution law* (T, Y, X, ∂_Y) is the evolution law with next state relation $(x, y, x') \in \partial_Y$ iff $\exists u$ such that relation $(x, (u, y), x') \in \partial$.

An *encoder trellis section* is the same as an I/S/O evolution law except that the state space is usually finite. An encoder trellis section can be viewed as a labeled graph where the label of an edge $(x, (u, y), x')$ is (u, y); the corresponding input (resp. output) evolution law may be regarded as an *input labeling* $\mathcal{I}(x, (u, y), x') = u$ (resp., an *output labeling* $\mathcal{O}(x, (u, y), x') = y$); according to (1) and (2) above, the input labeling is deterministic, and so given an initial state the future input sequence determines the future output sequence, symbol-by-symbol.

The term *finite-state code* (a term from constrained coding) is used to mean an encoder trellis section for which the output labeling is right closing. So, given an initial state, the input sequence can be recovered from the output sequence, with finite delay. Sometimes, the term *finite-state encoder* is used instead.

The term *transducer* is usually used to mean a labeled graph whose labels are pairs of symbols, sometimes with additional conditions imposed on the labelings.

FACT. An I/S/O system is complete iff it is represented by an I/S/O evolution law.

VI-3.
ST. —-
CT. Encoder with finite-memory decoder
SD. Sliding-block-decodable finite-state code
AT. —-

DEFINITION. A finite-state code is *sliding block decodable* if the input can be recovered from the output via a sliding block code; more precisely, there is a sliding block code $\phi : Y^\infty \to U^\infty$ such that $\phi \circ \mathcal{O}_\infty = \mathcal{I}_\infty$ (recall that $\mathcal{I}_\infty, \mathcal{O}_\infty$ are the sliding block codes generated by the input, output labelings $\mathcal{I}, \mathcal{O}$).

VI-4.
ST. —-
CT. Noncatastrophic encoder
SD. Noncatastrophic finite-state code
AT. —-

DEFINITION. A finite-state code is *noncatastrophic* if for any pair of output sequences that differ in finitely many places, any corresponding pair of input sequences must also differ in finitely many places; more precisely, whenever z, z' are bi-infinite paths in the underlying graph of the finite-state code and $\mathcal{O}_\infty(z)$ differs from $\mathcal{O}_\infty(z')$ in only finitely many places, then $\mathcal{I}_\infty(z)$ differs from $\mathcal{I}_\infty(z')$ in only finitely many places.

When the underlying graph is primitive, this definition agrees with the usual definition in coding theory. Otherwise, a slight modification is needed.

FACT. Sliding-block decodability $\Rightarrow$ noncatastrophic, but the converse is false.

VII. Concepts of linearity

Sect.	System Theory	Coding Theory	Symbolic Dynamics	Automata Theory
VII-1	Linear System	Convolutional code	Linear shift space	—
VII-2	Linear state-space system	Linear realization	—	—
VII-3	Linear evolution law	Linear trellis section	—	—
VII-4	Linear I/S/O system	Convolutional encoder	Linear finite-state code	—
VII-5	—	Polynomial convolutional encoder	Linear sliding block code	—
VII-6	Group system	Group code	Group shift	—
VII-7	Group state-space system	Group realization	—	—
VII-8	Group evolution law	Group trellis section	—	—
VII-9	—	Orbit code, Geometrically uniform code,	Homogeneous shift	—

VII-1.
ST. Linear system
CT. Convolutional code
SD. Linear shift space
AT. —-

DEFINITION. A *linear system* is a linear subspace of $V^{\mathcal{Z}}$, where V is a vector space over a field F.

The term 'linear system' usually assumes F is the field of real numbers or the field of complex numbers.

The term *convolutional code* usually assumes F is a finite field.

Of course, the term *linear shift space* assumes 'shift space.'

VII-2.
ST. Linear state space system
CT. Linear realization
SD. —-
AT. —-

DEFINITION. A *linear state space system* $(T, W, X, \mathcal{B}_s)$ is a state space system in which W and X are vector spaces and the behavior $\mathcal{B}_s$ is a linear subspace of $W^T \times X^T$.

VII-3.
ST. Linear evolution law
CT. Linear trellis section
SD. —-
AT. —-

DEFINITION. A *linear evolution law* is an evolution law in which the next state relation is a linear subspace.

FACT. The external behavior of a linear evolution law with finite-dimensional state space is always complete.

VII-4.
ST. Linear input/state/output system
CT. Convolutional encoder
SD. Linear finite-state code
AT. —-

DEFINITION. An I/S/O system $(T, U \times Y, X, \mathcal{B})$ is *linear* if U, Y and X are vector spaces and $\mathcal{B}$ is a linear subspace of $(U \times Y \times X)^T$.

When U, Y, and X are vector spaces over a finite field, a linear I/S/O system is called a *convolutional encoder*. Often, this refers to the induced mapping which maps input to output.

FACT. For a finite-state convolutional encoder, Sliding block decodability $\Leftrightarrow$ Non-catastrophic.

VII-5.
ST. —-

CT. Polynomial convolutional encoder
SD. Linear sliding-block code
AT. —

DEFINITION. Let F be a field, and k, n be positive integers. A *polynomial convolutional encoder* is a causal linear sliding block encoder from the full F^k-shift to the full F^n-shift (viewing the domain and range as vector spaces over F).

FACT. A shift space is the image of a linear sliding-block code iff it is a linear subspace and irreducible.

VII-6.
ST. Group system
CT. Group code
SD. Group shift
AT. —

DEFINITION. Let $\mathcal{A}$ be a group. Then $\mathcal{A}^{\mathcal{Z}}$ is a group with respect to the coordinatewise group structure. A *group code* (over $\mathcal{A}$) is a subgroup of $\mathcal{A}^{\mathcal{Z}}$. A group code which is also a shift space is called a *group shift*.

FACT. Every irreducible group shift is conjugate to a full shift.

VII-7.
ST. Group state space system
CT. Group realization
SD. —
AT. —

DEFINITION. A *group state space system* $(T, W, X, \mathcal{B}_s)$ is a state space system in which W and X are groups and the behavior $\mathcal{B}_s$ is a subgroup of $W^T \times X^T$.

VII-8.
ST. Group evolution law
CT. Group trellis section
SD. —
AT. —

DEFINITION. A *group evolution law* is an evolution law in which the next state relation is a subgroup.

FACT. The external behavior of a group evolution law whose state space satisfies the Descending Chain Condition is always complete.

VII-9.
ST. —
CT. Orbit code
SD. —
AT. —

DEFINITION. Let $\mathcal{A}$ be a group acting on a set S, and let $s \in S$. An *orbit code* is a code of the form

$$Y \equiv \{\ldots x_{-1}(s) x_0(s) x_1(s) \ldots : x = \ldots x_{-1} x_0 x_1 \ldots \in C\}$$

where C is a group code over $\mathcal{A}$.

When S is a metric space and $\mathcal{A}$ is a group of isometries, an orbit code is called a *geometrically uniform code*.

A *homogeneous shift* is a shift space on which a group shift acts (coordinatewise) transitively.

FACT. Any mixing homogeneous shift is an orbit code.

Note on convolutional codes: the core meaning of "convolutional" is "linear time-invariant," even though this meaning does not directly convey the notion of convolution. The alphabet is usually finite with algebraic structure: e.g., a finite field or a finite-dimensional vector space over a finite field. Coding theory has not traditionally been concerned with completeness; often a convolutional code is defined as the output of a linear time-invariant encoder where the input ranges over all semi-infinite input sequences (formal Laurent series), and such a code is not complete. More recent work has focused on polynomial encoders in which case inputs can range over all bi-infinite sequences, and the code is complete.

VIII. Other graph concepts

Sect.	System Theory	Coding Theory	Symbolic Dynamics	Automata Theory
VIII-1	—	—	Adjacency matrix	—
VIII-2	—	Parallel transitions	Multiple edges	—
VIII-3	—	—	Higher edge graph	—
VIII-4	—	Trellis section of length N	Higher power graph	—
VIII-5	—	Shift register graph	Higher edge graph of 1-state graph	DeBruijn graph

Recall the definitions of graph and labeled graph from III-4.

VIII-1.
ST. —
CT. —
SD. Adjacency matrix
AT. —

DEFINITION. The *adjacency matrix* of a graph G is the square matrix A, indexed by the vertices of G, and defined by:

$$A_{IJ} \equiv \text{number of edges from } I \text{ to } J.$$

Concepts of irreducibility and primitivity of graphs are usually expressed in terms of adjacency matrices.

VIII-2.
ST. —-
CT. Parallel transitions
SD. Multiple edges
AT. —-

DEFINITION. A set of *parallel transitions* is a set of edges with the same initial and terminal state.

VIII-3.
ST. —-
CT. —
SD. Higher edge graph
AT. —-

DEFINITION. The *N-th Higher edge graph* of a graph G is the graph $G^{[N]}$ with vertices consisting of all paths of length $N-1$ in G and a single edge from $e_1 \ldots e_{N-1}$ to $f_1 \ldots f_{N-1}$ iff $e_2 \ldots e_{N-1} = f_1 \ldots f_{N-2}$.

VIII-4.
ST. —-
CT. Trellis section of length N
SD. Higher power graph
AT. —-

DEFINITION. The *N-th Higher power graph* of a graph G is the graph G^N with the same vertices as G, and an edge from I to J for each path of length N in G from I to J.

VIII-5.
ST. —-
CT. Shift register graph
SD. Higher edge graph of 1-state graph
AT. DeBruijn graph

DEFINITION. Higher edge graph of a 1-state graph

FACT. The underlying graph of a group code which is also a graph shift is a product of DeBruijn graphs.

IX. Entropy

IX-1.
ST. —-
CT. —-
SD. Entropy or Capacity
AT. —-

DEFINITION. The *entropy* of a shift space X (viewed as a system $(\mathcal{Z}, W, \mathcal{B})$) is

$$h(X) = \lim_{n \to \infty} \frac{\log(\#\mathcal{B}|_{[0,n)})}{n}.$$

Shannon effectively considered sofic shifts and called them discrete noiseless channels; he used the term *capacity* instead of entropy, since he reserved the latter for random processes. The constrained coding and magnetic recording communities have adopted the term capacity. But *entropy*, short for topological entropy, was adopted by symbolic dynamics.

Entropy (capacity) governs the maximal rate at which you can invertibly encode sequences from a full shift into sequences of a sofic shift.

Index of Terms

MOTOROLA, 20 CABOT BOULEVARD, MANSFIELD, MA 02048
E-mail address: Luse27@email.mot.com

IBM K53-802, 650 HARRY RD., SAN JOSE, CA 95120
E-mail address: marcus@almaden.ibm.com

QUALCOMM INC., 6455 LUSK BLVD., SAN DIEGO, CA, 92121
E-mail address: nsindhushayana@qualcomm.com

DEPARTMENT OF ELECTRICAL ENGINEERING, MIT 35-213, CAMBRIDGE, MA, 02139
E-mail address: trott@lids.mit.edu

Proceedings of Symposia in Applied Mathematics
Volume **50**, 1995

Algebraic Geometric Codes

Henning Stichtenoth

ABSTRACT. In the seventies, the Russian mathematician Valeri D. Goppa found a surprising link between coding theory and algebraic geometry. Namely, he used algebraic curves to construct codes over a finite field. These codes are now called *algebraic geometric* codes (AG codes) or *geometric Goppa* codes. A few years later, in 1982, M. A. Tsfasman, S. G. Vladut and T. Zink [**21**] showed that there exist sequences of linear codes over $\mathbb{F}_q$ of increasing length, which are asymptotically better than the Gilbert-Varshamov bound (for q a square, $q \geq 49$). Their proof is based on Goppa's construction and deep results from algebraic geometry. This result motivated many mathematicians to study coding theory. And in the reverse direction, engineers began to learn algebraic geometry. There are several excellent survey articles on algebraic geometric codes which can serve as an introduction to this fascinating subject; see [**7**], [**8**], [**10**], [**12**], [**13**], [**15**] and [**22**]. A more comprehensive treatment can be found in the monographs [**6**], [**16**], [**19**] and [**20**].

In this paper, we discuss in some detail a simple but typical example of an algebraic geometric code. This code (known in the literature as the Hermitian code) can be described in an elementary way. We will explain some of the basic results of the theory of algebraic geometric codes (their definition, their parameters, their decoding) by means of this example. The general theory is a straightforward generalization of our example.

There are two (essentially equivalent) approaches to algebraic geometric codes. The first of them uses algebraic geometry. The second one is more elementary; it uses the theory of algebraic function fields. In Sec. 6, we provide a brief survey of algebraic geometric codes based on function fields. The basic facts from the theory of algebraic function fields are summarized in Sec. 5. Finally, we discuss in Sec. 7 the above-mentioned result of Tsfasman, Vladut and Zink, together with a recent simplification of the proof due to Garcia and Stichtenoth.

1. Preliminaries and Notation

We use the standard terminology of coding theory, cf. [**11**], [**14**]. $\mathbb{F}_q$ is the finite field with q elements. Given two vectors $u = (u_1, \ldots, u_n)$ and $v = (v_1, \ldots, v_n)$ in $\mathbb{F}_q^n$, their *distance* is defined as $d(u, v) = |\{i \mid u_i \neq v_i\}|$. The *weight* of u is given by $wt(u) = d(u, 0)$, the number of nonzero components of u.

1991 *Mathematics Subject Classification.* Primary 94B27; Secondary 12E20.

A *code of length* n over $\mathbb{F}_q$ is a linear subspace $C \subseteq \mathbb{F}_q^n$ (we consider only linear codes). The elements of C are called *codewords*. If $C \neq \{0\}$, the *minimum distance* $d(C)$ is defined as

$$d(C) = \min\{wt(c) \mid c \in C, c \neq 0\} = \min\{d(a,b) \mid a, b \in C, a \neq b\}.$$

The *dimension* of C is denoted by $\dim C$. The numbers n = length of C, $k = \dim C$ and $d = d(C)$ are the *parameters* of C, and we will refer to C as an $[n, k, d]$-code. Applications call for codes where both parameters k and d are large (with respect to n). However, there are some restrictions. The simplest one is the *Singleton bound*

$$(1) \qquad\qquad\qquad k + d \leq n + 1,$$

which can easily be proved as follows: Consider the space

$$U = \{u = (u_1, \dots, u_n) \in \mathbb{F}_q^n \mid u_i = 0 \ \text{ for all } \ i \geq d\}.$$

Clearly $\dim U = d - 1$, and any $u \in U \setminus \{0\}$ has weight $wt(u) \leq d - 1$. Hence $U \cap C = \{0\}$, and it follows that $\dim U + \dim C \leq n$. This gives the desired inequality $d - 1 + k \leq n$.

There are other, more restrictive bounds for the parameters of a code, for instance the Griesmer bound, the Plotkin bound, the Elias bound and the Linear Programming bound due to McEliece, Rodemich, Rumsey and Welch (see [11], [14]). These bounds involve also the size of the underlying field $\mathbb{F}_q$.

The *inner product* of two vectors $u = (u_1, \dots, u_n)$ and $v = (v_1, \dots, v_n)$ in $\mathbb{F}_q^n$ is given by

$$< u, v > = \sum_{i=1}^{n} u_i v_i \ .$$

The vectors u and v are said to be *orthogonal* if $< u, v > = 0$. Given a code $C \subseteq \mathbb{F}_q^n$, the *dual code* $C^\perp$ consists of all vectors which are orthogonal to C. The dimension of $C^\perp$ is $\dim C^\perp = n - \dim C$.

An $[n, k, d]$-code C can correct up to $(d - 1)/2$ errors. This means that for any $a \in \mathbb{F}_q^n$, there is at most one codeword $c \in C$ such that $d(a, c) \leq (d - 1)/2$. However, the code is useless if one does not have a method of finding this closest codeword (for a given vector $a \in \mathbb{F}_q^n$) that can be implemented in practice. Thus, the construction of good *decoding algorithms* is important.

2. Reed-Solomon Codes

This class of codes is well-known in coding theory. Reed-Solomon codes have good parameters, and one knows very efficient decoding algorithms for these codes (for instance, the Berlekamp decoder or the Euclidian algorithm, cf. [14]). Reed-Solomon codes can be defined as follows: Let $\alpha_1, \dots, \alpha_n$ be n distinct elements of $\mathbb{F}_q$. For $r \in \mathbb{N}$ consider the vector space

$$L_r = \{f(z) \in \mathbb{F}_q[z] \mid \deg f \leq r\}.$$

Define the *evaluation map* $ev : L_r \to \mathbb{F}_q^n$ by

$$ev(f) = (f(\alpha_1), \dots, f(\alpha_n)).$$

This is a linear map, and it is injective for $r < n$. The image

$$C = \{ev(f) \mid f \in L_r\} \quad , \text{ for } r < n,$$

is called a *Reed-Solomon* code. Obviously, the dimension of C is $\dim C = r + 1$. What about the minimum distance? Let $c = ev(f)$ be a codeword for which the weight equals the minimum distance $d = d(C)$. Then $f(\alpha_i) = 0$ for $n - d$ elements $\alpha_i \in \{\alpha_1, \ldots, \alpha_n\}$, so $n - d \leq \deg f \leq r$. It follows that $d \geq n - r$. This inequality is in fact an equality because there exist nonzero polynomials of degree r having r distinct zeros. Thus C has parameters

$$[n, r + 1, n - r].$$

This shows that the Singleton bound (1) is attained; i.e., Reed-Solomon codes are *optimal* in this sense. However, these codes have a drawback: their length n is restricted to be less than or equal to q, the size of the field $\mathbb{F}_q$.

The above construction can be generalized, by using polynomials in several variables. A polynomial $f(x_1, \ldots, x_m) \in \mathbb{F}_q[x_1, \ldots, x_m]$ can be evaluated at all points $P = (\gamma_1, \ldots, \gamma_m)$ of the affine m-space $\mathbb{A}_m = \mathbb{F}_q^m$, thus defining a vector $(f(P))_{P \in \mathbb{A}_m} \in \mathbb{F}_q^N$, with $N = q^m$. However, the minimum distance of such a code will in general be fairly small, compared with the length and the dimension of the code. The main idea in Goppa's construction is to evaluate f only at the points of a certain curve in $\mathbb{A}_m$. This gives in many cases codes with excellent parameters. We shall introduce these codes by means of an example, in the next section.

3. Construction of Hermitian Codes

For simplicity we discuss a particular case where the size of the field is $q = 16$. We consider the *Hermitian* curve; this is the plane curve defined by

$$\mathcal{C} = \{P = (\alpha, \beta) \in \mathbb{A}_2 \mid \beta^4 + \beta = \alpha^5\};$$

i.e., $\mathcal{C}$ is the set of zeros of the irreducible polynomial $\varphi(x, y) = y^4 + y + x^5$. For $\alpha \in \mathbb{F}_{16}$, the element α^5 lies in the subfield $\mathbb{F}_4 \subseteq \mathbb{F}_{16}$ (it is the *norm* of α with respect to the extension $\mathbb{F}_{16}/\mathbb{F}_4$). Since the *trace map* $\beta \mapsto \beta + \beta^4$ is a surjective $\mathbb{F}_4$-linear map from $\mathbb{F}_{16}$ to $\mathbb{F}_4$ we see that, given $\alpha \in \mathbb{F}_{16}$, there are 4 elements $\beta \in \mathbb{F}_{16}$ such that $\beta^4 + \beta = \alpha^5$. Hence the curve $\mathcal{C}$ has $16 \cdot 4 = 64$ points.

A polynomial $f(x, y)$ in two variables will be considered as a function $f : \mathcal{C} \to \mathbb{F}_{16}$. Thus the functions y^4 and $y + x^5$ are identical. For $r \geq 0$, let $\mathcal{L}_r$ be the space of functions on $\mathcal{C}$ spanned by the elements

(2) $x^i \cdot y^j \quad , \text{ with } 4i + 5j \leq r.$

The factors 4 and 5 come from the equation $\varphi(x,y) = y^4 + y + x^5 = 0$ which defines $\mathcal{C}$. For instance, the space $\mathcal{L}_{27}$ is spanned by the following functions:

$$1, \quad x, \quad x^2, \quad x^3, \quad x^4, \quad x^5, \quad x^6,$$
$$y, \quad xy, \quad x^2y, \quad x^3y, \quad x^4y, \quad x^5y,$$
$$y^2, \quad xy^2, \quad x^2y^2, \quad x^3y^2, \quad x^4y^2,$$
$$y^3, \quad xy^3, \quad x^2y^3, \quad x^3y^3,$$
$$y^4, \quad xy^4,$$
$$y^5.$$

The functions in the last two rows are linearly dependent on the preceding entries, because $y^4 = y + x^5$, $xy^4 = xy + x^6$ and $y^5 = y(y + x^5) = y^2 + x^5y$. Hence the dimension of $\mathcal{L}_{27}$ is at most 22, and any $f \in \mathcal{L}_{27}$ can be written as

(3) $f(x,y) = f_6(x) + f_5(x) \cdot y + f_4(x) \cdot y^2 + f_3(x) \cdot y^3,$

with $\deg f_i(x) \le i$.

Next we define an evaluation map $ev : \mathcal{L}_r \to \mathbb{F}_{16}^n$, with $n = |\mathcal{C}| = 64$, by

$$ev(f) = (f(P))_{P \in \mathcal{C}}.$$

This gives us a code

(4) $C_r = \{ev(f) \mid f \in \mathcal{L}_r\}$

of length $n = 64$ over $\mathbb{F}_{16}$. This code C_r is called a *Hermitian* code. The similarity with the definition of Reed-Solomon codes is obvious.

In order to compute the dimension and the minimum distance of Hermitian codes, we shall use Bezout's theorem, cf. [4]. Let us briefly recall this result: There is given a field K and two non-zero polynomials $f_1(X,Y)$, $f_2(X,Y) \in K[X,Y]$. Let $\mathcal{X}_i = \{P = (a,b) \in K \times K \mid f_i(a,b) = 0\}$ denote the corresponding (affine) curves $(i = 1, 2)$. Suppose that $f_1(X,Y)$ and $f_2(X,Y)$ have no common factor $g(X,Y) \in K[X,Y]$ of degree $\deg g(X,Y) > 0$. Then, the intersection $\mathcal{X}_1 \cap \mathcal{X}_2$ is finite, and

(5) $|\mathcal{X}_1 \cap \mathcal{X}_2| \le \deg f_1 \cdot \deg f_2.$

As an example, consider the polynomials

$$f_1(X,Y) = X^2 + Y^2 - 4 \quad \text{and} \quad f_2(X,Y) = XY - 1,$$

both of degree 2. In the case $K = \mathbb{R}$, the corresponding curves intersect in 4 $(= \deg f_1 \cdot \deg f_2)$ points. If $K = \mathbb{F}_{2^m}$, the intersection has only one point (namely $P = (1,1)$).

Now we would like to determine the parameters of the Hermitian code C_r in the case $r = 27$. Let $f(x,y) \in \mathcal{L}_{27}$ be given as in (3). As a polynomial in 2 variables, f has degree ≤ 6. Since $\varphi(x,y) = y^4 + y + x^5$ is irreducible, it has no factor in common with $f(x,y)$, and it follows from Bezout's theorem that f has at most $\deg f \cdot \deg \varphi \le 6 \cdot 5 = 30$ zeros on $\mathcal{C}$, unless f is the zero polynomial. From this we obtain that $\dim \mathcal{L}_{27} = 22$ and that the evaluation map $ev : \mathcal{L}_{27} \to \mathbb{F}_{16}^n$ is injective, hence $\dim C_{27} = 22$. The same argument shows that any nonzero codeword $c = ev(f) \in C_{27}$ has weight $wt(c) \ge 64 - 30 = 34$, so C_{27} is a $[64, 22, d \ge 34]$-code.

Actually the minimum distance of C_{27} is $d = 37$. One can prove (see [19], Prop. VII.4.3) that the code C_r has parameters

(6) $$[64, r - 5, 64 - r] \ , \quad \text{for } 12 \leq r \leq 52.$$

The dual code of a Hermitian code is also Hermitian. More precisely, we have (see [19], Prop. VII.4.2)

(7) $$C_r^{\perp} = C_{74-r} \ , \quad \text{for all } r \geq 0.$$

4. Decoding Hermitian Codes

We will continue to discuss the Hermitian code $C = C_{27}$. Its minimum distance is $d = 37$, so one can correct up to $(d - 1)/2 = 18$ errors. The following decoding scheme (due to Skorobogatov and Vladut [18], following ideas of Justesen et al. [9]) decodes up to 15 errors.

Fix an ordering $P_1, \ldots, P_n$ of the points of $\mathcal{C}$ (i.e., $n = 64$). For $b = (b_1, \ldots, b_n) \in \mathbb{F}_{16}^n$ and a function $h : \mathcal{C} \to \mathbb{F}_{16}$ we define the *syndrome*

$$[b, h] = \sum_{\nu=1}^{n} b_{\nu} \cdot h(P_{\nu}).$$

As the dual of C is the code C_{47}, by (7), we have that

(8) $$[b, h] = 0 \ \text{ for all } \ b \in C \ \text{ and } \ h \in \mathcal{L}_{47}.$$

Decoding the code C means that given a vector $a \in \mathbb{F}_{16}^n$ (the *received message*) which differs from some codeword $c \in C$ (the *true message*) in at most 15 coordinates, we have to determine c. We write

$$a = c + e,$$

where the *error vector* e is assumed to have weight $wt(e) \leq 15$. Let

$$e = (e_1, \ldots, e_n) \ \text{ and } \ I = \{\nu \mid 1 \leq \nu \leq n \ \text{ and } \ e_{\nu} \neq 0\}.$$

I is the set of *error locations*, and $|I| = wt(e) \leq 15$, by assumption.

The decoding algorithm consists of 2 steps. The first is to find the error locations using an *error-locator function*. This is a function $f : \mathcal{C} \to \mathbb{F}_{16}$ such that

(9) $$f(P_{\nu}) = 0 \ \text{ for all } \ \nu \in I,$$

and which does not have too many additional zeros. In our situation, there exists an error-locator function $f \neq 0$ in $\mathcal{L}_{21}$, because $\dim \mathcal{L}_{21} = 16$, and (9) yields at most 15 linear conditions. How does one find f ? Note that for all functions $g \in \mathcal{L}_{26}$, the product $f \cdot g$ is in $\mathcal{L}_{47}$, hence (8) implies that

$$[c, f \cdot g] = 0 \ \text{ for all } \ g \in \mathcal{L}_{26}.$$

On the other hand, $[e, f \cdot g] = 0$ because $f(P_{\nu}) = 0$ whenever $e_{\nu} \neq 0$. Since $[a, f \cdot g] = [c + e, f \cdot g] = [c, f \cdot g] + [e, f \cdot g]$, we have the following conditions on f:

(10) $$[a, f \cdot g] = 0 \ \text{ for all } \ g \in \mathcal{L}_{26}.$$

After fixing bases for $\mathcal{L}_{21}$ and $\mathcal{L}_{26}$, (10) gives a system of linear equations (here: $21 = \dim \mathcal{L}_{26}$ equations in $16 = \dim \mathcal{L}_{21}$ unknowns). Any nonzero solution of this system yields an error-locator function $f \in \mathcal{L}_{21}$. Note that f has at most 21 zeros in all; therefore (9) places strong restrictions on the (yet unknown) error locations.

In the second step we calculate the error values e_ν, for $\nu \in I$. Having found an error-locator function f, put

$$N(f) = \{\nu \mid 1 \le \nu \le n \text{ and } f(P_\nu) = 0\}.$$

This set can be determined by evaluating f at all points $P \in \mathcal{C}$. Note that $N(f) \supseteq I$. From (8) we know that for all functions $h \in \mathcal{L}_{47}$,

$$[a, h] = [c + e, h] = [c, h] + [e, h] = [e, h] = \sum_{\nu \in N(f)} h(P_\nu) \cdot e_\nu.$$

When h runs through a basis $\{h_1, \ldots, h_{42}\}$ of $\mathcal{L}_{47}$, we obtain a system of linear equations

(11)
$$\sum_{\nu \in N(f)} h_j(P_\nu) \cdot X_\nu = [a, h_j], \quad \text{for } 1 \le j \le 42.$$

It turns out that the vector $(e_\nu)_{\nu \in N(f)}$ is the *unique* solution of (11).

We have thus shown that decoding a Hermitian code can be performed by solving the two systems of linear equations (10) and (11).

5. Algebraic Function Fields

For the convenience of the reader we give here some basic notations and facts from the theory of algebraic function fields, which will be used in Sec. 6. However, this is not an exhaustive exposition; details and proofs can be found in [2], Ch.I,II or in [19], Ch.I.

An extension field F of $\mathbb{F}_q$ is said to be an *algebraic function field* over $\mathbb{F}_q$ if

(i) There is an element $x \in F$ which is transcendental over $\mathbb{F}_q$ so that F is a finite extension of $\mathbb{F}_q(x)$.
(ii) All elements of F that are algebraic over $\mathbb{F}_q$ belong to $\mathbb{F}_q$.

One can always find an element $y \in F$ such that $F = \mathbb{F}_q(x, y)$. This gives us an irreducible polynomial (depending on the choice of x and y in F as above) $\varphi(X, Y) \in \mathbb{F}_q[X, Y]$ such that $\varphi(x, y) = 0$.

A *valuation ring* $\mathcal{O}$ of $F/\mathbb{F}_q$ is a proper subring $\mathbb{F}_q \subset \mathcal{O} \subset F$ having the property

$$z \in F \setminus \mathcal{O} \Rightarrow z^{-1} \in \mathcal{O}.$$

Any valuation ring $\mathcal{O}$ of $F/\mathbb{F}_q$ is a local principal ideal domain; i.e., $\mathcal{O}$ has a unique maximal ideal $P \subset \mathcal{O}$, and P is generated by some element t. We call P the *place* of $F/\mathbb{F}_q$ corresponding to $\mathcal{O}$, and a generator t of P is said to be a *prime element* for P. Any $z \in F \setminus \{0\}$ can the be written as $z = t^n \cdot u$ with $n \in \mathbb{Z}$ and a unit $u \in \mathcal{O}$ (i.e., $u \in \mathcal{O}$ and $u^{-1} \in \mathcal{O}$). The map $v_P : F \to \mathbb{Z} \cup \{\infty\}$ given by $v_P(z) := n$ (where

n is defined as above) and $v_P(0) := \infty$ is called the *valuation* of F associated with the place P. The valuation v_P determines $\mathcal{O}$ and P since

$$\mathcal{O} = \{z \in F \mid v_P(z) \geq 0\} \quad \text{and} \quad P = \{z \in F \mid v_P(z) > 0\}.$$

The *residue class field* F_P of the place P is the field $F_P := \mathcal{O}/P$. We have a canonical embedding $\mathbb{F}_q \subseteq F_P$, and one shows that the degree $[F_P : \mathbb{F}_q]$ is always finite. We define the *degree* of P by $\deg P := [F_P : \mathbb{F}_q]$. Suppose that P has degree one; then its residue class field is $F_P = \mathbb{F}_q$, and for $h \in \mathcal{O}$ (the corresponding valuation ring) we define

$$h(P) \in \mathbb{F}_q$$

to be the residue class of h in $\mathcal{O}/P = \mathbb{F}_q$.

As a simple example, we consider the *rational function field* $F = \mathbb{F}_q(x)$. For any irreducible, monic polynomial $p(x) \in \mathbb{F}_q[x]$, the set

$$\mathcal{O}_{p(x)} = \{f(x)/g(x) \in F \mid f(x), g(x) \in \mathbb{F}_q[x] \text{ and } p(x) \text{ does not divide } g(x)\}$$

is a valuation ring of F; its maximal ideal $P_{p(x)}$ contains all elements $f(x)/g(x)$ such that $p(x)$ divides $f(x)$ (but not $g(x)$). This place $P_{p(x)}$ has degree one if and only if $p(x) = x - \alpha$ for some $\alpha \in \mathbb{F}_q$. Suppose that $h(x) = f(x)/g(x) \in \mathcal{O}_{x-\alpha}$ (where $f(x), g(x) \in \mathbb{F}_q[x]$ and $x - \alpha$ does not divide $g(x)$). Then

$$h(P_{x-\alpha}) = h(\alpha) := f(\alpha)/g(\alpha) \in \mathbb{F}_q.$$

It can be shown that there is just one other place in the rational function field $\mathbb{F}_q(x)$. This is the so-called *infinite* place P_∞ (with respect to the choice of the generating element $x \in F$). Its valuation ring $\mathcal{O}_\infty$ is given by

$$\mathcal{O}_\infty = \{f(x)/g(x) \mid \deg f(x) \leq \deg g(x)\}.$$

Also, $\deg P_\infty = 1$. Summing up, we have that the rational function field $\mathbb{F}_q(x)$ has $q + 1$ places of degree one: the place P_∞ and, for any $\alpha \in \mathbb{F}_q$, the place $P_{x-\alpha}$ corresponding to the irreducible polynomial $p(x) = x - \alpha$.

We consider again an arbitrary function field $F/\mathbb{F}_q$. A place P of F is said to be a *zero* of the element $f \in F$ if $v_P(f) > 0$; it is a *pole* of F if $v_P(f) < 0$. Any non-zero element $f \in F$ has only a finite number of zeros and poles.

A *divisor* of F is a formal sum $A = \sum a_P P$, where $a_P \in \mathbb{Z}$ and $a_P = 0$ except for finitely many places P. The *degree* of A is defined by $\deg A := \sum a_P \cdot \deg P$. The *principal divisor* of a non-zero element $f \in F$ (denoted (f)) is given by

$$(f) = \sum v_P(f)P,$$

the sum being over all places P of F. One can show that principal divisors always have degree zero (roughly speaking: any $f \neq 0$ has "as many zeros as poles", provided zeros and poles are counted properly).

A divisor $A = \sum a_P P$ is said to be positive (denoted $A \geq 0$) if $a_P \geq 0$ for all places P. For a divisor A, we consider the following set:

$$\mathcal{L}(A) := \{f \in F \mid (f) + A \geq 0\} \cup \{0\}.$$

This is a finite-dimensional vector space over $\mathbb{F}_q$. *Riemann's theorem* asserts that there is a non-negative integer $g = g(F)$, depending only on the function field $F/\mathbb{F}_q$ such that, for all divisors A, we have

$$(12) \qquad \dim \mathcal{L}(A) \geq \deg A + 1 - g,$$

with equality if $\deg A$ is sufficiently large. This integer $g \geq 0$ is called the *genus* of the function field; it is the most important numerical invariant of F. For instance, $F/\mathbb{F}_q$ is the rational function field iff its genus is $g = 0$.

If $\deg A > 2g - 2$ then equality holds in (12). The *Riemann-Roch theorem* says that there exists a divisor W of $F/\mathbb{F}_q$ (called a *canonical* divisor) such that, for all divisors A, we have

$$(13) \qquad \dim \mathcal{L}(A) = \deg A + 1 - g + \dim \mathcal{L}(W - A).$$

We illustrate the above notions by two examples. First, let $F = \mathbb{F}_q(x)$ be a rational function field and $A = rP_\infty$, where P_∞ is the infinite place of $\mathbb{F}_q(x)$ and $r \geq 0$. Then,

$$\mathcal{L}(rP_\infty) = \{f(x) \in \mathbb{F}_q[x] \mid \deg f \leq r\}.$$

Next, we consider the Hermitian function field $F = \mathbb{F}_{16}(x, y)$ with $y^4 + y + x^5 = 0$. There is a unique place Q of $F/\mathbb{F}_{16}$ which is a common pole of x and y. For $r \geq 0$, the space $\mathcal{L}(rQ)$ is spanned by the elements $x^i y^j$ with

$$0 \leq i, \qquad 0 \leq j \leq 3, \qquad 4i + 5j \leq r$$

(see [19], Ch.VII.4). We see that the spaces $\mathcal{L}(A)$ generalize the spaces of functions L_r (resp. $\mathcal{L}_r$) which were used for the construction of Reed Solomon codes (resp. Hermitian codes) in Sec. 2 (resp. Sec. 3).

6. Algebraic Geometric Codes

The definition of algebraic geometric codes is along the same lines as the definition of Reed-Solomon and Hermitian codes in Sec. 2 and 3: there is given a finite set $S = \{P_1, \ldots, P_n\}$ and a space $\mathcal{L}$ of functions from S to $\mathbb{F}_q$. For $f \in \mathcal{L}$, one sets $ev(f) = (f(P_1), \ldots, f(P_n)) \in \mathbb{F}_q^n$; then the code is given by

$$C = \{ev(f) \mid f \in \mathcal{L}\}.$$

The parameters of this code are intimately related to the cardinality of S, the dimension of $\mathcal{L}$ and the number of zeros of f, for $f \in \mathcal{L}$.

Let F be a function field over $\mathbb{F}_q$. Fix a set $S = \{P_1, \ldots, P_n\}$ of places of $F/\mathbb{F}_q$ of degree one and a divisor G that does not contain any place $P_i \in S$. Then $f(P_i) \in \mathbb{F}_q$ (the residue class of f at P_i) is defined for all $f \in \mathcal{L}(G)$. The code

$$(14) \qquad C = C(G) = \{(f(P_1), \ldots, f(P_n)) \mid f \in \mathcal{L}(G)\} \subseteq \mathbb{F}_q^n$$

is called the *algebraic geometric* (or *geometric Goppa*) code associated to the divisor G and the places $P_1, \ldots P_n$.

What are the parameters of C ? Its length is the number of places of degree one which were used in the construction. Assuming the degree of G satisfies $\deg G < n$, the evaluation map $ev : \mathcal{L}(G) \to C$ sending f to $(f(P_1), \ldots, f(P_n))$ is injective, hence $\dim C = \dim \mathcal{L}(G)$. The latter dimension is given by Riemann's theorem

$$(15) \qquad \dim C = \dim \mathcal{L}(G) \geq \deg G + 1 - g,$$

where g denotes the genus of F. Note that equality holds in (15) if $\deg G > 2g - 2$.

Let $c = ev(f) \in C$ be a codeword whose weight equals the minimum distance $d = d(C)$. Then f has $n - d$ zeros in S, say $f(P_1) = \ldots = f(P_{n-d}) = 0$. This means that $f \in \mathcal{L}(G - (P_1 + \ldots + P_{n-d}))$, and therefore $\deg G - (n - d) = \deg(G - (P_1 + \ldots + P_{n-d})) \geq 0$. Thus we have proved the *Goppa bound*

$$(16) \qquad d \geq n - \deg G.$$

The right hand side of (16) is called the *designed distance* of $C(G)$. Now we combine (15) and (16), set $k = \dim C$ and obtain

$$(17) \qquad n + 1 - g \leq k + d \leq n + 1$$

for algebraic geometric codes (with $\deg G < n$). Hence we have a global lower bound for $k + d$, depending only on the genus of the function field.

It is a consequence of the duality theorem (which is related to the Riemann-Roch theorem) that the dual code of $C(G)$ is also algebraic geometric:

$$(18) \qquad C(G)^\perp = C(H),$$

where $H = P_1 + \ldots + P_n - G + W$ and W is an appropriate canonical divisor of F (see [**19**], Ch.II).

Reed-Solomon codes and Hermitian codes are special algebraic geometric codes; we show this for Hermitian codes over $\mathbb{F}_{16}$. Here one considers the function field

$$F = \mathbb{F}_{16}(x, y) \ , \quad \text{with} \ \ y^4 + y = x^5.$$

The genus of F is $g = 6$. Let Q be the (unique) common pole of x and y. For any pair $(\alpha, \beta) \in \mathbb{F}_{16} \times \mathbb{F}_{16}$ satisfying $\beta^4 + \beta = \alpha^5$ there is a unique place $P_{\alpha\beta}$ of F which is a common zero of $x - \alpha$ and $y - \beta$. All these $65 \ (= 1 + 16 \cdot 4)$ places of F are of degree one, and we set

$$S = \{P_{\alpha\beta} \mid \beta^4 + \beta = \alpha^5\}.$$

The space $\mathcal{L}(rQ)$ is nothing other than the space $\mathcal{L}_r$ which was considered in (2), and therefore the Hermitian code C_r (as defined in (4)) is

$$C_r = C(rP_\infty).$$

The formula (6) for the parameters of Hermitian codes corresponds to the general formulas (15), (16) which hold for all algebraic geometric codes. The fact that the dual of a Hermitian code is also Hermitian (Sec. 3, equation (7)) is a special case of (18).

We conclude this section with two remarks.

(a) The decoding algorithm which we discussed for Hermitian codes in Sec. 4 can be generalized to all algebraic geometric codes. It decodes in general only up to $(d^* - 1 - g)/2$ errors, where d^* denotes the designed minimum distance of the

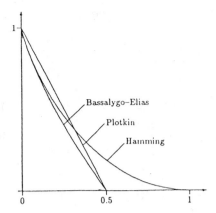

FIGURE 1. Upper bounds for $\alpha_q(\delta)$, for $q = 2$.

code. Recently, Feng and Rao [**3**] found an algorithm which decodes up to half the designed minimum distance. Another approach uses Gröbner bases for decoding cyclic and algebraic geometric codes [**1**].

(b) One can show that all codes are algebraic geometric, see Pellikaan et al. [**17**], in the following sense: given a code C over $\mathbb{F}_q$, one can always find a function field $F/\mathbb{F}_q$, a set of places of degree one and a divisor G of F, such that $C = C(G)$. However, the genus of this function field will be very large in general, so the estimate (17) for the parameters will give no information about the code.

7. Asymptotically Good Algebraic Geometric Codes

In order to compare the performance of codes of different lengths, we define the *rate* R and the *relative minimum distance* δ of an $[n, k, d]$ code C over $\mathbb{F}_q$ by

$$R = R(C) = \frac{k}{n} \quad \text{and} \quad \delta = \delta(C) = \frac{d}{n}.$$

Let

$$V_q = \{(\delta(C), R(C)) \in [0, 1]^2 \mid C \text{ is a code over } \mathbb{F}_q\},$$

and

$$U_q = \text{ set of limit points of } V_q.$$

Thus, for a point $(\delta, R) \in U_q$ there exist codes over $\mathbb{F}_q$ of arbitrarily large length whose rate and relative minimum distance are close to R and δ. It is not hard to prove that there is a continuous, decreasing function $\alpha_q : [0, 1] \to [0, 1]$ such that

$$U_q = \{(\delta, R) \mid 0 \le \delta \le 1 \text{ and } 0 \le R \le \alpha_q(\delta)\}.$$

For $1 - q^{-1} \le \delta \le 1$, one has $\alpha_q(\delta) = 0$. For $0 < \delta < 1 - q^{-1}$ however, the exact value of $\alpha_q(\delta)$ is not known. From bounds on the parameters of codes (such as the Singleton bound (1)) one gets *upper* bounds for $\alpha_q(\delta)$. Some of these are plotted in Fig. 1.

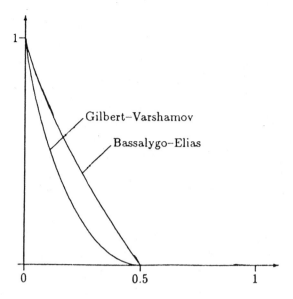

FIGURE 2. Bounds for $\alpha_q(\delta)$, for $q = 2$.

More interesting are *lower* bounds on $\alpha_q(\delta)$, because they imply the existence of long codes over $\mathbb{F}_q$ having good parameters. For many years, the only known non-trivial lower bound for $\alpha_q(\delta)$ was the *Gilbert-Varshamov bound*

(19) $$\alpha_q(\delta) \geq 1 - H_q(\delta) , \quad \text{for } 0 \leq \delta \leq 1 - q^{-1},$$

where

$$H_q(\delta) = \delta \cdot \log_q(q - 1) - \delta \cdot \log_q \delta - (1 - \delta) \cdot \log_q(1 - \delta)$$

denotes the *q-ary entropy function*. In Fig. 2, the Gilbert-Varshamov (lower) bound and the *Bassalygo-Elias* (upper) bound for $\alpha_q(\delta)$ are plotted.

Now we are in a position to explain the result of Tsfasman, Vladut and Zink [**21**]. Their starting point was the inequality given as (17):

$$k + d \geq n + 1 - g,$$

where $k = k(C)$ and $d = d(C)$ are the parameters of an algebraic geometric code C which is defined by means of a function field $F/\mathbb{F}_q$ of genus g that has (at least) n places of degree one. Dividing (17) by n, we obtain

(20) $$R + \delta \geq 1 + \frac{1}{n} - \frac{g}{n}.$$

Suppose we have a sequence of function fields $F_i/\mathbb{F}_q$ having genus g_i and n_i places of degree one, such that $g_i \to \infty$ and

(21) $$\lim_{i \to \infty} \frac{n_i}{g_i} = \gamma > 1.$$

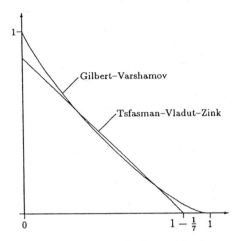

FIGURE 3. Lower bounds for $\alpha_q(\delta)$, for $q = 64$.

Then, for an appropriate choice of divisors G_i of F_i, the sequence of codes $C_i = C(G_i)$ of length n_i yields a point in U_q which lies on or above the line

$$R + \delta = 1 - \gamma^{-1}.$$

For q a square, Tsfasman, Vladut and Zink showed that there exist sequences of function fields over $\mathbb{F}_q$ such that

$$(22) \qquad \lim_{i \to \infty} \frac{n_i}{g_i} = \sqrt{q} - 1.$$

For small values of q, the line

$$(23) \qquad R + \delta = 1 - \frac{1}{\sqrt{q} - 1}$$

lies below the Gilbert-Varshamov curve $R = 1 - H_q(\delta)$. For all $q \geq 49$ however, there is a non-empty interval $M_q \subseteq [0, 1]$ where the line (23) lies above the Gilbert-Varshamov bound. Hence, the *Tsfasman-Vladut-Zink bound*

$$(24) \qquad \alpha_q(\delta) \geq (1 - \frac{1}{\sqrt{q} - 1}) - \delta$$

improves the Gilbert-Varshamov bound, for all squares $q \geq 49$ and $\delta \in M_q$.

We note that one cannot do better than (22): a result of Drinfeld and Vladut states that

$$\limsup_{i \to \infty} \frac{n_i}{g_i} \leq \sqrt{q} - 1,$$

for any sequence of function fields over $\mathbb{F}_q$.

The construction of a sequence of function fields given by Tsfasman, Vladut and Zink uses deep results from algebraic geometry: it is based on properties of certain *modular curves* which parametrize elliptic curves, see [16], [20] for details. However, this approach is not quite satisfactory for coding theory because the construction of modular curves is far from being explicit. Therefore it is desirable to have other sequences of function fields satisfying (22).

Recently Garcia and Stichtenoth [5] found such a sequence; it is defined as follows: Let $q = r^2$ be a square. Put $F_1 = \mathbb{F}_q(x_1)$ and, for $i \geq 1$,

$$F_{i+1} = F_i(z_{i+1}),$$

where z_{i+1} satisfies the equation

$$z_{i+1}^r + z_{i+1} = x_i^{r+1},$$

with

$$x_i = z_i/x_{i-1} \in F_i \quad \text{(for } i > 1\text{)}.$$

Observe that F_2 is the Hermitian function field, cf. Sec. 3 and Sec. 5. One can show that the genus g_i (resp. the number n_i of places of degree one) of the above function field $F_i/\mathbb{F}_q$ is given by

$$g_i = \begin{cases} r^i + r^{i-1} - r^{\frac{i+1}{2}} - 2r^{\frac{i-1}{2}} + 1, & \text{if } i \equiv 1 \mod 2, \\ r^i + r^{i-1} - \frac{1}{2}r^{\frac{i}{2}+1} - \frac{3}{2}r^{\frac{i}{2}} - r^{\frac{i}{2}-1} + 1, & \text{if } i \equiv 0 \mod 2 \end{cases}$$

and

$$n_i \geq (r^2 - 1) \cdot r^{i-1}.$$

Hence,

$$\lim_{i \to \infty} \frac{n_i}{g_i} = r - 1 = \sqrt{q} - 1.$$

We hope it will be possible to construct *explicitly* sequences of codes over $\mathbb{F}_q$ which are better than the Gilbert-Varshamov bound, based on the above function fields.

References

[1] Chen, X., Reed, I. S., Helleseth, T. and Truong, T. K.: Use of Gröbner Bases to Decode Binary Cyclic Codes up to the True Minimum Distance. IEEE Trans. on Inform. Th. **40** (1994), 1654-1661.

[2] Chevalley, C.: Introduction to the Theory of Algebraic Functions of One Variable. AMS Math. Surveys, New York, 1951.

[3] Feng, G.-L. and Rao, T. R. N.: Decoding of Algebraic Geometric Codes up to the Designed Minimum Distance. IEEE Trans. on Inform. Th. **39** (1993), 37-46.

[4] Fulton, W.: Algebraic Curves. Benjamin, New York - Amsterdam, 1969.

[5] Garcia, A., Stichtenoth, H.: A Tower of Artin-Schreier Extensions of Function Fields Attaining the Drinfeld-Vladut Bound. Submitted to Invent. Math.

[6] Van der Geer, G. and Van Lint, J. H.: Introduction to Coding Theory and Algebraic Geometry. DMV Seminar, Vol. **12**. Birkhäuser, Basel-Boston-Berlin, 1988.

[7] Goppa, V. D.: Algebraico-Geometric Codes. Math. USSR-Izv. **21** (1983), 75-91.

[8] Hirschfeld, J.: Linear Codes and Algebraic Curves. In: Geometrical Combinatorics. Conf. Milton Keynes (1984), Res. Notes Math. **114** (1984), 35-53.

[9] Justesen, J., Larsen, K. J., Jensen, H. E., Havemose, A. and Høholdt, T.: Construction and Decoding of a Class of Algebraic Geometric Codes. IEEE Trans. on Inform. Theory **35** (1989), 811-821.

[10] Lachaud, G.: Les Codes Géométriques de Goppa. Sem. Bourbaki, exp. **641** (1985).

[11] Van Lint, J. H.: Introduction to Coding Theory. Graduate Texts in Math., Vol. **86**. Springer, New York-Heidelberg-Berlin, 1982.

[12] Van Lint, J. H.: Algebraic Geometric Codes. In: Coding Theory and Design Theory. IMA Vol. in Mathematics and its Applications **20** (1988), 137-162.

[13] Van Lint, J. H. and Springer, T. A.: Generalized Reed-Solomon Codes from Algebraic Geometry. IEEE Trans. on Inform. Theory **33** (1987), 305-309.

[14] Mac Williams, F. J. and Sloane, N. J.: The Theory of Error-Correcting Codes. North-Holland, Amsterdam, 1977.

[15] Michon, J. F.: Codes de Goppa. Sém. de Théorie des Nombres de Bordeaux, exp. **7** (1983-84).

[16] Moreno, C.: Algebraic Curves over Finite Fields. Cambridge Tracts in Math., Vol. **97**. Cambridge University Press, Cambridge, 1991.

[17] Pellikaan, R., Shen, B. Z. and van Wee, G. J. M.: Which Linear Codes are Algebraic Geometric ? IEEE Trans. on Inform. Theory **37** (1991), 583-602.

[18] Skorobogatov, A. N. and Vladut, S. G.: On the Decoding of Algebraic Geometric Codes. IEEE Trans. on Inform. Theory **36** (1990), 1461-1463.

[19] Stichtenoth, H.: Algebraic Function Fields and Codes. Universitext. Springer, Berlin-Heidelberg-New York, 1993.

[20] Tsfasman, M. A. and Vladut, S. G.: Algebraic-Geometric Codes. Kluwer Academic Publ., Dordrecht-Boston-London, 1991.

[21] Tsfasman, M. A., Vladut, S. G. and Zink, T.: On Goppa Codes which are Better than the Gilbert-Varshamov Bound. Math. Nachr. **109** (1982), 21-28.

[22] Wolfmann, J.: Recent Results on Coding and Algebraic Geometry. Lect. Notes Comp. Sci. **229** (1986), 167-184.

FACHBEREICH 6 MATHEMATIK UND INFORMATIK, UNIVERSITÄT ESSEN, D-45117 ESSEN, GERMANY

E-mail address: stichtenoth@uni-essen.de

Proceedings of Symposia in Applied Mathematics
Volume **50**, 1995

Codes, Quadratic Forms and Finite Geometries

William M. Kantor

ABSTRACT. We study nonlinear binary error–correcting codes closely related
to finite geometries and quadratic forms, and having links with extremal Euclidean line–sets and with recently introduced codes over $\mathbb{Z}_4$. Our emphasis
is on geometric and combinatorial properties of highly structured families of
codes.

The following diagram gives an indication of the main topics and interconnections arising in this paper.

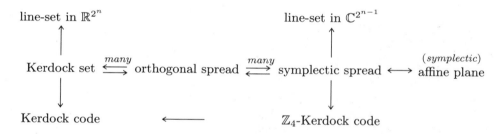

1. Introduction

A binary error–correcting code C of length N is just a subset of the vector space
$\mathbb{Z}_2^N$, the most standard ones being *linear codes*: subspaces of $\mathbb{Z}_2^N$. The *Hamming
distance* d_H between two vectors is the number of places they differ:

$$d_H\big((x_i),(y_i)\big) = (\#i : x_i \neq y_i).$$

One of the basic problems in the theory of error–correcting codes is to construct
and study codes C of length N and large size $|C|$ subject to the condition that the
minimum of the distances between any two different "codewords" in C is some given
integer d, the *minimum distance* of the code. Of particular interest are those codes
that are extremal subject to such a condition. Evidently, such questions are highly
combinatorial. Our purpose is to discuss aspects that are also within finite geometry
and algebra. We will only touch on one type of connection of coding theory with
finite geometry, one rich in a number of additional directions (projective planes,

---

1991 *Mathematics Subject Classification.* Primary 94B27, 51A40; Secondary 05B25, 51A35.
The preparation of this paper was supported in part by the NSF.

I am grateful to A. R. Calderbank and M. E. Williams for many helpful remarks concerning
preliminary versions of this paper.

quadratic forms, Euclidean geometry, and groups). Many other connections with finite geometry are provided in [**MS**].

Another way to view a code of length N is as a set of subsets of an N-element set. The transition between these views is elementary, just using an ordering of the N–set to associate an N-tuple (i.e., vector) with each subset. Addition becomes symmetric difference, and the Hamming distance is just the size of the symmetric difference of the corresponding subsets. The size of a subset is the *weight* of the corresponding word: the number of nonzero coordinates.

One way to search for families of subsets of a set is to impose additional structure on the set. We will assume throughout that the underlying set is itself a vector space $\mathbb{Z}_2^n$, so that $N = 2^n$. The most obvious family of subsets consists of all affine hyperplanes: all $n - 1$–dimensional subspaces and their translates. It is easy to see that, if the empty set and the whole space $\mathbb{Z}_2^n$ are also included, the result is a subspace of $\mathbb{Z}_2^{2^n}$, called the *first order Reed–Muller code $RM(1, n)$*. Note that $RM(1, n)$ is closely tied to the binary *affine space $AG(n, 2)$* based on $\mathbb{Z}_2^n$: the analogue, in this binary setting, of real affine space based on a real vector space. Thus, we will never be far from this binary affine space.

Forms other than linear ones can be used. An especially rich source of "good" codes is the *second order Reed–Muller code $RM(2, n)$*, consisting of all of the zero–sets of all binary polynomials of degree at most 2 in n variables. That is, $RM(2, n)$ has subcodes that behave in interesting manners, and in particular, extremal subcodes; historically, this has been the reason for the time devoted to subcodes of $RM(2, n)$ by numerous authors. We will focus on some of those arising from unions of cosets of $RM(1, n)$ in $RM(2, n)$.

These Reed–Muller codes can be written as follows in terms of coordinates (where some ordering is chosen for $\mathbb{Z}_2^n$):

$$RM(1, n) = \{\, (s \cdot v + \varepsilon)_{v \in \mathbb{Z}_2^n} \mid s \in \mathbb{Z}_2^n, \varepsilon \in \mathbb{Z}_2 \,\}$$

$$RM(2, n) = \{(Q(v) + s \cdot v + \varepsilon)_{v \in \mathbb{Z}_2^n} \mid Q \text{ is a quadratic form on } \mathbb{Z}_2^n, s \in \mathbb{Z}_2^n, \varepsilon \in \mathbb{Z}_2\},$$

where quadratic forms will be defined in the next section. Quadratic forms will then be used to construct (nonlinear) subcodes of $RM(2, n)$ called *Kerdock codes*. In §§3,4 we will see entirely different views of these codes in terms of orthogonal geometries and projective planes, which will lead us to structural properties and nonuniqueness results for the codes and for the various geometric objects associated with them.

The codes we focus on are *nonlinear*: they are not subgroups of $\mathbb{Z}_2^n$. Historically, linear codes have been the most important codes, since they are easier to discover, describe, encode and decode. On the other hand, the nonlinear codes studied here have the advantage of being superior from a combinatorial point of view: they have at least twice as many codewords as any linear code with same length and minimum distance. A surprising breakthrough in coding theory is that some of these nonlinear codes can be viewed as linear codes over $\mathbb{Z}_4$, rather than $\mathbb{Z}_2$ [**CHKSS**], and hence have the best of both worlds: superior description and implementation, and yet combinatorial optimality.

Much of this paper can be viewed as an introduction to Kerdock and other interesting subcodes of $RM(2, n)$ described in detail in [**MS**], codes which have just been investigated anew in [**CHKSS**] and [**CCKS**] from the vantage point of $\mathbb{Z}_4$ (cf. §6). The smallest example is the Nordstrom-Robinson code, described in Calderbank's paper in these Proceedings. Subcodes of $RM(2, n)$ also arose in the study, by Cameron and Seidel [**CS**], of extremal line–sets in Euclidean spaces (cf. §§5,6).

We will describe large numbers of codes by means of projective planes and nonassociative "algebras". This will lead to a better understanding of some of the mathematical underpinnings of the newly–discovered aspects of codes over $\mathbb{Z}_4$, besides producing new connections with other areas of mathematics.

2. Quadratic forms and Kerdock codes

Quadratic forms are standard in algebra and geometry. Care is needed when dealing with characteristic 2, but is well worth the effort: large numbers of important geometric and combinatorial objects (as well as groups) arise from them (cf. [**MS**] for many examples).

Quadratic and alternating forms. A *quadratic form* on a binary vector space V is a map $Q\colon V \to \mathbb{Z}_2$ such that

(2.1) $$(u,v)\colon = Q(u+v) - Q(u) - Q(v)$$

is a symmetric bilinear form on V. In terms of coordinates, if $V = \mathbb{Z}_2^n$ then Q looks like

$$Q(x_1,\dots,x_n) = \sum_{i \leq j} a_{ij} x_i x_j$$

for some scalars a_{ij}, and $((x_i),(y_i)) = \sum_{ij} b_{ij} x_i x_j$, where $b_{ij} = b_{ji} = a_{ij}$ for $i < j$ and $b_{ii} = 0$. The *rank* of Q, or of its associated bilinear form, is just the rank of the matrix $B = (b_{ij})$ representing the bilinear form; this is also the codimension of the subspace consisting of all of the vectors v such that $(v,V) = 0$. Also, Q and the bilinear form are called *nonsingular* if B is (equivalently, if $((v,V) = 0 \Longrightarrow v = 0)$).

The matrix B is *skew–symmetric* (symmetric with 0 diagonal); its rank necessarily is even. The associated bilinear form is called an *alternating bilinear form* $(\, , \,)\colon (u,v) = (v,u)$ and $(v,v) = 0$ for all u,v.

A vector space equipped with a nonsingular alternating bilinear form $(\, , \,)$ is called a *symplectic space*. By a linear change of variables, any such form on $\mathbb{Z}_2^{2r}$ can be transformed into the form $\sum_{i=1}^{r}(x_i y_{i+r} - x_{i+r} y_i)$ (i.e., any nonsingular alternating bilinear form is *equivalent* to the indicated one). An *isometry*, or a *symplectic transformation*, is a nonsingular linear transformation g of the vector space that preserves the form: $(ug, vg) = (u,v)$ for all vectors u,v.

Singular vectors of quadratic forms. It is easy to count the number of zeros (*singular vectors*) of quadratic forms over finite fields. Here we will only deal with the field $\mathbb{Z}_2$.

Let Q_{2r} denote the quadratic form on $\mathbb{Z}_2^r \oplus \mathbb{Z}_2^r$ defined by $Q_{2r}(x,y) = x \cdot y$ for all $x,y \in \mathbb{Z}_2^r$ (ordinary dot product). Any quadratic form on $\mathbb{Z}_2^n$ can be transformed, using an affine change of coordinates (i.e., a transformation $v \mapsto vA + c$ for some invertible $n \times n$ matrix A and some $c \in \mathbb{Z}_2^n$) to one of the following:

$$Q_{2r}, \ Q_{2r} + 1 \ or \ Q_{2r} + z,$$

where z is a variable not among those used for Q_{2r} ("Dickson's Theorem" [**Dic**, p. 197], cf. [**MS**, p. 438]). This makes it very easy to determine the number of zeros (*singular vectors*) of Q: an easy calculation shows that

(2.2)

$$Q_{2r} \quad and \quad Q_{2r} + 1 \quad have, \; respectively, \; exactly$$

$$2^{n-1} + 2^{n-1-r} \quad and \quad 2^{n-1} - 2^{n-1-r} \quad zeros \; in \quad \mathbb{Z}_2^n.$$

It is straightforward to deduce that any *coset* $(Q(v))_v + RM(1, n)$, where Q has rank $2r$, has weight distribution as follows:

weight	# of vectors of that weight
$2^{n-1} - 2^{n-r-1}$	2^{2r}
2^{n-1}	$2^{n+1} - 2^{2r+1}$
$2^{n-1} + 2^{n-r-1}$	2^{2r}

(Note that the complements of the vectors of weight $2^{n-1} + 2^{n-r-1}$ are those of weight $2^{n-1} - 2^{n-r-1}$.)

We will be interested in the largest possible weights, and hence will restrict to the case in which $n = 2r$. Then any quadratic form of rank n in n variables can be transformed, as above, to either Q_n or $Q_n + 1$, in which case our coset becomes $(Q_n(v))_v + RM(1, n)$. Moreover, the above weight distribution is then even simpler (there are no vectors of weight 2^{n-1}).

Cosets. Since our characteristic is 2, unlike the familiar situation with real quadratic forms it is not possible to recover Q from the bilinear form (u, v): many different quadratic forms determine the same symmetric bilinear form. For any quadratic form Q on $\mathbb{Z}_2^n$, the coset $(Q(v))_v + RM(1, n)$ "contains" all quadratic forms Q' determining the same bilinear form as Q. Namely, if Q and Q' determine the same bilinear form, then

$$(u, v) = Q(u + v) - Q(u) - Q(v) = Q'(u + v) - Q'(u) - Q'(v)$$

for all $u, v \in \mathbb{Z}_2^n$, and then $Q - Q'$ is clearly a linear functional $\mathbb{Z}_2^n \to \mathbb{Z}_2$; this argument can be reversed.

We now turn to the behavior of a *union* of cosets $(Q(v))_v + RM(1, n)$, where Q is allowed to run over a family $\mathcal{F}$ of quadratic forms on $\mathbb{Z}_2^n$ *each* of which has rank n. However, we require even more: we want the distance between the zero sets of any two different forms $Q, Q' \in \mathcal{F}$ to be large, which means that $Q - Q'$ should be another quadratic form of rank n. This condition is easier to understand in terms of the corresponding bilinear forms–or, better yet, in terms of the skew–symmetric matrices B, B' determined by these bilinear forms: our requirement is that $B - B'$ is nonsingular. Thus, we are led to consider a set $\mathcal{K}$ of skew–symmetric $n \times n$ matrices the difference of any two of which is nonsingular. Then any two of these matrices have different first rows, so that there can be at most 2^{n-1} such matrices. The extremal case is the one of special interest here.

Kerdock sets and Kerdock codes. Kerdock sets and their associated codes and geometries are the principal subject of this paper.

A *Kerdock set* of $n \times n$ binary matrices is a family $\mathcal{K}$ of 2^{n-1} skew–symmetric $n \times n$ binary matrices, containing O, such that the difference of any two is nonsingular. (Note that n is even since we are dealing with skew–symmetric matrices.) For the reason indicated above, this number 2^{n-1} is extremal. In combinatorial settings, extremal configurations frequently have rich structures. This is very much the case with Kerdock sets. We will construct such sets very soon, but first we construct codes using them.

Each Kerdock set $\mathcal{K}$ determines a *Kerdock code* $C(\mathcal{K}) = \bigcup_{B \in \mathcal{K}}[(Q_B(v))_v + RM(1, n)]$, where Q_B denotes any quadratic form whose associated bilinear form is uBv^t. Thus, if $B = (b_{ij})$ and if U denotes the upper triangular matrix obtained from B by replacing all entries below the diagonal by 0 (so that $U + U^t = B$), then we may assume that $Q_B(v) = vUv^t$. Explicitly, in terms of vectors we then have

$$(2.3) \qquad C(\mathcal{K})\colon = \{\, (Q_B(v) + s \cdot v + \varepsilon)_{v \in \mathbb{Z}_2^n} \mid B \in \mathcal{K}, s \in \mathbb{Z}_2^n, \varepsilon \in \mathbb{Z}_2 \,\}.$$

$C(\mathcal{K})$ is a code of length $N = 2^n$ (where n is even), consisting of $2^{n-1}2^n2 = 2^{2n}$ codewords (i.e., vectors). Any $c \in C(\mathcal{K})$ partitions $C(\mathcal{K})$ in terms of distances, as follows:

distance from c	# of words at that distance	comments
0	1	c
$2^{n-1} - 2^{(n-2)/2}$	$2^n(2^{n-1} - 1)$	
2^{n-1}	$2^{n+1} - 2$	
$2^{n-1} + 2^{(n-2)/2}$	$2^n(2^{n-1} - 1)$	
2^n	1	$c + $ (the all-1 vector)

Minimum distance: $2^{n-1} - 2^{(n-2)/2}$.

The property that the distribution of distances is independent of the choice of c is called *distance–invariance*. It as an approximation to the linearity of a code, this property being trivial for such codes. (That is, if C is a linear code then the translations $v \mapsto v + c$ form a group of automorphisms transitive on the set of codewords, so that distance–invariance is obvious.) as we will see below (Theorem 5.1), $C(\mathcal{K})$ is nonlinear.

Recovering $\mathcal{K}$ from $C(\mathcal{K})$. $RM(1, n)$ is the set of codewords of weight 0, 2^{n-1} or 2^n. $C(\mathcal{K})$ is a union of cosets of $RM(1, n)$, each of which corresponds to a unique skew–symmetric matrix. These matrices comprise $\mathcal{K}$.

Examples of Kerdock sets. Here is an example of a set of 2^{4-1} quadratic forms when $n = 4$:

$$\{0, \; x_1x_2 + x_3x_4, \; x_1x_3 + x_1x_4 + x_2x_3 + x_2x_4,$$

$$x_1x_3 + x_2x_4 + x_3x_4, \; x_1x_2 + x_1x_3 + x_1x_4 + x_2x_4, x_1x_4 + x_2x_3 + x_2x_4 + x_3x_4,$$

$$x_1x_2 + x_1x_4 + x_2x_3, \; x_1x_2 + x_1x_3 + x_2x_3 + x_2x_4\}.$$

This description is opaque. It is not motivated (nor will our other examples be well–motivated until later, when we get to projective planes), and it is tedious to verify that all differences of these quadratic forms are nonsingular (cf. [**Li**]).

All remaining examples discussed here will be obtained from the field $\mathrm{GF}(2^m)$, where m is *odd* (this will be "$n - 1$" in our previous notation). Let $T : \mathrm{GF}(2^m) \to \mathrm{GF}(2)$ be the trace map: $T(x) = \sum_{i=0}^{m-1} x^{2^i}$. This determines an inner product $T(xy)$ on $\mathrm{GF}(2^m)$. There is an orthonormal basis that lets us identify $\mathrm{GF}(2^m)$ equipped with this inner product and $\mathbb{Z}_2^m$ equipped with its usual dot product.

We are searching for Kerdock sets, which require even–dimensional spaces whereas m is odd. Hence, we boost the dimension by 1, and consider $\mathrm{GF}(2^m) \oplus \mathbb{Z}_2$, equipped with the inner product $((x,a),(y,b)) := T(xy) + ab$. In place of skew–symmetric matrices we will use linear operators $M \colon \mathrm{GF}(2^m) \oplus \mathbb{Z}_2 \to \mathrm{GF}(2^m) \oplus \mathbb{Z}_2$ such that $((x,a),(x,a)M) = 0$ for all $(x,a) \in \mathrm{GF}(2^m) \oplus \mathbb{Z}_2$. We will construct families of such linear operators M by using suitable binary operations on $\mathrm{GF}(2^m)$.

EXAMPLE 2.1. Consider the set $\mathcal{K}$ of 2^m linear operators $M_s \colon \mathrm{GF}(2^m) \oplus \mathbb{Z}_2 \to \mathrm{GF}(2^m) \oplus \mathbb{Z}_2$ given by

$$(x,a)M_s = \left(xs^2 + sT(sx) + as, T(sx) \right).$$

This definition has been pulled out of the blue, and will be motivated later in terms of projective planes (§4). For now, we note that *these matrices M_s form a Kerdock set $\mathcal{K}$*. First, M_s is skew–symmetric:

$$\left((x,a),(x,a)M_s\right) = T\left(x[xs^2 + sT(sx) + as]\right) + aT(sx) = 0$$

since $T(xxs^2) = T(xs)^2 = T(xsT(sx))$. Next, $M_r - M_s$ is nonsingular whenever $r \neq s$: if

$$(xr^2 + rT(rx) + ar, T(rx)) = (xs^2 + sT(sx) + as, T(sx)),$$

then $T(rx) = T(sx)$ and $xr^2 + rT(sx) + ar = xs^2 + sT(sx) + as$, so that

$$x(r+s)^2 + (r+s)T(sx) + a(r+s) = 0,$$

$$rx + sx + T(sx) + a = 0,$$

$$T(rx) + T(sx) + T(sx) + a = 0$$

(this uses the fact that m is odd, so that $T(1) = 1$), and hence

$$rx + sx = 0 = T(sx) + a.$$

Thus, $M_r - M_s$ is nonsingular, as required.

By (2.3), this Kerdock set produces a Kerdock code $C(\mathcal{K})$. This is the original code discovered by Kerdock [**Ke**] in 1972 (in rather different language); cf. [**Dil, MS, Ka1**]. When $m = 3$ this is the Nordstrom–Robinson code of length 16. Moreover, we now see that *a Kerdock code of length 2^n exists for every even n*.

Kerdock set equivalence. Kerdock sets $\mathcal{K}_1$ and $\mathcal{K}_2$ of $n \times n$ matrices are *equivalent* if there is an invertible $n \times n$ matrix A and a skew–symmetric matrix M such that $A^t \mathcal{K}_1 A + M = \mathcal{K}_2$. One of our goals is to describe large numbers of inequivalent Kerdock sets (and corresponding codes) by means of projective planes and nonassociative "algebras".

Example 2.1 used field multiplication (the term xs^2). As we will seen in §4, important types of projective planes are described using more general types of binary operations. Hence, we are led to introduce those operations important in our coding–theoretic context. These have the advantage of being the quickest way to write down what amount to *all* Kerdock sets (cf. Theorem 4.2).

Binary operations. Consider a binary operation $*$ on $\mathrm{GF}(2^m)$ related to field multiplication by the following conditions (for all $x, y, z \in \mathrm{GF}(2^m)$):

(i) $(x + y) * z = x * z + y * z$ (left distributivity),
(ii) $x * y = x * z \implies x = 0$ or $y = z$,
(iii) $T(x(x * y)) = T(xy)$, and
(iv) $x * y = 0 \iff x = 0$ or $y = 0$.

Also, (iii) implies

(v) $T(x(y * z)) = T(y(x * z))$

(namely, in (iii) replace x by $x + z$, x and z, and subtract). This condition is more useful for our purposes; but if (v) holds and (iii) does not, it is easy to modify $*$ insignificantly so that (iii) will hold.

A fundamental aspect of the subject matter in this paper is that (i) and (ii) are familiar in the theory of projective planes (cf. §4). These amount to some distorted versions of fields; for example, if both distributive laws hold then we are dealing with a special type of (nonassociative) division algebra (except for the lack of an identity element). It is just such field–like algebras that arise in the coordinatization of projective planes. Thus, one can expect that there will be further interactions between coding theory and planes, with a great deal to be learned in each discipline from the other one.

In Example 2.1, $x * y = xy^2$ (note that $T(x(x * y) = T(x^2y^2) = T(xy)$, which explains the use of xy^2 instead of the more natural–looking xy). The argument used in that example essentially shows that

PROPOSITION 2.2. *The maps*

$$M_s \colon (x, a) \mapsto \big(x * s + sT(sx) + as, T(sx)\big), \ s \in GF(2^m),$$

form a Kerdock set.

Namely, proceed exactly as before in order to obtain the equation $x*r+x*s = (r + s)[T(sx) + a]$. If (x, a) also satisfies $T(sx) + a = 0$ then, by (v), $x = 0$. It follows that the dimension of the kernel of $M_r - M_s$ is at most 1, and hence is 0 since $m + 1$ is even and $M_r - M_s$ is skew–symmetric.

EXAMPLE 2.3. Let T_1 denote the trace map from $\mathrm{GF}(2^m)$ to some proper subfield $F \neq \mathbb{Z}_2$. Then

$$x * s \colon = xs^2 + T_1(x)s + T_1(xs)$$

satisfies (i-v). (N.B.—If we allowed $F = \mathbb{Z}_2$ here, then the Kerdock set obtained in this manner would be the same as the one obtained in Example 2.1.)

Once again, these maps appear to have come from nowhere, but will turn out to be motivated by projective planes.

EXAMPLE 2.4. Let T_1 again denote the trace map from $\mathrm{GF}(2^m)$ to some proper subfield $F \neq \mathbb{Z}_2$, let $\alpha \in F - \mathbb{Z}_2$, and write

$$x * s \colon = xs^2 + \alpha sT_1(xs).$$

Then this operation satisfies (i-v), but this time only one distributive law is satisfied. Once again a Kerdock set is obtained using the preceding proposition.

It might appear that the above conditions **(i-v)** are so strong as to prevent the existence of many examples. This is not the case. Every Kerdock set is, in a suitable sense, equivalent to one of those in Proposition 2.2 (see the Remark following Proposition 3.7). One can, of course, ask whether $\mathcal{K}$ determines the "algebra" $(\mathrm{GF}(2^m), +, *)$ uniquely up to something like isomorphism. However, this also is not the case if $m \geq 5$: there is a strong version of non-uniqueness, which is essentially the content of Theorem 4.4. Moreover, there are large numbers of inequivalent Kerdock sets (cf. Theorem 3.5).

3. Finite orthogonal geometries[1]

Quadratic forms arise for us in two different ways. On the one hand, we have used them in order to construct codes (second order Reed–Muller codes and Kerdock codes). On the other hand, we will use them in order to construct a very different-looking type of configuration in larger vector spaces ("orthogonal spreads"). We will also see that the two ways to use quadratic forms are nicely linked, albeit in a somewhat indirect manner.

An orthogonal geometry. In order to have a more geometric view of skew–symmetric matrices, we will double the dimension and consider one concrete type of orthogonal geometry. Let $V = \mathbb{Z}_2^{2n} = X \oplus Y$ for subspaces X and Y both of which are identified with $\mathbb{Z}_2^n$. Equip V with the quadratic form $Q = Q_{2n}$ (so that $Q(x, y) = x \cdot y$), with associated bilinear form (,). The notion of perpendicularity is as usual. However, note that every vector is perpendicular to itself (since $(u, u) = 0$). If W is any subspace of V then $W^\perp \colon = \{v \in V \mid (v, W) = 0\}$ is a subspace of dimension $\dim V - \dim W$. For example, $X^\perp = X$ and $Y^\perp = Y$.

Totally singular subspaces. A subspace W is *totally singular* if $Q(W) = 0$, in which case it also is perpendicular to itself (i.e., $W \subseteq W^\perp$ since $(W, W) = 0$), and hence $\dim W \leq n$ (since $2n = \dim W + \dim W^\perp \geq 2 \dim W$). Thus, X and Y are examples of totally singular n–spaces.[2]

Orthogonal spreads. By (2.2), V has $(2^n - 1)(2^{n-1} + 1)$ nonzero singular vectors. Each totally singular n–space consists of singular vectors, and contains $2^n - 1$ nonzero ones. This number divides the number of singular vectors and suggests that there might be families Σ of totally singular n–spaces that partition the set of all nonzero singular vectors. Such a family of $2^{n-1} + 1$ subspaces is called an *orthogonal spread*. We will see soon that such a family cannot exist unless n is even, and that there is always at least one such family when n is even.

Isometries. An *isometry* of V is a nonsingular linear transformation preserving $Q = Q_{2n}$ (i.e., a nonsingular linear transformation T such that $Q(vT) = Q(v)$ for all $v \in V$); these form a group, the *orthogonal group* $O^+(2n, 2)$ of V. (Here, the "+" refers to the fact that V has totally singular n–spaces.) This group is transitive on the ordered pairs of totally singular n–spaces having only 0 in common: from the point of view of this orthogonal geometry of V, the pair X, Y we started with is indistinguishable from any other such pair.

---

[1] Much of this section only uses the fact that the field is finite of characteristic 2, rather than $\mathbb{Z}_2$. The exception is the part of Theorem 3.4 that concerns codes.

[2] Similarly, in the case of a $2m$–dimensional symplectic space, a subspace W is *totally isotropic* if $W \subseteq W^\perp$, in which case $\dim W \leq m$.

Fix a basis $x_1, \ldots, x_n$ of X and let $y_1, \ldots, y_n$ be the dual basis of Y: $(x_i, y_j) = \delta_{ij}$. Write matrices with respect to the basis $x_1, \ldots, x_n, y_1, \ldots, y_n$.

LEMMA 3.1.   (i) *The isometries of V that fix every vector of Y are just those linear transformations whose matrices are $\left(\begin{smallmatrix} I & M \\ O & I \end{smallmatrix}\right)$ for some binary skew–symmetric $n \times n$ matrix M.*

(ii) *These isometries form a group isomorphic to the additive group of all binary skew–symmetric $n \times n$ matrices.*

(iii) *The isometries fixing Y are just those linear transformations whose matrices are $\left(\begin{smallmatrix} A^{-t} & O \\ O & A \end{smallmatrix}\right)\left(\begin{smallmatrix} I & M \\ O & I \end{smallmatrix}\right)$, where A runs through the group $GL(n,2)$ of all nonsingular $n \times n$ binary matrices and M is as in (i).*

PROOF.   (i) Any such isometry must look like $\left(\begin{smallmatrix} I & M \\ O & B \end{smallmatrix}\right)$ for some $n \times n$ matrices M and B. Then Q is preserved if and only if $x \cdot (xM + yB) = x \cdot y$ for all x, y, which is the case if and only if M is skew–symmetric (use $y = 0$) and $B = I$.

(ii) $\left(\begin{smallmatrix} I & M \\ O & I \end{smallmatrix}\right)\left(\begin{smallmatrix} I & N \\ O & I \end{smallmatrix}\right) = \left(\begin{smallmatrix} I & M+N \\ O & I \end{smallmatrix}\right)$.

(iii) Any such isometry g induces a linear transformation on Y, with matrix A, say. The matrix $\left(\begin{smallmatrix} A & O \\ O & A^{-t} \end{smallmatrix}\right)$ arises from an isometry h of V, and $h^{-1}g$ is as in (ii). $\square$

LEMMA 3.2.   (i) *Every totally singular n–space Z of V such that $Y \cap Z = 0$ has the form $X\left(\begin{smallmatrix} I & M \\ O & I \end{smallmatrix}\right)$ for a unique skew–symmetric matrix M. Conversely, if M is a skew–symmetric binary $n \times n$ matrix, then $X\left(\begin{smallmatrix} I & M \\ O & I \end{smallmatrix}\right)$ is a totally singular n–space having only 0 in common with Y.*

(ii) *The dimension of the intersection of any two such n–spaces $X\left(\begin{smallmatrix} I & M \\ O & I \end{smallmatrix}\right)$ and $X\left(\begin{smallmatrix} I & N \\ O & I \end{smallmatrix}\right)$ is $n - rank(M - N)$*

PROOF.   (i) We can write $Z = \{(x, xM) \mid x \in X\}$ for a unique $n \times n$ matrix M. The requirement that Z be totally singular is equivalent to having $x \cdot xM = 0$ for all $x \in X$; and this is precisely the condition of skew–symmetry.

(ii) The desired dimension is that of the set of solutions to the following system of linear equations: $(x, xM) = (x, xN)$. $\square$

Part (i) says that Z consists of all of the vectors of the form (x, xM); or, in more familiar terms, Z is the subspace "$y = xM$". Note that the group in Lemma 3.1(ii) is transitive on the set of subspaces Z occurring in Lemma 3.2(i). By Lemma 3.2(ii), *if some such pair of subspaces meet only at 0, then n must be even.*

In view of the definition of Kerdock sets in §2, we have the

COROLLARY 3.3.   (i) *If $\mathcal{K}$ is a Kerdock set of $n \times n$ skew–symmetric binary matrices, then*

$$\Sigma := \{Y\} \bigcup \left\{ X\left(\begin{smallmatrix} I & M \\ O & I \end{smallmatrix}\right) \;\middle|\; M \in \mathcal{K} \right\}$$

is an orthogonal spread of V.

(ii) *Conversely, every orthogonal spread of V that contains both X and Y arises as in (i).*

Evidently, in (ii) Σ depends on $\mathcal{K}$. Is it possible that inequivalent choices for $\mathcal{K}$ produce "equivalent" orthogonal spreads Σ? The answer is "yes": see Theorem 3.4 and the remark following it. In any event, we now see that *an orthogonal spread exists if and only if n is even.*

Equivalence of equivalences. We now turn to the relationships between pairs of Kerdock codes, pairs of Kerdock sets, and pairs of orthogonal spreads.

An *equivalence* between binary codes of length N is a permutation of coordinates sending one to the other. Automorphisms of codes are then equivalences of a code with itself. Since our coordinates are indexed by vectors in $\mathbb{Z}_2^n$, an equivalence will look like $(a_v)_{v \in \mathbb{Z}_2^n} \mapsto (a_{v\sigma})_{v \in \mathbb{Z}_2^n}$ for a permutation σ of $\mathbb{Z}_2^n$. For example, each translation $v \mapsto v + c$ of $\mathbb{Z}_2^n$ is an automorphism of $C(\mathcal{K})$ since it leaves invariant each coset $(Q(v))_v + RM(1, n)$. (Namely, $Q(v + c) = Q(v) + Q(c) + (v, c)$, where $(Q(c) + (v, c))_v \in RM(1, n)$.)

A *quasi-equivalence* between binary codes of length N is a map of the form $(a_v)_v \mapsto (a_{v\sigma} + c_v)_v$, sending one to the other, where σ is a permutation of coordinates and $(c_v)_v$ is some vector in $\mathbb{Z}_2^N$. Thus, two codes are quasi–equivalent if and only each is the image of the other by means of an isometry of the underlying metric space $(\mathbb{Z}_2^N, \text{Hamming metric})$. In the case of linear codes, this notion is almost the same as equivalence. For a nonlinear code C, even one containing 0, it is noticeably weaker: if $w \in C$, then C and $C + w$ are quasi–equivalent but not equivalent, and yet clearly they are not "significantly" different.

Equivalence of Kerdock sets was defined earlier.

Orthogonal spreads Σ_1 and Σ_2 of V are *equivalent* if there is an isometry of V sending Σ_1 to Σ_2.

THEOREM 3.4. *Let $\mathcal{K}_1$ and $\mathcal{K}_2$ be Kerdock sets of $n \times n$ binary matrices. Then the following are equivalent:*

(i) *$\mathcal{K}_1$ and $\mathcal{K}_2$ are equivalent;*

(ii) *$C(\mathcal{K}_1)$ and $C(\mathcal{K}_2)$ are quasi–equivalent;*

(iii) *The orthogonal spreads Σ_1 and Σ_2 of V, determined, respectively, by $\mathcal{K}_1$ and $\mathcal{K}_2$ via Corollary 3.3(i), are equivalent by an isometry of V sending Y to itself.*

PROOF. (ii)$\Rightarrow$(i) Suppose that $g\colon (a_v)_v \mapsto (a_{v\sigma} + c_v)_v$ is a quasi-equivalence sending $C(\mathcal{K}_1)$ to $C(\mathcal{K}_2)$. Then $(0)_v g = (c_v)_v$ is in $C(\mathcal{K}_2)$, and hence has the form $(Q(v) + s \cdot v + \varepsilon)_v$ for some quadratic form Q, some $s \in \mathbb{Z}_2^n$, and $\varepsilon = \pm 1$. Let h be the map $(a_v)_v \mapsto (a_v + c_v)_v$. Then gh sends $(a_v)_v \mapsto (a_{v\sigma})_v$, and sends $C(\mathcal{K}_2)$ to $C(\mathcal{K}_2) + (c_v)_v = C(\mathcal{K}_2) + (Q(v))_v$, which still contains $RM(1, n)$.

The words in $C(\mathcal{K}_1)$ of weight 2^{n-1}, and the words in $C(\mathcal{K}_2) + (Q(v))_v$ of weight 2^{n-1}, are the hyperplanes of $AG(n, 2)$, corresponding to $RM(1, n)$. It follows that σ has the form $v \mapsto vA + w$ for some invertible $n \times n$ matrix A and some $w \in \mathbb{Z}_2^n$; we may assume that $w = 0$ since $v \mapsto v + w$ is an automorphism of $C(\mathcal{K}_1)$. Each word of $C(\mathcal{K}_1)$ or $C(\mathcal{K}_2)$ containing 0 (i.e., having 1 in the 0 position) arises from a quadratic form. Hence, each quadratic form Q_1 giving rise to a codeword of $C(\mathcal{K}_1)$ produces, via A, a quadratic form $Q_2 + Q$ giving rise to a codeword of $C(\mathcal{K}_2) + (Q(v))_v$; that is, $Q_1(vA) = (Q_2 + Q)(v)$ for all $v \in \mathbb{Z}_2^n$. If M and B_i are the matrices of the alternating bilinear forms produced by Q and Q_i, then this means that $(uA)B_1(vA)^t = u(B_2 + M)v^t$ for all u, v, and hence that $AB_1 A^t = B_2 + M$.

(i)$\Rightarrow$(ii) Reverse the above argument.

(i)⇔(iii) If A is an invertible $n \times n$ matrix and M is a skew–symmetric matrix such that $A^t \mathcal{K}_2 A + M = \mathcal{K}_1$, then the matrix pictured in Lemma 3.1(iii) sends Σ_2 to Σ_1. For the converse, reverse the argument.   □

The above theorem needs to be examined carefully. Inequivalent Kerdock sets can produce equivalent orthogonal spreads, a possibly confusing fact that has that has occasionally been overlooked [**Li**, **CL**]. Many examples of this phenomenon exist. In fact, this situation is the norm: it occurs whenever the group $G(\Sigma)$ of orthogonal transformations preserving an orthogonal spread Σ is intransitive on Σ, and there appear to be few examples where $G(\Sigma)$ is actually transitive on Σ.

Inequivalent codes. Assume that m is odd and $m \geq 5$. In [**Ka1**] it is shown that Kerdock codes arising from Examples 2.3 and 2.4 are not quasi–equivalent; and that two codes arising from Example 2.3 or 2.4 are quasi–equivalent if and only if they are equivalent under a permutation of $\mathrm{GF}(2^m)$ of the form $x \mapsto ax^\sigma + b$ for some $a, b \in \mathrm{GF}(2^m)$, $a \neq 0$, and some $\sigma \in \mathrm{Aut}\,\mathrm{GF}(2^m)$. By using intermediate fields in order to vary these constructions (a hint of this is in Examples 2.3 and 2.4), the following much stronger result has been proved by Williams:

THEOREM 3.5. [**Wi**] *Let m be an odd integer > 1. Let $m, m_1, \dots, m_r, 1$ be a sequence of $r+2 \geq 3$ divisors of m such that each is a proper divisor of the preceding one. If $m \geq 7m_1$ then there are more than $2^{(r-1)m}/m$ pairwise inequivalent Kerdock sets of $(m+1) \times (m+1)$ matrices, and hence at least that many pairwise quasi-inequivalent Kerdock codes of length 2^{m+1}.*

A similar result from [**Wi**] is found below in Theorem 6.5. Williams expects to prove similar results for analogues of Example 2.4, producing Kerdock sets admitting a cyclic automorphism group fixing one member and transitive on the remaining ones (and, more generally, producing orthogonal spreads admitting a cyclic automorphism group fixing two members and transitive on the remaining ones). Much weaker versions of this type of result are contained in [**Ka1, Ka2**]. There is also the following related result:

THEOREM 3.6. [**KW**] *Let m be an odd integer > 1. Let $m, m_1, \dots, m_r, 1$ be a sequence of $r + 2 \geq 3$ divisors of m such that each is a proper divisor of the preceding one. Then there are at least $[\Pi_1^r(2^{m_i} + 1)]/2m_1$ pairwise inequivalent orthogonal spreads Σ in the usual binary orthogonal $2m + 2$–space such that $G(\Sigma)$ has a cyclic subgroup transitive on Σ.*

These results, and the determination of the automorphism groups of the Kerdock sets or codes as well as the automorphism groups of the orthogonal spreads, rest on Theorem 3.4 together with Theorem 4.4 below. First we need to see how to construct orthogonal spreads from other geometric objects.

To symplectic spreads. Let z denote any nonsingular 1–space of V, so that $Q(z) \neq 0$. If Z is any totally singular n–space of V then $Z^\perp = Z$, so that $Z \nsubseteq z^\perp$. Consequently, if Σ is any orthogonal spread of V, then

$$\{Z \cap z^\perp \mid Z \in \Sigma\}$$

is a family of totally singular $n - 1$–spaces of $z^\perp$ such that every nonzero singular vector is in exactly one of these subspaces.

Recall that z is contained in the hyperplane $z^\perp$. The $2n-2$–space $z^\perp/z$ inherits the nonsingular alternating bilinear form from V (but not the quadratic form):

$$(u + z, v + z): = (u, v)$$

is well-defined on $z^\perp$ (but "$v+z \mapsto Q(v)$" is not). This turns $z^\perp/z$ into a symplectic space. (Recall from the fourth paragraph of §2 that any two symplectic spaces of the same dimension are equivalent.)

Now we can "project" Σ into $z^\perp/z$, obtaining a set

$$\Sigma_z: = \{\langle Z \cap z^\perp, z\rangle/z \mid Z \in \Sigma\}$$

consisting of $|\Sigma| = 2^{n-1} + 1$ totally isotropic $n-1$–spaces of $z^\perp/z$ such that any two meet only in 0. This is called a *symplectic spread* of the symplectic space $z^\perp/z$: each nonzero vector of $z^\perp/z$ is contained in exactly one member of Σ_z.

From symplectic spreads. The preceding construction can be reversed, proceeding from symplectic spreads to orthogonal ones. This can be accomplished geometrically or in terms of matrices. We will use the latter approach, since it requires no additional background.

Let $V': = X' \oplus Y'$ be the direct sum of two m–dimensional subspaces X' and Y', each of which we identify with $\mathbb{Z}_2^m$. Equip V' with a nonsingular alternating bilinear form $\big((x_1', y_1'), (x_2', y_2')\big) = x_1' \cdot y_2' - x_2' \cdot y_1'$ for $x_1', x_2' \in X'$, $y_1', y_2' \in Y'$, so that both X' and Y' are totally isotropic m–spaces. Fix dual bases $x_1', \dots, x_m'$ and $y_1', \dots, y_m'$ of X' and Y'; write matrices with respect to the basis $x_1', \dots, x_m', y_1', \dots, y_m'$. As in Lemma 3.2, every totally isotropic m–space Z' such that $X' \cap Z' = 0$ can be written as $\left(\begin{smallmatrix} I & P \\ O & I \end{smallmatrix}\right)$ for a unique *symmetric* matrix P. Two such m–spaces $X'\left(\begin{smallmatrix} I & P \\ O & I \end{smallmatrix}\right)$ and $X'\left(\begin{smallmatrix} I & R \\ O & I \end{smallmatrix}\right)$ have only 0 in common if and only if $P - R$ is nonsingular.

Thus, a symplectic spread in V' containing X' and Y' arises from a set $\mathcal{S}$ of 2^m symmetric matrices, containing O, such that the difference of any two is nonsingular. We have seen above that any orthogonal spread Σ of V, together with a nonsingular 1-space z, determines a symplectic spread Σ_z in the symplectic space $z^\perp/z$ of dimension $2m = 2n - 2$. In terms of the basis for V introduced earlier, assume that $z = \langle x_n + y_n\rangle$. We identify X' and Y' with $\langle X \cap z^\perp, z\rangle/z$ and $\langle Y \cap z^\perp, z\rangle/z$, respectively; let the basis chosen for $z^\perp/z$ consist of the vectors $x_i' = x_i + z$ and $y_i' = y_i + z$, $1 \le i \le m = n - 1$.

PROPOSITION 3.7. [**CCKS**]

$$\mathcal{S} = \left\{ M_1 + d^t d \; \middle| \; \begin{pmatrix} M_1 & d^t \\ d & 0 \end{pmatrix} \in \mathcal{K} \right\} \quad and$$

$$\mathcal{K} = \left\{ \begin{pmatrix} P + d(P)^t d(P) & d(P)^t \\ d(P) & 0 \end{pmatrix} \; \middle| \; P \in \mathcal{S} \right\},$$

where $d(P)$ is the vector in $\mathbb{Z}_2^m$ whose coordinates are the diagonal entries of P in their natural order.

SKETCH. Consider a totally singular subspace

$$\{(x, xM) \mid x \in X\} = \left\{ \left((x', a), (x', a)\begin{pmatrix} M_1 & d^t \\ d & 0 \end{pmatrix}\right) \; \middle| \; (x', a) \in X \oplus \mathbb{Z}_2 \right\}$$

as in Lemma 3.2(i). Its intersection with $z^{\perp} = (0, 1, 0, 1)^{\perp}$ consists of those vectors $(x', a, x'M_1 + ad, x'd^t)$ such that $a = x'd^t$, and hence is the union of the cosets $(x', 0, x'M_1 + x'd^t d, 0) + z = (x', 0, x'[M_1 + d^t d], 0) + z$ with $(x', 0) \in X$.   □

REMARK 3.8. The equation $M = \begin{pmatrix} P + d(P)^t d(P) & d(P)^t \\ d(P) & 0 \end{pmatrix}$ defines a bijection $P \mapsto M$ from symmetric $m \times m$ matrices P to skew–symmetric $(m+1) \times (m+1)$ matrices M. Indeed, given a skew–symmetric $(m+1) \times (m+1)$ matrix M, let its last row be $(d\ 0)$ and find P from the principal minor indicated in the above equation. Conversely, given a symmetric $m \times m$ matrix P, observe that the matrix M defined above is, indeed, skew–symmetric (the diagonal of $d(P)^t d(P)$ is that of P since our field is $\mathbb{Z}_2$). This bijection $P \mapsto M$ is not linear. It is an easy exercise to show that, since n is even, if $P \mapsto M$ and $P' \mapsto M'$, then $P - P'$ is nonsingular if and only if $M - M'$ is.

Proposition 3.7 is very closely related to Proposition 2.2: see Theorem 4.2.

EXAMPLE 3.9. Suppose that Σ' is a *desarguesian spread*: the set of 1-spaces of $\mathrm{GF}(2^m)^2$. There is an obvious alternating bilinear form on $\mathrm{GF}(2^m)^2$, given by $\det \begin{pmatrix} u \\ v \end{pmatrix}$. When followed by the trace map $\mathrm{GF}(2^m) \to \mathbb{Z}_2$, this produces a nonsingular alternating bilinear form on $\mathbb{Z}_2^{2m}$ such that Σ' is still a symplectic spread. Now identify $\mathbb{Z}_2^{2m}$ with $z^{\perp}/z$. Then Corollary 3.3 produces an orthogonal spread Σ of V, which is in fact the orthogonal spread arising from the Kerdock set in Example 2.1. This reflects the prominence of field multiplication there (the term xs^2). The group $SL(2, 2^m)$ that acts on $\mathrm{GF}(2^m)^2$, preserving its set Σ' of 1-spaces, also preserves the alternating bilinear form on $\mathbb{Z}_2^{2m} \equiv z^{\perp}/z$, and lifts to a subgroup of $O^+(2m+2, 2)$ that acts on Σ as it does on the set of 1-spaces of $\mathrm{GF}(2^m)^2$ (in particular, this subgroup is 3-transitive on Σ).

Up and down. The Kerdock sets arising from Examples 2.3 and 2.4 are obtained from a slight variation on the example, using different choices of z and taking into account an intermediate field between $\mathrm{GF}(2^m)$ and $\mathbb{Z}_2$ in order to get a different orthogonal spread Σ.

Starting with a symplectic spread Σ' in a $2m$–dimensional binary symplectic space, we now can produce an orthogonal spread in a $2m+2$–dimensional orthogonal space, in such a way that there is a nonsingular 1-space z for which Σ_z is Σ'. Once we have Σ, we can then form a *different* symplectic spread $\Sigma_{z'}$ using a *different* nonsingular 1-space z'. When combined with passage to subfields [Ka1], this type of up and down process leads to the proof of Theorem 3.5.

4. Projective planes

We now wander even further from the traditional coding theory questions we started with: an entirely different type of geometric view of symplectic spreads is provided by projective planes. For this purpose we first need to ignore, temporarily, the word "symplectic".

From spreads to projective planes. Let V' be a $2m$–dimensional vector space over $\mathrm{GF}(q)$ (no restriction is placed even on the parity of q or m).

A *spread* of V' is a family Σ' of $q^m + 1$ subspaces of dimension m whose union is all of V'. This means that every nonzero vector is in a unique member of Σ'. *Any family of $q^m + 1$ m-spaces in a $2m$-space, any two of which have only 0 in* *common, is a spread.* (N.B.—An orthogonal spread is not a spread in this sense, but a symplectic spread is.)

Affine planes. The importance of spreads is that they produce affine planes: Let $\mathbf{A}(\Sigma')$ denote the point–line geometry whose points are vectors and whose lines are the cosets $W + v$ with $W \in \Sigma', v \in V'$. Then $\mathbf{A}(\Sigma')$ is an *affine plane of order* q^m:

- Any two different points u, v are on a unique line (namely, the line $W + v$ where $u - v \in W \in \Sigma'$);
- Given a line L and a point v not on it, there is a unique line through v disjoint from L (namely, $W + v$ if L is a coset of $W \in \Sigma'$); and
- Each line has exactly q^m points.

There is an obvious notion of parallelism, and by adjoining a new "line at infinity" that "contains" all parallel classes we obtain a projective plane (of order q^m). For each $c \in V$ the translation $v \mapsto v + c$ is an automorphism fixing every parallel class. These affine planes (and their associated projective planes) are called *translation planes.* Any isomorphism between two such planes is induced by a semilinear transformation of the underlying vector spaces.

EXAMPLE 4.1. If V' is a 2-dimensional vector space over $\mathrm{GF}(q)$, its set Σ' of 1-spaces is a desarguesian spread (cf. Example 3.17), and $\mathbf{A}(\Sigma')$ is called a *desarguesian plane.* This plane is pictured in the following figure. The figure also suggests why it makes no difference whether we view lines as the sets "$y = xs$" or the sets "$y = xs^2$" (i.e., $s \mapsto s^2$ is bijective).

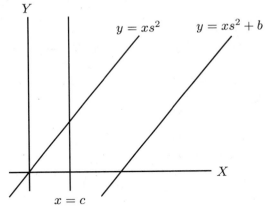

Needless to say, the study of translation planes focuses on nondesarguesian planes. Nevertheless, within the context of this paper desarguesian planes play very special roles: firstly, they produce the original Kerdock codes [**Ke**] (cf. Example 2.1); and secondly, the translation planes constructed via Examples 2.3 and 2.4, as well as those in Theorem 3.5, all are very closely related to desarguesian planes.

Spreads $\leftrightarrow$ spread sets. As in Lemma 3.2, write $V' = X' \oplus Y'$ with $X', Y' \in \Sigma'$, and write matrices with respect to a basis of V' consisting of a basis of X' together with one of Y'. Then every member of $\Sigma' - \{Y\}$ can be written uniquely in the form $X' \left(\begin{smallmatrix} I & P \\ O & I \end{smallmatrix} \right) =$ "$y = xP$" for an $m \times m$ matrix P. The set $\mathcal{S}$ of such matrices is essentially what is called a *spread set,* and lets the plane be described in a very familiar manner, using the lines

$$\text{"}x = c\text{" and "}y = xP + b\text{"}, \ b, c \in V', \ P \in \mathcal{S}.$$

Σ' and $\mathcal{S}$ determine one another in an obvious manner.

Binary operations $\leftrightarrow$ spreads. A binary operation $*$ satisfying conditions (**i**) and (**ii**) in §2 also determines a spread, consisting of Y' and the subsets "$y = x * s$" of $\mathrm{GF}(2^m) \oplus \mathrm{GF}(2^m)$. The lines of the associated affine plane have a familiar appearance:

$$\text{"}x = c\text{" and "}y = x * s + b\text{"}, \ b, c, s \in GF(2^m).$$

Here, $\mathcal{S}$ consists of matrices of the maps $x \mapsto x * s$. Conversely, starting with a spread Σ' in a vector space of characteristic 2, and distinct $X', Y' \in \Sigma'$, choose any bases for X' and Y', and obtain obtain a spread set $\mathcal{S}$ of $m \times m$ matrices as above. Fix an arbitrary bijection $s \mapsto P_s$ of $\mathrm{GF}(2^m) \to \mathcal{S}$ with $P_0 = 0$, and define $x * s := xP_s$ for all $x, y \in \mathrm{GF}(2^m)$. Then conditions (**i**) and (**ii**) are straightforward to check. See [**De**, §5.1] for this and additional information concerning these ways of representing translation planes, as well as for a survey of projective planes of this type.

Symplectic translation planes. Now that we have seen how to go back and forth between spreads, spread sets, translation planes and binary operations, it is time to see how this works for symplectic spreads Σ' and the corresponding planes $\mathbf{A}(\Sigma')$, called *symplectic translation planes.*

EXAMPLE 4.1 *continued.* Starting with a desarguesian spread Σ' in $\mathbb{Z}_2^{2m}$, where m is odd, by Corollary 3.3 and Proposition 3.7 we obtain an orthogonal spread Σ in $\mathbb{Z}_2^{2m+2}$, and hence a Kerdock set and Kerdock code. This latter Kerdock set just the one in Example 2.4: the one giving rise to the original Kerdock code of length $m + 1$.

Symplectic spreads $\leftrightarrow$ symmetric spread sets. Suppose we start with a symplectic spread Σ'. Fix distinct $X', Y' \in \Sigma'$, and a basis of X', but this time choose the basis of Y' to be the dual basis (as was also done just before Lemma 3.1). Then the resulting spread set $\mathcal{S}$ consists of symmetric matrices. Conversely, each spread set consisting of symmetric matrices produces a symplectic spread.

Binary operations $\leftrightarrow$ Kerdock sets. Now suppose that we start with a binary operation $*$ satisfying condition (**v**) in §2. Then the transformations $x \mapsto x * s$ are self–adjoint with respect to the inner product $T(xy)$ on $\mathrm{GF}(2^m)$. In terms of an orthonormal basis of $\mathrm{GF}(2^m)$, this means that $x \mapsto x * s$ is represented by a symmetric matrix P_s. Consequently, we obtain a spread set consisting of symmetric matrices, and we have seen that this produces a symplectic spread. Lift $\mathcal{S}$ to a Kerdock set $\mathcal{K}$ using Proposition 3.7. A calculation shows that *this Kerdock set is precisely the one appearing in* Proposition 2.2.

Conversely, starting with a Kerdock set $\mathcal{K}$, pass to the set $\mathcal{S}_\mathcal{K}$ given in Proposition 3.7, fix a bijection $s \mapsto P_s$ of $\mathrm{GF}(2^m) \to \mathcal{S}_\mathcal{K}$ with $P_0 = 0$, and again define $x * s := xP_s$ for all $x, y \in \mathrm{GF}(2^m)$. Then conditions (**i,ii,iv,v**) are straightforward to check, and (**iii**) can be made to hold by suitably modifying the bijection $s \mapsto P_s$. In other words,

THEOREM 4.2. *Every Kerdock set of $(m + 1) \times (m + 1)$ binary matrices is equivalent to one obtained in Proposition 2.2 using some binary operation.*

We have now seen how to go back and forth between various objects:

$$\text{orthogonal spread} \leftrightarrow \text{symplectic spread}$$
$$\text{orthogonal spread} \leftrightarrow \text{Kerdock set}$$
$$\text{Kerdock set} \qquad \leftrightarrow \text{symmetric spread set}$$
$$\text{Kerdock set} \qquad \leftrightarrow \text{binary operation}$$

With each object on the left are associated many on the right; with each on the right is associated essentially just one on the left. Here "many" and "one" mean "up to whatever notion of equivalence is appropriate". Choices are made in each case, though this is is most evident in the first two listed instances, where a choice of nonsingular point z or of $Y \in \Sigma$ was explicitly made. In Proposition 3.7 we chose a basis, and even distinguished the last basis vector. In Proposition 2.2 and Theorem 4.2 a specific identification was chosen between an $m + 1$–dimensional vector space and $\mathrm{GF}(2^m) \oplus \mathbb{Z}_2$.

EXAMPLE 4.3. Start with a desarguesian symplectic spread, go up and then down (at the end of Section 3). This produces another symplectic spread. The binary operations in Examples 2.3 and 2.4 were obtained in this manner [**Ka1**].

Isomorphisms between planes. Each orthogonal spread appears to produce large numbers of symplectic spreads Σ_z. This leads us to the isomorphism question: when are two planes $\mathbf{A}(\Sigma_z)$ obtained in this manner isomorphic? If there is a symplectic transformation sending one spread to the other, the planes are certainly isomorphic. It seems surprising that the converse is both true and easy to prove:

THEOREM 4.4. [**Ka1**] *For $i = 1, 2$, let Σ_i be a symplectic spread in a $2m$–dimensional symplectic space V_i over $\mathbb{Z}_2$. Let $g \colon \mathbf{A}(\Sigma_1) \to \mathbf{A}(\Sigma_2)$ be an isomorphism that sends the point 0 to the point 0. Then there is an invertible linear transformation $s \colon V_1 \to V_2$ such that the following hold:*

(i) $(\Sigma_1)s = \Sigma_2$,
(ii) *s is an isometry (i.e., $(us, vs) = (u, v)$ for all $u, v \in V_1$), and*
(iii) *$g^{-1}s$ fixes every member of Σ_2.*

The set of all nonsingular linear transformations fixing every member of Σ_2 (as in (iii)), together with O, is a field. It is the largest field over which the plane can most readily be viewed.

COROLLARY 4.5. *Two translation planes $\mathbf{A}(\Sigma_{z_1})$ and $\mathbf{A}(\Sigma_{z_2})$ arising from the same orthogonal spread Σ are isomorphic if and only if z_1 and z_2 are in the same orbit of the group $G(\Sigma)$ of all orthogonal transformations preserving Σ.*

Theorem 4.4 also permits the determination of the full automorphism groups of many of these planes with little or no effort. Further information concerning some of these planes is given in [**Ka1**]. For now we merely note that the construction techniques for planes, using Kerdock sets and orthogonal and symplectic spreads, are very flexible. They have produced planes with relatively large automorphism groups [**Ka1**] as well as planes with unexpectedly small automorphism groups [**Ka5**, **Wi**].

5. Further aspects of Kerdock codes

Nonlinearity. *Each code $C(\mathcal{K})$ is nonlinear.* This is not at all obvious. What is easy to see is that linearity would be the same as $\mathcal{K}$ being closed under addition, which is not the case when $n > 2$. In fact, a much stronger result is true, in view of the following elegant result of Cameron (cf. [**Ka5**]):

THEOREM 5.1 (Cameron). *Let W be a subspace of the space of all $2r \times 2r$ skew–symmetric matrices over a finite field. If every nonzero member of W is nonsingular, then $\dim W \leq r$.*

PROOF. If $(a_{ij}) \in W$ then $\det(a_{ij}) = \text{Pf}(a_{ij})^2$, where $\text{Pf}(a_{ij})$ is the Pfaffian of (a_{ij}) and is a polynomial of degree r in the a_{ij} [**La**, p. 373]. Let $A_1, \ldots, A_d$ be a basis of W. If $A = \sum_i x_i A_i$ for scalars x_i, then $\text{Pf}(A) = f(x_1, \ldots, x_d)$ for a polynomial f of degree r. By the Chevalley-Warning Theorem [**La**, p. 140], f has more than one zero if $d > r$. Thus, we must have $d \leq r$. □

Extremal subspaces (i.e., of dimension r) have yet to be investigated. In particular, it is not known whether there might be interesting examples.

Strongly regular graphs. Once again consider a $2n$–dimensional binary vector space V equipped with the quadratic form Q_{2n}, where $n \geq 4$ and n is even. There is a natural graph $(S, \not\perp)$ defined on the set S of nonzero singular vectors. This is a strongly regular graph: it is regular of degree $2(2^{n-1} - 1)(2^{n-2} + 1)$; any two adjacent vertices are adjacent to $1 + 4(2^{n-2} - 1)(2^{n-3} + 1)$ others; and any two nonadjacent vertices are adjacent to $(2^{n-1} - 1)(2^{n-2} + 1)$ others.

Any orthogonal spread Σ in V also leads to a strongly regular graph having the exact same parameters (i.e., the same constants, associated with adjacent and nonadjacent pairs of vertices, as in the preceding paragraph). Namely, the vertices of this graph are the hyperplanes of the members of Σ; two vertices V_1, V_2 are adjacent if and only if $V_1 \cap V_2^\perp = 0$ [**DDT, Ka3**]. This graph is isomorphic to the previous one if $2n = 8$, and probably not if $2n > 8$, but this is open.

There are analogues of these graphs obtained from symplectic spreads, and similar graphs obtained over other fields [**Ka3**].

Bounds for line–sets in $\mathbb{R}^N$ with prescribed angles. There is a simple way to embed $\mathbb{Z}_2^N$ into $\mathbb{R}^N$, induced by the obvious isomorphism $\mathbb{Z}_2^N \to \{\pm 1\}^N$. In this manner, a code C of length N produces an example of a set of unit vectors; and extremal properties of sets of unit vectors imply ones for codes. This point of view is somewhat related to that of Sloane in these Proceedings.

Line–sets from Kerdock codes. For example, start with any Kerdock set $\mathcal{K}$ of matrices, let $C(\mathcal{K})$ be as in (2.3), and write $N = 2^n$. Then we can form the following unit vectors in $\mathbb{R}^N$ (where coordinates are again indexed by vectors in $\mathbb{Z}_2^n$ and the exponents again are just the Kerdock codewords):

$$\frac{1}{2^{n/2}}\left((-1)^{Q_B(v) + s \cdot v + \varepsilon}\right)_{v \in \mathbb{Z}_2^n} \quad \text{where } B \in \mathcal{K}, \ s \in \mathbb{Z}_2^n, \ \varepsilon \in \mathbb{Z}_2;$$

and

the $N = 2^n$ standard basis vectors and their negatives.

Total number of vectors: $N^2 + 2N$ in $\mathbb{R}^N$.

Another way to view this is as a set of *lines* in $\mathbb{R}^N$, namely the 1-spaces spanned by the vectors in the above list:

$$\left\langle \left((-1)^{Q_B(v)+s\cdot v+\varepsilon} \right)_{v \in \mathbb{Z}_2^n} \right\rangle \quad \text{where } B \in \mathcal{K}, \ s \in \mathbb{Z}_2^n, \ \varepsilon \in \mathbb{Z}_2;$$
and
the 1-spaces spanned by the N standard basis vectors.
Total number of lines: $(N^2 + 2N)/2$ in $\mathbb{R}^N$.

The distances between codewords in the Kerdock code imply that *any two of these lines are either perpendicular or are at an angle of* $\cos^{-1} 1/\sqrt{N}$. In fact, these lines fall into $(N+2)/2$ orthonormal frames such that the angle between members of different frames is always $\cos^{-1} 1/\sqrt{N}$. This construction is due to König [**Ko**], based on ideas in [**CS**]. Applications of these line–sets to approximation theory and to isometric embeddings of Euclidean spaces into ℓ_p-spaces are given in [**Ko**].

One of the starting points of the paper [**CCKS**] was the observation that there is a tantalizing similarity between the construction of this set of lines from $\mathcal{K}$ and the construction orthogonal spreads from $\mathcal{K}$ in Corollary 3.3. Namely, in both situations there is an apparent asymmetry to the description, in which one member of the spread, or one frame (the standard one), appears to be somehow distinguished. In both situations, this asymmetry is merely apparent, caused by an initial choice of basis. If we had chosen one of the other orthonormal frames and written all the others in terms of it, we would have obtained a similar description. This is studied in great detail in [**CCKS**], where it is shown that these $|\mathcal{K}|+1$ orthonormal frames arise in a *natural* way from the $|\mathcal{K}|+1$ members of the orthogonal spread determined by $\mathcal{K}$. Moreover, it is shown how to go back from the line-set to $\mathcal{K}$ using a group (the stabilizer of the line–set in the real orthogonal group).

More general line–sets. In general, consider a set Ω of unit vectors spanning $\mathbb{R}^N$, use the usual dot product in $\mathbb{R}^N$, and assume that $|a\cdot b| \in \{0, \alpha\}$ for all $a \neq b$ in Ω, where $0 < \alpha < 1$ is a constant: the angles between the lines of $\mathbb{R}^N$ determined by the pairs of distinct members of Ω take on only two values, one of which is $90°$ (so $\Omega \cap (-\Omega) = \emptyset$). Delsarte, Goethals and Seidel [**DGS**] proved that $|\Omega| \leq \binom{N+2}{3}$ for any α. They also showed that $|\Omega| \leq \frac{N(N+2)(1-\alpha^2)}{3-(N+2)\alpha^2}$, provided that the denominator is positive.

It is the case of equality here that especially concerns us, where we have an *extremal line–set*. In that case, define a graph on Ω, joining two vectors if they are perpendicular. Then this is a strongly regular graph (cf. [**CCKS**]). The special case $\alpha = 1/\sqrt{N}$, $|\Omega| = \frac{N(N+2)(1-\alpha^2)}{3-(N+2)\alpha^2} = N^2(N+2)/2$, arises when the original code is a Kerdock code $C(\mathcal{K})$ of length $N = 2^{m+1}$. In that case, Ω is a union of $(N+2)/2 = 2^m + 1 = |\mathcal{K}| + 1$ orthonormal bases, with vectors in different bases not perpendicular. (N. B.—It is not known whether the extremal case $\alpha = 1/\sqrt{N}$ can *only* arise from a Kerdock set $\mathcal{K}$ as above.)

There are many other extremal results concerning Euclidean line–sets (or sets of vectors) due to Delsarte, Goethals and Seidel [**DGS**] and Levenštein [**Le**], among others. For example, the results in [**Le**] merely make assumptions about the largest value of $|a \cdot b|$ for distinct $a, b \in \Omega$, rather than the exact nature of the set of dot products. The arguments in these papers use classical Jacobi polynomials. Besides being beautiful, the methods have the added advantage of being highly flexible, permitting natural extensions to a variety of different contexts. For example, in §6 we will be concerned with line–sets in complex vector spaces.

6. $\mathbb{Z}_4$–codes

A $\mathbb{Z}_4$–*code* of length N is just a subset C_4 of $\mathbb{Z}_4^N$; it is *linear* if it is an additive subgroup. While one could use the Hamming metric here, an important discovery in [**CHKSS**] was that the *Lee metric* $d_L(u, v)$ leads to lovely results. This metric is defined as follows. The *Lee weights* of $0, 1, 2, 3 \in \mathbb{Z}_4$ are $0, 1, 2, 1$ respectively, the Lee weight $wt_L(v)$ of $v \in \mathbb{Z}_4^N$ is the integral sum of the Lee weights of its coordinates, and $d_L(u, v) := wt_L(u - v)$.

Gray map. Next we need to recall the definition of the Gray map used in [**CHKSS**]. The following figure shows the Gray encoding of the elements of $\mathbb{Z}_4$ (or of the points $1, i, -1, -i$ in the complex plane) as pairs of *binary* digits.

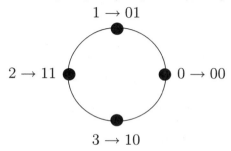

The 2–adic expansion $c = c_1 + 2c_2$ of $c \in \mathbb{Z}_4$ defines maps $c \mapsto c_1$ and $c \mapsto c_2$ from $\mathbb{Z}_4$ to $\mathbb{Z}_2$. Extend these in an obvious way to maps $v \mapsto v_i$ from $\mathbb{Z}_4^N$ to $\mathbb{Z}_2^N$. Then binary codes are obtained from $\mathbb{Z}_4$–codes as their images under the *Gray map* $\varphi \colon \mathbb{Z}_4^N \to \mathbb{Z}_2^{2N}$ given by

$$v\varphi = (v_2, v_1 + v_2), \ v \in \mathbb{Z}_4^N$$

[**CHKSS**]. The key property of this map is the following observation:

THEOREM 6.1. [**CHKSS**] *The Gray map is an isometry* ($\mathbb{Z}_4^N$, Lee metric) $\to$ ($\mathbb{Z}_2^{2N}$, Hamming metric).

There is really more than one Gray map: one can be followed by a permutation of the coordinates of $\mathbb{Z}_2^{2N}$ in order to obtain another one. This is significant in [**CHKSS**] and [**CCKS**] since rearrangements of coordinates are implicitly allowed or needed when Gray maps are used.

Duality. Starting with a *linear* code $C_4 \subseteq \mathbb{Z}_4^N$, there is a natural definition of the *dual* linear code $C_4^\perp$, using the usual dot product on $\mathbb{Z}_4^N$. The standard MacWilliams identity [**MS**, p. 127], and the fact that the Gray map is an isometry, produce detailed information concerning the metric properties of $C_4^\perp$ and of its binary image under any Gray map φ. Namely, define the *Hamming weight enumerator* of a distance–invariant *binary* code C to be the following polynomial in two variables W and X:

$$\text{Ham}_C(W, X) = \sum_{c' \in C} W^{N - d_H(c, c')} X^{d_H(c, c')},$$

which is independent of the choice of $c \in C$. The standard MacWilliams identity asserts that, for a *linear binary code* C,

$$\mathrm{Ham}_{C^\perp}(W, X) = \frac{1}{|C|}\mathrm{Ham}_C(W + X, W - X).$$

The following variant of this was proved using Theorem 6.1:

THEOREM 6.2. [**CHKSS**] *If C is a binary code such that $C\varphi^{-1}$ is linear, then the binary codes C and $((C\varphi^{-1})^\perp)\varphi$ are distance–invariant and satisfy*

$$Ham_{((C\varphi^{-1})^\perp)\varphi}(W, X) = \frac{1}{|C|}Ham_C(W + X, W - X).$$

$$\begin{array}{ccc}
\mathbb{Z}_4\text{-code} & C\varphi^{-1} & \xrightarrow{\text{dual}} & (C\varphi^{-1})^\perp \\
& \downarrow \text{Gray} & \uparrow \varphi^{-1} & \downarrow \varphi \\
\text{binary code} & C & & ((C\varphi^{-1})^\perp)\varphi
\end{array}$$

We will apply this below to some of the Kerdock codes $C(\mathcal{K})$.

$\mathbb{Z}_4$–valued quadratic forms. *Each symmetric $m \times m$ binary matrix P determines a map $F_P\colon \mathbb{Z}_2^m \to \mathbb{Z}_4$.*

The definition of F_P is based on the observation that $\mathbb{Z}_4^m/2\mathbb{Z}_4^m \cong \mathbb{Z}_2^m$. For each $v \in \mathbb{Z}_2^m$ let $\hat{v} \in \mathbb{Z}_4^m$ project onto $v \bmod 2$. View the entries of P as elements $0, 1$ of $\mathbb{Z}_4$, and write $F_P(v)\colon = \hat{v}P\hat{v}^t$. In detail, if $P = (p_{ij})$ with $p_{ij} \in \{0, 1\}$, and if $\hat{v} = (x_i)$, then

$$F_P(v) = \sum_i p_{ij}x_i^2 + 2\sum_{i<j} p_{ij}x_i x_j.$$

It is easy to see that this is independent of the choice of "lift" $\hat{v} = (x_i)$ of v. Of course, we could just choose $\hat{v}$ to have coordinates equal to those of v, but with 0 and 1 viewed as elements of $\mathbb{Z}_4$ (as was done for P). However, we need to be able to state the following basic property of the $\mathbb{Z}_4$–*valued quadratic form F_P* associated with P:

$$F_P(u + v) = F_P(u) + F_P(v) + 2\hat{u}P\hat{v}^t$$

for all $u, v \in \mathbb{Z}_2^n$. This equation should be compared with the similar one (2.1) relating binary quadratic forms and alternating bilinear forms.

$\mathbb{Z}_4$–Kerdock codes. By Proposition 3.7, each Kerdock set $\mathcal{K}$ is related to a set $\mathcal{S}_\mathcal{K}$ of symmetric matrices. (N.B.—Note, however that relationship presupposes that a row and column have been specified.) Equation (2.3) suggests that we consider the following subset of $\mathbb{Z}_4^{2^m}$:

(6.1) $\quad C_4(\mathcal{S}_\mathcal{K})\colon = \big\{ (F_P(v) + 2\hat{s} \cdot \hat{v} + \varepsilon)_{v\in\mathbb{Z}_2^m} \mid P \in \mathcal{S}_\mathcal{K}, s \in \mathbb{Z}_2^m, \varepsilon \in \mathbb{Z}_4 \big\}.$

This is called the $\mathbb{Z}_4$–*Kerdock code* associated with $\mathcal{K}$. One of the main results in [**CCKS**] is the following

THEOREM 6.3. *$C(\mathcal{K})$ is the image of $C_4(\mathcal{S}_\mathcal{K})$ under a suitable Gray map.*

In particular, these two codes are isometric when equipped, respectively, with the Hamming and Lee metrics. Note that the Gray map in the theorem depends on the manner in which $\mathcal{S}_\mathcal{K}$ was obtained from $\mathcal{K}$ in Proposition 3.7. Namely, we arbitrarily chose to single out the nth row and column; but we could just as well used the jth row and column for any j. Thus, some care is needed so as not to be mislead by notation. In view of the preceding theorem, $\mathbb{Z}_4$–valued quadratic forms are natural objects. They were first introduced within topology [**Br**].

The preceding theorem may leave the impression that the definition of $C_4(\mathcal{S_K})$ might first have been calculated by applying φ^{-1} to $C(\mathcal{K})$. This was not the case: $\mathbb{Z}_4$–valued quadratic forms, and the definition of $C_4(\mathcal{S_K})$, arose by viewing the real and complex representation theory of extraspecial 2–groups from unusual perspectives, guided by real and complex line–sets. However, we will not delve into the group–theoretic aspects of these codes, or into the structure of these line–sets, which were essential ingredients in the discovery of $\mathbb{Z}_4$–Kerdock codes. (cf. [**CCKS**]).

$\mathbb{Z}_4$–linear Kerdock and Preparata codes. We have seen that $C(\mathcal{K})$ is never linear (Theorem 5.1). One of the most striking discoveries in [**CHKSS**] was that the $\mathbb{Z}_4$–version $C_4(\mathcal{S_K})$ of $C(\mathcal{K})$ can be linear. That paper studied this in the case of the original Kerdock code, where $\mathcal{S_K}$ arises, as in Example 2.4, using the field multiplications $\mathrm{GF}(2^m) \to \mathrm{GF}(2^m)$ (although this code was written in an entirely different manner in that paper). In that case, $\mathcal{S_K}$ is clearly closed under addition, so that $C_4(\mathcal{S_K})$ is a linear $\mathbb{Z}_4$–code. This was generalized in [**CCKS**]:

THEOREM 6.4. *If $\mathcal{K}$ is a Kerdock set arising as in Proposition 2.2 by means of a binary operation $*$, then $C_4(\mathcal{S_K})$ is a linear $\mathbb{Z}_4$–code if and only if $*$ is* **2–sided** *distributive.*

The next observation in [**CHKSS**] was that, if $C_4(\mathcal{S_K})$ is linear, then $C_4(\mathcal{S_K})^\perp$ also is linear, and Theorem 6.2 gives the exact weight distribution of the *nonlinear* binary code $P_m(\mathcal{S_K})$ of length 2^{m+1} that is the Gray image of $C_4(\mathcal{S_K})^\perp$. The codes $P_m(\mathcal{S_K})$ are examples of *Preparata codes*: their weight distributions are the same as that of code P_m of length 2^{m+1} discovered by Preparata in 1968 [**Pr**] (cf. [**MS**]). The fact that the weight distribution of the latter codes is related to that of (the original) Kerdock codes has been a perplexing fact for many years. The introduction of $\mathbb{Z}_4$–linear codes and the Gray map have narrowed this gap, providing codes in some precise sense dual to Kerdock codes. If $m = 3$ then $P_m(\mathcal{S_K})$ and P_m are equivalent to the Nordstrom–Robinson code. However, if $m \geq 5$ then $P_m(\mathcal{S_K})$ has the property that the $\mathbb{Z}_2$–subspace of $\mathbb{Z}_2^{2^{m+1}}$ it spans has vectors of weight 2, which is not the case for the original Preparata codes: the codes P_m and $P_m(\mathcal{S_K})$ *are never quasi–equivalent if $m \geq 5$* (proved in [**CHKSS**] for the case studied there, and for any Kerdock set $\mathcal{K}$ in [**CCKS**]). The fact that $P_m(\mathcal{S_K})$ is a sort of dual of $C_4(\mathcal{K})$ prompted the authors of [**CHKSS**] to "propose that this is the 'correct' way to define these codes" (i.e., codes with Preparata's weight distribution).

Extremal property. The importance of Preparata codes (either the original versions P_m or the new ones $P_m(\mathcal{S_K})$) takes us back to the start of this paper. These codes are extremal in the following sense. They have length $N = 2^{m+1}$, minimum distance 6, and as many codewords as possible subject to these conditions, namely, $2^{N-2(m+1)}$. Moreover, no linear code can be extremal in this sense [**GS**]. Since the size of any linear code is a power of 2, it follows that *any linear code with minimum distance at least 6 has at most half as many codewords as Preparata codes of the same length.*

In [**CHKSS**] it is also shown that other nonlinear subcodes of $RM(2, n)$ are Gray images of $\mathbb{Z}_4$–linear codes. This groundbreaking paper has produced an outpouring of further research on $\mathbb{Z}_4$–codes. This has led to the consideration of codes over $\mathbb{Z}_{2^l}$ for all l, and even more recently to codes over the ring of 2-adic integers by using classical Hensel lifts.

As already observed in §1, Kerdock and other $\mathbb{Z}_4$–linear codes have the striking properties of being optimal from a combinatorial point of view and yet having linear descriptions that simplify both their study and implementation.

Equivalence. Two $\mathbb{Z}_4$–codes are *equivalent* if one can be gotten from the other by a permutation of coordinates followed by multiplication by a single diagonal matrix of ± 1's. Two $\mathbb{Z}_4$–codes of length N are *quasi–equivalent* if one is equivalent to a $\mathbb{Z}_4^N$–translate of the other.

Equivalences among the codes $C_4(\mathcal{S}_\mathcal{K})$ and among the codes $P_m(\mathcal{S}_\mathcal{K})$ are discussed at length in [**CCKS**]. The results are similar to Theorem 3.4. It is also shown that, when m is composite, there is a $\mathbb{Z}_4$–linear Kerdock code $C_4(\mathcal{S}_\mathcal{K})$ and a Preparata code $P_m(\mathcal{S}_\mathcal{K})$ not quasi–equivalent to the ones studied in [**CHKSS**]. More recently, Williams proved the following far stronger result:

THEOREM 6.5. [**Wi**] *If m is odd and has $r \geq 2$ prime factors, at least one of which is ≥ 7, then there are at least $2^{(r-1)m}/m$ pairwise quasi–inequivalent $\mathbb{Z}_4$–linear Kerdock and Preparata codes of length 2^{m+1}.*

These codes are constructed as follows. There is a sequence $\mathrm{GF}(2^m) \supset F_1 \supset \cdots \supset F_{r-1} \supset \mathrm{GF}(2)$ of fields. For each $i \geq 1$ let $T_i \colon \mathrm{GF}(2^m) \to F_i$ be the trace map and let $\zeta_i \in F$. Williams greatly generalized Example 2.3 by repeated use of the up and down process at the end of Section 3. He showed that the following 2–sided distributive binary operation on $\mathrm{GF}(2^m)$ satisfies (**i-v**):

$$x * s = xs^2 + \sum_{1}^{r-1} \Big(T_i(\zeta_i x)s + \zeta_i T_i(xs) \Big).$$

He then handled the quasi–equivalence of all of the resulting $\mathbb{Z}_4$–linear Kerdock codes (obtained using Propositions 2.2 and 3.7 together with (6.1)) in order to prove Theorem 6.5. Planes were a crucial tool in this, using Theorem 4.4. Thus, planes enter not only into the construction of the codes $C(\mathcal{K})$, $C_4(\mathcal{S}_\mathcal{K})$ and $P_m(\mathcal{S}_\mathcal{K})$, but also into the study of their structure.

Bounds for line–sets in $\mathbb{C}^{N'}$ with prescribed angles. As in the case of the usual Kerdock codes, the $\mathbb{Z}_4$–Kerdock codes produce line–sets in $\mathbb{C}^{N'}$ via the isomorphism $\mathbb{Z}_4^{N'} \cong \langle i \rangle^{N'}$, where $N' = 2^m$. Thus, the $\mathbb{Z}_4$–Kerdock code (6.1) produces the following set of lines of $\mathbb{C}^{N'}$ (where the exponents are just the $\mathbb{Z}_4$–Kerdock codewords):

$$\Big\langle \big(i^{F_P(v)+2\hat{s}\cdot\hat{v}+\varepsilon}\big)_{v \in \mathbb{Z}_2^m} \Big\rangle \text{ where } P \in \mathcal{S}_\mathcal{K}, s \in \mathbb{Z}_2^m, \varepsilon \in \mathbb{Z}_4;$$

and

the 1–spaces spanned by the $N' = 2^m$ standard basis vectors.

Total number of lines: $2N'^2 + 2N'$ in $\mathbb{C}^{N'}$.

This time the distances between codewords in the $\mathbb{Z}_4$–Kerdock code imply that *any two of these lines are either perpendicular or are at an angle of* $\cos^{-1} 1/\sqrt{N'}$. These lines fall into $N' + 1$ orthonormal frames such that the angle between members of different frames is always $\cos^{-1} 1/\sqrt{N'}$. One can pass back and forth between these line-sets and those in $\mathbb{R}^{2^{m+1}}$ discussed earlier, each complex line–set producing an essentially unique real one but each real one producing many inequivalent complex ones [**CCKS**].

Once again there are general bounds on complex line–sets in [**DGS**] and [**Le**]; strongly regular graphs arise in suitable cases of equality; and the line–sets obtained from $\mathbb{Z}_4$–Kerdock codes are examples of *extremal line–sets* (cf. [**CCKS**]). Once again there are also applications to approximation theory and to isometric embeddings [**Ko**].

Quaternionic codes. These ideas are pursued slightly further in [**Ka7**], where *quaternionic* line–sets are examined. Extremal ones are constructed in quaternionic space $\mathbb{H}^{N''}$, where $N'' = 2^{m-1}$. These arise, in turn, from quaternionic Kerdock codes of length N'', which are suitable subsets of $Q_8^{N''}$ obtained using Kerdock sets of $m + 1 \times m + 1$ matrices.

In general, a *quaternionic code* of length N is simply a subset of Q_8^N. The study of such codes suffers from various apparent disadvantages. There is no way to convert to additive notation, and in particular no reasonable way to introduce a ring structure on the coordinates, as in the cases of codes over $\mathbb{Z}_2$ or $\mathbb{Z}_4$. Thus, they also lack one of the most basic aspects of codes over $\mathbb{Z}_2$ or $\mathbb{Z}_4$, the notion of a dual code: there is no natural inner product on subsets of Q_8^N that generalizes the dot product on $\mathbb{Z}_2^N$ or $\mathbb{Z}_4^N$, since only one binary operation is available. Therefore, it is not surprising that, as yet, there are almost no results concerning quaternionic codes.

7. Further directions

In §5 we discussed subsets of $\mathbb{R}^N$ arising from binary codes C, obtained by replacing $\mathbb{Z}_2$ by $\{\pm 1\}$. In a similar manner, subsets of $\mathbb{C}^N$ arise from $\mathbb{Z}_4$–codes by replacing $\mathbb{Z}_4$ by $\{\pm 1, \pm i\} = \langle i \rangle$. The obvious metric in $\mathbb{C}^N$ is the one induced by the usual hermitian inner product. The natural metrics on $\mathbb{R}^N$ and $\mathbb{C}^N$ are also natural within coding theory:

- the Hamming metric on $\mathbb{Z}_2^N \equiv \{\pm 1\}^N$ is half of the square of the Euclidean metric restricted to the subset $\{\pm 1\}^N$ of $\mathbb{R}^N$; and
- the Lee metric on $\mathbb{Z}_4^N \equiv \langle i \rangle^N$ is half of the square of the hermitian metric restricted to the subset $\langle i \rangle^N$ of $\mathbb{C}^N$.

These statements are entirely elementary to check. Nevertheless, they suggested in [**Ka7**] that

- "the natural metric" on Q_8^N is half of the square of the hermitian metric restricted to the subset Q_8^N of $\mathbb{H}^N$.

(Note that this "hamiltonian metric" restricts to the Lee metric on $\langle i \rangle^N$.) A tentative discussion of this can be found in that reference.

We have merely hinted at group–theoretic aspects of the subject of this paper; see [**Ka1, CCKS**]. A connection with simple complex Lie algebras is surveyed in [**Ka6**].

We also have not spent much time discussing the affine planes $\mathbf{A}(\Sigma_z)$.

The methods in [**CHKSS**] involve the use of a ring of size 4^m in place of $GF(2^m)$. This leads into the realm of cyclic codes over $\mathbb{Z}_4$. This fundamental new direction in coding theory has not been dealt with at all in the present survey.

References

[Br]   E. H. Brown, *Generalizations of Kervaire's invariant*, Annals of Math. **95** (1972) 368–383.

[CCKS]   A. R. Calderbank, P. J. Cameron, W. M. Kantor and J. J. Seidel, *$\mathbb{Z}_4$–Kerdock codes, orthogonal spreads, and extremal Euclidean line–sets* (submitted).

[CHKSS]   A. R. Calderbank, A. R. Hammons, Jr., P. V. Kumar, N. J. A. Sloane, and P. Solé, *The $\mathbb{Z}_4$–linearity of Kerdock, Preparata, Goethals and related codes*, IEEE Trans. Inform. Theory **40** (1994) 301–319.

[CL]   P. J. Cameron and J. H. van Lint, *Designs, graphs, codes and their links*, Cambridge Univ. Press, Cambridge, 1991.

[CS]   P. J. Cameron and J. J. Seidel, *Quadratic forms over $GF(2)$*, Indag. Math. **35** (1973), 1–8.

[DDT]   F. DeClerck, R. H. Dye and J. A. Thas, *An infinite class of partial geometries associated with the hyperbolic quadric in $PG(4n-1,2)$*, Europ. J. Combinatorics **1** (1980) 323–326.

[DGS]   P. Delsarte, J. M. Goethals and J. J. Seidel, *Bounds for systems of lines and Jacobi polynomials*, Philips Res. Repts. **30** (1975) 91–105.

[De]   P. Dembowski, *Finite geometries*, Springer, Berlin-Heidelberg-New York, 1968.

[Dic]   L. E. Dickson, *Linear groups, with an exposition of Galois theory*, Teubner, Leipzig 1901; reprint Dover, New York, 1958.

[Dil]   J. F. Dillon, *Elementary Hadamard difference sets*. Ph.D. thesis, U. of Maryland, 1974.

[GS]   J. M. Goethals and S. L. Snover, *Nearly perfect binary codes*, Discrete Math. **3** (1972) 65–88.

[Ka1]   W. M. Kantor, *Spreads, translation planes and Kerdock sets. I,II*, SIAM J. Alg. Discr. Meth. **3** (1982) 151–165 and 308–318.

[Ka2]   W. M. Kantor, *An exponential number of generalized Kerdock codes*, Inform. Control **53** (1982) 74–80.

[Ka3]   W. M. Kantor, *Strongly regular graphs defined by spreads*, Israel J. Math **41** (1982), 298–312.

[Ka4]   W. M. Kantor, *On the inequivalence of generalized Preparata codes*, IEEE Trans. Inform. Theory **29** (1983), 345–348.

[Ka5]   W. M. Kantor, *Projective planes of order q whose collineation groups have order q^2*, J. Algebraic Combinatorics **3** (1994), 405–425.

[Ka6]   W. M. Kantor, *Some Lie algebras, finite groups and finite geometries* (to appear in: Proc. Ohio State U. Groups and Geometries Conference).

[Ka7]   W. M. Kantor, *Quaternionic line–sets and quaternionic Kerdock codes* (submitted).

[KW]   W. M. Kantor and M. E. Williams, *New flag–transitive affine planes of even order* (to appear in JCT(A)).

[Ke]   A. M. Kerdock, *A class of low-rate nonlinear binary codes*, Inform. Control **20** (1972), 182–187.

[Ko]   H. König, *Isometric embeddings of euclidean spaces into finite-dimensional ℓ_p-spaces* (manuscript).

[La]   S. Lang, *Algebra*, Addison-Wesley, Reading, 1971.

[Le]   V. I. Levenštein, *Bounds on the maximal cardinality of a code with bounded modulus of the inner product*, Soviet Math. Dokl. **25** (1982), 526–531.

[Li]   J. H. van Lint, *Kerdock and Preparata codes*, Cong. Numerantium **39** (1983), 25–41.

[MS]   F. J. MacWilliams and N. J. A. Sloane, *The theory of error-correcting codes*, North–Holland, Amsterdam, 1977.

[Pr]   F. P. Preparata, *A class of optimum nonlinear double-error correcting codes*, Inform. Control. **13** (1968), 378–400.

[Wi]   M. E. Williams, $\mathbb{Z}_4$–linear Kerdock codes, orthogonal geometries, and non–associative division algebras, Ph.D. thesis, University of Oregon 1995.

DEPARTMENT OF MATHEMATICS, UNIVERSITY OF OREGON, EUGENE, OR 97403
E-mail address: `kantor@math.uoregon.edu`

Proceedings of Symposia in Applied Mathematics
Volume **50**, 1995

Codes (Spherical) and Designs (Experimental)

R. H. Hardin and N. J. A. Sloane

ABSTRACT. An overview of the authors' work (partly in collaboration with
W. D. Smith) on the problems of packing equal nonoverlapping spherical caps
on a sphere in d dimensions, covering the sphere with equal caps in the most
economical way, finding sets of points on a sphere with minimal energy, or
whose convex hull has the greatest volume, or which can be used for numerical
integration on the sphere (spherical t-designs), etc., as well as the problems
of choosing good sets of points in the ball or cube to be used as experimental
designs.

1. Preamble

A lot has been written about the connections between classical codes and combinatorial designs [1], [44], [58], [65]. That is *not* what this lecture is about! The codes we will discuss are sets of points on the unit sphere

$$\Omega_d = S^{d-1} = \{(x_1, \dots, x_d) \in \mathbb{R}^d : x_1^2 + \cdots + x_d^2 = 1\} ,$$

and the designs are those used by experimenters: statisticians' designs, not mathematicians'.

There is a curious story behind our work on experimental designs. An article about the second author, dealing especially with the perhaps surprising connections between the problems of finding good packings of equal spheres in $\mathbb{R}^d$ and of finding good signaling sets for digital communications, appeared in the October 1990 issue of the magazine *Discover* [5]. This article resulted in a large number of letters from readers. A few quotations will indicate why most of them could be tossed aside with a laugh:

> "Amazing. Dr. K____ breaks through $\sqrt{2}$. Solves one of Science's Unbreakable Enigmas ..."

> "On page 697 of this report, you will find the single most important statement in the history of physics ..."

> "It is convenient to assume that your 'Handbook of Integer Sequences' is the single most important mathematical 'discovery' in the last 3000

1991 *Mathematics Subject Classification.* Primary 62K05; Secondary 05B40, 11P05.

years [He is referring to [**71**].] ... Get ready for your annual paid vacation to Stockholm."

One letter, however, looked extremely interesting. It was written by a statistician, David Doehlert, of the Experiment Strategies Foundation in Seattle. He had come across the article by chance in an airplane, and immediately dashed off a note saying: Since you know how to pack spheres, I wish you would solve this problem, that has interested me for many years, and is of some importance in statistics: can you place 14 (or 15, or 16) points "nicely" on a sphere in four dimensions? What about 20 (or 21, or 22) points on a sphere in five dimensions, and so on?

2. Placing points on a sphere and related problems

Doehlert's letter had come to the right place. For many years the authors and Warren D. Smith have been building up tables of nice arrangements of points on spheres. The three of us call ourselves the 'Codemart' team, and our logo is shown in Figure 1. In fact we have even designed our own T-shirt, a photograph of which can be seen on page 308 of [**30**].

Another code from

CODEMART

R. H. Hardin, N. J. A. Sloane and W. D. Smith

AT&T Bell Laboratories
Room 2C-376, Murray Hill, New Jersey 07974 USA

FIGURE 1. The 'Codemart' logo.

What does a "nice" arrangement mean? We have considered several different criteria.

(P1) The packing problems. Place N points $P_1, \ldots, P_N$ on the sphere Ω_d so as to maximize the minimal distance between them. The distance is chordal distance, but an equivalent and nicer formulation is to choose $P_1, \ldots, P_N$ so as to

$$(1) \qquad \text{minimize} \max_{i \neq j} P_i \cdot P_j \,,$$

regarding the points as unit vectors from the center of the sphere. A third formulation, also equivalent, is to maximize the minimal angle between the points, measuring angles from the center.

(P2) The covering problem. Choose $P_1, \ldots, P_N$ on Ω_d so as to minimize the maximal distance from a point of Ω_d to the nearest P_i:

$$\text{minimize} \max_{X \in \Omega_d} \max_{i=1,\ldots,N} X \cdot P_i$$

One may think of the P_i as locations of fuel supplies on the moon, to be placed so that no matter where one lands on the moon, the distance to the nearest fuel supply is not too great.

The difference between the packing and covering problems is sometimes described in terms of convenience stores ("7–11" stores in some parts of the U.S.A.). From the point of view of the managers of the stores, they should be placed as far apart as possible, i.e. they should be a packing. But from the customers' point of view, the stores should be placed so that no one has too far to walk to the nearest store, i.e. they should form a covering.

(P3) The quantizing problem. Choose $P_1, \ldots, P_N$ on Ω_d so as to minimize the mean squared error when the points are used as a quantizer or analog-to-digital converter. A point X is chosen at random on Ω_d, and replaced by the closest $P_i(X)$. The P_i should be chosen so that the average error

$$\int_{X \in \Omega_d} |X - P_i(X)|^2 d\mu(X)$$

is minimized, where μ is uniform measure on the sphere.

(P4) The minimal error probability problem. Now the P_i represent signals in a communication system. When P_i is transmitted, the received signal is a neighboring point X on the sphere, where $|X - P_i|$ has a Gaussian distribution with mean 0 and variance σ^2. The decoder replaces X by the closest P_j, and therefore makes an error if $j \neq i$. The problem is to choose $P_1, \ldots, P_N \in \Omega_d$ so that the average probability of error is minimized.

(P5) The maximal volume problem. Choose $P_1, \ldots, P_N \in \Omega_d$ so that the volume of their convex hull is maximized. The polytope formed by the convex hull of such a set of points has sometimes been used as an answer to the question: which N-vertex polytope inscribed in the unit sphere gives the best approximation to the sphere?

(P6) Best set of points for numerical integration. The idea is that we will approximate the integral of a function on the sphere by its average over our set of points:

$$(2) \qquad \int_{\Omega_d} f(x) d\mu(x) \approx \frac{1}{N} \sum_{i=1}^{N} f(P_i) \ .$$

(It is also possible to allow coefficients or *weights* on the right-hand side of (2), but we shall not consider this here.)

We say that $P_1, \ldots, P_N \in \Omega_d$ form a *spherical t-design* if equality holds in (2) for all polynomials f of degree $\leq t$. For given values of d and t, the problem is to find what values of N are possible, and in particular to determine the minimal value of N.

There are several related problems: for example, replace the sphere on the left-hand side of (2) by the ball $B_d = \{(x_1, \ldots, x_d) \in \mathbb{R}^d : x_1^2 + \cdots + x_d^2 \leq 1\}$, and choose $P_1, \ldots, P_N \in B_d$ on the right-hand side.

Alternatively, there is the **interpolation problem:** we wish to interpolate f over Ω_d from its values at $P_1, \ldots, P_N$. How should the P_i be chosen?

(P7) Minimal energy arrangements. Choose $P_1, \ldots, P_N \in \Omega_d$ so as to minimize the potential energy

$$\sum_{i \neq j} \frac{1}{|P_i - P_j|^m}$$

for a given value of m (usually taken to be 2).

After Doehlert's letter arrived, we added another criterion:

(P8) Best statistical design. A simple version of this problem is: choose $P_1, \ldots, P_N \in \Omega_d$ so that, when supplemented by an appropriate number of measurements at the center of the sphere, they form an optimal design for fitting a quadratic response surface.

Of course, as we shall discuss in Section 4, this is just one special case of a very large class of problems.

Two further problems should be mentioned, since we have successfully applied the same methods to them.

(P9) Construction of Isometric Embeddings. A set of points $P_1, \ldots, P_N$ in $\mathbb{R}^d$ is said to form an *isometric embedding* of degree $2s$ if the following identity holds:

$$(3) \qquad (x \cdot x)^{2s} = \sum_{i=1}^{N} (P_i \cdot x)^s \, ,$$

where $x = (x_1, \ldots, x_d)$ is a vector of indeterminates. This problem is also connected with numerical integration on the sphere (see [56], [66], [70]). We will discuss our results on this problem in Section 6.

(P10) Minimal energy arrangements of balls. Choose $P_1, \ldots, P_N \in \mathbb{R}^d$ so that $|P_i - P_j| \geq 2$ for $i \neq j$ (so the balls have radius 1 and do not overlap) and the second moment

$$\sum_{i=1}^{N} |P_i - \overline{P}|^2$$

is minimized, where $\overline{P} = (1/N) \sum P_i$ is the centroid of the points. For our results on this problem, see [72].

The packing problem, (P1), is the most widely studied. It is sometimes known as the **Tammes problem** after the Dutch botanist P.M.L. Tammes who was led to this question by studying the distribution of pores on pollen grains [74]. The following rather long list of references has been chosen from a much greater list (see the bibliography in [42]) to illustrate the richness of this subject: [11], [13], [15], [17], [19], [28], [29], [31]–[35], [36], [50], [53], [54], [55], [57], [59], [67], [68], [69], [73], [75]–[78], [81].

Our own work on all these problems, and on the packing problem in particular, will be described in our book-in-preparation [42] (see also the next section).

Problems (P2), (P3) and (P4) are related in that they can all be expressed in terms of the Voronoi regions of the points. Problem (P2) asks that the greatest circumradius of any Voronoi cell should be minimized, problem (P3) that the average second moment of the Voronoi cells be minimized, and so on. Not so much has been written about these problems (see [14], [79]). For problem (P5) see [6], [42] and the following section. We defer discussion of problems (P6) and (P8) to Sections 5 and 4 respectively.

The minimal energy problem, (P7), also has an extensive literature: see [4], [24], [26], [52], [59], [64], [80], and especially [42] and the following section.

Spherical codes. Strictly speaking, by analogy with classical coding theory, only the solutions to problems (P1) and (P4) should be called *spherical codes*. However, we often use the term more generally to refer to any nice arrangement of points on Ω_d.

Comparison of problems. At first one expects that the answers to all these problems will be the same: a good packing of 24 points should also be a good covering, and so on. Nothing could be further from the truth. Except in very special cases, the answers to most of these problems are different. The case of 12 points in 3 dimensions is one of the exceptions: we believe the set of twelve vertices of a regular icosahedron solves all these problems. But in general it seems that each of problems (P1), (P2), (P5), (P6) and (P7) requires a different arrangement of points for its solution. (We have not investigated problems (P3) and (P4), and problem (P8) in the form we have stated it is very similar to the case $t = 4$ of (P6), the construction of spherical 4-designs; so we exclude problems (P3), (P4) and (P8) from this discussion.)

We illustrate by discussing the case of $N = 24$ points in 3 dimensions, since this is one of the few cases where the optimal solution to any of these problems has been established theoretically. Robinson [67] showed in 1961 that the best packing of 24 points is achieved by the vertices of a regular snub cube, one of the Archimedean solids (cf. [20]). According to our tables, however (see the next section), the 24-point solutions to the covering problem (P2), the maximal volume problem (P5), and the minimal energy configuration (P7) are all different from each other and from the regular snub cube. Furthermore the vertices of the regular snub cube form only a spherical 3-design (see Problem (P6)). We have recently discovered [41] that by modifying the shape of the snub cube slightly the vertices can be made to form a spherical 7-design: we call this the "improved snub cube".

The following table compares the different solutions, giving both the minimal angle between the points and the order of the symmetry group.

Problem	Min. angle	Group
Packing (P1)	43.691°	24
Min. energy (P7)	42.065°	24
t-design (P6)	41.376°	24
Max. volume (P5)	40.512°	4
Covering (P2)	36.673°	4

The first three solutions are all snub cubes, consisting of the 24 points that can be obtained from a single point (A, B, C) by applying any even permutation followed by changing any even number of signs, or any odd permutation followed by changing any odd number of signs. For the packing problem A, B, C are respectively .8503, .4623, .2514, giving the regular snub cube; for the minimal energy problem they are .8616, .4416, .2503; and for our new spherical 7-design, the "improved snub cube", they are .8662, .4225, .2666 (see [**41**] for details). The last two configurations in the table have a completely different structure, being both less symmetrical and having only triangular faces. Figure 2 shows the 24-point packing (left-hand picture), covering (center picture) and maximal volume arrangement (right-hand picture). The pictures show the convex hulls of the points. The regular snub cube in the left-hand picture has a diagonal drawn on each of its square faces. The "improved snub cube" and the 24-point minimal energy configurations are not shown, but in appearance are almost indistinguishable from the regular snub cube.

Although we do not know for certain that these are the optimal solutions to the minimal energy, maximal volume, and covering problems with 24 points, we strongly believe that they are. (It should not be difficult to show that there cannot be a single 24-point arrangement that beats the three designs mentioned for these three problems.)

We find this very convincing evidence that in general these problems have different solutions.

Incidentally it would be useful to have some theorems connecting the different problems. For example, if θ_p (resp. θ_c) is the maximal angular separation in the best N-point packing (resp. covering), then of course $\theta_c \leq \theta_p$. How small can θ_c be with respect to θ_p? Similar questions can be asked about the other problems.

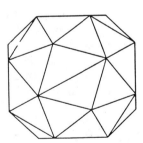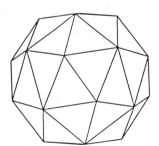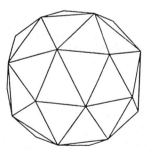

FIGURE 2. Best 24-point packing and putatively best 24-point covering and maximal-volume arrangements.

3. Our tables

Our initial response to Doehlert's letter was to extract an appropriate collection of packings from our tables and send them to him. (We will discuss his answer in the next section.)

Our tables have been constructed using a variety of techniques, and include putative solutions to problems (P1)–(P10) (except (P2) and (P3), which we have not yet considered) for various dimensions (d) and numbers of points (N).

Our main tool, at least for 'small' numbers of points (say with $Nd \leq 500$), is an optimizer that is a modification of the Hooke and Jeeves [**43**] *pattern search*, and which is described in greater detail in [**38**] (see also [**3**]). We have made effective use of suitably modified versions of this optimizer for attacking all of these problems.

Our tables extend far beyond any others that have been published. We have several reasons for believing that are solutions are either optimal or very close to optimal: (a) in the case of the packing problem, where there has been a considerable amount of prior work, our solutions (with seven exceptions[1]) are at least as good as the old records; (b) in the case of experimental designs for fitting linear models, where again a considerable amount was already known about optimal solutions, our optimizer was usually able to find these solutions in the range $Nd \leq 500$ (see [**38**] for details); and (c) as we shall discuss in Section 5, similar remarks apply to the case of quadratic response surface designs in the sphere.

We are in the process of publishing all these tables, principally in the book [**42**] that we are preparing. But in view of the considerable recent interest in these problems, we are making these tables available before the book is completed.

The tables are in netlib, and can be accessed via email, ftp or Mosaic. In the netlib archive the directories

> att/math/sloane/packings
> att/math/sloane/coverings
> att/math/sloane/maxvolumes
> att/math/sloane/sphdesigns
> att/math/sloane/electrons
> att/math/sloane/gosset
> att/math/sloane/iedir
> att/math/sloane/cluster

contain solutions to problems P1, P2, P5–P10 respectively, and

> att/math/sloane/icosahedral

contains solutions to problems P1, P2 and P5 with icosahedral symmetry. Incidentally there are similar directories for Hadamard matrices, orthogonal arrays, minimal Lennard-Jones potential packings, and constant weight codes, as well as a directory att/math/sloane/doc that contains many of our papers.

We first describe how to access the archive by email. One can find out what is available by sending a message to netlib@research.att.com containing lines like

> send index for att/math/sloane/packings
> send index for att/math/sloane/packings/dim4
> send index for att/math/sloane/doc

The return mail will have a list of available material. For example, here is one of the items from att/math/sloane/packings/dim4:

> file   att/math/sloane/packings/dim4/pack.4.24
> by   R.H. Hardin, N.J.A. Sloane & W.D. Smith
> for   File pack.4.24 contains the coords of the putatively optimal
>   packing of 24 points on a sphere in 4 dimensions
> # For more information see att/math/sloane/packings/readme
> # Copyright 1994 by R.H. Hardin, N.J.A. Sloane and W.D. Smith

---

[1]For $d = 3$ and $N = 21, 27, 33, 66, 74, 81$ and 86, Kottwitz's packings [**50**], [**51**] were better than ours. With his permission, we have added his packings, duly credited, to our tables.

To order this item, send the message

send att/math/sloane/packings/dim4/pack.4.24

or equivalently

send pack.4.24 from att/math/sloane/packings/dim4

to netlib@research.att.com. The file will be sent in one or more pieces. The mail header should be stripped from each piece to produce a shell file. The shell files may be run in any order; the original document will be created as the last shell file is run. (Of course this particular example would fit in a single file.)

For example, you might receive a large file in four chunks, which could arrive in any order. Strip off the mail headers, and call them say temp1, ..., temp4, in any order. Then do $ sh temp1, ..., $ sh temp4. At the end, the requested file will have been created.

The default limit for the size of each chunk is just under one megabyte. If this is too large for your mail program to handle, include a line such as

mailsize 40k

in your request. This will limit the size of the chunks to 40 KB.

The request

send getting.stuff from att/math

will produce further instructions.

Second, ftp access. Connect by ftp to netlib.att.com, login as anonymous, and use your email address as password. Now type

binary
cd netlib/att/math/sloane/packings

for example. You can then use "ls" to see what files are available, "get" to fetch them, "cd" to move to subdirectories, etc., and "quit" to quit.

(The files you receive will be compressed, and end with .Z, e.g. pack.4.24.Z. Do $ uncompress pack.4.24.Z to uncompress them.)

Third, from a Mosaic document viewer, you can get directly to the material. Open an URL address such as:

ftp://netlib.att.com/netlib/att/math/sloane/doc/index.html.Z
ftp://netlib.att.com/netlib/att/math/sloane/packings/index.html.Z
ftp://netlib.att.com/netlib/att/math/sloane/packings/dim4/index.html.Z

This will give you a screen of short descriptions of all the items available. Clicking on one gives you the document, which can then be saved in a file.

At the present time the archive contains packings in dimensions 3, 4, 5 with $N \leq 130$ points, as well as an extensive table of larger 3-dimensional packings with icosahedral symmetry. We are in the process of adding a much larger table of packings in up to 24 dimensions that we have constructed by other techniques.

We would greatly appreciate hearing[2] of improvements to any of these tables, and will be glad to include them in the archive, giving credit to the discoverer.

Figures 3–10 show some examples of our spherical codes. Figure 3 shows our best packings, coverings and maximal volume arrangements for 72 and 100 points.

---

[2]Send them to N.J.A. Sloane, preferably by electronic mail to njas@research.att.com, or by fax to (908) 582 3340, or by regular mail to N.J.A. Sloane, Room 2C-376, AT&T Bell Labs, Murray Hill, NJ 07974, USA.

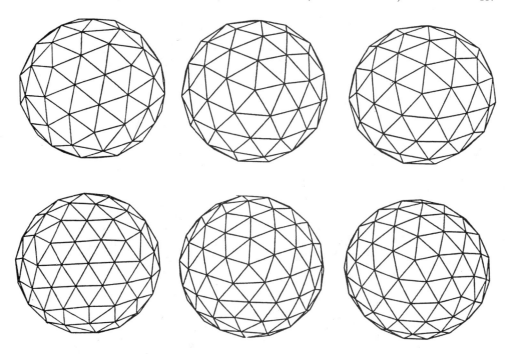

FIGURE 3. From left to right, top to bottom, the putatively best packings, coverings and maximal volume arrangements for 72 and 100 points respectively.

In Figure 3 (as in Figure 2) the pictures show the convex hulls of the arrangements. Figures 4–9 show packings with icosahedral symmetry and various numbers of points in the range 300 to 2000. In Figs. 4 and 5 we see the contact graph of the points (i.e. only points at the minimal separation are joined). The pictures have been projected stereographically with a horizon of 50° North. The 1952-point packing shown in Fig. 5 is on the front of the Codemart T-sheet. On the back is an 8192-point covering, shown in Fig. 6. Unlike the earlier pictures, which all show the best arrangements found, Fig. 6 was chosen for its aesthetic appearance, and is not the best 8192-point covering found. It has covering radius 1.408641°, which is very slightly inferior to the arrangement shown in Fig. 7, which has covering radius 1.404871°. The best 8192-*packing* found (Fig. 8) is much less pleasing to the eye.

We have found this to be true in general: coverings look nicer (and have larger symmetry groups) than packings.

After seeing Figs. 6–8 the reader may ask, why not simply cover the sphere completely with a grid of triangles, with six lines meeting at each point? Or why not simply place the points "uniformly" on the sphere, so that every point looks like every one (as in the icosahedron, for example)? The answers are that the first suggestion is simply impossible (it would violate Euler's theorem, see [20], §3.6), and the second suggestion is only viable for small numbers of points. Jordan's theorem (see for example [23], §30) gives an upper limit on how many points can be placed on Ω_d (for $d \geq 3$) in such a way that their symmetry group acts transitively.

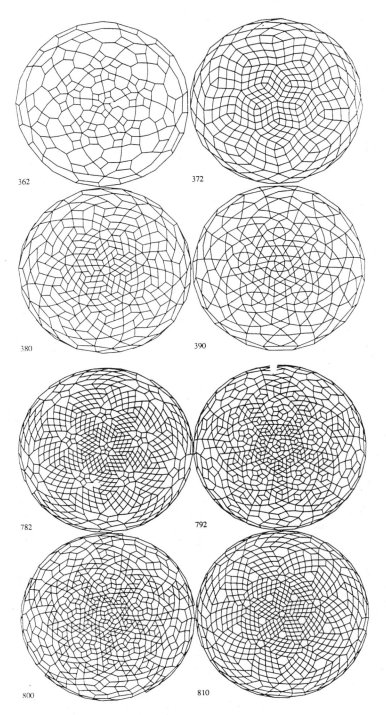

FIGURE 4. Best packings found of 362, 372, 380, 390, 782, 792, 800, 810 points assuming icosahedral symmetry.

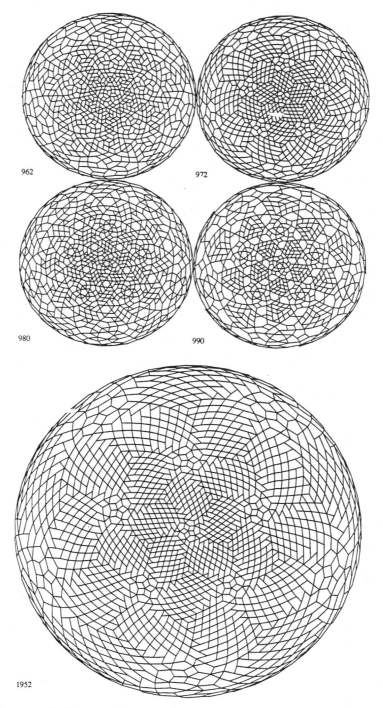

FIGURE 5. Best packings found of 962, 972, 980, 990 and 1952 points assuming icosahedral symmetry.

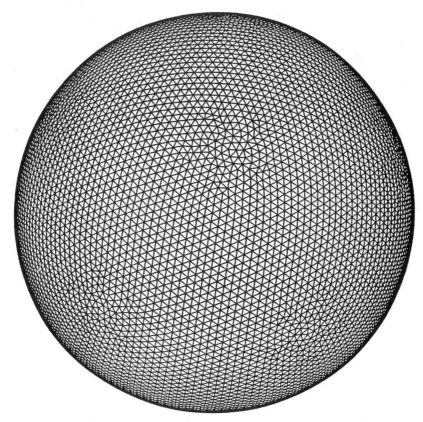

FIGURE 6. Second-best 8192-point covering with icosahedral symmetry.

For nondegenerate arrangements the limits in dimensions 3, 4, 5, 8 are respectively

$$120, \ 14400, \ 720, \ 696729600 \ .$$

Except for degenerate arrangements — such as placing them all on the equator — there is no way to place 121 or more points on Ω_3 so that they are all equivalent. Completely symmetric spherical codes with large numbers of points are impossible in any dimension above 2. On the one hand this means that the solutions aren't always pretty; on the other hand it makes the problems interesting.

4. Experimental designs and "Gosset"

We now return to our discussion of Doehlert's letter. We sent him a number of our best packings (of 14 to 20 points in 4 dimensions, 20–25 points in 5 dimensions, and so on), which he was very happy to receive and started using right away in his consulting work. However, he then explained that the problem he was really interested in was not exactly the packing problem, but rather the question of finding optimal experimental designs.

The following is a brief introduction to the subject of Design of Experiments. Further information can be found in any one of a large number of books — see for example [2], [9], [21], [46], [48], [63].

Your client is in charge of a refinery that produces oil (Fig. 9). The oil

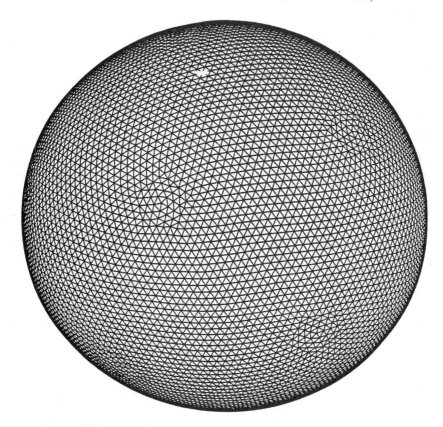

FIGURE 7. Best 8192-point covering with icosahedral symmetry.

output y depends on the settings of four variables, which we will pretend are $x_1 = $ temperature, $x_2 = $ pressure, $x_3 = $ cooking time, $x_4 = $ percentage of nitrogen. The client's problem is to adjust the settings of these variables so as to maximize the output. We suppose that the client has a rough idea of the best operating region, so that after rescaling the variables we may assume that the sought-for best operating point (the "sweet spot") is in a ball of radius 1 around the origin.

Let us assume now that the oil output y is well-represented by the constant, linear and quadratic terms of its Taylor series expansion in terms of the x_i. Thus our model for the refinery is

(4)
$$y = \beta_0 + \beta_1 x_1 + \cdots + \beta_4 x_4 + \beta_{11} x_1^2 + \cdots + \beta_{44} x_4^2$$
$$+ \beta_{12} x_1 x_2 + \cdots + \beta_{34} x_3 x_4 + \epsilon \,,$$

where the β_i are unknown coefficients, and ϵ is an error term. There are 15 coefficients β_i in this model (and more generally $\binom{n+2}{2}$ for a quadratic model involving n variables). So we will certainly have to make at least 15 measurements (or "runs") to determine the coefficients. In fact a minimal design would consist of one measurement at the center of the ball and 14 measurements on the boundary of the ball — this explains Doehlert's initial question about placing 14 points on a sphere in four dimensions!

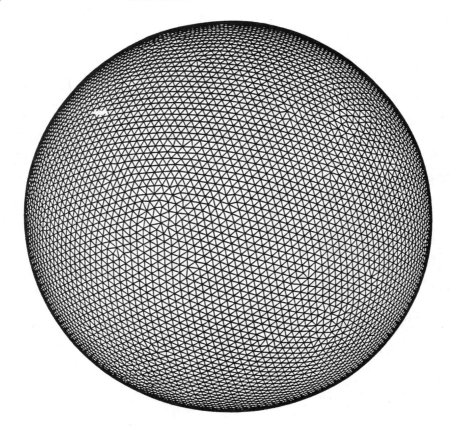

FIGURE 8. Best 8192-point packing with icosahedral symmetry.

But minimal designs are risky, for a variety of reasons, and a good design here would use some greater number p (say) of measurements, where $p \geq 15$, perhaps $p = 18$ or 20. On the other hand p cannot be made too large, because the experiments are expensive and time consuming.

The problem in designing the experiment is to determine the "best" location for these p measurements. "Best" can be interpreted in many ways, and there is no universal agreement on which sense is best. Our own preference is very strongly in favor of what are called I-optimal designs.

In order to explain this, it is necessary to discuss what happens after the measurements have been made. We continue to use the quadratic model (4), although a similar analysis applies to other models.

Equation (4) can be written as

$$y = f(x)\beta^{tr} + \epsilon ,$$

where $f(x) = (1, x_1, x_2, \ldots, x_3 x_4)$ is a vector listing the monomials that appear in the model, $\beta = (\beta_0, \beta_1, \ldots, \beta_{34})$ is a vector of unknown coefficients, and tr denotes transpose. We will assume that the error ϵ can be represented as a random variable with mean 0 and variance σ^2, and that the errors in different measurements are independent.

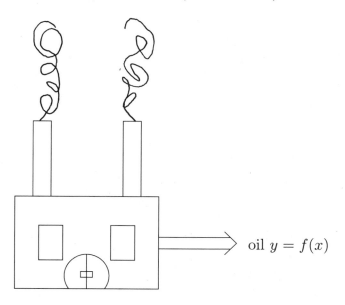

FIGURE 9

Suppose we make p measurements of y at the points

$$x^{(i)} = (x_1^{(i)}, x_2^{(i)}, x_3^{(i)}, x_4^{(i)}), \ i = 1, \ldots, p \ ,$$

obtaining the values

$$Y = (y(x^{(1)}), \ldots, y(x^{(p)})) \ .$$

Then we have

$$Y^{tr} = X\beta^{tr} + Z^{tr} \ ,$$

where Z is a vector of errors, and the $p \times 15$ *design matrix* X is given by

$$X = \begin{pmatrix} f(x^{(1)}) \\ \vdots \\ f(x^{(p)}) \end{pmatrix} \ .$$

The best (least squares) estimate of β is then

$$\widehat{\beta} = (X^{tr}X)^{-1}X^{tr}Y \ ,$$

which has mean $E\widehat{\beta} = \beta$, and covariance

$$\begin{aligned} \mathrm{Cov}(\widehat{\beta}) &= E(\widehat{\beta} - \beta)^{tr}(\widehat{\beta} - \beta) \\ &= \sigma^2(X^{tr}X)^{-1} \ . \end{aligned}$$

Our estimate for y is

$$\widehat{y} = f(x)\widehat{\beta}^{tr} \ ,$$

which has variance

$$\begin{aligned} \mathrm{Var}(\widehat{y}) &= E(\widehat{y} - \overline{y})^2 \\ (5) \qquad &= \sigma^2 f(x)(X^{tr}X)^{-1}f(x)^{tr} \ . \end{aligned}$$

This is the *prediction variance*.

An *I*-optimal design (see [7], [8]) is one which minimizes the *average* (or *integrated*) prediction variance over the region where we are fitting the model. Actually it is important to distinguish two difference regions: there is the *measurement* (or *operating*) region O, where we can make observations, and the *modeling region R*, where we want to fit the model. (In our program `gosset`, described below, these two regions can be specified independently.)

More precisely, an *I*-optimal design is one which minimizes the "integrated variance"

$$
\begin{aligned}
IV &= \int_R \frac{1}{\sigma^2} \text{Var } \widehat{y}(x) d\mu(x) \\
&= \int f(x)(X^{tr}X)^{-1}f(x)^{tr} d\mu(x) \\
&= \text{trace}\left\{ M(X^{tr}X)^{-1} \right\},
\end{aligned}
$$

where

$$
M = \int_R f(x)^{tr} f(x) d\mu(x)
$$

is the moment matrix of the modeling region. The *I-efficiency* of a design is the ratio IV_∞/IV, where IV_∞ denotes the limiting value of IV as $p \to \infty$.

In short, for an *I*-optimal design, we wish to choose p points in O so as to minimize

$$
IV = \text{trace } M(X^{tr}X)^{-1}.
$$

Other criteria that have often been used in the past include *D-optimality*, which minimizes $\det(X^{tr}X)^{-1}$, and *A-optimality*, which minimizes $\text{trace}(X^{tr}X)^{-1}$. Neither of these involve M, and we have found them to be unsatisfactory (except when the model is a polynomial of degree 1) for a number of reasons (see [38]). For later use we define the *D-value* of the design to be

$$
D = (\det X^{tr}X)^{-1/p},
$$

and the *D-efficiency* to be D_∞/D, where D_∞ is the limiting value of D as $p \to \infty$.

Doehlert's initial letter was followed by many subsequent ones, asking about optimal placements of points in the cube, in the simplex, then in more complicated regions, and for models which were not the full quadratic model shown in (4) but also quadratics with some terms omitted, cubics, etc. Over the course of the next three years we built up an ever-more complicated program that will attempt to find optimal designs for a very wide range of problems.

The program is called `gosset`, is written in C, and runs on any Unix[TM]platform. It is still being developed even today. However, we would like to hear from readers who might be interested in testing the present version of the program for us.

The program is named after the amateur mathematician *Thorold Gosset* (1869–1962), who was one of the first to study polytopes in six, seven and eight dimensions [16, p. 164], and his contemporary, the statistician *William Seally Gosset* (1876–1937), who was one of the first to use statistical methods in the planning and interpretation of agricultural experiments [62]. Although from our geometric viewpoint their work is related, we do not know if the paths of Thorold (Cambridge, London, lawyer), and William Seally (Oxford, Dublin, brewer) ever crossed.

Some of the program's features are the following. Only a few can be described here — for further information see [38], [39].

Problem specification. Problems are presented to the program using a very simple language, rather like "BASIC" — examples can be seen below. Because the program contains a built-in parser, the format is extremely flexible and user-friendly.

Variables. Variables may be discrete or continuous. Continuous variables may range over a sphere or a cube (or both). Discrete variables may be quantitative or qualitative (or both). Example:

$$10 \text{ range Temp Pressure } 100 \text{ } 200$$

means that Temp and Pressure are continuous variables ranging between 100 and 200.

Constraints. The variables may be required to satisfy linear equalities and/or inequalities, so mixtures and constraints present no difficulty. Example:

$$20 \text{ constraint Temp} + \text{Pressure} < 150$$

or

$$30 \text{ constraint } A + B + C + D = 100$$

Models. The user can specify a model in a quite general way. In principle, almost any model at all can be used, provided it can be described by a C program! In most applications so far the models used have been low degree polynomials, but we expect this to change as this feature becomes more widely known. Example:

$$40 \text{ model } (1 + \text{Temp} + \text{Pressure}) \uparrow 2$$

defines a full quadratic model of the form

$$
\begin{aligned}
\beta_0 \quad &+ \quad \beta_1 \text{ Temp} + \beta_2 \text{ Pressure} \\
&+ \quad \beta_{11} \text{ Temp}^2 + \beta_{12} \text{ Temp Pressure} + \beta_{22} \text{ Pressure}^2 \\
&+ \quad \text{error term },
\end{aligned}
$$

while

$$40 \text{ model } (1 + x + \sin(y)) \uparrow 2 - \sin(y) \uparrow 2$$

specifies that the terms in the model are $1, x, x^2, \sin(y)$ and $x\sin(y)$.

If no model is available: packings. If no model is known, the user can simply ask for a "packing", that is, request the program to place N points in the operating region so that they are well-separated. As far as we know, this is the first time a program has been available that will search for packings in fairly arbitrary regions. Here is a simple 2-dimensional example, showing 100 points packed into a wedge-shaped region. The region was specified by

$$10 \text{ range } a \text{ } b \text{ } 0 \text{ } 1$$

$$20 \text{ constraint } a < 4 * b$$

The result is shown in Fig. 10.

Sequential designs. The design can be required to include a specified set of points. Thus a sequence of optimal designs can be constructed, each one building on the previous experiments.

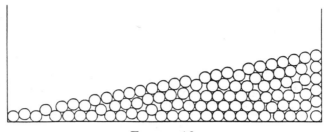

FIGURE 10

Measuring region and modeling region can be different: There are many situations where this feature is useful:

- some variables may take only discrete values (e.g. 5, 10, 25 or 100 grams), but it is desired to fit a model over the whole range
- measurements can be made over a large region, but we want an accurate model fitted over a smaller region
- extrapolation or prediction: we can make measurements only in a small region, but want to fit a model over a larger region.

Number of runs. The user can specify how many runs (or observations) the design will include. The user also has control over how hard the program works in attempting to find a good design. Example:

$$\text{design runs} = 20 \; n = 30 \; \text{processors} = 6$$

would instruct the program to look for a 20-run design, taking the best of 30 tries, and running 6 processors simultaneously. (Of course the latter feature is useful only on a multiprocessor machine.)

Optimality criteria. The program can search for A-, D-, E- or I-optimal designs. As already mentioned, our experience indicates that I-optimality is the most useful of these criteria, since all the others have serious drawbacks.

We have also introduced some further optimality criteria, useful in situations where it is possible that one of the measurements will fail, or otherwise be lost for some reason (we are told by experimenters that in practice this is not at all unusual).

For example, a J-optimal design with N runs has the property that the worst of the $N+1$ designs (the original design and those obtained by dropping one run in all possible ways) is I-optimized. In other words, J-optimal is "I-optimal given that an experiment may be lost". There are similar criteria for A-, D- and E-optimality.

Designs for situations where the errors are correlated. If the errors in the measurements, instead of being independent, have a known (or estimated) correlation, the program can take this into account. For example, Fig. 11 shows some designs intended for a situation in which successive pairs of measurements are correlated (the application was to an experiment making measurements on eyes, first the left eye, then the right eye). The design is specified by

$$10 \text{ sphere } X \; Y \; -1 \; 1$$

$$20 \text{ model } (1 + X + Y) \uparrow 2$$

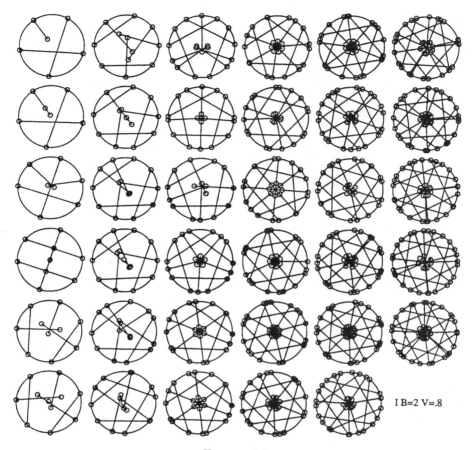

I B=2 V=.8

FIGURE 11

that is, a full quadratic model in a circle, in which the covariance matrix for the samples is

$$
\begin{bmatrix}
1 & .8 & 0 & 0 & \cdots \\
.8 & 1 & 0 & 0 & \cdots \\
0 & 0 & 1 & .8 & \cdots \\
0 & 0 & .8 & 1 & \cdots \\
\cdot & \cdot & \cdot & & \\
\end{bmatrix}
$$

The putatively I-optimal designs with 6, 7, 8, ... runs are as follows. (Pairs of successive design points are joined by lines.)

Blocked designs. A feature that has had many applications is the ability to look for a design in which the measurements are made in blocks. See the manual [39] for examples.

Applications. So far there have been two main uses for gosset.

(i) We have attempted to construct optimal (especially I-optimal) designs for a number of "classical" situations, for example linear, quadratic or cubic response-surface designs with n continuous variables in a cube or ball with p experiments, over quite a large range of values of n and p, typically $1 \leq n \leq 12$ and p ranging from the minimal value to 6 (or more) greater than the minimal value. We have also computed designs for similar models and regions in which the variables are discrete. An extensive library of these designs is now built into gosset. Our work on these "classical" problems can be regarded as an attempt to provide optimal "exact" designs with small numbers of runs to complement the "asymptotic" designs of Kiefer et al. (see [48]).

We have also used this collection of designs as data for theoretical investigations. Two results are worth mentioning here.

(a) There is a simple lower bound on the integrated variance of an I-optimal design for quadratic models with p measurements in an n-dimensional ball (see the next section). A number of interesting designs meet the bound. There is a similar bound for D-optimal designs.

(b) It is known that for large numbers of experiments D- and G-optimal designs are equivalent [49]. Our results show that I-optimal designs are strictly different. For example, I-optimal designs make more measurements at the center of the region and fewer at the boundary. For quadratic models in an n-dimensional ball, n large, an I-optimal design makes about $4/n^2$ of the measurements at the center of the sphere, compared with about $2/n^2$ for D- and G-optimal designs. I-optimality also appears to be a more strict condition than D-optimality. In situations where the criteria produce similar designs (such as certain linear designs), we commonly find that although I-optimal designs are D-optimal, the converse is not necessarily true.

(ii) We have constructed designs for a large number of industrial applications. These include:

- optimizing the production of wafers for integrated circuits (see for example [60])
- placing laser beams for treatment of tumors in the brain
- growing protein crystals
- maximizing the thermal conductivity of heat-spreading diamond film
- designing potted meat
- designing a cellular ceramic substrate used in catalytic converters
- designing coated photographic paper

5. The construction of spherical 4-designs

One of the most interesting things to have come out of our work with gosset is a series of discoveries that has led to the construction of many new spherical 4-designs (see Problem (P6) of Section 2). These results are described in more detail in [37] and [38].

These discoveries came about when we were comparing I- and D-optimal designs in the ball for the full quadratic model of (4), using the extensive library of designs that we had computed using gosset. Let $\mathcal{I}(n, p)$ (resp. $\mathcal{D}(n, p)$) denote any I-optimal (resp. D-optimal) design for this model, where n is the number of variables and p is the number of experiments, with $p \geq \binom{n+2}{2}$.

First, it appears that there is a unique design $\mathcal{I}(3, 14)$ (apart from orthogonal transformations), which consists of three copies of a point distant .003622 from the center of the ball and eleven points on the surface of the ball. The precise design may be found in the gosset library. However, restricting $\mathcal{I}(3, 14)$ to points at the center and on the surface of the ball incurs a loss of only about .00006% in I-efficiency. A similar phenomenon occurs for other values of n and p.

In contrast, for D-optimal designs, it seems that the only points that occur are at the center and on the surface. We formalize these observations in the following conjecture, still unproved.

Conjecture. *For all n and p, $\mathcal{D}(n, p)$ contains only points at the center and on the surface of the ball. This is not true for $\mathcal{I}(n, p)$, but restricting $\mathcal{I}(n, p)$ to designs with this property incurs a loss in I-efficiency of less than .01%.*

In the rest of this section we therefore restrict attention to designs supported only at the center and the surface of the ball. For any such design, not necessarily optimal, let B and C respectively denote the number of points on the surface (or boundary) and at the center, so that $p = B + C$.

Our second discovery was that the IV-value of the best designs was often given by the formula

$$(6) \qquad \frac{1}{(n+2)(n+4)} \left\{ \frac{n^2(n^2 + 5n + 10)}{2\beta} + \frac{8}{\gamma} \right\} ,$$

where $\beta = B/p$, $\gamma = C/p$. This was an empirical formula, found simply by examining our collection of designs (we observed that obviously rational IV-values were arising from many geometrically distinct designs, suggesting that there was a formula to be found). This formula was the key to everything that followed.

Our observations were that this formula is always a lower bound to the IV-value of a design, and that it could be attained once the number of experiments was sufficiently large. We were then able to prove these results, by considering the moments of the design points. Let ξ denote the discrete measure, normalized to have total measure 1, defined by the B surface points of the design. The B surface points form a spherical 4-design if and only if the moments of ξ up through order 4 agree with the moments of uniform measure on the sphere. The fact that (6) is a lower bound on IV is a consequence of the following result

THEOREM 5.1. *For fixed values of n, p, B and C, both the I- and D-efficiencies are maximized if the B surface points can be arranged to form a spherical 4-design.*

The proof for I-efficiency is given in [**37**], while for D-efficiency this follows from the work of Box and Hunter [**10**] and Kiefer [**47**] (see also [**27**], [**61**]).

If the surface points do form a spherical 4-design, the IV- and D-values of the design can be calculated analytically, and turn out to be given by (6) for the IV-value, thus confirming our empirical observations, and by

$$(7) \qquad \frac{n}{\beta}(n+2)^{(n-1)/(n+2)} \left\{ \frac{\beta}{n\gamma 2^{n-1}} \right\}^{2/((n+1)(n+2))}$$

for the D-value. It follows from Theorem 5.1 that these are indeed lower bounds.

One can now select the values of β and γ to minimize (6) or (7) for any fixed value of n. For large n, (6) implies that in an I-optimal design the fraction of points at the center is

$$(8) \qquad \gamma = \frac{4n\sqrt{n^2 + 5n + 10} - 16}{(n-1)(n+2)(n^2 + 4n + 8)} .$$

(7) implies that in a D-optimal design this fraction is

$$(9) \qquad\qquad \gamma = \frac{2}{(n+2)(n+4)} \ ,$$

which is a theorem of Kiefer [47].

By substituting these expressions in (6) and (7) we obtain the limiting values

$$(10) \qquad IV_\infty \ = \ \frac{n+2}{2(n+4)} \left\{ \frac{(n-1)(n^2+4n+8)}{n\sqrt{n^2+5n+10}-4} \right\}^2 \ ,$$

$$(11) \qquad D_\infty \ = \ \frac{(n+1)(n+2)^{2n/(n+1)}}{n+3} \left(\frac{n+3}{2^n}\right)^{2/((n+1)(n+2))} \ ,$$

which enable us to determine the I- and D-efficiencies of any given design.

It follows from a result of Neumaier and Seidel [61] that a design has D-value given by (7) if and only if the B surface points form a spherical 4-design. There is a similar result for I-values.

THEOREM 5.2. *A quadratic design in the ball has IV-value given by (6) if and only if the B surface points form a spherical 4-design.*

Thus whenever **gosset** is able to find a design that meets the bound (6), the surface points form a spherical 4-design. And the nonexistence of designs meeting the bound imply the nonexistence of the 4-design. Since our program is very good at finding these designs, we take this as compelling evidence that the corresponding 4-designs do not exist.

In summary, we believe that spherical 4-designs containing B points in n dimensions exist for the following values of B and n:

$$
\begin{array}{cl}
n & B \\
1 & 2,4,6,8,\dots \\
2 & \geq 5 \\
3 & 12, 14, \geq 16 \\
(12) \qquad 4 & \geq 20 \\
5 & \geq 29 \\
6 & 27, 36, \geq 39 \\
7 & \geq 53 \\
8 & \geq 69 \\
\end{array}
$$

See [37] and [38] for further information about these spherical 4-designs, as well as [41] for our more recent work on the extension of this investigation to spherical t-designs for larger values of t.

6. Isometric embeddings

Finally, we discuss problem (P9), the construction of isometric embeddings. We will give just one example, and show that there exists a 23-point isometric embedding in $\mathbb{R}^4$. Equivalently, we will show that $(x_1^2 + x_2^2 + x_3^2 + x_4^2)^3$ can be written as a sum of 23 sixth powers of linear forms. This is one less than is required in a famous 1912 identity of Kempner. The discussion is based on [40], while further examples can be found in [12].

In connection with Waring's problem of expressing integers as a sum of sixth powers, Lucas published in 1876 the incorrect identity

$$(x_1^2 + x_2^2 + x_3^2 + x_4^2)^3 = \frac{1}{10} \sum_{i<j}^{(12)} (x_i \pm x_j)^6 \, ,$$

and in the following year replaced it by

$$(x_1^2 + x_2^2 + x_3^2 + x_4^2)^3 = \frac{2}{5} \sum^{(4)} x_i^6 + \frac{1}{10} \sum_{i<j}^{(12)} (x_i \pm x_j)^6 \, ,$$

also incorrect (cf. Dickson [22], p. 718). A correct version,

$$
\begin{aligned}
(13) \quad (x_1^2 + x_2^2 + x_3^2 + x_4^2)^3 &= \tfrac{8}{15} \sum^{(4)} x_i^6 + \tfrac{1}{15} \sum_{i<j}^{(12)} (x_i \pm x_j)^6 \\
&+ \tfrac{1}{120} \sum^{(8)} (x_1 \pm x_2 \pm x_3 \pm x_4)^6
\end{aligned}
$$

was apparently given for the first time by Kempner [45] in 1912.

More generally, for any even number q, we look for N points $P^{(i)} = [P_1^{(i)}, \ldots, P_d^{(i)}] \in \mathbb{R}^d$ and positive coefficients $c_i \in \mathbb{R}$, $1 \le i \le N$, such that there is an identity

$$(14) \qquad (x_1^2 + \cdots + x_d^2)^{q/2} = \sum_{i=1}^{N} c_i \left(\sum_{j=1}^{d} P_j^{(i)} x_j \right)^q .$$

The existence of such identities, for all d and even q, with c_i and $P_j^{(i)}$ rational, was a key step in Hilbert's (1909) general solution of Waring's problem (Ellison [25]). Chapter XXV of Dickson [22] surveys the classical results concerning such identities. They have recently resurfaced in works by Lyubich and Vaserstein [56], Reznick [66] and Seidel [70], where many new results are given as well as connections with numerical quadrature, designs, and isometric embeddings of one space in another.

Let $N(d, q)$ denote the smallest value of N for which an identity (14) is possible. Equation (13) shows that $N(4, 6) \le 24$, and Proposition 9.2 of [66] shows that $N(4, 6) \ge 21$. We will present an identity of the form

$$(15) \qquad (x_1^2 + x_2^2 + x_3^2 + x_4^2)^3 = \sum_{i=1}^{23} c_i \left(\sum_{j=1}^{4} P_j^{(i)} x_j \right)^6 ,$$

which establishes $N(4, 6) \le 23$. The points $P^{(i)}$ and coefficients c_i are given in Table 1. (However, since some of the c_i and $P^{(i)}$ are irrational, (15) does not contribute to Waring's problem.)

Equation (15) was discovered in the following way. Let us rewrite it as $\left(\sum_{i=1}^{4} x_i^2 \right)^3 = \sum_{i=1}^{23} \left(\sum_{j=1}^{4} Q_j^{(i)} x_j \right)^6$, where $Q_j^{(i)} = c_i^{1/6} P_j^{(i)}$. We used the computer to find sets of $Q_j^{(i)}$'s which satisfied this identity to within a small tolerance. The algorithm was simply a further modification of the one mentioned in Section 3. These sets of 23 points were then analyzed by hand. There appear to be many inequivalent solutions, and it was not easy to find a set of points with enough symmetry to identify their coordinates $Q_j^{(i)}$ as algebraic numbers. Having identified the $Q_j^{(i)}$, there is still the problem of finding a convenient way to factorize them

TABLE 1(A). The points $P^{(1)}, \dots, P^{(23)}$ in the identity (15). Double parentheses indicate that all cyclic shifts of the last three components are to be included.

[1	0	0	0	]	=	[1	0	0	0	]
[α	((0	± 1	$\pm\tau$))]		=	[1.473370	((0	± 1	± 1.618034))]		
[0	1	1	1	]	=	[0	1	1	1	]
[0	((1	$\tau - 1$	$-\tau$))]		=	[0	((1	.618034	-1.618034))]		
[0	(($-\tau$	β	$\beta\tau + 1$))]		=	[0	((-1.618034	1.868517	4.023324))]		
[0	(($-\tau$	γ	$\gamma\tau + 1$))]		=	[0	((-1.618034	$-.535184$	.134054))]		

as $c_i^{1/6} P_j^{(i)}$. There is no unique way to do this, and our aim was to make the final answer as simple as possible. The computer took a couple of hours to find each approximate solution, but "beautification" of the points by hand took a couple of weeks. We will not attempt to describe this fairly mysterious process, but just give our best answer, which emerged after a series of miraculous simplifications, in Table 1.

The $P^{(i)}$ and c_i are listed in Table 1, both exactly (as algebraic numbers) and approximately (as decimal numbers, rounded to six significant figures). The geometric structure of the points is as follows (there is a picture in [37]). $P^{(1)}$ is at the north pole, and $P^{(2)}$ to $P^{(13)}$ form a regular icosahedron (with x_1 coordinate $\sqrt{3\tau}\, 5^{-1/4}$, where $\tau = (1 + \sqrt{5})/2$). The remaining ten points lie on the equatorial hyperplane $x_1 = 0$ and consist of a singleton and three equilateral triangles. The vertices of those equilateral triangles lie on the edges (possibly produced) of the icosahedron (with x_1 coordinate omitted). The only symmetries of the configuration are the cyclic shifts of the last three components. However, if the negatives or antipodes of the points are included, the resulting 46-point configuration has symmetry group of structure $C_2 \times C_2 \times D_6$, where D_6 is a dihedral group of order 6. This group contains the cyclic shift just mentioned and the reflection in $[0, 1, 1/\tau, -\tau]$, which together generate a three-dimensional triangular antiprismatic group (denoted by $[2^+, 6]$ in the notation of [18], by $2 * 3$ in the Conway-Thurston orbifold notation, and with structure $C_2 \times D_6$). The full group is generated by this subgroup and negation of the first coordinate. where $\alpha = \sqrt{3\tau}\, 5^{-1/4}$, $\beta = (2 + \sqrt{13})/3$, $\gamma = (2 - \sqrt{13})/3$.

The points $P^{(i)}$ lie on six different spheres, one for each of the six rows of Table 1(a). (So in the notation of [66], equation (15) is a sixth-caliber representation of $(x_1^2 + \cdots + x_4^2)^3$.)

As to the proof that (15) is an identity: the verification could be carried out by hand, but would be rather tedious. The c_i and $P^{(i)}$ are now simple enough, however, that a computer algebra system such as Maple is able to verify the identity exactly in a few seconds. Additional confirmation is provided by the fact that floating point evaluations of the coefficients on each side of (15) agree very closely.

Our computer investigations have failed to produce a 22-term identity, and we conjecture that $N(4, 6) = 23$.

TABLE 1(B). The coefficients $c_1, \ldots, c_{23}$ in the identity (15).

$$\frac{16}{25} \quad = \quad .64 \text{ (once)} ,$$

$$\frac{1}{36\tau^3\sqrt{5}} \quad = \quad .00293258 \text{ (twelve times)} ,$$

$$\frac{16}{735} \quad = \quad .0217687 \text{ (once)} ,$$

$$\frac{1}{120} \quad = \quad .00833333 \text{ (three times)} ,$$

$$-\frac{1460 + \sqrt{5} - \sqrt{13}(577 - 76\sqrt{5})}{2^4\, 3^2\, 5\, 7^2\sqrt{13}} \quad = \quad .0000427301 \text{ (three times)}$$

$$\frac{1460 + \sqrt{5} + \sqrt{13}(577 - 76\sqrt{5})}{2^4\, 3^2\, 5\, 7^2\sqrt{13}} \quad = \quad .0230332 \text{ (three times)}$$

We have also found sets of points which suggest that

$$N(3, 10) \le 24, \ N(3, 12) \le 32, \ N(3, 14) \le 41, \ N(3, 16) \le 52, \ N(3, 18) \le 66,$$

$$N(4, 8) \le 43, \ N(6, 6) \le 63, \ N(7, 6) \le 91, \ N(8, 4) \le 45, \ N(9, 4) \le 59 .$$

We are currently in the process of formally establishing these identities. Details will be found in [**12**].

References

[1] E. F. Assmus, Jr. and J. D. Key, *Designs and Their Codes*, Cambridge Univ. Press, 1992.

[2] A. C. Atkinson and A. N. Donev, *Optimum Experimental Designs*, Oxford Univ. Press, 1992.

[3] C. S. Beightler, D. T. Phillips, and D. J. Wilde, *Foundations of Optimization*, Prentice-Hall, Englewood Cliffs, New York, 2nd edition, 1987.

[4] A. A. Berezin, Asymptotics of the maximum number of repulsive particles on a spherical surface, *J. Math. Phys.* **27** (1986), 1533–1536.

[5] D. Berreby, Math in a million dimensions, *Discover*, **11** (October, 1990), 58–66.

[6] J. D. Berman and K. Hanes, Volumes of polyhedra inscribed in the unit sphere in E^3, *Math. Ann.* **188** (1970), 78–84.

[7] G. E. P. Box and N. R. Draper, A basis for the selection of a response surface design, *J. American Statistical Association* **54** (1959), 622–654.

[8] G. E. P. Box and N. R. Draper, The choice of a second order rotatable design, *Biometrika* **50** (1963), 335–352.

[9] G. E. P. Box and N. R. Draper, *Empirical Model-Building and Response Surfaces*, Wiley, New York, 1987.

[10] G. E. P. Box and J. S. Hunter, Multi-factor experimental designs for exploring response surfaces, *Annals of Mathematical Statistics* **28** (1957), 195–241.

[11] V. Brun, On regular packing of equal circles touching each other on the surface of a sphere, *Comm. Pure Appl. Math.* **29** (1976), 583–590.

[12] A. R. Calderbank, R. H. Hardin, J. J. Seidel and N. J. A. Sloane, New isometric embeddings, preprint.

[13] B. W. Clare and D. L. Kepert, The closest packing of equal circles on a sphere, *Proc. Royal Soc. London* **A405** (1986), 329–344.

[14] J. H. Conway and N. J. A. Sloane, *Sphere Packings, Lattices and Groups*, Springer-Verlag, New York, 2nd edition, 1993.

[15] H. S. M. Coxeter, The problem of packing a number of equal nonoverlapping circles on a sphere, *Trans. N.Y. Acad. Sci.* **24** (No. 3, 1962), 320–331.

[16] H. S. M. Coxeter, *Regular Polytopes*, Dover, New York, 3rd edition, 1973.

[17] H. S. M. Coxeter, A packing of 840 balls of radius $9°\ 0'\ 19''$ on the 3-sphere, in *Intuitive Geometry*, ed. K. Böröczky and G. Fejes Tóth, North-Holland, Amsterdam, 1987.

[18] H. S. M. Coxeter and W. O. J. Moser, *Generators and Relations for Discrete Groups*, Springer-Verlag, NY, Fourth edition, 1984.

[19] L. Danzer, Finite point-sets on S^2 with minimum distance as large as possible, *Discrete Math.* **60** (1986), 3–66.

[20] H. M. Cundy and A. P. Rollett, *Mathematical Models*, Oxford Univ. Press, 2nd ed., 1961.

[21] W. J. Diamond, *Practical Experimental Designs for Engineers and Scientists*, Wadsworth, Belmont, CA, 1981.

[22] L. E. Dickson, *History of the Theory of Numbers*, Chelsea, NY, 1966, Vol. II.

[23] L. Dornhoff, *Group Representation Theory*, Dekker, NY, 2 vols., 1971.

[24] J. R. Edmundson, The distribution of point charges on the surface of a sphere, *Acta Cryst.*, **A 48** (1992), 60–69.

[25] W. J. Ellison, Waring's problem, *Amer. Math. Monthly* **78** (1971), 10–36.

[26] T. Erber and G. M. Hockney, Equilibrium configurations of N equal charges on a sphere, *J. Phys.*, **A 24** (1991), L1369–L1377.

[27] R. H. Farrell, J. Kiefer, and A. Walbran, Optimum multivariate designs, in *Proc. 5th Berkeley Sympos. Math. Statist. and Probability*, Univ. Calif. Press, Berkeley, Calif., **1** (1967), pp. 113–138.

[28] G. Fejes Tóth and L. Fejes Tóth, Dictators on a planet, *Studia Sci. Math. Hung.* **15** (1980), 313–316.

[29] L. Fejes Tóth, *Lagerungen in der Ebene, auf der Kugel und in Raum*, Springer-Verlag, 2nd ed., 1972.

[30] S. Garfunkel (coordinator), *For All Practical Purposes: Introduction to Contemporary Mathematics*, Freeman, NY, 3rd edition, 1994.

[31] M. Goldberg, Packing of 18 equal circles on a sphere, *Elem. Math.* **20** (1965), 59–61.

[32] M. Goldberg, Packing of 19 equal circles on a sphere, *Elem. Math.* **22** (1967), 108–110.

[33] M. Goldberg, An improved packing of 33 equal circles on a sphere, *Elem. Math.* **22** (1967), 110–111.

[34] M. Goldberg, Axially symmetric packing of equal circles on a sphere, *Ann. Univ. Sci.* Budapest **10** (1967), 37–48; **12** (1969), 137–142.

[35] M. Goldberg, Stability configurations of electrons on a sphere, *Math. Comp.* **23** (1969), 785–786.

[36] W. Habicht and B. L. van der Waerden, Lagerung von Punkten auf der Kugel, *Math. Ann.* **123** (1951), 223–234.

[37] R. H. Hardin and N. J. A. Sloane, New spherical 4-designs, *Discrete Mathematics*, Vol. 106/107, 1992, pp. 255–264. (*Topics in Discrete Mathematics*, Vol. 7, "A Collection of Contributions in Honor of Jack Van Lint," ed. P. J. Cameron and H. C. A. van Tilborg, North-Holland, 1992.)

[38] R. H. Hardin and N. J. A. Sloane, A new approach to the construction of optimal designs, *J. Statistical Planning and Inference*, Vol. 37, 1993, pp. 339–369.

[39] R. H. Hardin and N. J. A. Sloane, *Operating Manual for Gosset: A General-Purpose Program for Constructing Experimental Designs (Second Edition)*, Statistics Research Report No. 98, AT&T Bell Labs, Murray Hill, NJ, Nov. 15, 1991. Also DIMACS Technical Report 93–51, August 1993, Center for Discrete Math. and Computer Science, Rutgers Univ., New Brunswick, NJ.

[40] R. H. Hardin and N. J. A. Sloane, Expressing $(a^2 + b^2 + c^2 + d^2)^2$ as a sum of 23 sixth powers, *Journal of Combinatorial Theory*, Series A, **68** (1994), 481–485.

[41] R. H. Hardin and N. J. A. Sloane, McClaren's improved snub cube and other new spherical t-designs in three dimensions, *Discrete and Computational Geometry*, submitted.

[42] R. H. Hardin, N. J. A. Sloane, and Warren D. Smith, *Spherical Codes*, in preparation.

[43] R. Hooke, and T. A. Jeeves, 'Direct Search' Solution of Numerical and Statistical Problems, *Journal Association for Computing Machinery* **8** (1961), 212–229.

[44] D. Jungnickel and S. A. Vanstone, editors, *Coding Theory, Design Theory, Group Theory*, Wiley, NY, 1993.

[45] A. J. Kempner, *Über das Waringsche Problem und einige Verallgemeinerungen*, Dissertation, Göttingen, 1912.

[46] A. I. Khuri and J. A. Cornell, *Response Surfaces: Designs and Analyses*, Dekker, NY, 1987.

[47] J. Kiefer, Optimum experimental designs V, with applications to systematic and rotatable designs, in *Proc. 4th Berkeley Sympos. Math. Statist. and Probability*, Univ. Calif. Press, Calif., **1** (1960), pp. 381–405.

[48] J. C. Kiefer, *Collected Papers III: Design of Experiments*, L. D. Brown et al., editors, Springer-Verlag, New York, 1985.

[49] J. Kiefer and J. Wolfowitz, The equivalence of two extremum problems, *Canadian Journal of Mathematics* **12** (1960), 363–366.

[50] D. A. Kottwitz, The densest packing of equal circles on a sphere, *Acta Cryst.*, **A 47** (1991), 158–165.

[51] D. A. Kottwitz, personal communication.

[52] J. Leech, Equilibrium of sets of particles on a sphere, *Math. Gazette* **41** (1957), 81–90.

[53] J. Leech and T. Tarnai, Arrangements of 22 circles on a sphere, *Ann. Univ. Sci. Budapest Ser. Math.* **31** (1988), 27–37.

[54] A. Lubotzky, R. Phillips, and P. Sarnak, Hecke operators and distributing points on the sphere I, *Comm. Pure Appl. Math.* **39** (1986), S149–S186.

[55] A. Lubotzky, R. Phillips, and P. Sarnak, II: *Comm. Pure Appl. Math.* **40** (1987), 401–420

[56] Y. I. Lyubich and L. N. Vaserstein, *Isometric embeddings between classical Banach spaces, cubature formulas, and spherical designs*, Report PM 128, Penn. State Univ., Philadelphia PA, 1992.

[57] A. L. Mackay, The packing of three-dimensional spheres on the surface of a four-dimensional hypersphere, *J. Phys.* **A13** (1980), 3373–337.

[58] F. J. MacWilliams and N. J. A. Sloane, *The Theory of Error-Correcting Codes*, North-Holland, Amsterdam, 1977.

[59] T. W. Melnyk, O. Knop, and W. R. Smith, Extremal arrangements of points and unit changes on a sphere: equilibrium configurations revisited, *Can. J. Chem.* **55** (1977), 1745–1761,

[60] O. Nalamasu, A. Freeny, E. Reichmanis, N. J. A. Sloane, and L. F. Thompson, *Optimization of Resist Formulation and Processing with Disulfone Photo Acid Generators Using Design of Experiments*. AT&T Bell Labs Memorandum, 1993.

[61] A. Neumaier and J. J. Seidel, Measures of strength 2e, and optimal designs of degree e, *Sankhyā*, (1992), to appear.

[62] E. S. Pearson and J. Wishart, editors, *"Students" Collected Papers*, University College London, 1942.

[63] F. Pukelsheim, *Optimal Design of Experiments*, Wiley, NY, 1993.

[64] E. A. Rakhmanov, E. B. Saff and Y. M. Zhou, Minimal discrete energy on the sphere, preprint, 1994.

[65] D. Ray-Chaudhuri editor, *Coding Theory and Design Theory*, Springer-Verlag, 2 vol., 1990.

[66] B. Reznick, *Sums of Even Powers of Real Linear Forms*, Memoirs Amer. Math. Soc., No. 463, March 1992.

[67] R. M. Robinson, Arrangement of 24 points on a sphere, *Math. Ann.* **144** (1961), 17–48.

[68] R. M. Robinson, Finite sets of points on a sphere with each nearest to five others, *Math. Ann.* **179** (1969), 296–318.

[69] K. Schütte and B. L. van der Waerden, Auf welcher Kugel haben 5, 6, 7, 8, oder 9 Punkte mit Mindesabstand Eins Platz?, *Math. Ann.* **123** (1951), 96–124.

[70] J. J. Seidel, Isometric embeddings and geometric designs, *Trends in Discrete Mathematics*, to appear.

[71] N. J. A. Sloane, *A Handbook of Integer Sequences*, Academic Press, NY 1973. (An expanded version, *The Encyclopedia of Integer Sequences*, by N. J. A. Sloane and S. Plouffe, will be published by Academic Press in 1995.)

[72] N. J. A. Sloane, R. H. Hardin, T. S. Duff, and J. H. Conway, Minimal-energy clusters of hard spheres, *Discrete Computational Geom.*, 1995 to appear.

[73] E. Székely, Sur le problème de Tammes, *Ann. Univ. Scia Budapest. Eötvös, Sect. Math.* **17** (1974), 157–175.

[74] P. M. L. Tammes, On the origin of number and arrangements of the places of exit on the surface of pollen-grains, *Recueil des travaux botaniques néerlandais* **27** (1930), 1–84.

[75] T. Tarnai, Packing of 180 equal circles on a sphere, *Elem. Math.* **38** (1983), 119–122; **39** (1984), 129.

[76] T. Tarnai, Note on packing of 19 equal circles on a sphere, *Elem. Math.* **39** (1984), 25–27.

[77] T. Tarnai, Spherical circle-packing in nature, practice and theory, *Structural Topology* **9** (1984), 39–58.

[78] T. Tarnai and Z. Gáspár, Improved packing of equal circles on a sphere and rigidity of its graph, *Math. Proc. Cambr. Phil. Soc.* **93** (1983), 191–218.

[79] T. Tarnai and Z. Gáspár, Covering a sphere by equal circles, and the rigidity of its graph, *Math. Proc. Cambr. Phil. Soc.* **110** (1991), 71–89.

[80] J. B. Weinrach, K. L. Carter, D. W. Bennett and H. K. McDowell, Point charge approximations to a spherical charge distribution, *J. Chem. Educ.*, **67** (1990), 995–999.

[81] L. L. Whyte, Unique arrangements of points on a sphere, *Amer. Math. Monthly* **59** (1952), 606–611.

MATHEMATICAL SCIENCES RESEARCH CENTER, AT&T BELL LABORATORIES, MURRAY HILL, NJ 07974-0636

E-mail address: rhh@research.att.com
E-mail address: njas@research.att.com

Proceedings of Symposia in Applied Mathematics
Volume **50**, 1995

The Use of Coding Theory in Computational Complexity

Joan Feigenbaum

ABSTRACT. The interplay of coding theory and computational complexity theory is a rich source of results and problems. This article surveys three of the major themes in this area:
- the use of codes to improve algorithmic efficiency
- the theory of program testing and correcting, which is a complexity theoretic analogue of error detection and correction
- the use of codes to obtain characterizations of traditional complexity classes such as NP and PSPACE; these new characterizations are in turn used to show that certain combinatorial optimization problems are as hard to approximate closely as they are to solve exactly.

1. Introduction

Complexity theory is the study of efficient computation. Faced with a computational problem that can be modelled formally, a complexity theorist seeks first to find a solution that is provably efficient and, if such a solution is not found, to prove that none exists. Coding theory, which provides techniques for "robust representation" of information, is valuable both in designing efficient solutions and in proving that efficient solutions do not exist.

This article surveys the use of codes in complexity theory. The improved upper bounds obtained with coding techniques include bounds on the number of random bits used by probabilistic algorithms and the communication complexity of cryptographic protocols. In these constructions, codes are used to design small sample spaces that approximate the behavior of large sample spaces. Codes are also used to prove lower bounds on the complexity of approximating numerous combinatorial optimization functions. Finally, coding theory plays an important role in new characterizations of traditional complexity classes, such as NP and PSPACE, and in an emerging theory of program testing.

Section 2 reviews the concepts from both complexity theory and coding theory that we will need in the following sections. Section 3 demonstrates how codes are used to prove complexity theoretic upper bounds. The theory of program testing and correcting is presented in Section 4. Lower bound applications and new characterizations of standard complexity classes are presented in Section 5.

1991 *Mathematics Subject Classification.* Primary 68Q25; Secondary 68P25, 68Q15, 94A60, 94B05.

2. Preliminaries

This section briefly reviews the basic elements of the two disciplines under consideration, i.e., complexity theory and coding theory. If more than a brief review is needed, refer to one of the standard textbooks [**27**, **40**, **39**, **43**].

2.1. Complexity Theory. We assume that the reader is familiar with the Turing machine (TM) model of computation. (A formal definition of this model can be found in any introductory book on computational complexity, e.g., Garey and Johnson [**27**] or Papadimitriou [**43**].) However, most of the definitions presented in this section require only an intuitive understanding of the notions of "time complexity" or "space complexity" of a computational problem; readers unfamiliar with the definition of a TM can understand our main points in terms of the number of operations performed or the number of memory locations used by a standard computer program.

In general, a function we are interested in computing is defined on some infinite domain I. There is a sequence of subdomains $I_1, I_2, \ldots$, such that $I = \cup_{n \geq 1} I_n$ and a constant c such that, for all $x \in I_n$, $n^{1/c} \leq |x| \leq n^c$, where $|x|$ is the number of bits in some suitable binary encoding of x. For example, we may have $I = \{0, 1\}^+$ and $I_n = \{0, 1\}^n$, in which case we can take $c = 1$. If p_n is an n-bit prime, then I_n may consist of n-tuples of elements in $GF(p_n)$, in which case we can take $c = 2$. We refer to elements of I_n as *inputs of size* n. So "size" is a generalization of binary length.

A *polynomial-time Turing machine* is a TM for which there is a specific polynomial, say $p(n)$, that bounds the running time; that is, on inputs of size n, the machine always halts after at most $p(n)$ steps. We denote by FP the class of functions computable by polynomial-time TMs. Note that a TM that computes a boolean function can also be interpreted as recognizing a language. For example, "computing f," where $f(x) = 1$ if x encodes a planar graph and $f(x) = 0$ otherwise, is the same as "recognizing the language of planar graphs." In general, the deterministic Turing machine M is said to recognize the language $\{x \mid f(x) = 1\}$, which is denoted $L(M)$. Thus, FP is a generalization of the complexity class P of polynomial-time recognizable languages. *Polynomial-space Turing machines* and the complexity classes FPSPACE and PSPACE are defined in exactly the same manner as polynomial-time TMs, FP, and P, except that the computational resource that is bounded by the polynomial $p(n)$ is space instead of time. *Exponential-time Turing machines* and the complexity classes FEXP and EXP are defined analogously to polynomial-time TMs, FP, and P, except that all occurrences of "polynomial" and "$p(n)$" are replaced by "exponential" and "$2^{p(n)}$."

A *nondeterministic polynomial-time Turing machine* is a polynomial-time TM that, at each step in the computation, has several choices for its next move. The set of all possible computations of such a machine M on input $x \in I_n$ can be viewed as a tree. Because the total running time of M is bounded by $p(n)$, the paths from the root to the leaves of the computation tree may all be taken to have length exactly $p(n)$; short computation paths may be padded with "dummy steps" if necessary. Each leaf in the computation tree is labelled with the output that M produces on input x if, during the computation, it makes the sequence of choices represented by the path to this leaf. If all of the labels are 0s and 1s, then we can define the language $L(M)$ accepted by M. The input x is in $L(M)$ if there is at least one leaf in the computation tree that is labelled 1. The path to such a leaf is called an *accepting computation of M on input x* or a *witness that* $x \in L(M)$. The set of all languages accepted by nondeterministic polynomial-time TMs constitutes the complexity class NP.

NP plays a prominent role in computational complexity. Indeed the central unsolved problem in complexity theory is the P = NP? question. The main reason for the centrality of the complexity class NP is the large number of natural computational problems that can be formalized as NP languages. Examples include:

- Satisfiability of propositional formulae: The NP language SAT consists of strings that encode satisfiable propositional formulae in conjunctive normal form (CNF). For example, $(x_1 \vee \overline{x_2}) \wedge (\overline{x_1} \vee x_2)$ is an element of the language SAT, because the assignment $x_1 =$ T, x_2=T satisfies both clauses. On the other hand, $(x_1 \vee x_2) \wedge (x_1 \vee \overline{x_2}) \wedge \overline{x_1}$ is not in SAT, because none of the four truth assignments to the variables x_1 and x_2 satisfies all three clauses simultaneously. In most settings, it suffices to consider the language 3SAT, in which the formulae are conjuncts of clauses that are themselves disjuncts of three literals.
- Colorability of graphs: The NP language COLOR consists of pairs (G, k) such that the graph G is k-colorable. That is, (G, k) is in COLOR if and only if there is a mapping σ from $V(G)$ to $\{1, \ldots, k\}$ such that, if $\{v, w\} \in E(G)$, then $\sigma(v) \neq \sigma(w)$.
- Clique number of graphs: The NP language CLIQUE consists of pairs (G, k) such that the graph G has a k-clique. That is, (G, k) is in CLIQUE if and only if there is a subset $\{v_1, \ldots, v_k\}$ of $V(G)$ such that $\{v_i, v_j\} \in E(G)$, for $1 \leq i < j \leq k$.

These three NP languages, along with thousands of others that arise naturally in applications, are *NP-complete*. A language L is NP-complete if it is in NP and, for any other language L' in NP, there is a function R in FP (called a *polynomial-time reduction*) such that $x \in L'$ if and only if $R(x) \in L$. This means, for example, that if there were a polynomial-time decision algorithm for 3SAT, there would be a polynomial-time algorithm for every L in NP: To decide whether x is in L, compute $R(x)$ and test whether it is in 3SAT. Thus, the NP-complete languages are "as hard as any language in NP," and, barring an unexpected resolution of the P = NP? question in the affirmative, they cannot be decided by deterministic polynomial-time algorithms. See Garey and Johnson [27] for a comprehensive formal treatment of the theory of NP-completeness.

The concept of NP-completeness and the proof that SAT is NP-complete were put forth in the seminal paper of Cook [20]. Similar ideas were developed independently by Levin [36]. Shortly thereafter, Karp [34] established the fundamental importance of the concept by proving the NP-completeness of many languages that arise naturally in applications, including 3SAT, CLIQUE, and COLOR. In the ensuing years, thousands of NP-completeness results were proven. A standard question (along with a body of technique for answering it) was established in the computer science repertoire: When confronted with a combinatorial problem for which you cannot find a good algorithm, formulate it as a language-recognition problem, and try to prove that the language is NP-complete. Such problems are now divided into those for which polynomial-time algorithms are known (e.g., maximum matching and network flow), those that are NP-complete, and a few (e.g., graph isomorphism[1]) whose status is unknown. Before Cook and Karp established the concept of NP-completeness, there was no coherent explanation for the fact that certain problems (like matching) had efficient algorithms, while others that did not seem very different at first glance (like CLIQUE), did not. With the theory of NP-completeness in hand, such an explanation is easy: A polynomial-time algorithm for, say, CLIQUE would resolve the P = NP? question in the affirmative and hence is not something we expect to find.

In many applications, it is more natural to formalize a computational task as an NP "search problem" or an NP "optimization function," rather than as an NP language-recognition problem. The search problems corresponding to the languages defined above are:

- Given a CNF or 3CNF formula, find a truth assignment that satisfies as many of the clauses as possible.
- Given a graph, color its vertices using as few colors as possible so that no two adjacent vertices are the same color.
- Find a maximum-sized clique in a given graph.

The corresponding optimization functions are:

- Given a CNF or 3CNF formula ϕ, what is the largest k such that k clauses of ϕ are simultaneously satisfiable by a truth assignment? (These are the optimization functions MAX-SAT and MAX-3SAT, respectively.)
- Given a graph, what is the smallest number of colors needed to color its vertices such that no two adjacent vertices are the same color? (This is the optimization function *chromatic number.*)
- Given a graph, what is number of vertices in its largest clique? (This is the optimization function *clique number.*)

These optimization functions are *NP-hard*, just as the languages on which they are based are NP-complete. This means that the task of deciding membership in any NP language can be reduced in polynomial time to the task of computing one of these optimization functions. Thus, none of these optimization functions is in FP, unless P = NP.

One natural question to ask is whether these optimization problems can be solved approximately in polynomial time. An *ϵ-approximation algorithm* for an NP optimization function f takes an instance x and outputs an estimate E such that $E/(1 + \epsilon) \leq f(x) \leq E(1 + \epsilon)$. For example, if there were a polynomial-time $(1/2)$-approximation algorithm for the chromatic number function χ (as there seems not to be – see [**38**]), it would take a graph G as input and output a number E such that $2E/3 \leq \chi(G) \leq 3E/2$. A *polynomial-time approximation scheme* (PTAS) for an NP optimization function f takes as input a parameter $\epsilon > 0$ and outputs an ϵ-approximation algorithm for f; the running time of this approximation algorithm is polynomial in the size of inputs to f, but it may depend superpolynomially on ϵ.

We say that *ϵ-approximating a function f is NP-hard* if the task of deciding membership in any NP language can be reduced in polynomial time to the task of ϵ-approximating f. Just as it is natural to try to prove that an optimization function is NP-hard if one has failed to find a polynomial-time algorithm for it, it is also natural to try to prove that ϵ-approximating this function is NP-hard if one has

---

[1]Although there is no *proof* that graph isomorphism is not NP-complete (nor is one expected any time soon, because such a proof would imply that P $\neq$ NP), there is some evidence that it is not – see Boppana, Håstad, and Zachos [**15**] or Schöning [**50**].

failed to find a polynomial-time ϵ-approximation algorithm for it. While general techniques for proving NP-hardness of exact computations have been known since the early 1970s (see [27]), none were known for proving NP-hardness of approximate computations until recently. Coding theory plays a surprising role in these new techniques, as explained in Section 5 below.

The reason that standard NP-completeness theory does not help in proving nonapproximability of NP optimization functions is that typical polynomial-time reductions between NP-complete language-recognition problems do not preserve approximability. That is, if L_1 and L_2 are NP languages with associated optimization functions f_1 and f_2, and R is a polynomial-time reduction from L_1 to L_2, then an approximation to $f_2(R(x))$ is typically of no help in computing an approximation to $f_1(x)$. A major step forward in the development of a general theory of approximability was taken by Papadimitriou and Yannakakis [44] in their seminal paper on the complexity class MAX-SNP. Before the introduction of MAX-SNP, approximability of NP-hard optimization functions was in the same state that exact optimization was in before the establishment of NP-completeness: Good approximation methods could be found for some problems (such as bin packing) but not for others (such as chromatic number), and there was no coherent explanation of which was which. Papadimitriou and Yannakakis's paper established the framework in which to classify approximation problems in the same way that the early work of Cook and Karp established a framework for exact optimization problems.

We give a definition (due to Sudan [57]) of MAX-SNP that is convenient for the results discussed in Section 5; it is equivalent to the original definition given in [44]. A *constraint of arity* c is a mapping from c boolean variables to the range $\{0, 1\}$. A constraint is *satisfied* by a truth assignment if it evaluates to 1 at that assignment. The *constraint satisfaction problem* (CSP) is a family of optimization functions parameterized by the arity c and is defined as follows. An instance of c-CSP is a set $\{C_1, \dots, C_m\}$ of constraints of arity c on variables $x_1, \dots, x_n$. The value of the function c-CSP on instance $\{C_1, \dots, C_m\}$ is the largest integer k such that there is a truth assignment to $x_1, \dots, x_n$ that simultaneously satisfies k of the input constraints.

An optimization function is in the complexity class MAX-SNP if and only if it can be expressed as c-CSP for some c. For example, it is easy to see that the function MAX-3SAT is in MAX-SNP; just let $c = 3$ and the clauses in an input formula be the constraints. In fact, MAX-3SAT is complete for the class MAX-SNP with respect to *linear reductions* [44]. These are reductions that are "approximability-preserving," in the sense that, if MAX-SNP functions f and g are such that f is linearly reducible to g and g has a polynomial-time ϵ-approximation algorithm, then f has a polynomial-time $d\epsilon$-approximation algorithm, for some constant d; exactly which constant d is achievable depends on how efficiently the reduction preserves approximability. (See [1, 44, 57] for a precise definition of linear reductions and many more examples of problems that are complete for MAX-SNP.) Papadimitriou and Yannakakis [44] show that every function in MAX-SNP is ϵ-approximable for some constant ϵ. They pose the basic question "do MAX-SNP-complete functions have PTASs?" This is the central question in the theory of approximability of NP optimization functions, because the definitions are such that all MAX-SNP functions have PTASs if the complete ones do. The theory of probabilistically checkable proof systems (see Section 5), in which coding techniques play a crucial role, has essentially resolved this question in the negative: MAX-SNP functions do not have PTASs unless P = NP.

A *nondeterministic exponential-time Turing machine* is defined exactly the same way as a nondeterministic polynomial-time Turing machine, except that all occurrences of "polynomial" and "$p(n)$" are replaced by "exponential" and "$2^{p(n)}$." The languages accepted by nondeterministic exponential-time TMs constitute the complexity class NEXP.

A *probabilistic polynomial-time Turing machine* is a polynomial-time TM that has an extra "random tape" of 0s and 1s that can be read as necessary. The bits on this tape are the outcomes of independent, unbiased coin tosses. Let M be a probabilistic polynomial-time TM with running time $p(n)$. On any input $x \in I_n$, M tosses at most $p(n)$ coins (i.e., reads at most $p(n)$ bits from the random tape), because it always halts after at most $p(n)$ steps. If the output of M is a single bit, we require that, on any input $x \in I_n$, M either output 1 with probability at least 3/4 or output 0 with probability at least 3/4; this probability is computed over the uniform distribution on $\{0,1\}^{p(n)}$ (i.e., over the probability space of all coin-toss sequences that M may make on input x). The language L recognized by such a machine M, i.e., the inputs x on which M outputs 1 with probability at least 3/4, is said to be in the complexity class BPP. The probability of error can be reduced from 1/4 to $2^{-q(n)}$, for any polynomial q, at the expense of increasing the number of coin tosses and the running time by a corresponding polynomial factor. (The issue of how many random bits a BPP machine uses is revisited in Section 3.1 below.) Note that the definition of BPP allows for two-sided error: The TM may give a wrong answer both in the case that $x \in L$ and in the case that $x \notin L$. Probabilistic polynomial-time TMs that admit only one-sided error and other formal definitions of probabilistic computation are treated at length in, e.g., [31, 58].

An *oracle Turing machine* M has access to an auxiliary "oracle tape" from which it can get answers to computations that it may not be able to perform itself. The "base machine" M may be deterministic, nondeterministic, or probabilistic. The oracle may itself be a machine or program of any of these three types, or it may be a nonrecursive function, i.e., a function that is not computable by any TM with any amount of computational resources. When M asks for the value of the oracle on some string y, this is referred to as an "oracle call," and it costs M one unit of time. The reason that it makes sense to charge a machine M only one unit of time for information that may be very expensive (or even impossible) to compute is that it allows us to model formally the notion of separating a computational task into its constituent parts. We can encapsulate part of the task in the oracle O and then ask what else the base machine M has to do in order to "reduce" the computational task to a sequence of calls to O.

The notation $M(x)$ denotes the output of Turing machine M on input x. If M is a deterministic machine, then it defines a computable function, and $M(x)$ is just the value of this function at x. If M is a nondeterministic machine, then it defines a multivalued partial function. If $x \in L(M)$, then the partial function's value at x is the set of accepting computations that witness this fact; if $x \notin L(M)$, then the function is undefined at x. If M is a probabilistic machine, then $M(x)$ is a random variable. We use $M^O(x)$ to denote the output of oracle Turing machine M on input x when run with oracle O. If O is a probabilistic oracle, then the output distribution is determined by the algorithms and the coin-toss sequences of both M and O.

The shorthand $m = poly(n)$ means that there is a polynomial p such that, for all sufficiently large n, $m \leq p(n)$. It is used when the existence of such a polynomial is what is important, rather than the specific polynomial p.

2.2. Coding Theory. We now review a small number of definitions from basic coding theory that are needed in Sections 3, 4, and 5. A thorough introduction to the subject can be found in, e.g., MacWilliams and Sloan [**39**] or McEliece [**40**].

A *code* over the alphabet Σ is a function E from Σ^k to Σ^n. A *binary code* is one in which $\Sigma = \{0, 1\}$. Words in the domain of E are *messages*, and words in the image of E are *codewords*. If B and B' are two elements of Σ^n, the *distance* between them is the number of places in which they differ. Computing $E(A)$, given the message A, is called *encoding*. Given a word $B \in \Sigma^n$, determining whether there exists a message A such that $E(A) = B$ is called *error detection*. Finding a valid codeword B' that is closest to B is called *error correction*. If B is a codeword, then finding the message A such that $E(A) = B$ is called *decoding*.

The *minimum distance* of a code E is the minimum, over all pairs of codewords, of the distance between them. The *relative distance* between codewords B and B' is the distance between B and B' divided by n, and the relative distance of the code E is its minimum distance divided by n. The ratio k/n is called the *rate* of the code.

An (n, k) *linear code* C over the finite field F is a k-dimensional subspace of the n-dimensional vector space over F. A *generator matrix* G for C is a $k \times n$ matrix whose k rows are linearly independent vectors in F^n. To encode a word $x \in F^k$, simply perform the matrix multiplication $x^T G$. If $F = \mathrm{GF}(2)$, then C is called a *binary linear code*.

The following lemma states a fundamental fact about polynomials that is important in our uses of coding theory.

Schwartz's Lemma [51]: Two distinct m-variable polynomials over the finite field F, each of total degree at most d, must assume different values on at least $(1 - d/|F|) \cdot |F|^m$ of the $|F|^m$ points in their domain.

An equivalent statement of Schwartz's Lemma is that a polynomial in $F[X_1, \ldots, X_m]$ of total degree at most d is either identically zero or has at most $d \cdot |F|^{m-1}$ distinct roots. This fact is well known in the case $m = 1$; the proof of the more general fact is by induction on m.

In a *polynomial code* over a finite field F, the messages $A = (a_1, \ldots, a_k)$ are interpreted as coefficients of a polynomial $p(x_1, \ldots, x_m)$ over F. The codeword corresponding to A is obtained by writing down the value of p at each m-tuple in F^m or in some subset of F^m. A fundamental example of polynomial codes are those of Reed and Solomon. A message $A = (a_0, \ldots, a_k)$, where $a_i \in F$, is interpreted as the univariate polynomial $p(x) = a_0 + a_1 x + \cdots + a_k x^k$ in $F[x]$, where $|F| = n = ck$, for some constant $c > 1$. It is encoded by writing down the value of p at each of the points $b_1, \ldots, b_n$ in F.

Because two degree-k polynomials can agree on at most k points, the minimum distance of this code is at least $(c-1)k = \Omega(n)$. Note, however, that this is "distance over F" in that two symbols in a codeword are considered "different" if they differ as field elements. If we view this as a binary code, then the distance between two codewords is the number of bits in which they differ; because $\log n$ bits are required to write down a field element, the relative distance of the code can tend to 0 as n grows.

Justesen [32] uses Reed-Solomon codes to construct an infinite family of binary, linear codes of constant rate and constant relative distance. Justesen's basic trick is to compose the Reed-Solomon code with codes in which the messages have length $\log n$, and both the rate and the relative distance are constant. It is known that, with high probability, if b is chosen uniformly at random from F, the mapping $x \mapsto (x, bx)$ has constant relative distance. (All such maps have rate $1/2$ and messages of length $\log n$.) Let $E_i(x) = (x, b_i x)$. Then the Justesen encoding E is defined as

$$E(a_0, \ldots, a_k) \equiv (E_1(p(b_1)), \ldots, E_n(p(b_n))),$$

where $p(x) = a_0 + a_1 x + \cdots + a_k x^k$. Because a high fraction of the codes E_i have constant relative distance, E has constant relative distance, for $n \to \infty$. For more details about Reed-Solomon and Justesen codes, see [32, 39, 40].

Finally, we recall the Berlekamp-Welch decoding theorem.

Berlekamp-Welch Decoding [11]: Given pairs $(x_1, y_1), \ldots, (x_n, y_n)$ of points in a finite field F, there is an algorithm that finds a univariate polynomial p of degree at most d such that $p(x_i) = y_i$ for all but k pairs (x_i, y_i), provided $2k + d < n$ and such a p exists. The running time of the algorithm is polynomial in n and l, where l is the size of elements of F.

The Berlekamp-Welch algorithm and a complete proof of its correctness are given in the paper of Gemmell and Sudan [28]. The essence of the algorithm is to find polynomials w and p such that $degree(w) \leq k$, $degree(p) \leq d$, w is not identically zero, and $w(x_i) \cdot y_i = w(x_i) \cdot p(x_i)$, for $1 \leq i \leq n$. Berlekamp and Welch reduce this task to that of finding polynomials w and q such that $degree(w) \leq k$, $degree(q) \leq k + d$, w is not identically zero, $w(x_i) \cdot y_i = q(x_i)$ for $1 \leq i \leq n$, and w divides q. They show that two pairs of polynomials q, w and l, u that satisfy the first four requirements also satisfy $q/w = l/u$. Thus one can translate the first four requirements plus the requirement that w divide q into a set of linear equations in the coefficients of q and w and find an arbitrary solution to this set of equations.

3. Using Good Linear Codes to Improve Computational Efficiency

This section provides examples of how coding theory is used to improve computational efficiency. What is needed is an infinite family $\{E_{k_i}\}_{i \geq 1}$ of binary linear codes that have constant rate, constant relative distance, and a uniform efficient encoding algorithm. That is, there is one FP encoding function that, for any k_i, takes a string x in $\{0, 1\}^{k_i}$ and produces $E_{k_i}(x)$. Note that efficient decoding, although not a disadvantage, is not needed in this application. Linear code families with these properties exist, and in fact the Justesen codes described in Section 2.2 above are such a family.

3.1. Efficient Use of Randomness as a Resource. Randomized algorithms play an important role in both theory and practice of computation. As first suggested by Karp and Pippenger [35], it is complexity theoretically natural to view random bits as a resource analogous to time or space and to design algorithms that use as few of them as possible. There is also a practical motivation to use few random bits, because such bits have to be generated by a physical device, such as a Geiger counter or a Zener diode, and these devices are slow. We now

THE USE OF CODING THEORY IN COMPUTATIONAL COMPLEXITY

describe an elegant construction of Naor and Naor [**42**] that uses good linear codes to save random bits.

Suppose that a probabilistic polynomial-time machine M uses n independent random bits. This means that it samples from a probability space of size 2^n. Naor and Naor use linear codes to construct a smaller probability space that, for certain machines M, can be used to solve the same problem that M solves. Because this space is smaller, the machine that samples from it uses fewer independent random bits than M uses. The starting point for their construction is the equivalence of the following two statements.

1. The $\{0,1\}$-random variables $x_1, \ldots, x_n$ are independent and, for all i, $\text{Prob}[x_i = 0] = \text{Prob}[x_i = 1] = 1/2$.

2. For every nonempty subset S of $\{1, \ldots, n\}$, the probability that $\sum_{i \in S} x_i = 1$ and the probability that $\sum_{i \in S} x_i = 0$ are both $1/2$. Here Σ is the mod-2 sum.

Suppose that statement 2 is relaxed to require only that every nonempty subset S of $\{1, \ldots, n\}$ be ϵ-*biased*. This means that

$$\left| \text{Prob}[\sum_{i \in S} x_i = 0] - \text{Prob}[\sum_{i \in S} x_i = 1] \right| \leq \epsilon.$$

Then $x_1, \ldots, x_n$ are called ϵ-biased random variables, and the sample space that they give rise to is of size $2^{O(\log(n) + \log(1/\epsilon))}$. If ϵ is $1/poly(n)$, then the sample space associated with these variables is polynomially small.

Let v and r be elements of $\{0,1\}^n$, and let $v \cdot r$ be the usual mod-2 dot product. The vector r is said to be a *distinguisher with respect to* v if $v \cdot r = 1$. Naor and Naor's construction of ϵ-biased random variables has three stages. In the first stage, they construct a set $\mathcal{F}$ of vectors in $\{0,1\}^n$ that can be sampled once using $O(\log(n))$ random bits; this set has the additional property that, for any nonzero $v \in \{0,1\}^n$, an r chosen uniformly at random from $\mathcal{F}$ is a distinguisher with respect to v with probability at least β, for some constant $\beta > 0$. In the second stage, these variables are sampled l times, where l depends on ϵ. In the third stage, these l samples are combined in a way that produces an ϵ-biased set of variables. The second and third stages do not use coding theory and hence are not explained here; refer to [**42**] for a complete explanation.

The theory of combinatorial and spherical designs provides another way to view the construction of $\mathcal{F}$. Geometrically, the set $v^\perp \equiv \{r \mid r \cdot v = 0\}$ is a hyperplane in the vector space $\{0,1\}^n$. A set of random vectors would be split equally between $v^\perp$ and its complement. The set $\mathcal{F}$ approximates the behavior of a random set. Approximations of random sets motivate many designs in this field; see, for example, the article in this volume by Sloane [**55**].

Let E_n be a binary linear code with constant rate and constant relative distance. That is, $E_n : \{0,1\}^n \longrightarrow \{0,1\}^m$, where $m = O(n)$, and the minimum weight of a codeword in $\{0,1\}^m$ is βm, for some constant $\beta > 0$. Let G_n be the generator matrix for E_n, and let $\mathcal{F}$ be the set of columns of G_n. The fact that, for any nonzero $v \in \{0,1\}^n$, the codeword $E_n(v)$ has weight at least βm means precisely that, for any such v, a column r of G_n chosen uniformly at random is a distinguisher with respect to v with probability at least β. Because $m = O(n)$, a column of G_n can be chosen uniformly at random using $O(\log(n))$ random bits. (Actually, for this property, it would suffice to have $m = poly(n)$.)

This construction can be generalized to allow v and r to be vectors over an arbitrary ring, rather than over GF(2), and $v \cdot r$ to denote the dot product in this ring. This generalization is applied in many areas of computer science, including combinatorial algorithms, parallel computation, fault diagnosis, and communication complexity. (See [**42**, Section 3].) Here we discuss two applications that entail saving random bits in a probabilistic algorithm.

Suppose that three $n \times n$ boolean matrices A, B, and C are given, and we wish to determine whether $AB = C$ without performing matrix multiplication. (The fastest known matrix multiplication algorithms have asymptotic complexity $O(n^c)$, where $2 < c < 3$, but the constants implied in the $O()$ notation are so huge that these algorithms run more slowly than straightforward $O(n^3)$ algorithms for any plausible size n; thus the "real" time complexity of current matrix multiplication methods is $O(n^3)$.) Freivalds [**26**] suggests the following probabilistic test: Choose a vector r uniformly at random from $\{0,1\}^n$ and check whether $(r^T A)B - r^T C = 0$. This test has time complexity $O(n^2)$, uses n random bits, always says "yes" if $AB = C$, and says "no" with probability at least $1/2$ if $AB \neq C$. The proof that this test says "no" with probability at least $1/2$ when $AB \neq C$ amounts to the observation that, if v is a nonzero column vector in $AB - C$, then an r chosen uniformly at random from $\{0,1\}^n$ is a distinguisher for v with probability at least $1/2$. Thus, to reduce the number of random bits needed by Freivalds's test to $O(\log(n))$, while maintaining the $O(n^2)$ running time and the $1/2$ probability of detecting an error, we need a set of vectors in $\{0,1\}^n$ that can be sampled using $O(\log(n))$ bits with the property that, for an arbitrary v, the sampled vector r is a distinguisher for v with some constant probability $\beta > 0$. The set $\mathcal{F}$ constructed above with linear codes has exactly this property. Explicitly, on $n \times n$ matrices, the improved algorithm chooses a column r of G_n uniformly at random and uses it exactly as the vector r is used in Freivalds's original algorithm. Because G_n is an $n \times m$ matrix and $m = O(n)$, the vector r is of length n, and the sampling requires $\log m = O(\log n)$ random bits.

The second example also concerns verification that a computation has been done correctly, this time in a finite field. The input is a prime p, a number a, and a list of pairs (x_1, y_1), ..., (x_n, y_n). We wish to verify that $a^{x_i} = y_i \bmod p$, for $1 \leq i \leq n$. The following test, due to Fiat and Naor, is presented in [**42**]: Choose $r = (r_1, \ldots, r_n)$ uniformly at random from $\{0,1\}^n$; let $t = \sum_{i=1}^{n} r_i x_i \bmod (p-1)$ and $m = \prod_{i=1}^{n} y_i^{r_i} \bmod p$; check whether $a^t = m \bmod p$. This test requires $O(n + \log(p))$ modular multiplications instead of the $O(n \log(p))$ required to check each equality separately. If all equalities hold, the test always says "yes," and if at least one does not hold, it says "no" with probability at least $1/2$. Its cost in random bits is n. The proof that it detects a faulty input with probability at least $1/2$ reduces to a proof that a random r is a distinguisher for $w = (w_1, \ldots, w_n)$ with probability at least $1/2$, where $a^{z_i} = y_i \bmod p$ and $w_i = x_i - z_i \bmod (p-1)$. As in the previous example, sampling from the family $\mathcal{F}$ derived from a good linear code produces a distinguisher with constant probability and requires only $O(\log(n))$ random bits.

3.2. Efficient Use of Communication Bits. Cryptographic complexity theory studies the efficiency of procedures that protect privacy and integrity of information. Most of these tasks are accomplished by protocols that involve two or more communicating machines. To be of practical use, a protocol must be efficient not only in its use of time and space but also in its use of communication bandwidth.

In this section, we show how good linear codes are used to lower the communication complexity of a fundamental cryptographic protocol.

A *bit-commitment* protocol, executed by two probabilistic polynomial-time machines called the *committer* C and the *receiver* R, has two stages:

- The *commit stage*: C has a bit b that she commits to R. C and R exchange messages, and after this exchange, R has some information that represents b.

- The *reveal stage*: C and R exchange messages and, after this exchange, R knows b.

The expense of the protocol, in terms of local computation costs of C and R and number of bits exchanged, depends on a "security parameter" n. That is, the guarantees embodied in the following two properties that the protocol must satisfy can be made stronger or weaker by choosing a larger or smaller n. Thus the input to the protocol is the pair $(b, 1^n)$, and it makes sense to say that C and R are probabilistic polynomial-time TMs. This statement would not make sense if the input were just the single bit b. The notation 1^n is used to mean a string of n 1's; it provides a way of writing the security parameter "in unary" so that the length of the input is n, and one can use "polynomial time" to mean "polynomial in n" as usual.

Let C' and R' denote probabilistic polynomial-time TMs that play the roles of C and R; they may follow the protocol faithfully, or they may try to cheat in order to gain some advantage over the other party. The protocol must satisfy the following two properties for all probabilistic polynomial-time C' and R', all polynomials p, and sufficiently large n.

- The *privacy property*: After the commit stage, b is private. That is, R' can guess b with probability at most $1/2 + 1/p(n)$.
- The *integrity property*: After the commit stage, b is fixed. That is, C' can reveal only the b that was committed to during the commit stage; if she tries to reveal the opposite bit, she is caught with probability at least $1 - 1/p(n)$.

Executing the commit stage is thus analogous to having C write b on a piece of paper, put the paper into a locked box to which only C has a key, and give the box to R. Executing the reveal stage is analogous to having C unlock the box. C knows that R cannot guess b, because only C has a key to the box. R knows that C has not changed the value of b after the commit stage, because the box has been in R's possession. Bit-commitment protocols are essential building blocks in user-authentication schemes and many of the other tasks that are needed in secure systems.

Let $m(n) > n$ be a polynomially bounded function. The probabilistic polynomial-time machine G is a *cryptographically strong pseudorandom number generator* if, for all polynomials p and all probabilistic polynomial-time machines A,

$$|\text{Prob}[A(y) = 1] - \text{Prob}[A(G(s)) = 1]| < \frac{1}{p(n)},$$

for all sufficiently large n, where y and s are chosen uniformly from $\{0,1\}^{m(n)}$ and $\{0,1\}^n$, respectively. Here A is a polynomial-time statistical test that is trying to distinguish the length-$m(n)$, pseudorandom output of G on a random seed s of length n from the truly random string y of length $m(n)$. The generator G is cryptographically strong if no such test A succeeds with nonnegligible probability.

Naor [41] shows how to use any such generator G to build a bit-commitment scheme. The importance of this result is that it provides flexibility in the design of secure systems that require bit-commitment, because pseudorandom generators have been proven to exist under very general conditions [29, 30]. In the following statement of Naor's protocol, $B_i(s)$ denotes the ith bit, $1 \leq i \leq m(n)$, in the pseudorandom sequence $G(s)$ generated from random seed $s \in \{0,1\}^n$. The symbol $\oplus$ denotes the exclusive-or operation; it can be applied to a single bit or, componentwise, to a vector of bits. In the following protocol, we can set $m(n) = 3n$, because this is sufficient to make the chance of catching a cheating C' at least $1 - 2^{-n}$. We will modify this choice of m below when we design a protocol to commit to many bits simultaneously.

Bit-Commitment$(b, 1^n)$:

- Commit stage:
    1. R chooses $r = (r_1, \dots, r_{3n})$ uniformly at random from $\{0,1\}^{3n}$ and sends r to C.
    2. C chooses s uniformly at random from $\{0,1\}^n$ and sends $d = (d_1, \dots, d_{3n})$ to R, where $d_i = B_i(s)$ if $r_i = 0$ and $d_i = B_i(s) \oplus b$ if $r_i = 1$.
- Reveal stage: C sends b and s to R, who verifies that all of the bits of d are correct.

The proof that this protocol satisfies the definition of bit-commitment is give in [41].

Linear codes come into the picture when C needs to commit to many bits at once. In fact, this is exactly what is needed in practical applications of bit commitment. When committing to one bit using the above protocol, C and R incur a communication cost of $O(n)$, where n is the security parameter. A naïve use of the protocol to commit to a set of bits $b_1, \dots, b_k$ would incur a communication cost of $O(kn)$. Codes allow us to reduce this cost substantially.

For simplicity of exposition, suppose that $k = 3n/2$; the following construction actually works whenever $k = O(n)$. As in the previous section, $E_k : \{0,1\}^k \longrightarrow \{0,1\}^{\alpha k}$ is a linear code with constant rate $1/\alpha$ and constant relative distance β. More precisely, there is an infinite family of such codes, one for each k of the form $3n/2$, $n \geq 1$, and an FP function that, on input $x \in \{0,1\}^k$, computes $E_k(x)$. We require that $\alpha k \log(2/(2 - \beta))$ be at least $3n$, and once again the Justesen codes satisfy these requirements.

Let $G : \{0,1\}^n \longrightarrow \{0,1\}^{m(n)}$ be a cryptographically strong pseudorandom generator for some $m(n) \geq 3\alpha n$; in the following discussion, we will only be concerned with the first $3\alpha n = 2\alpha k$ bits of a pseudorandom sequence $G(s)$, $s \in \{0,1\}^n$. For any t, $\alpha k \leq t \leq m(n)$ and any 0-1 vector $r = (r_1, \dots, r_t)$ in which exactly αk of the r_i's are 1, let $G_r(s)$ denote the vector $(a_1, \dots, a_{\alpha k})$, where $s \in \{0,1\}^n$ is a random seed, $j(i)$ is the index of the ith 1 in r, and $a_i = B_{j(i)}(s)$.

Many-Bit-Commitment$((b_1, \dots, b_k), 1^n)$:

- Commit stage:
    1. R chooses $r = (r_1, \dots, r_{2\alpha k})$ uniformly at random from the set of vectors in $\{0,1\}^{2\alpha k}$ in which exactly αk of the r_i's are 1. R sends r to C.

  2. C computes $c = E_k(b_1, \ldots, b_k)$. C chooses s uniformly at random from $\{0,1\}^n$ and computes $e = c \oplus G_r(s)$. C sends to R the vector e and the bit $B_i(s)$ for every i, $1 \le i \le 2\alpha k$, such that $r_i = 0$.

- Reveal stage: C sends $(b_1, \ldots, b_k)$ and s to R, who verifies that all of the bits he received are correct.

The number of bits exchanged during the execution of Many-Bit-Commitment is $O(\max(k,n))$, which is as promised a substantial improvement over $O(kn)$. The proof that it has the privacy property uses the definition of pseudorandom number generation and does not involve codes. The proof that it satisfies the integrity property starts with the observation that C' can only cheat if she can find two seeds s and s' in $\{0,1\}^n$ and an input sequence $(b'_1, \ldots, b'_k) \ne (b_1, \ldots, b_k)$ such that $B_i(s) = B_i(s')$ whenever $r_i = 0$ and the sequences $G_r(s) \oplus E_k(b_1, \ldots, b_k)$ and $G_r(s') \oplus E_k(b'_1, \ldots, b'_k)$ are identical. Consider any pair of seeds s, s'. Because the distance between the codewords $E_k(b_1, \ldots, b_k)$ and $E_k(b'_1, \ldots, b'_k)$ is at least $\alpha\beta k$, the pseudorandom sequences $G_r(s)$ and $G_r(s')$ must also be at least $\alpha\beta k$ apart for C' to be able to cheat successfully. This means that there are at least $\alpha\beta k$ indices i for which $B_i(s) \ne B_i(s')$. The indices i for which $r_i = 0$ form a random subset of $\{1, \ldots, 2\alpha k\}$ of size αk; thus, the probability that all such i satisfy $B_i(s) = B_i(s')$ is at most

$$\left(\frac{2\alpha k - \alpha\beta k}{2\alpha k} \right)^{\alpha k} = \left(1 - \frac{\beta}{2} \right)^{\alpha k} .$$

Because $\alpha k \log(2/(2-\beta)) \ge 3n$, this probability is at most 2^{-3n}. Now multiply by 2^{2n}, the total number of pairs s, s', to see that the probability that C' can convince R to accept a wrong sequence is at most 2^{-n}.

Good linear codes are used in a very similar way in the *digital signature* schemes of Even, Goldreich, and Micali [23] and Dwork and Naor [22]. Digital signature schemes consist of a *signing* algorithm S and a *verification* algorithm V. They capture the paper world's notion of "signature" in that, if signer A constructs a signature $s = S(x)$ of document x, then, by running V, anyone can verify that s is a legitimate signature of x and that it was A who constructed it. Because signatures are often verified by resource-limited devices like smart cards, it is important that signature schemes make efficient use of random bits and communication bits.

4. Program Testing and Correction

This section presents a natural complexity theoretic analogue of error-detection and -correction, namely the testing and correction of computer programs. Program testers and correctors are similar to error-detecting and -correcting codes in their overall purpose: A tester is supposed to output PASS or FAIL, depending upon whether the program is correct; a corrector is supposed to take an input x and a program P that has been declared by the tester to be at least "nearly correct" and output the correct value for $P(x)$. Before giving a formal definition of program testers and correctors, we note two ways in which they are different from traditional error-detecting and -correcting codes.

The first difference is that only asymptotically good testers and correctors matter. A "program" is assumed to compute a function whose domain is infinite. When we speak of the "running time" of the program, it is implicit that we mean the asymptotic running time. As we will see in the formal definition given below, a tester or corrector is supposed to work on the entire domain of the function. Thus, while specially designed codes $E : \Sigma^k \longrightarrow \Sigma^n$ for particular small values of k and n are of interest in coding theory, even when they are not part of an infinite family of codes with the same properties, testers and correctors that only work on some finite subdomain of the program in question are not even defined.

The second difference is that probabilistic algorithms play a much more central role in program testing and correction than they do in traditional coding theory. A program can pass the tester if it is correct on most of its inputs, but not all, and a corrector guarantees only that the program is correct with high probability on each input, not that it is correct with probability one. Tolerance for a small probability of error allows for the development of very efficient testing and correction algorithms and the application of these algorithms in seemingly unrelated problem areas in complexity theory, as explained in Section 5.2 below.

The precise definition of program testing and correction that we will use here was given by Babai, Fortnow, and Lund [6], who built upon the general approach first taken by Blum, Luby, and Rubinfeld [14]. The work in [14] was in turn inspired by work on program "checking" by Blum and Kannan [12, 13, 33]. A thorough treatment of all of these notions can be found in, e.g., [1, 25, 33, 47, 57].

The probabilistic polynomial-time oracle Turing machines T and C form a *self-testing/correcting pair for f* if they behave as follows. The output of T is always PASS or FAIL. For any n, $T^f(1^n) =$ PASS with probability at least $3/4$. If the probability that $T^Q(1^n) =$ PASS is at least $1/4$, then for any input x of size n, the probability that $C^Q(x) = f(x)$ is at least $3/4$. In other words, the tester T takes a program Q that purports to compute f and a size parameter n, written in unary. If Q is an everywhere-correct program for f, then T should output PASS with high probability, for all sizes n. On the other hand, if there is a nonnegligible probability that T passes Q on input size n, then Q may in fact have errors somewhere, but for any input x of size n, the corrector C must be able, possibly by making repeated calls to the program Q, to produce the right value $f(x)$ with high probability. As usual, the $3/4$ probability of correctness and the $1/4$ threshold for correctability can be increased or decreased if one is willing to use slower, but still polynomial-time, testers and correctors.

Rubinfeld and Sudan [49] generalize the notion of a tester for a function f to that of a tester for a function family $\mathcal{F}$. Let f and g be two functions defined on the same domain, and let $d_n(f, g)$ denote the fraction of inputs of size n on which functions f and g differ. If $\mathcal{F}$ is a family of functions defined on the same domain as the function f, then $\Delta_n(f, \mathcal{F})$ is the minimum, over all $g \in \mathcal{F}$, of $d_n(f, g)$. The probabilistic polynomial-time oracle Turing machine T is a *tester for the function family $\mathcal{F}$* if, for all n and all $f \in \mathcal{F}$, $T^f(1^n)$ outputs PASS with probability at least $3/4$ and, for all n and all programs Q such that $\Delta_n(Q, \mathcal{F}) \geq 1/4$, $T^Q(1^n)$ outputs FAIL with probability at least $3/4$.

Blum, Luby, and Rubinfeld [14] provided the first example of a family of functions that can be tested and corrected – linear functions over finite fields. We describe this example here, because it is used in Section 5.1 below. Recall that f is a linear, n-variable function over the finite field F if there are n coefficients a_1, ..., a_n in F such that

$$f(x_1, \ldots, x_n) = \sum_{i=1}^{n} a_i \cdot x_i,$$

for $(x_1, \ldots, x_n) \in F^n$. Let $\{F_n\}_{n \geq 1}$ be a sequence of finite fields, $\mathcal{F}_n$ be the family of linear, n-variable functions over F_n, and $\mathcal{F} = \cup_{n \geq 1} \mathcal{F}_n$. Blum, Luby, and Rubinfeld observe the following useful fact.

Linearity testing and correcting [14]: Suppose that $0 \leq \delta \leq 1/3$ and that the function $g : F_n^n \longrightarrow F_n$ has the property that two elements x and y both chosen uniformly at random from F_n^n satisfy the equation $g(x + y) = g(x) + g(y)$ with probability at least $1 - \delta/2$. Then $\Delta_n(g, \mathcal{F}) \leq \delta$. On the other hand, if $\Delta_n(g, \mathcal{F}) \leq \delta$, then, for any $x \in F_n^n$, the probability is at least $1 - 2\delta$ that a y chosen uniformly at random from F_n^n satisfies $g(x) = g(x + y) - g(y)$.

From this basic observation, it is straightforward to construct a self-testing/correcting pair for any sequence of linear functions over finite fields. The essence of the testing strategy is to check that the program Q satisfies the identity $Q(x + y) = Q(x) + Q(y)$ at a constant number of random sample points and that it satisfies some "initial conditions" that define the particular linear function that Q is supposed to compute. Exactly what this constant number of sample points is depends on the error probability one is willing to tolerate. The fact that these testers and correctors require only a constant number of calls to the program being tested or corrected is crucial in Section 5 below. We give some details about a more general tester, i.e., one of the total-degree, multivariate polynomial testers provided by Rubinfeld and Sudan [49]. More details about the linearity tester can be found in [14].

These testers for multivariate linear functions and polynomials are based on "robust characterizations" of function families. The basic idea of such a characterization is to take an exact characterization of the family (such as $g(x+y) = g(x)+g(y)$ for the family of linear functions) and prove that the "for all" quantifier of the variables x and y can be replaced by a "for most" quantifier. A robust characterization can be used to build a tester, because polynomially many samples suffice to show that a property holds for most elements of the domain of the function, whereas the entire (exponential-sized) domain would have to be tested to establish that the property held for all elements. Rubinfeld and Sudan [49] provide a detailed treatment of this notion as well as several alternative robust characterizations of multivariate polynomials that can be used to build testers. Subsequent robust characterizations of some non-algebraic function classes, as well as program testers and correctors based on these characterizations, can be found in [48].

Let $\{\mathrm{GF}(p_n)\}_{n \geq 1}$, where p_n is prime, be a sequence of finite fields. Let $\mathcal{F}_n$ be the family of n-variable polynomials over $\mathrm{GF}(p_n)$ that have total degree at most d_n, and let $\mathcal{F}$ denote $\cup_{n \geq 1} \mathcal{F}_n$. We require that p_n be at least $d_n + 2$. Throughout this discussion, the coefficient $\alpha_{n,i} = (-1)^{i+1} \binom{d_n+1}{i}$. The computation of $\alpha_{n,i}$, as well as all other computations in this example, is done modulo p_n. Note that $\alpha_{n,i}$ depends only on i and the degree d_n, not on the particular polynomial being tested.

The starting point for this tester is the following (well known) exact characterization of multivariate polynomials. The fundamental algebra underlying this and other exact characterizations of polynomials can be found in, e.g., the classic book of Van der Waerden [21].

Evenly spaced points characterization – exact: The function $g_n : \mathrm{GF}(p_n)^n$ $\longrightarrow \mathrm{GF}(p_n)$ is in $\mathcal{F}_n$ if and only if $g_n(x) = \sum_{i=1}^{d_n+1} \alpha_{n,i} g_n(x + iy)$, for all x and y in $\mathrm{GF}(p_n)^n$.

The crucial fact used by the tester is that this characterization is robust.

Evenly spaced points characterization – robust [49]: Let $\delta_0 = 1/2(d_n + 2)^2$. If the function $Q_n : \mathrm{GF}(p_n)^n \longrightarrow \mathrm{GF}(p_n)$ has the property that

$$\delta \equiv \mathrm{Prob}(Q_n(x) \neq \sum_{i=1}^{d_n+1} \alpha_{n,i} Q_n(x + i \cdot y)) \leq \delta_0,$$

where the probability is induced by (independently) choosing x and y uniformly at random from $\mathrm{GF}(p_n)^n$, then $\Delta_n(Q_n, \mathcal{F}) \leq 2\delta$.

Let $g_n(x) \equiv \mathrm{maj}_{y \in \mathrm{GF}(p_n)^n} \{\sum_{i=1}^{d_n+1} \alpha_{n,i} Q_n(x + iy)\}$, where "maj" of a multiset picks the most common element, breaking ties arbitrarily. The fact that g_n is within distance 2δ of Q_n follows immediately from the definitions of g_n and δ. Rubinfeld and Sudan [49, Section 4] provide a clever proof that $g_n \in \mathcal{F}_n$. First they show that, for all x,

$$(1) \qquad \mathrm{Prob}(g_n(x) = \sum_{i=1}^{d_n+1} \alpha_{n,i} Q_n(x + iy)) \leq 1 - 2(d_n + 1)\delta,$$

where the probability is induced by choosing y uniformly at random from $\mathrm{GF}(p_n)^n$. This implies that

$$(2) \quad \mathrm{Prob}(g_n(x + iy) = \sum_{j=1}^{d_n+1} \alpha_{n,j} Q_n((x + iy) + j(h_1 + ih_2))) \geq 1 - 2(d_n + 1)\delta,$$

for any fixed i, where the probability is induced by (independently) choosing h_1 and h_2 uniformly at random from $\mathrm{GF}(p_n)^n$ – just set $y = h_1 + ih_2$ in Inequality (1). Furthermore for all $1 \leq j \leq d_n + 1$,

$$(3) \qquad \mathrm{Prob}(\sum_{i=0}^{d_n+1} \alpha_{n,i} Q_n((x + jh_1) + i(y + jh_2)) = 0) \geq 1 - \delta,$$

where the probability is again computed over independently chosen h_1 and h_2. This follows from the definition of δ and the fact that $x + jh_1$ and $y + jh_2$ are both uniformly distributed over $\mathrm{GF}(p_n)^n$. We can use Inequalities (2) and (3) to show that g_n satisfies $\sum_{i=0}^{d_n+1} \alpha_{n,i} g_n(x + iy) = 0$, for all x and y. Because of the (exact) evenly spaced points characterization, this means that $g_n \in \mathcal{F}_n$.

In the following calculations, all probabilities are induced by choosing h_1 and h_2 independently and uniformly at random from $\mathrm{GF}(p_n)^n$. First replace $g_n(x + iy)$ by $\sum_{j=1}^{d_n+1} \alpha_{n,j} Q_n((x + iy) + j(h_1 + ih_2))$. Then, by Inequality (2), we have

(4)

$\mathrm{Prob}(\sum_{i=0}^{d_n+1} \alpha_{n,i} g_n(x + iy)$

$\neq \sum_{i=0}^{d_n+1} \alpha_{n,i} \sum_{j=1}^{d_n+1} \alpha_{n,j} Q_n((x + iy) + j(h_1 + ih_2))) \leq 2(d_n + 1)(d_n + 2)\delta.$

Switch the order of summation and regroup the terms in the inner summation of Inequality (4). That give us

(5)

$\mathrm{Prob}(\sum_{i=0}^{d_n+1} \alpha_{n,i} g_n(x + iy)$

$\neq \sum_{j=1}^{d_n+1} \alpha_{n,j} \sum_{i=0}^{d_n+1} \alpha_{n,i} Q_n((x + jh_1) + i(y + jh_2))) \leq 2(d_n + 1)(d_n + 2)\delta.$

For any fixed j, Inequality (3) gives us that the inside summation $\sum_{i=0}^{d_n+1} \alpha_{n,i} Q_n((x+ jh_1) + i(y + jh_2))$ in Inequality (5) is 0 with probability at least $1 - \delta$. Putting this all together, we see that the probability that $\sum_{i=0}^{d_n+1} \alpha_{n,i} g_n(x + iy)$ is 0 is at least $1 - (2(d_n + 1)(d_n + 2)\delta + (d_n + 2)\delta)$. Because $\delta \leq 1/2(d_n + 2)^2$, this probability is positive. Note, however, that this probability is computed over random choices of h_1 and h_2, while the statement "the probability that $\sum_{i=0}^{d_n+1} \alpha_{n,i} g_n(x + iy)$ is 0" is independent of both h_1 and h_2. Thus, because this probability is positive, it must in fact be 1; the conclusion that $g_n \in \mathcal{F}_n$ follows.

From this robust characterization, it is straightforward to build a tester. The input to the tester consists of a size parameter 1^n, a program Q that purports to compute a sequence of multivariate polynomials $\{f_n\}_{n \geq q}$ in $\mathcal{F}$, a set of pairs $(x_1, f_n(x_1)), \ldots, (x_t, f_n(x_t))$ that define the particular polynomial that Q is supposed to compute on inputs of size n, and some constants that specify the error probability that we can tolerate in the tester. The tester first chooses $O(1)$ pairs (x, y) and checks for each one whether $\sum_{i=0}^{d_n+1} \alpha_{n,i} Q_n(x + iy) = 0$; if this check fails for a high enough fraction of the pairs (x, y), the tester outputs FAIL and quits. If it does not quit at this point, the tester has concluded that the function computed by Q on inputs of size n is sufficiently close to a polynomial in $\mathcal{F}_n$. It now proceeds to test whether Q is computing a function that is close to the particular polynomial defined by $(x_1, f_n(x_1)), \ldots, (x_t, f_n(x_t))$. For each j, $1 \leq j \leq t$, it (independently) chooses $O(1)$ points y uniformly at random from $GF(p_n)^n$ and checks that $f_n(x_j) = \sum_{i=1}^{d_n+1} \alpha_i Q_n(x_j + iy)$. It PASSes Q if and only if a high enough fraction of these checks succeed. For details, including values of all of the relevant constants, see Rubinfeld and Sudan [49, Section 6.1].

The best-known multivariate correctors (which are indeed the best possible) are provided by Gemmell and Sudan [28]. They are based not on robust characterizations but rather on Berlekamp-Welch decoding.

Multivariate polynomial self-correction [28]: On inputs $x = (x_1, \ldots, x_n)$ $\in F_n^n$, for some finite field F_n, a program Q purports to compute an n-variable polynomial g_n over F_n of degree d_n. Suppose that Q has passed a tester T on inputs of size n and that the particular guarantee given by T is that $\Delta_n(Q, g_n) \leq 1/2 - \delta$. Suppose further that, for all n, $|F_n| = \Omega((1/\delta + d_n)^2)$. Then there is a self-corrector C for Q; that is, on input x, C outputs $g_n(x)$ with high probability.

Gemmell and Sudan's reduction of multivariate polynomial correction to Berlekamp-Welch decoding works as follows. They construct a subdomain J_n of F_n^n that is parameterized by a single variable t, i.e., $J_n = \{D(t) \mid t \in F_n\}$, that has the following properties:
1. The function $g_n(D(t))$ is a polynomial in t of degree $O(d_n)$.
2. The input point $x = (x_1, \ldots, x_n)$ is contained in J_n, and $D(0) = x$.
3. With high probability, the fraction of J_n on which Q differs from g_n is approximately $\Delta_n(Q, g_n)$. That is, sampling on J_n yields approximately the same error rate for Q as sampling on all of F_n^n.
Note that this construction suffices for the reduction, because the Berlekamp-Welch algorithm can be used to reconstruct the univariate polynomial $g_n(D(t))$, which can then be evaluated at $t = 0$.

The definition of J_n given by Gemmell and Sudan is beautifully simple: Let $D(t)$ be a random degree-2 curve that passes through x. That is, choose $2n$ elements

$\alpha_1, \beta_1, \dots, \alpha_n, \beta_n$ each uniformly at random from F_n, and let the ith coordinate of $D(t)$ be $\alpha_i t^2 + \beta_i t + x_i$. Because each coordinate of D is a polynomial of degree 2 in t, and $degree(g_n) = d_n$, it is clear that J_n satisfies property 1. Similarly, property 2 is satisfied trivially, because the ith coordinate of $D(0)$ is $\alpha_i(0^2) + \beta_i(0) + x_i$, which is x_i. To establish property 3, Gemmell and Sudan show that J_n forms a pairwise independent sample of F_n^n and then apply Chebyshev's inequality; details can be found in [28].

This technique of replacing the n variables in a multivariate polynomial g_n by a random curve that passes through the point at which g_n is being evaluated has been used before in cryptographic complexity theory. For example, it enables computations on public servers in which the users do not have to reveal their private data – see, e.g., [7, 8, 10, 16]. The technique's intellectual roots are in the "secret sharing" scheme of Shamir [52]. In such a scheme, a "secret" must be distributed among n parties so that any $t + 1$ of them can reconstruct it, but t or fewer cannot. This is accomplished in [52] by representing the secret s as an element in a finite field F, choosing t elements $\beta_1, \dots, \beta_t$ uniformly at random from F, and giving each party a pair $(a, p(a))$, where $a \in F$ and $p(x) = \beta_t x^t + \cdots + \beta_1 x + s$; because $t + 1$ points are required to determine the degree-t polynomial p (or even to infer any information about its constant term), the definition of a secret sharing scheme is satisfied.

We close this section by remarking that there is a self-testing/correcting pair for any function that is complete for FPSPACE or FEXP [6]. A detailed discussion of these structural complexity theoretic results on testing/correcting and of their relationship to the algebraic testers and correctors discussed in this section can be found in [25].

5. Using Polynomial Codes to Characterize Complexity Classes and to Prove Lower Bounds

Babai, Fortnow, and Lund [6] obtained a new characterization of the complexity class NEXP by showing that every language accepted by a nondeterministic exponential-time TM is also accepted by a multiprover interactive proof (MIP) system [9]. In an MIP system, two or more computationally unbounded "provers" convince a probabilistic polynomial-time "verifier" that an input string x is in a language L. If L is an arbitrary language in NEXP, then accepting computation paths of a nondeterministic TM for L have length exponential in the length of x, and it seems counterintuitive that the correctness of such a computation could be verified by a polynomial-time machine; in particular, such a machine cannot examine the entire computation. The provers in an MIP system overcome this by encoding an accepting computation using polynomial codes; the crucial property of a correct encoding is that it uses multivariate polynomials of the appropriate total degree over the appropriate field. The probabilistic polynomial-time verifier then uses multivariate polynomial testing techniques similar to those discussed in Section 4 in order to verify that the codewords correspond to an accepting computation. Such a tester proceeds by sampling the polynomial at random points in its domain and does not have to read the whole (exponential-length) encoding. In fact, the first multivariate polynomial tester was developed by Babai, Fortnow, and Lund [6] precisely for the purpose of encoding long accepting computations so that they could be verified by a probabilistic polynomial-time machine; the testers of

Rubinfeld and Sudan [**49**] discussed in Section 4 came later and are more efficient than those in [**6**].

Prior to [**6**], the new characterization of PSPACE as the class of languages accepted by one-prover interactive proof systems [**37, 53**] had used simpler properties of polynomial codes. The results discussed in Section 5.1 refine the techniques of [**6**] considerably and represent the full flowering of the use of coding theory in new characterizations of traditional complexity classes.

From a coding theoretic point of view, it is striking that, while these results do need infinite families of polynomial codes that have constant relative distance, there is no need for the rate of the codes to be large. Indeed, the length of a codeword may be any polynomially bounded function of the length of a message.

In Section 5.2, we show how the characterizations of NP and PSPACE discussed in Section 5.1 can be used to prove lower bounds on the complexity of approximating certain combinatorial optimization functions. More precisely, they are used to show that there are ratios ϵ for which ϵ-approximating these functions is NP-hard or PSPACE-hard, i.e., just as hard as computing the function exactly. This is a "lower bound" in the same sense that an NP-completeness or PSPACE-completeness result is a lower bound – unless P = NP (resp. P = PSPACE), these approximation problems cannot be solved in polynomial time.

5.1. Probabilistically Checkable Proof Systems.

A nondeterministic polynomial-time Turing machine M may be regarded as a "proof system" in which the polynomial-time verifier is deterministic, and the statements proved are of the form "$x \in L(M)$." If x is indeed in $L(M)$, then any accepting computation of M on input x is a "proof" of this fact, and if x is not in $L(M)$, then no such proof exists. The proofs provided by such a system are very fragile: If one bit in the description of a computation is changed, the verifier's decision to accept or reject x on this computation may also change. The goal of the proof systems defined in this section is to make proofs of membership in NP languages more robust: If a correct proof is altered slightly, it should still be recognizable as "essentially correct," and any input x that is not in the language should only give rise to computation paths that are "far from correct." This is closely related to the goals of error-detection and error-correction that are addressed by traditional coding theory.

Robust versions of NP proof systems were first sought explicitly by Babai et al. [**5**]. The formalism in [**5**] modifies the definition of a nondeterministic TM's proof system by allowing the verifier to be probabilistic and restricting its running time to polylogarithmic in n, the size of x. Because the running time of the verifier was sublinear in n, [**5**] explicitly required the input x to be presented via an error-correcting code. This was very influential and allowed [**5**] to achieve robust proofs as they are described above, but it is insufficient for the applications described in Section 5.2.

The membership proofs that we define here are called *probabilistically checkable proofs* and were first defined formally by Arora and Safra [**4**]. A language L is in $PCP(r(n), q(n))$ if there is a probabilistic polynomial-time machine V (called the verifier) with the following properties. The input to V is a pair (x, π); the string x is claimed to be a member of L, and π is the purported proof of this claim. During the course of its computation on input (x, π), V flips $O(r(n))$ coins and examines $O(q(n))$ bits of the proof string π, where n is the size of x. If $x \in L$, then there is a proof string π such that V outputs 1 with probability 1 on input (x, π). If $x \notin L$, then, for all strings π, V outputs 1 with probability at most $1/2$ on input (x, π).

Note that, by definition, $\mathrm{NP} = \mathrm{PCP}(0, poly(n))$. That is, a proof system in which the verifier flips no coins and reads the entire proof string is simply an NP machine. (In this case, the probability is 0, not $1/2$, that a string x not in L is accepted by the verifier.) The PCP Theorem shows that there is a dramatic tradeoff between the parameters $r(n)$ and $q(n)$; by allowing the verifier to flip a small number of coins, one can drastically lower the number of "query bits" that the verifier requires.

PCP Theorem [3, 4]: $\mathrm{NP} = \mathrm{PCP}(\log(n), 1)$.

If a verifier is to detect that a prover's claim is invalid by examining only a constant number of bits, the proof must be encoded in a way that "spreads" errors throughout the proof string π. This is similar in spirit to the traditional design goals of error-detecting codes, and the testing algorithms presented in Section 4 go part of the way toward allowing us to achieve this goal for proofs of membership in NP languages. The full proof of the PCP Theorem also uses the following Composition Lemma; in fact, a few restrictions on probabilistically checkable proof systems are required if they are to satisfy this lemma, but we omit discussion of them here – see, e.g., [**1, 3, 4, 57**] for a detailed treatment.

Composition Lemma [4]: If L is in both $\mathrm{PCP}(r_1(n), q_1(n))$ and $\mathrm{PCP}(r_2(n), q_2(n))$, then there are constants c_1 and c_2 such that L is in $\mathrm{PCP}(r(n), q(n))$, where $r(n) = r_1(n) + r_2(q_1(n)^{c_1})$ and $q(n) = q_2(q_1(n)^{c_2})$.

Arora et al. [**3**] combine the following "long, robust proof system" and "transparent proof system" to get the PCP Theorem.

Long, Robust Proofs [3]: $\mathrm{NP} \subseteq \mathrm{PCP}(poly(n), 1)$.

Transparent Proofs [5, 6]: There is a constant c such that $\mathrm{NP} \subseteq \mathrm{PCP}(\log(n), \log(n)^c)$.

We give an overview of the $\mathrm{PCP}(poly(n), 1)$ proof system for the NP-complete language 3SAT. Details can be found in [**1, 3, 57**].

Recall that an instance of 3SAT consists of a collection $\{v_1, \ldots, v_n\}$ of boolean variables and a collection $\{C_1, \ldots, C_m\}$ of clauses. Each C_j is a disjunction of three literals, where a literal is either a variable or its negation. A "satisfying assignment" $(a_1, \ldots, a_n)$, $a_i \in \{0, 1\}$, is one that makes all of the clauses true simultaneously when v_i is assigned the truth value a_i; here 1 and 0 denote True and False. The long, robust proof system uses the fact that one can choose a random degree-3 polynomial $\phi_r \in \mathrm{GF}(2)[X_1, \ldots, X_n]$ in such a way that, if $(a_1, \ldots, a_n)$ is a satisfying assignment, then $\phi_r(a_1, \ldots, a_n) = 0$ with probability 1 and, if $(a_1, \ldots, a_n)$ is not a satisfying assignment, then $\phi_r(a_1, \ldots, a_n) = 0$ with probability at most $1/2$; here 1 and 0 denote the elements of $\mathrm{GF}(2)$. This is done by "arithmetizing" each C_j: A positive literal v_i is arithmetized as $(1 - X_i)$ and a negative literal $\overline{v_i}$ as X_i, and the three arithmetized literals in a clause are multiplied; for example, the clause $C_j = v_1 \vee v_2 \vee \overline{v_3}$ is arithmetized as the monomial $\tilde{C}_j = (1 - X_1)(1 - X_2)X_3$. Note that $\tilde{C}_j$ evaluates to 0 for any assignment that satisfies C_j. To choose a random polynomial ϕ_r with the desired properties, choose r uniformly at random from $\{0, 1\}^m$ and let $\phi_r(X_1, \ldots, X_n) = \sum_{j=1}^m r_j \tilde{C}_j$.

Any vector $(a_1, \ldots, a_n)$ in $\mathrm{GF}(2)^n$ defines three linear functions $A : \mathrm{GF}(2)^n \longrightarrow \mathrm{GF}(2)$, $B : \mathrm{GF}(2)^{n^2} \longrightarrow \mathrm{GF}(2)$, and $C : \mathrm{GF}(2)^{n^3} \longrightarrow \mathrm{GF}(2)$ as follows.

$$A(x) \equiv \sum_{i=1}^{n} a_i x_i$$

$$B(y) \equiv \sum_{i=1}^{n} \sum_{j=1}^{n} a_i a_j y_{i,j}$$

$$C(z) \equiv \sum_{i=1}^{n} \sum_{j=1}^{n} \sum_{k=1}^{n} a_i a_j a_k z_{i,j,k}$$

Explicit function tables for A, B, and C have size singly exponential in n. Thus the index of a table entry can be written down using $poly(n)$ bits.

The prover in a long, robust proof system is supposed to write down the tables corresponding to an assignment $(a_1, \ldots, a_n)$ that he claims satisfies the original 3SAT instance. Given three tables, the verifier V can test that they indeed represent three linear functions, or at least three functions that are close to linear. To do this, V uses the linearity testing method of Blum, Luby, and Rubinfeld [14] discussed in Section 4 above: Instead of making calls to a "program" that purports to compute a linear function, V simply looks up the functional values in the table provided by the prover. If the tables pass this test, then V still cannot be sure that they represent linear functions completely accurately; if he could be sure of this, then he could obtain any desired functional value $A(x)$, $B(y)$, or $C(z)$ simply by looking it up. However, the definition of a tester does guarantee that, if the tables pass the test, there are unique linear functions A, B, and C that are very close to the functions given by the tables; furthermore, V can obtain accurate functional values $A(x)$, $B(y)$, or $C(z)$ by using the linearity self-corrector of [14]. It is crucial that the resources needed for linearity testing and correcting are exactly those available to the verifier in a $\mathrm{PCP}(poly(n), 1)$ proof system: $poly(n)$ random bits are required to specify random elements x, y, and z in the domains of A, B, and C, but only $O(1)$ table entries need be queried, each of which is a single bit, because the range of A, B, and C is $\mathrm{GF}(2)$.

V can also use $poly(n)$ random bits and $O(1)$ query bits to verify that the linear functions A, B, and C determined by a legitimate set of tables are related to each other in the proper way. Interestingly, a convenient way to do this uses the Freivalds matrix product technique discussed in Section 3.1. Let $\hat{a} = (a_1, \ldots, a_n)$, $\hat{b} = (b_{1,1}, \ldots, b_{n,n})$, and $\hat{c} = (c_{1,1,1}, \ldots, c_{n,n,n})$ be the coefficient vectors for these functions. What must be verified is that $\hat{b} = \hat{a} \circ \hat{a}$ and $\hat{c} = \hat{a} \circ \hat{b}$, where $\circ$ denotes the outer product operation. Both $\hat{a} \circ \hat{a}$ and $\hat{b}$ can be viewed as $n \times n$ matrices; denote them by M_1 and M_2. Let r and s be uniformly chosen random vectors in $\mathrm{GF}(2)^n$. If $M_1 \neq M_2$, then $r^T M_1 s \neq r^T M_2 s$ with probability at least $1/4$. By definition, $r^T M_1 s = A(r) \cdot A(s)$, where $\cdot$ is just multiplication in $\mathrm{GF}(2)$ and $r^T M_2 s = B(r \circ s)$. Thus, if there is a flaw in the relationship between A and B, V can detect it with probability at least $1/4$ by choosing two polynomial-length random vectors and evaluating three functional values; these evaluations can be done with the linearity corrector and require only a constant number of queries to the tables. The test can be repeated a constant number of times to increase the probability of detecting flaws. The test that $\hat{c} = \hat{a} \circ \hat{b}$ is analogous.

It remains to be seen how V can use the linear functions A, B, and C to test that the assignment $(a_1, \ldots, a_n)$ from which they were derived satisfies the original 3SAT instance. The essential point is that A, B, and C permit V to evaluate any degree-3 polynomial $f \in \mathrm{GF}(2)[X_1, \ldots, X_n]$ at the point $(a_1, \ldots, a_n)$. For any such f, there are index sets $S_1 \subseteq \{1, \ldots, n\}$, $S_2 \subseteq \{(1,1), \ldots, (n,n)\}$, and $S_3 \subseteq \{(1,1,1), \ldots, (n,n,n)\}$ and a constant term $\alpha \in GF(2)$ such that

$$f(a_1, \ldots, a_n) = \alpha + \sum_{i \in S_1} a_i + \sum_{(i,j) \in S_2} a_i a_j + \sum_{(i,j,k) \in S_3} a_i a_j a_k.$$

Using the definition of A, B, and C, we can rewrite this as

$$f(a_1, \ldots, a_n) = \alpha + A(\chi(S_1)) + B(\chi(S_2)) + C(\chi(S_3)).$$

Note that α, S_1, S_2, and S_3 are determined completely by which of the coefficients of the polynomial f are 0 and which are 1; that is, they do not depend on the point $(a_1, \ldots, a_n)$ at which f is being evaluated.

To summarize, the PCP($poly(n)$, 1) proof system for 3SAT proceeds as follows. To prove that the instance $(\{v_1, \ldots, v_n\}, \{C_1, \ldots C_m\})$ is satisfiable, the prover takes a satisfying assignment $(a_1, \ldots, a_n)$ and constructs the corresponding function tables A, B, and C. The verifier checks that the tables have all of the desired properties, using the linearity tester and corrector and the Freivalds technique as explained above. If any of these checks fails, V outputs 0 and stops. If A, B, and C have all of the desired properties, V chooses r uniformly at random from $\{0,1\}^m$ and derives the corresponding degree-3 polynomial ϕ_r from the instance $(\{v_1, \ldots, v_n\}, \{C_1, \ldots C_m\})$. V then uses the tables A, B, and C to evaluate $\phi_r(a_1, \ldots, a_n)$ and outputs 1 if and only if $\phi_r(a_1, \ldots, a_n) = 0$.

The construction of PCP($\log(n)$, $\log(n)^c$) proof systems for NP is quite intricate and is beyond the scope of this article. Multivariate polynomial testing plays a crucial role. The terminology of PCP had not yet been developed when [5, 6] were written, but a thorough explanation of the relationships among multivariate polynomial testing, transparent proofs, and PCP, along with a translation of the results of [5, 6] into PCP terms can be found in, e.g., [1, 4, 46, 49, 57]. As in the long, robust proof system, the proof strings π encode witnesses from the original NP machine for the language via polynomial codes. Here the codes have higher degree and a smaller number of variables than those in the long, robust proofs.

Two applications of the Composition Lemma now give the PCP Theorem. First let $r_1(n) = r_2(n) = \log(n)$ and $q_1(n) = q_2(n) = \log(n)^c$. That yields NP $\subseteq$ PCP($\log(n), \log\log(n)^{c'}$), for some constant c'. Then let $r_1(n) = \log(n)$, $q_1(n) = \log\log(n)^{c'}$, $r_2(n) = poly(n)$, and $q_2(n) = 1$; composing these two sets of parameters yields the theorem. (To be precise, it yields one direction of the theorem, namely NP $\subseteq$ PCP($\log(n)$, 1); the inclusion PCP($\log(n)$, 1) $\subseteq$ NP follows trivially from the definitions of the two classes.)

For some potential applications, it is desirable to have PCP($\log(n)$, 1) proof systems in which the proof strings π are as short as possible. For example, automated theorem-proving tools often produce proofs that are too long to be verified by a human reader. PCP techniques may provide an approach to this problem: Encode the automatically generated proof via the PCP Theorem, and have a PCP verifier check it by reading only a constant number of bits. Because theorem-proving tools produce proofs that are already too long to store and transmit conveniently, it is important that the PCP encoding process increase the proof length as little as possible. The construction of Polishchuk and Spielman [46] can be combined with the improved multivariate polynomial testers of [49] to construct $PCP(\log(n), 1)$ proof systems in which the proof strings are considerably shorter than those in [3].

Although less central than NP, the complexity class PSPACE also plays a prominent role in theoretical computer science, and many natural problems are PSPACE-complete. Condon et al. [18, 19] use PCP techniques to derive new characterizations of PSPACE. A Probabilistically Checkable Debate System (PCDS) for a language L consists of a probabilistic polynomial-time verifier V and a debate between Player 1, who claims that the input x is in L, and Player 0, who claims that the input x is not in L (cf. [18]). An RPCDS is a PCDS in which Player 0 follows a very simple strategy: On each turn, Player 0 chooses uniformly at random from the set of legal moves [19]. A language is in the class $PCD(r(n), q(n))$ (resp. $RPCD(r(n), q(n))$) if it has a PCDS (resp. RPCDS) in which V flips $O(r(n))$ random coins and reads $O(q(n))$ bits of the debate. It is shown in [18, 19] that both $PCD(\log(n), 1)$ and $RPCD(\log(n), 1)$ are equal to PSPACE.

5.2. Application to Nonapproximability of Optimization Functions.
We now show how the PCP Theorem is used to prove nonapproximability results for NP-hard optimization functions. Because approximability of hard optimization functions is a core concern of theoretical computer science, these results demonstrate decisively that coding theory provides useful techniques for mainstream theoretical computer scientists.

The connection between proof systems and hardness of approximation was first drawn by Condon [17]. Feige et al. [24] were the first to connect proof systems to a well-known, basic optimization problem, namely the clique number function defined in Section 2 above. This connection ignited the flurry of work on probabilistically checkable proofs that culminated in the PCP Theorem described in Section 5.1. Here we present a proof that the PCP Theorem implies that MAX-SNP-hard optimization functions do not have PTASs unless P = NP; this version of the proof is taken from Sudan [57].

We begin by defining an optimization function MAX-PCP whose domain consists of pairs (x, L), where L is a language in NP and x is an input, say of size n, for which one may want to determine membership in L. The language L is represented by the description of a $PCP(\log(n), 1)$ proof system for L. Note that such a proof system must exist by the PCP Theorem and that its description has size $O(1)$. The question of whether x is in L can be transformed into an optimization question as follows. Proof strings in this $PCP(\log(n), 1)$ system have polynomial length, say $s(n)$. Each bit of a proof string π is regarded as a boolean variable π_i. The verifier in the proof system tosses a sequence of coins that has length $c \log(n)$, for some constant c. Thus there are polynomially many possible coin-toss sequences r. Let $C_{x,r}$ be a constraint on a subset of the variables $\pi_1, \ldots, \pi_{s(n)}$ that evaluates to 1 if the verifier accepts x when it tosses sequence r and evaluates to 0 otherwise. Because the verifier in a $PCP(\log(n), 1)$ proof system only reads $O(1)$ bits of the proof π, the arity of the constraints $C_{x,r}$ is a constant. The value of the MAX-PCP optimization function on input (x, L) is thus the maximum, over $\pi \in \{0, 1\}^{s(n)}$, of the number of simultaneously satisfied constraints $C_{x,r}$.

Now we argue that $(1/10)$-approximating MAX-PCP is NP-hard. This follows directly from the existence of a "gap" in acceptance probabilities in the definition of a probabilistically checkable proof system. If $x \in L$, then MAX-PCP$(x, L) = n^c$, i.e., there is some proof string π for which the verifier accepts on all coin-toss sequences r, and hence all constraints can be satisfied simultaneously. On the other hand, if $x \notin L$, then MAX-PCP$(x, L) \leq .5n^c$, because, for all proof strings π, the verifier accepts on at most $1/2$ the coin-toss sequences r, and hence at most $1/2$ of the constraints are simultaneously satisfied. A $(1/10)$-approximation algorithm for MAX-PCP would thus always return a value that was at least $(1/1.1)n^c \approx .9n^c$ or at most $.55n^c$, thus allowing us to distinguish between the cases $x \in L$ and $x \notin L$. Because L is an arbitrary NP language, this implies that $(1/10)$-approximating MAX-PCP is NP-hard.

Finally, note that MAX-PCP is in the class MAX-SNP, because it is a constant-arity constraint-satisfaction problem. This means that there is a linear reduction from MAX-PCP to any optimization problem that is MAX-SNP-hard. Thus, any such problem is NP-hard to ϵ-approximate, for some constant ϵ. This means that no such problem has a PTAS, unless P = NP.

The PCP Theorem has been used to derive nonapproximability results for many natural optimization functions, including chromatic number, clique number, MAX-3SAT, shortest vector, nearest vector, and halfspace learning. See [**1**, **57**] for a thorough discussion of these applications. Similarly, the results of Condon et al. [**18**, **19**] are used to derive nonapproximability results for PSPACE-hard optimization functions, including finite-automaton intersection, MAX-Quatified-3SAT, dynamic graph reliability, and games such as generalized geography and mahjongg. See [**18**, **19**] for details.

6. Concluding Remarks

We conclude with pointers to several other connections between coding theory and complexity.

All of the material covered in Sections 3, 4, and 5 deals with the Turing machine model of computation and hence with uniform complexity measures. Coding theory is also used in the study of circuits, formulae, and other nonuniform complexity models. Pippenger [**45**] provides a thorough overview of this subject.

We have also restricted consideration to results in complexity that make use of or are inspired by coding theory. In fact, the interplay between the two subjects has led to new developments in coding theory as well. For example, Spielman [**56**] has recently designed an infinite family of codes with constant rate and constant relative distance that can be both encoded and decoded in linear sequential time or logarithmic parallel time with a linear number of processors. Earlier, the "expander codes" of Sipser and Spielman [**54**] achieved linear-time decoding and quadratic-time encoding algorithms, using the theory of "expander graphs" that is central to many results in complexity theory; the quadratic encoding time makes expander codes inappropriate for on-line communications, but they may be useful for storage on write-once media, because of their efficient decoding algorithms. Both of these recent developments were inspired by the influential role that codes play in the theory of probabilistically checkable proof systems.

In a forthcoming paper, Arora [**2**] explores this role in depth. His work formalizes the notion of a "code-like reduction," observes that the nonapproximability results discussed in Section 5.2 use such reductions, and shows that these reductions have certain limitations.

References

[1] S. Arora, *Probabilistic Checking of Proofs and Hardness of Approximation Problems*, PhD Thesis, University of California, Computer Science Division, Berkeley CA, 1994.

[2] S. Arora, *Reductions, Codes, PCPs, and Inapproximability*, manuscript, December 1994.

[3] S. Arora, C. Lund, R. Motwani, M. Sudan, and M. Szegedy, *Proof Verification and Hardness of Approximation Problems*, Proc. 33rd Symposium on Foundations of Computer Science, IEEE Computer Society Press, Los Alamitos, 1992, pp. 14–23.

[4] S. Arora and M. Safra, *Probabilistic Checking of Proofs*, Proc. 33rd Symposium on Foundations of Computer Science, IEEE Computer Society Press, Los Alamitos, 1992, pp. 2–13.

[5] L. Babai, L. Fortnow, L. Levin, and M. Szegedy, *Checking Computations in Polylogarithmic Time*, Proc. 23rd Symposium on Theory of Computing, ACM, New York, 1991, pp. 21–31.

[6] L. Babai, L. Fortnow, and C. Lund, *Nondeterministic Exponential Time has Two-prover Interactive Protocols*, Computational Complexity, 1 (1991), pp. 3–40.

[7] D. Beaver and J. Feigenbaum, *Hiding Instances in Multioracle Queries*, Proc. 5th Symposium on Theoretical Aspects of Computer Science, Lecture Notes in Computer Science, vol. 415, Springer, Berlin, 1990, pp. 37–48.

[8] D. Beaver, J. Feigenbaum, J. Kilian, and P. Rogaway, *Security with Low Communication Overhead*, in Advances in Cryptology – Crypto '90, Lecture Notes in Computer Science, vol. 537, Springer, Berlin, 1991, pp. 62–76.

[9] M. Ben-Or, S. Goldwasser, J. Kilian, and A. Wigderson, *Multiprover Interactive Proof Systems: How to Remove Intractability Assumptions*, Proc. 20th Symposium on Theory of Computing, ACM, New York, 1988, pp. 113–131.

[10] M. Ben-Or, S. Goldwasser, and A. Wigderson, *Completeness Theorems for Non-Cryptographic Fault-Tolerant Distributed Computation*, Proc. 20th Symposium on Theory of Computing, ACM, New York, 1988, pp. 1–10.

[11] E. Berlekamp and L. Welch, *Error Correction of Algebraic Block Codes*, US Patent Number 4,633,470, 1986. Proof appears in [**28**].

[12] M. Blum, *Program Result Checking: A New Approach to Making Programs More Reliable*, Proc. 20th International Colloquium on Automata, Languages, and Programming, Lecture Notes in Computer Science, vol. 700, Springer, Berlin, 1993, pp. 2–14. First appeared in preliminary form in International Computer Science Institute Technical Report 88-009, Berkeley CA, 1988.

[13] M. Blum and S. Kannan, *Designing Programs that Check their Work*, J. ACM, to appear. Extended abstract in Proc. 21st Symposium on the Theory of Computing, ACM, New York, 1989, pp. 86–97.

[14] M. Blum, M. Luby, and R. Rubinfeld, *Self-testing/correcting with Applications to Numerical Problems*, J. Comput. Sys. Scis., 47 (1993), pp. 549–595.

[15] R. Boppana, J. Håstad, and S. Zachos, *Does co-NP Have Short Interactive Proofs?*, Inf. Proc. Letters, 25 (1987), pp. 127–133.

[16] D. Chaum, C. Crépeau, and I. Damgård, *Multiparty Unconditionally Secure Protocols*, Proc. 20th Symposium on Theory of Computing, ACM, New York, 1988, pp. 11–19.

[17] A. Condon, *The Complexity of the Max Word Problem and the Power of One-Way Interactive Proof Systems*, Computational Complexity, 3 (1993), pp. 292–305. First appeared in preliminary form in Proc. 8th Symposium on Theoretical Aspects of Computer Science, Lecture Notes in Computer Science, vol. 480, Springer, Berlin, 1991, pp. 456–465.

[18] A. Condon, J. Feigenbaum, C. Lund, and P. Shor, *Probabilistically Checkable Debate Systems*, Proc. 25th Symposium on Theory of Computing, ACM, New York, 1993, pp. 305–314. Journal version has been submitted and is available as DIMACS TR 93-10.

[19] A. Condon, J. Feigenbaum, C. Lund, and P. Shor, *Random Debaters and the Hardness of Approximation Stochastic Functions*, Proc. 9th Structure in Complexity Theory Conference, IEEE Computer Society Press, Los Alamitos, 1994, pp. 280–293. Journal version has been submitted and is available as DIMACS TR 93-79.

[20] S. Cook, *The Complexity of Theorem-Proving Procedures*, in Proc. 3rd Symposium on the Theory of Computing, ACM, New York, 1971, pp. 151–158.

[21] Van der Waerden, *Algebra*, vol. 1, Frederick Ungar Publishing, New York, 1970.

[22] C. Dwork and M. Naor, *An Efficient Existentially Unforgeable Signature Scheme and its Application*, to appear. Extended abstract in Advances in Cryptology – Crypto '94, Lecture Notes in Computer Science, vol. 839, Springer, Berlin, 1994, pp. 234–246.

[23] S. Even, O. Goldreich, and S. Micali, *On-Line/Off-Line Digital Signatures*, J. Cryptology, to appear. Extended abstract in Advances in Cryptology – Crypto '89, Lecture Notes in Computer Science, vol. 435, Springer, Berlin, 1990, pp. 263–275.

[24] U. Feige, S. Goldwasser, L. Lovász, M. Safra, and M. Szegedy, *Approximating Clique is Almost NP-Complete*, Proc. 32nd Symposium on Foundations of Computer Science, IEEE Computer Society Press, Los Alamitos, 1991, pp. 2–12.

[25] J. Feigenbaum, *Locally Random Reductions in Interactive Complexity Theory*, in Advances in Computational Complexity Theory, DIMACS Series in Discrete Mathematics and Theoretical Computer Science, vol. 13, J.-y. Cai (ed.), AMS, Providence, 1993, pp. 73–97.

[26] R. Freivalds, *Fast Probabilistic Algorithms*, in Mathematical Foundations of Computer Science, Lecture Notes in Computer Science, vol. 74, Springer, Berlin, 1979, pp. 57–69.

[27] M. Garey and D. Johnson, *Computers and Intractability: A Guide to the Theory of NP-Completeness*, Freeman, San Francisco, 1979.

[28] P. Gemmell and M. Sudan, *Highly Resilient Correctors for Polynomials*, Inf. Proc. Letters, 43 (1992), pp. 169–174.

[29] J. Håstad, *Pseudo-Random Generators under Uniform Assumptions*, Proc. 22nd Symposium on the Theory of Computing, ACM, New York, 1990, pp. 395–404.

[30] R. Impagliazzo, L. Levin, and M. Luby, *Pseudo-Random Generation from One-Way Functions*, Proc. 21st Symposium on the Theory of Computing, ACM, New York, 1989, pp. 12–24.

[31] D. Johnson, *A Catalog of Complexity Classes*, in Handbook of Theoretical Computer Science, vol. A: Algorithms and Complexity, J. van Leeuwen (ed.), The MIT Press/Elsevier, Cambridge/New York, 1990, pp. 67–162.

[32] J. Justesen, *A Class of Asymptotically Good Algebraic Codes*, IEEE Trans. Inf. Th., 18 (1972), pp. 652–656.

[33] S. Kannan, *Program Checkers for Algebraic Problems*, PhD Thesis, University of California, Computer Science Division, Berkeley CA, 1989.

[34] R. Karp, *Reducibility Among Combinatorial Problems*, in Complexity of Computer Computations, R. Miller and J. Thatcher (eds.), Plenum, New York, 1972, pp. 85–103.

[35] R. Karp and N. Pippenger, *A Time-Randomness Tradeoff*, talk at the AMS Conference on Probabilistic Computation and Complexity, 1983.

[36] L. Levin, *Universal Sorting Problems*, Problemy Peredaci Informacii, 9 (1973), pp. 115-115 (in Russian). English translation in Problems of Information Transmission, 9, pp. 265–266.

[37] C. Lund, L. Fortnow, H. Karloff, and N. Nisan, *Algebraic Methods for Interactive Proof Systems*, J. ACM, 39 (1992), pp. 859–868.

[38] C. Lund and M. Yannakakis, *On the Hardness of Approximating Minimization Problems*, J. ACM, 41 (1994), pp. 960–981.

[39] J. MacWilliams and N. Sloane, *The Theory of Error-Correcting Codes*, North-Holland, Amsterdam, 1977.

[40] R. McEliece, *The Theory of Information and Coding*, vol. 3 of the Encyclopedia of Mathematics and its Applications, G. Rota (ed.), Addison Wesley, Reading, 1977.

[41] M. Naor, *Bit Commitment Using Pseudorandomness*, J. Cryptology, 4 (1991), 151-158.

[42] J. Naor and M. Naor, *Small-bias Probability Spaces: Efficient Constructions and Applications*, SIAM J. Comput., 22 (1993), pp. 838–856.

[43] C. Papadimitriou, *Computational Complexity*, Addison-Wesley, Reading, 1994.

[44] C. Papadimitriou and M. Yannakakis, *Optimization, Approximation, and Complexity Classes*, J. Comput. Sys. Scis., 43 (1991), pp. 425–440.

[45] N. Pippenger, *Developments in the Synthesis of Reliable Organisms from Unreliable Components*, Proc. AMS Symposia in Pure Maths., 50 (1990), pp. 311–324.

[46] A. Polishchuk and D. Spielman, *Nearly-linear Size Holographic Proofs*, Proc. 26th Symposium on Theory of Computing, ACM, New York, 1994, pp. 194–203.

[47] R. Rubinfeld, *A Mathematical Theory of Self-Checking, Self-Testing, and Self-Correcting Programs*, PhD Thesis, University of California, Computer Science Division, Berkeley CA, 1990.

[48] R. Rubinfeld, *On the Robustness of Functional Equations*, Proc. 35th Symposium on Foundations of Computer Science, IEEE Computer Society Press, Los Alamitos, 1994, pp. 288–299.

[49] R. Rubinfeld and M. Sudan, *Robust Characterization of Polynomials with Applications to Program Testing*, SIAM J. Comput., to appear. Extended abstract in Proc. 3rd Symposium on Discrete Algorithms, ACM/SIAM, New York/Philadelphia, 1992, pp. 23–43.

[50] U. Schöning, *Graph Isomorphisms is in the Low Hierarchy*, in Proc. 4th Symposium on Theoretical Aspects of Computer Science, Lecture Notes in Computer Science, vol. 247, Springer, Berlin, 1986, pp. 37–48.

[51] J. Schwartz, *Fast Probabilistic Algorithms for Verification of Polynomial Identities*, J. ACM, 27 (1980), pp. 701–717.

[52] A. Shamir, *How to Share a Secret*, C. ACM, 22 (1979), pp. 612–613.

[53] A. Shamir, IP = PSPACE, J. ACM, 39 (1992), pp. 869–877.

[54] M. Sipser and D. Spielman, *Expander Codes*, Proc. 35th Symposium on Foundations of Computer Science, IEEE Computer Society, Los Alamitos, 1994, pp. 566–576.

[55] N. Sloane, *Codes (Spherical) and Designs (Experimental)*, these proceedings.

[56] D. Spielman, *Linear-Time Encodable and Decodable Error-Correcting Codes*, in Proc. 27th Symposium on Theory of Computing, ACM, New York, 1995, to appear.

[57] M. Sudan, *Efficient Checking of Polynomials and Proofs and the Hardness of Approximation Problems*, PhD Thesis, University of California, Computer Science Division, Berkeley CA, 1992.

[58] S. Zachos, *Probabilistic Quantifiers and Games*, J. Comput. Sys. Sci., 36 (1988), pp. 433–451.

AT&T BELL LABORATORIES, MURRAY HILL, NJ 07974-0636
E-mail address: jf@research.att.com

Index

Other Titles in This Series

(Continued from the front of this publication)

ISBN 0-8218-0379-4

9 780821 803790